THE CAMBRIDGE COMPANION TO QU

The Cambridge Companion to Quakerism offers a fresh, up-to-date, and accessible introduction to Quakerism. Quakerism is founded on radical ideas and its history of constancy and change offers fascinating insights into the nature of nonconformity. In a series of eighteen essays written by an international team of scholars, and commissioned especially for this volume, the *Companion* covers the history of Quakerism from its origins to the present day. Employing a range of methodologies, it features sections on the History of Quaker Faith and Practice, Expressions of Quaker Faith, Regional Studies, and Emerging Spiritualities. It also examines all branches of Quakerism, including evangelical, liberal, and conservative, as well as non-theist Quakerism and convergent Quaker thought. This *Companion* will serve as an essential resource for all interested in Quaker thought and practice.

Stephen W. Angell is Leatherock Professor of Quaker Studies at the Earlham School of Religion. He has published extensively in the areas of Quaker Studies and African-American Religious Studies.

Pink Dandelion directs the work of the Centre for Research in Quaker Studies, Woodbrooke, and is Professor of Quaker Studies at the University of Birmingham and a Research Fellow at Lancaster University. He is the author and editor of a number of books, most recently (with Stephen Angell) *Early Quakers and Their Theological Thought*.

This is a series of companions to major topics and key figures in theology and religious studies. Each volume contains specially commissioned chapters by international scholars, which provide an accessible and stimulating introduction to the subject for new readers and nonspecialists.

OTHER TITLES IN THE SERIES

(continued after the Index)

The Cambridge Companion to Quakerism

Edited by

STEPHEN W. ANGELL

Earlham School of Religion

PINK DANDELION

University of Birmingham

CAMBRIDGE
UNIVERSITY PRESS

CAMBRIDGE
UNIVERSITY PRESS

University Printing House, Cambridge CB2 8BS, United Kingdom

One Liberty Plaza, 20th Floor, New York, NY 10006, USA

477 Williamstown Road, Port Melbourne, VIC 3207, Australia

314-321, 3rd Floor, Plot 3, Splendor Forum, Jasola District Centre, New Delhi - 110025, India

79 Anson Road, #06-04/06, Singapore 079906

Cambridge University Press is part of the University of Cambridge.

It furthers the University's mission by disseminating knowledge in the pursuit of education, learning and research at the highest international levels of excellence.

www.cambridge.org
Information on this title: www.cambridge.org/9781316501948
DOI: 10.1017/9781316480021

First published 2018

A catalogue record for this publication is available from the British Library

ISBN 978-1-107-13660-1 Hardback
ISBN 978-1-316-50194-8 Paperback

For the next generation of scholars

Contents

Contributors

HANS EIRIK AAREK is retired Assistant Professor at the University of Stavanger, Norway. His main area of research is the development and transformation of Norwegian Quakerism in the nineteenth and twentieth centuries. His published studies in English include "The Norwegian authorities' methods of restricting the Quaker influence, and the types of punishment meted out when regulations were transgressed" in Geir Skeie and Hans Eirik Aarek eds., *Religious Freedom as Seen from a Minority Perspective* (2015); "Conscription and conscientious objection in the experience of Norwegian Friends" in *Quaker Studies* 11/1, September 2006; "A short history of the Troms Quakers and their emigration to America" in *Norwegian-American Studies*, 35 (2000).

MARGERY POST ABBOTT has been traveling in the ministry, writing, and facilitating workshops of the Religious Society of Friends (Quakers) for more than twenty years. She has also served as presiding clerk of Friends Committee on National Legislation, the Quaker lobby on Capitol Hill. Her books include *A Certain Kind of Perfection* (1997); *The Historical Dictionary of the Friends* (with Pink Dandelion, Mary Ellen Chijioke, and John Oliver) (2007, 2012); *To Be Broken and Tender: A Quaker Theology for Today* (2010), and *Walk Worthy of Your Calling: Quakers and the Traveling Ministry* (with Peggy Senger Parsons) (2004). Her newest writing is *Everyday Prophets*, the Backhouse Lecture for Australia Yearly Meeting. She was a plenary speaker in 2016 at both Australia and Aotearoa/New Zealand Yearly Meetings and visited widely among Friends in both those nations.

STEPHEN W. ANGELL is Leatherock Professor of Quaker Studies at the Earlham School of Religion. His books include *Early Quakers and their Theological Thought* (with Pink Dandelion) (2015); *The Oxford Handbook of Quaker Studies* (with Pink Dandelion) (2013); and *Black Fire: African American Quakers on Spirituality and Human Rights* (with Harold D. Weaver Jr., and Paul Kriese) (2011). He is Associate Editor of *Quaker Studies* and *Quaker Theology*, and he has published extensively in the areas of Quaker Studies and African American Religious Studies. With Pink Dandelion, he is editor in chief of the new Brill series in Quaker studies.

MICHAEL BIRKEL is Professor of Christian Spirituality at Earlham School of Religion. His books include *The Lamb's War* (with John W. Newman) (1992), *The Inward Teacher* (2002), *"A Near Sympathy": The Timeless Quaker Wisdom of John Woolman* (2003), *Silence and Witness: Quaker Spirituality* (2004), *Engaging Scripture: Encountering the Bible with Early Friends* (2005), *Genius of the Transcendent: Mystical Writings of Jakob Boehme* (with Jeff Bach) (2010), and *Qur'an in Conversation* (2014). Other works include Pendle Hill Pamphlets, *The Messenger That Goes Before: Margaret Fell as Spiritual Nurturer* (2008), *The Mind of Christ: Bill Taber on Meeting for Business* (2010), *A Seal upon the Heart: Quaker Readings in the Song of Songs* (2016), and a translation of and introduction to Robert Barclay's *Christianae quaedam animadversiones* (*Quaker Theology* 11/1, 2012). He has contributed to the *Oxford Handbook of Quaker Studies* (2013), *Early Quakers and Their Theological Thought: 1647–1723* (2015), and *Contemplative Literature: A Comparative Sourcebook* (2015).

ELAINE BISHOP, a retired social worker, lives in Winnipeg, Manitoba, Canada on Treaty 1 territory and the homeland of the Manitoba Metis Nation. She practiced in several social justice areas including women's and Indigenous rights. She served Canadian Yearly Meeting in various capacities, including clerk, and Canadian Friends Service Committee as coordinator. Her PhD studies explored, through the lens of Quaker peace testimony, the roles of land in peace building. She currently serves on several boards and is working with an Indigenous/Settler circle to create a foundation to facilitate Settler engagement in reconciliation with Indigenous peoples. Publications include "'The Sacred Nature of Places'; Understanding Land as a Contribution to Peacebuilding" in *Seeking Cultures of Peace: A Peace Church Conversation* (2004); and "Share the Gifts: Honour the Treaties" in *Yours, Mine, Ours: Unravelling the Doctrine of Discovery – a special edition of Intotemak* (2016).

CLARE BROWN is an independent scholar whose research interests include nineteenth-century Quaker philanthropy and British and American abolitionism. She gained a first-class honors degree in Religious Studies with History in 1996 and received an MA with distinction in Religion and Society in 2000 from Cheltenham and Gloucester College of Higher Education (now the University of Gloucestershire). She was awarded her PhD from the University of Bristol, Trinity College, in 2015. Her doctoral thesis considered the contribution of Joseph Sturge to the British and American antislavery movement and examined the principles that motivated his work.

TIMOTHY BURDICK is Social and Human Services Professor at Edmonds Community College. He has served in leadership capacities with several Quaker ministries in Northwest Yearly Meeting, participated in mission projects with Quaker outreach groups in Brazil and Bolivia, and has an extensive vocational background in social service. His doctoral dissertation (2013) focused on the emerging neo-evangelical Quaker identity in early twentieth-century America. He has presented on Quaker issues at national conferences, and he has published various articles and reviews.

GEORGE BUSOLO is currently pastor of Chavakali Yearly Meeting of Friends Church (Quakers), attached to Kizivi Village (local) Meeting in Munugi Monthly Meeting. He also serves as chaplain of Friends School Demesi Secondary. From 2013 to 2016, he served as an adjunct tutor at Friends Theological College teaching residential program certificate and diploma classes at the Kaimosi main campus and also certificate classes at the Samburu-Maralal campus. Previous published work includes an article entitled "Pope Francis' Visit to Africa: Implications for the Church" and "Pope Francis' Visit to Africa: A Message of Hope," both in the *Africa Ecclesial Review*.

NANCY JIWON CHO is Assistant Professor of English Literature at Seoul National University, South Korea. Her work is located in the fields of religion and literature, English poetry, and women's writing. She has published journal articles and book chapters on the millenarian prophetic writings of Dorothy Gott, a Romantic-era (ex) Quaker visionary; the work of British women hymn writers (Anne Steele, Susanna Harrison, nineteenth-century Roman Catholic women, Ellen Lakshmi Goreh, and Amy Carmichael); and Evangelical children's literature.

JOHN CONNELL resides in Camby, Indiana. He holds AA and BS degrees in Religion from Liberty University, and an MA degree from the Earlham School of Religion with a concentration in Quaker Studies. His scholarship about Friends includes "Let the holy seed of life reign – Perfection, Pelagianism, and the early Friends," in *Quaker Theology*, 24 (2014); *Brethren of the Same Household of Faith – The Story of Division among Conservative and Revivalist Quakers at White Lick Quarterly Meeting of Friends* (2013); and *Subjection to the Seed – The Natural Man and the Supernatural Light in the Epistemology of Friends* (MA thesis, ESR, 2015).

PINK DANDELION directs the work of the Centre for Research in Quaker Studies, Woodbrooke. He is professor of Quaker Studies at the University of Birmingham and a Research Fellow at Lancaster University. He edits *Quaker Studies* and convenes the Quaker Studies Research Association. His books include *Early Quakers and Their Theological Thought* (with Stephen Angell)

(2015); *The Oxford Handbook of Quaker Studies* (with Stephen Angell) (2013); *The Quaker Condition* (with Peter Collins) (2009); *The Quakers: A Very Short Introduction* (2008); *Good and Evil: Quaker Perspectives* (with Jackie Leach Scully) (2007); *Introduction to Quakerism* (2007); *The Liturgies of Quakerism* (2005); *The Creation of Quaker Theory* (2004); the multi-authored *Towards Tragedy/Reclaiming Hope* (2004); and *The Sociological Analysis of the Theology of Quakers: The Silent Revolution* (1996). With Stephen Angell, he is editor in chief of the Brill series in Quaker studies.

C. WESS DANIELS is the William R. Rogers Director of Friends Center and Quaker Studies at Guilford College. He has a PhD in Intercultural Studies from Fuller Theological Seminary and served as a "released minister" at Camas Friends Church for six years. Daniels has traveled and taught widely among Friends, including courses at George Fox Seminary and Earlham School of Religion. His book, *A Convergent Model of Renewal: Remixing The Quaker Tradition in Participatory Culture* (2015), sets out to describe a model of renewal that takes into account both tradition and innovation while fostering a participatory community. Other publications include *Spirit Rising: Young Quaker Voices* (2010); "Convergent Friends: The Emergence of Postmodern Quakerism" in *Quaker Studies* (2010); "A Faithful Betrayal: The New Quakers" in *Quaker Life* (2010); and "I (Hope) I see Dead People" in *Friends Journal* (2012). He is one of the associate editors of the Brill series in Quaker studies.

THOMAS D. HAMM received his PhD in History from Indiana University in 1985 and since 1987 has been on the faculty of Earlham College, where he serves as Professor of History and Director of Special Collections. He is the author of several books and numerous articles on Quaker history, including *The Transformation of American Quakerism: Orthodox Friends, 1800–1907* (1988), *The Quakers in America* (2003), and *Quaker Writings, 1650–1920* (2010). He has just finished a book-length study of Hicksite Friends, 1827–1900.

ROBYNNE ROGERS HEALEY is Professor of History and co-director of the Gender Studies Institute at Trinity Western University in Langley, British Columbia, Canada. She convenes the Conference of Quaker Historians and Archivists and is publications chair for the Canadian Friends Historical Association. Her publications include chapters in *The Quakers, 1656–1723: The Evolution of an Alternative Community* (forthcoming), *Early Quakers and Their Theological Thought* (2015), *The Oxford Handbook of Quaker Studies* (2013), *American Churches and the First World War* (2016), *Canadian Churches and the First World War* (2014), and the book *From Quaker to Upper Canadian: Faith and Community Among Yonge Street Friends, 1801–1850* (2006). She is one of the associate editors of the Brill series in Quaker studies.

JISEOK JUNG directs the works of the Border Peace School and is director of Korea YMCA Peace-Life Centre. He is a member of the Committee of Theology of National Council of Churches in Korea. His books include four Korean books: *History of Christian Idea of Peace: Religion, Politics and Peace* (2015); *Invitation to Quakerism* (2014); *Peace in Diversity, Coexistence in Difference* (with Lee et al.) (2009); and *Seed Life Peace* (with Park et al.) (2007) – and one English book *Ham Sokhon's Pacifism and the Reunification of Korea, A Quaker Theology of Peace* (2006).

JON R. KERSHNER is Lecturer in Theology at Pacific Lutheran University and Honorary Researcher in Quakerism at the University of Lancaster (United Kingdom). He is co-chair of the Quaker Studies Program Unit at the American Academy of Religion and one of the associate editors of the Brill series in Quaker studies. His research has been published in *Quaker History, Quaker Studies*, and *Quaker Religious Thought*, and the multi-authored volumes *Quakers and Their Allies in the Abolitionist Cause, 1754–1808* (2015) and *Quakers and Literature* (2016).

STEPHANIE MIDORI KOMASHIN is a doctoral candidate in Religion at Hokkaido University. She was a recipient of the Japanese Government (MEXT) Research Student Scholarship. She holds an MDiv from Princeton Theological Seminary, where she was awarded the Senior Fellowship in History. Her publications include (with Andrew Komasinski) "How Relational Selfhood Rearranges the Debate between Feminists and Confucians" in *Feminist Encounters with Confucius* (2016); "How Ecology, Economics, and Ethics Brought Winstanley and Nitobe to Quakerism" in *Quaker Studies* 21(2) (2016); and "*Miyabe Kingo no Joseikan*" (Kingo Miyabe's View of Women) in *Kirisutokyou-Gaku (Studium Christianitatis)* 51 (2016). Komashin's current research is the Sapporo Band's view of women with a focus on Inazo Nitobe's and Kanzo Uchimura's personal, professional, and Quaker-related interactions with women, and Quakerism in the Asia-Pacific region.

EMMA JONES LAPSANSKY is Emeritus Professor of History and Curator of the Quaker Collection at Haverford College, where she continues to teach and to consult with students and with scholars who visit Haverford's Quaker Collections. She received her BA in History from the University of Pennsylvania, and her doctorate in American Civilization from the same institution. Her recent publications include *Quaker Aesthetics* (with Anne Verplanck) (2003); *Back to Africa: Benjamin Coates and the American Colonization Movement* (with Margaret Hope Bacon) (2005). She has contributed essays to *Benjamin Franklin: In Search of a Better World* (2006) and *Pennsylvania: A History of the Commonwealth* (2003) and was a contributing author to *The*

Oxford Handbook of Quaker Studies (2013), and to *Quakers and Abolition*, edited by Brycchan Carey and Geoffrey Plank (2014). She is currently at work on three projects: a history of a Bryn Mawr Quaker family; a study of a mid-twentieth-century Philadelphia multicultural intentional community; and an article on Quakers' "transition" period after the death of the seventeenth-century founding generation, to be published by Pennsylvania State University Press in an anthology edited by Richard Allen and Rosemary Moore.

RAMÓN GONZÁLEZ LONGORIA graduated with a Bachelor in Theology degree in 1976 from the Theological Evangelical Seminary (Matanzas, Cuba) and in Quaker Studies and Construction of Peace and Mediation from the Cuban Quaker Institute of Peace. He is principal and professor of the Cuban Quaker Institute of Peace. He has served as a Quaker pastor and recording minister since 1976, and as Presiding Clerk of CUBAYM for thirteen years. He has also served as Clerk of the Cuba YM Historical Committee and as a member of FWCC Central Executive Committee (1996–2000, 2013–2016, 2017–2019) and International Planning Committee (1996–2000, 2007–2012). He was Presiding Clerk of FWCC (2013–2016) and is now FWCC Assistant Clerk (2017–2019).

OSCAR MALANDE has served as a pastor in Kenya for twelve years at Vihiga Yearly Meeting of Friends. He taught and served as registrar and assistant academic dean at Friends Theological, Kaimosi, for three years. He is currently a graduate student at Earlham School of Religion in Richmond, Indiana.

ISAAC BARNES MAY is a doctoral candidate in Religious Studies at the University of Virginia. He holds a Master of Theological Studies degree from Harvard Divinity School, where he studied the religions of the Americas. His academic articles on Quakerism have appeared in *Quaker History, Quaker Studies*, and *Quaker Theology*, among other publications. In addition to studying Quakerism, his other research interests include religious liberalism, secularism, religion and law, and pacifism.

KATHERINE MURRAY is the Hospice Chaplain and Bereavement Coordinator at Hancock Regional Hospice in Greenfield, Indiana. She is also a longtime writer and editor, former publications director of Quaker Earthcare Witness, pastor of Noblesville First Friends Meeting, and adjunct faculty at Earlham School of Religion, where she teaches a course in Eco-Spirituality. Her books include *Listening to the Earth: Meditations on Experiencing and Belonging to Nature* (2011) and *A Simple Guide to Eco-Spirituality* (2012).

DAN CHRISTY RANDAZZO is Chester Reagan Chair of Quaker and Religious Studies at Moorestown Friends School in Moorestown, New Jersey. Randazzo serves as Graduate Student Representative at the American Academy of Religion and co-chair of the Quaker Theological Discussion Group. His publications include a forthcoming article in *Quaker Religious Thought* on Quaker hybridity through the lens of Ham Sok Heon's theology. He is a PhD candidate at the University of Birmingham. His dissertation, "The Interdependent 'Light': Quaker Models of God in Reconciliation Theology," explores liberal Quaker reconciliation theology and was submitted in Spring 2017.

ANN RIGGS was Principal (President) and Senior Lecturer in Theology at Friends Theological College from 2009 to 2014. She represents Friends on the Central Committee of the World Council of Churches and the planning committee for the WCC's 11th Assembly. Her publications include *Introduction to Ecumenism* (with Jeffrey Gros and Eamon McManus) (1998); *Seeking Cultures of Peace: A Peace Church Conversation* (2004); *Ancient Faith and American Born Churches* (with Ted Campbell and Gilbert Stafford) (2006); and *God's Love for the Poor and the Church's Witness to It* (with Shaun Casey, John Crossin, OSFS, Eric Crump, Katherine Grieb, and Beverly Mitchell) (2005). The theoretical bases for the case study on Africa in this volume were developed in her essays "The Global and Ecumenical Reach of Joseph Komonchak's Realist's Church" in *A Realist's Church: Essays in Honor of Joseph Komonchak* (2015) and "Building on the Legacy of Ecumenical Trailblazers: Ecumenical Ecclesiological Possibilities of Mutual Recognition of the Personal Witness and Good Works of the Redeemed" in *Ecumenical Trends*.

JULIA HINSHAW RYBERG is a tenth-generation Friend, born and raised in the United States, residing in Sweden since 1975. She serves as pedagogue to Sweden Yearly Meeting and as Ministry and Outreach Coordinator for the Europe and Middle East Section of the Friends World Committee for Consultation. She has served Woodbrooke Quaker Study Centre as European Project Coordinator and continues to serve as Associate Tutor. Her work includes teaching, retreat leadership, travel in the ministry, outreach, writing, and speaking engagements. A special focus is the development of online resources and learning opportunities for Friends. Her presentations over the years at Yearly Meeting sessions and other Quaker gatherings in Germany (Carey Lecture 2011), Britain, Poland, Sweden, and Ireland have been published in various contexts. She is ecumenically active in Sweden and contributed, on behalf of Swedish Friends, to the Swedish Christian Council's peace anthology *Att slå följe för fred*. She has been a regular columnist in the progressive Christian Swedish web magazine *Dagens Seglora*. She holds an MDiv from Earlham School of Religion.

THEONESTE SENTABIRE is a professional teacher and a peace activist. He served as a high school teacher at College George Fox de Butaro (Rwanda) for seven years. He has taught at Friends Theological College, Kaimosi, in Kenya and also served as an interim pastor in one of the Quaker local churches. Sentabire holds a Master of Arts in Religion: Peace Studies from Earlham School of Religion. Currently, he is a PhD candidate at the United Mandated University for Peace (Costa Rica).

DEBORAH L. SHAW serves as director of the Quaker Leadership Scholars Program and the assistant director of the Friends Center, both of Guilford College, Greensboro, North Carolina. She leads numerous retreats and workshops in America and Britain on Quaker Spirituality and exploring historic Quaker luminaries and their impact on Quaker faith and practice today. Her publications include chapters in *Good and Evil: Quaker Perspectives* (2007) and *The Quaker Bible Reader* (2006); "Being Fully Present to God," *Annual Michener Lecture* (Southeastern Yearly Meeting of the Religious Society of Friends, 2005); and numerous articles in *Journal of the North Carolina Yearly Meeting (Conservative)* and the *Pastoral Care Newsletter*.

NANCY THOMAS is currently researching and writing the 100-year history of Friends (INELA) in Bolivia, a five-year project. Nancy and her husband Hal have served alongside Bolivian Friends from 1972 to the present, living in Bolivia for most of that time. As part of her vocation she has trained Latin American Quaker writers in five countries. A poet as well as a scholar, Nancy has published four volumes of poetry, the latest being *Close to the Ground* (2016). Her other books include *La iglesia latinoamericana: su vida y su misión* ("The Latin American Church: It's Life and Mission," with Alberto F. Roldán and Carlos Van Engen, 2011); *Footprints of God: A Narrative Theology of Mission* (with Charles Van Engen and Robert Gallagher) (1999), and some ten theological titles in Spanish, published in La Paz, Bolivia. Nancy's PhD in Intercultural Studies is from Fuller Theological Seminary (1998). Nancy and Hal live in Newberg, Oregon.

GREG WOODS is a Quaker campus minister who has worked at Guilford College and is setting up a network of Quaker campus ministries at non-Quaker higher education institutions. He wrote the chapter entitled "The Sweat Lodge and Meeting for Worship" for *Spirit Rising: Young Quaker Voices* (2010). He lives in Greensboro, North Carolina, with his wife and daughter.

Introduction

Pink Dandelion and Stephen W. Angell

Quakerism is fascinating in its enduring ability to adapt to new contexts and yet retain a radical witness that has been inherent to its spirituality from the start. The Quakers (or Friends) today are a global faith composed of different branches, and the recent history has been one of schism, diversification, mission and varying degrees of intra-denominational ecumenism. For all but a few Quakers, there still exists a 'world family of Friends', rooted in a historical tradition of faith, practice and witness that transcends doctrinal, liturgical and political diversity. Quakerism begs our attention, not simply because of this dynamic between diversity and congruence but also because it is unique amongst Christian denominations in its theological emphases and practice.

BEGINNINGS

It was in 1647 that George Fox had an experience of God breaking into his life, a transformative experience that was to change his life and lead to the founding of the Quaker movement, even whilst he claimed others had had a similar experience before him. Fox had left his home village of Fenny Drayton in Leicestershire four years earlier and had been searching across England for someone who might help him with his religious quest. He had spent a year with a Baptist uncle in London and had visited the army camps of the English Civil War where the most radical religious ideas were circulating. This was a time of great religious expectation, of the world turned upside down, and yet no one gave Fox any solace. He later wrote that his 'hopes in all men were gone' and that he 'had nothing outwardly to help' him (Fox 1952, 11) In this bleak place of despair, Fox then hears a voice which claims 'there is one, even Christ Jesus, that can speak to thy condition.' Even or no less than Christ is to become Fox's spiritual guide and in that instant, Fox sees that he has been looking in the wrong places, to humanity and text, rather than to the living Word, Christ Jesus. He understands that he has been 'shut up in unbelief' and 'concluded under sin' but that now he 'may give Him all the glory' (Fox 1952, 11). He knows this 'experimentally' or through his experience.

This experience sets the mould for the formation of the Quaker movement based on a sense of intimacy with God. Quakerism emerges from this moment on, initially falteringly and then with great momentum in the north of England from 1652, as a group whose spiritual basis rests in an experience of direct encounter with God. This experience is salvific and also entails an ability to resist sin, a perfectability. Nothing frustrated other Christians more than these claims. Fox does not set himself apart as a particular prophet but understands that 'convincement', the conviction of his former faith and the power to live a regenerated life, is available to anyone who did not resist the in-working and indwelling of Christ. Thus a second radical aspect of Quaker spirituality is that of spiritual equality, whereby all are ministers.

Third, Fox understood that he had had nothing outwardly to help him because the location of authentic spirituality was inward. Rather than install a rota of ministers to lead worship, Quakers adopted a liturgy of silence and stillness in which God might use any one of those gathered as a mouthpiece. Worship would typically last three hours, sometimes totally silent, at other times laced with vocal ministry.

And Quakers quaked. The term 'Quaker' was originally an insult handed to Fox by a judge who derided the physical shaking that often accompanied this approach to the divine. Quakers have been a group founded on a powerful collective mystical experience. They understood this to be their instalment of the inward second coming of Christ and the beginning of the culmination of the Biblical timeline. They lived their faith as if in the Book of Revelation; Fox justified inward communion (after Revelation 3:20) and the use of silence (Revelation 8:1) using that Scripture. Quakers were the vanguard for God over England and all other nations heralding the coming of the kingdom. Necessarily, as the true church, they were impelled to decry all those who held humanity back from this new dispensation, and they interrupted church services and preached wherever they could. Quakerism would moderate its views towards other Christians within twenty years but only really become ecumenical in the nineteenth century.

Quaker faith was thus straightforward and optimistic, offering the idea of a universal elect. It was egalitarian within its theocratic or pneumocratic paradigm. It offered certainty and clarity about what was right and what, and who, was wrong. 'The world' was to be trampled under and a particular lifestyle quickly emerged that was visibly Quaker. Quakers started to adopt plain forms of dress and speech, use 'thee' and 'thou' to everyone instead of the deferential 'you' and number the days and months rather than use pagan-derived names. Quakers eschewed outward war that contradicted the gospels and the idea of spiritual equality. Quakers withdrew from the corrupting temptations of the world.

Structure and process would follow in time, Quakers adopting a collective process of discernment to seek God's will on any matter, based again on a theo-logic of silence and stillness as the way to approach the Divine. Minutes are written and agreed within the meetings to reflect the discernment of the group. Unity implies reliability; disunity may require the matter to be brought back and for Friends to once again set 'self aside' in their quest to know God's leadings. Local 'Meetings' were grouped into regional groupings which met quarterly, with substantial constituencies of geographically dis-crete areas forming a 'Yearly Meeting' which met annually. All of these meetings were open to all Friends although 'meetings for church affairs' became separated by gender beginning in 1675.

Witness was integrated into the spirituality. Quakers enacted signs, pro-tested and petitioned and sought social justice as well as spiritual victory. This early form of an enacted and embodied spirituality has remained the basis for Quakerism in all its forms since. Whilst different groups have given more or less authority to revelation and to Scripture and whilst, since the 1870s, an increasing number of Friends have adopted a pastoral 'pro-grammed' form of worship, the insights of George Fox and the other early Friends remain embedded in the faith, practice and witness of all Yearly Meetings. A pastor has no greater spiritual authority than any other Friend, just those Spirit-given gifts required for the role. Others serve as Elders, nurturing the worship and ministry of the group, still others as Clerks who help manage the meetings for worship for church affairs and who write the minutes reflecting the sense of God's will discerned by the group. Roles are often rotated, although some are 'released' financially to fulfil their ministry.

Quakerism remains a distinctive part of the religious landscape and a compelling subject. We hope this volume brings the nature of Quaker history and development and distinctives of the Quaker faith into clear relief.

CONTENTS

Whilst many introductory volumes have extended histories of the move-ment, we have compressed the 360 years into three chapters. The book then contains five chapters on expressions of Quaker faith, five on regional over-views and five on emerging spiritualities.

History

Robynne Healey covers the earliest period of Quakerism, how it fared during the persecution of the Restoration, how it managed emigration (notably to the Quaker colony of Pennsylvania) and how it developed in the eighteenth century. This latter period was one of relative stability, many of the earlier state-sponsored threats to the movement removed. Quakerism had become an acceptable part of the religious landscape. However, Quakers themselves were less spiritually confident and were wary of a corrupt and corrupting world. They aspired to the supernatural plane whilst fearing all that was 'natural'. At the same time, they were embedded in the wider society rather than removed from it and were active in commerce and social justice campaigns such as those for penal reform and the abolition of the slave trade.

Thomas Hamm and Isaac May cover the nineteenth century. This was the time when Quakerism started to disassemble, fracturing into two main branches (Hicksite and Orthodox) starting in 1827 and into three (Hicksite, Wilburite and Gurneyite) in the 1840s. Influenced by revival meetings that, for some, revealed the limitations of unprogrammed worship, a pastoral tradition emerged within Gurneyite Quakerism in 1875 with all but one Gurneyite Yearly Meetings maintaining pastoral meetings or Friends Churches by 1900. An uneasy tension between a modernist renewal tendency and Holiness revivalism beset this part of the Quaker tradition. At the same time, Gurneyite Yearly Meetings formed a strong coalition after a conference in Richmond, Indiana, in 1887 and by 1902 had founded an umbrella organisation, Five Years Meeting (FYM).

Timothy Burdick and Pink Dandelion cover the twentieth century. Modernist Quakerism emerged not only within parts of Gurneyite Quakerism but also within Hicksite Quakerism by the start of the twentieth century. Hicksite Friends founded Friends General Conference as an umbrella organisation in 1900. FYM continued to be divided between modernist and Holiness Friends and from the 1920s between modernist and fundamentalist Friends. First, fundamentalist Friends pushed for their Yearly Meetings to disengage from the newly formed American Friends Service Committee for its lack of soteriological goals; later they would leave FYM for its lack of doctrinal specificity. By the 1960s, the Evangelical Friends Alliance had been set up as a third umbrella organisation. Conservative Friends (linked to the earlier Wilburite tradition) created a fourth grouping. Burdick and Dandelion concentrate on majority Quakerism, the programmed tradition and its mission work, which had by the end of the twentieth century come to represent nearly 90 percent of global Quakerism. Kenya, following 1902 mission work, is now the most populous country in terms of Quakers. Modernist or Liberal Friends became increasingly detached from their Christian heritage and also increasingly diverse, theologically, as the century wore on.

Expression

Nancy Cho charts Quaker expression through literary and print culture, among British and American Friends. Whilst early Quakers distrusted literature and the arts, Cho shows how Quaker writers have increasingly accepted and utilised a wide variety of literary genres. Initially Quakers worried about how the production and use of fiction fit with the Quaker testimony of integrity. In the early decades, the production of literature among Quakers grew more conservative, as prophetic and ecstatic literature fell out of favour with them. In the nineteenth century, however, John Greenleaf Whittier gained wide recognition as a Quaker poet, but other Friends also adopted the genre, such as abolitionist Elizabeth Margaret Chandler. In the mid-nineteenth century, Quakers were prompted to recognise the presence of beauty in literature and reconsider their objections to that aspect of the human endeavour. Since that time, Quaker literary endeavours have flowered, and Cho looks at the contributions of Quaker writers such as Jessamyn West, Elizabeth Gray Vining, Chuck Fager and Joan Slonczweski.

Katherine Murray continues this theme of action in the world with an overview of Quaker social justice work and how that relates to more recent concerns for sustainability. She points out that seventeenth-century Friends were not dissuaded from Spirit-led actions, such as refusing to doff one's hat to monarchs and nobility, even when such actions were costly, landing them in prison or enduring other kinds of suffering. She briefly reviews the witness of Quakers such as John Woolman and Elizabeth Fry, as well as the contemporary work of organisations such as the American Friends Service Committee, the Friends Committee on National Legislation and the Quaker United Nations Office. She then examines various efforts by Friends in the 2010s on behalf of ecojustice, including the call issued by a worldwide conference in 2012 at Kabarak University in Kenya, asserting that Quakers 'are called to be patterns and examples in a 21st century campaign for peace and ecojustice'.

The section on expressions of Quaker faith continues with a chapter by Elaine Bishop and Jiseok Jung on the Quaker opposition to war. It usefully and deliberately begins, however, with a section on the nature of Quaker testimony, or faith-based expression, as a precursor for what follows. Bishop and Jung cover the history of the Quaker testimony against war and its evolution into a peace testimony. They introduce new work on five ways in which the Quaker peace witness has shifted in the past century and innovative scholarship on two ways in which that witness is now manifest, as peacemaking and as conflict transforming.

Stephen Angell and Clare Brown offer an overview of the Quaker involvement with education historically and in its global breadth today. They chart the changing attitudes and involvement in education over time as well as outline the scope of current Quaker educational provision. The first Quakers were distrustful of too much 'worldly' learning and focused on a 'practical curriculum'. In the eighteenth century, Quakers maintained a 'guarded' or 'select' education system for their children, keen to inculcate a Quaker curriculum in a purely Quaker environment. By the end of the nineteenth century as most Quakers began to see themselves as only a part of the true church rather than the true church itself, the desire to keep Quaker students away from non-Quakers waned, and the curriculum began to broaden. At this time too, Quaker schools outside of Britain and North America started to appear, for example, in Palestine, Lebanon and Japan. Both of these trends continued into the twentieth century with renewed vigour based on the fruits of full citizenship in Britain (Quakers and other nonconformists could go to Oxford and Cambridge after 1871) and missionary work in general. The past century has been one of a huge expansion of Quaker education, both at school and since the 1830s college levels. Questions of appropriate curriculum have continued and Quaker Bible Institutes opened in the early twentieth century as an alternative to a more worldly liberal arts education offered by some Quaker colleges. The ethics of private education has also been a twentieth-century concern. At the same time, Quakers have become keenly involved in helping with the education of non-Quakers, especially those on the margins. The history of Quaker involvement with education is a complex and fascinating topic as Angell and Brown demonstrate.

Emma Jones Lapsansky looks at Quaker material culture and the paradoxical attention to the outward (e.g. in terms of dress or buildings) from adherents to a group centred on an interiorised spirituality. According to most seventeenth- and eighteenth-century Quakers, 'vanity' and 'ostentation' were to be avoided, and an aesthetic of 'plainness' embraced as godly. Lapsansky enquires closely as to what such terms were taken to mean. For the first generation of Friends, it often meant dressing in 'unadorned, often undyed garb'. Quaker meeting houses were modest structures, very different from the ornate churches that arose in late seventeenth-century England. At the same time, wealthy Friends favoured 'meticulous craftsmanship', and in so doing they allowed themselves a certain degree of luxury, at least in terms of the quality of the product. Thus, they sought out consumer goods that were 'of the best sort, but plain'. The more low-cost fabrics of the twentieth and twenty-first centuries have meant that Quaker tastes in clothes have become 'less obvious', but still, like their earlier predecessors, many Friends tend to avoid 'high-fashion trends' as well as 'clothing produced under exploitative conditions'. Quaker architecture went through parallel processes, whereby Quaker plainness, or simplicity, has been reinterpreted over the centuries, but not rejected altogether. Lapsansky concludes with an examination of the ways that simplicity has shaped Quaker liturgy and decision-making processes.

Regional Studies

Our 'Regional Studies' section takes each area of the world and offers a present-day overview in the area as well as a specific case study.

Stephen Angell and John Connell cover North America (the United States and Canada). They focus in particular on the three largest groupings of Quakers, Friends General Conference, Friends United Meeting and Evangelical Friends Church International, charting numerical gains and losses in the recent past alongside the shifting dynamics between meetings of different branches, particularly reunification and schism. A specific case study covers Western Yearly Meeting, an organisation of Friends that is located in Western Indiana in the Midwest region of the United States, and how its fortunes appear in the short-term future. The chapter provides a useful insight into the way different Quaker traditions operate in parallel and where their differing points of vitality lie, as well as how the shape of global Quakerism is shifting away from the dominance of the global north.

Nancy Thomas and Ramon Longoria chart the mainly evangelical Quaker communities of Central and South America. Cuban Friends form the case study in their chapter. They tell a fascinating story that features many dedicated Friends missionaries hailing from a variety of American yearly meetings imbued with evangelical Christian Holiness fervour, but also sensitive profiles of many of the Latin American leaders themselves. In Bolivia, the nation with the most Friends in this region, most of the converts came from the Aymara people, a group that existed prior to the Incas and has its own language. Many Latin American Friends were not Christians prior to becoming Quakers; often they espoused animism. But the Friends in this region are strongly Christian and Quaker. They generally have a strong interest in Quaker testimonies and distinctives, but they also have adapted these to their often lively Latin American cultures.

George Busolo, Oscar Malande, Ann Riggs and Theoneste Sentabire focus on Quakerism in East Africa, with a focus on the Chavakali Yearly Meeting in western Kenya. There are more Quakers in Kenya, and in the East African region, than anywhere else in the world. Since the founding of the Kenyan mission in 1903, Quakers have grown markedly and matured under both colonial and post-colonial contexts. The authors note a variety of cultural and economic challenges as necessary background to their analysis. They also give an in-depth portrayal of African Quaker beliefs, providing contrasts with African traditional religions, and also noting variations between ethnic groups in Kenya. They provide a much needed 'thick' ethnographic description of faith and practice in Vozoli Village Meeting in Chavakali Yearly Meeting, part of the Luhya people dominant in Kenyan Quakerism. They conclude by pointing out that the maturity of Kenyan Quakerism has resulted in a transition from it being a 'mission receiving' to a 'mission sending' church. By 2017, Kenyan Quakers had sent missionaries to Congo, Tanzania and South Sudan, and then across the Atlantic Ocean to Belize, a Central American nation.

Hans Eirik Aarek and Julia Ryberg look at Quakerism in Europe with a particular focus on Friends in Norway and other Scandinavian countries. Quakers are to be found in thirty-five of forty-eight European countries, often in small numbers. In most places, modern liberal Quakerism is dominant, but in Hungary, Romania and Albania, there are significant numbers of evangelical Quakers. European Quakers have often been involved in significant humanitarian activities, especially during the two world wars and the intervening period, and in peace and reconciliation work, especially during the Cold War. In many contexts, European Quakers are experiencing growth and feel a special concern to nurture their small worship groups.

Finally, Stephanie Middori Komashin offers an overview of the highly diverse nature of Quakerism in Southeast Asia and Australasia (Asia Pacific) with a case study on Friends in Japan. While not ignoring other sorts of Friends churches and meetings, Komashin provides an important window into the origins and growth of evangelical Friends churches in Bhutan, Indonesia, the Philippines, Cambodia and elsewhere in the region. Komashin draws a parallel between Asian Friends churches and those Friends churches in Latin America and Africa, in that Friends churches in each of these regions are primed for rapid growth. She also provides vivid detail about differences between all of these Friends churches, even those within the same branch. Mission is a central theme throughout all of these chapters as well as the continual development of new local groups of Quakerism, adapting to new contexts, new challenges and new opportunities.

Emerging Spiritualities

The final section of the book is entitled 'Emerging Spiritualities'. Each of the five chapters considers an aspect of the variety of current Quaker spirituality. Michael Birkel and Deborah Shaw look at Conservative Quaker spirituality, its distinctive practices and its enduring appeal, and then the way some Liberal Friends have chosen dual affiliation, for example, maintaining Buddhist as well as Quaker practice. They uncover a Quaker tradition which is 'not static but rather unfolding'. Friends holding dual traditions have combined them in varying ways, and they seek to bring benefit to their Quaker communities in disparate ways. Often they point to a more direct teaching of these varieties of Quaker spiritualities than what commonly occurred in generations past. William Taber, for example, was mindful of the Conservative tradition of intuitive acquisition of spiritual traits, but, believing that there was insufficient resources for contemporary Friends to gain spiritual depth by such means, he 'departed from Conservative tradition and wrote boldly' about a variety of spiritual concerns and practices.

Dan Christy Randazzo looks at one aspect of the spectrum of Liberal Quaker belief, non-theism, and the debates that have emerged within liberal Quakerism, mostly in Britain and the United States, during recent decades over the use of the term 'God' as necessary or appropriate. He charts a great variety of arguments. Some non-theists, for example, use certain Quaker concepts to argue against others which they see as intrinsically theist. Others attempt to honour the Christian roots of Quakers by working systematically to bridge the original Christian understandings and the non-theism of some contemporary Quakers. Randazzo perceives room for Quaker non-theism to grow but adds that it will need to remain in dialogue with other types of Liberal Quakerism to 'make effective contributions to the development of Liberal Quakerism' going forward.

Jon Kershner gives an overview of present-day evangelical Quaker spirituality. He provides a thorough overview of several types of evangelical Quaker spirituality, focusing especially on differences between North American evangelical Quakerism and the evangelical Quakerism of the Global South. He also points to commonalities and variations in worship forms among evangelical Quakers. He provides helpful summaries of some disputes that were current in the 2010s, especially in the manner that evangelical regard for biblical authority-oriented evangelical Quakers when confronting issues of homosexuality.

Wess Daniels and Greg Woods build on Daniels's earlier work on 'Convergent Quakerism', a movement of mainly younger Friends from different Quaker traditions keen to conserve Quaker distinctives and yet engage with wider culture as part of the emergent church movement. This chapter typifies the continual dynamic interplay between constancy and change that we find throughout Quaker history and which has so dominated the past century.

Margery Post Abbott reviews the pioneering work of the North Pacific Women's Theological Discussion Group, which has successfully bridged different Quaker traditions in a powerful example of intra-Quaker ecumenism. She then broadens her analysis geographically by looking at ways that women in other parts of the Quaker world – most notably, Indiana (United States) and Kenya – have acted to empower women in the face of their exclusion from decision-making roles, or to preserve and to nurture Quaker unity when divisions have been threatened or actually have occurred. She proposes that this work by women is a concrete manifestation in the contemporary world of the ministry and teachings of Jesus.

Many books outline the history and expression of the Quaker movement, but this volume is distinct in at least three ways. First, it presents a new range of authors, many writing their first book chapters. Each is an accomplished scholar but as editors we have deliberately sought out those with a fresh and innovative edge to their work. This is not a book of 'settled scholarship' but of new ideas and ways of approaching the study of Quakerism. The section on 'Emerging Spiritualities' enables the volume to be timely and relevant.

Second, we trust that this volume redresses the erstwhile bias towards Liberal Quakerism inherent in the way that many earlier histories have been written by Liberal Friends rather than Evangelical ones.

Third, and crucially, we believe this volume is the first that is explicitly global in its authorship and coverage of the different branches of Quakerism. Too often, Quaker studies have been centred on Anglo-American history and experience. We hope this book goes some way to redress this deficit.

∾

PART I

HISTORY OF QUAKER FAITH AND PRACTICE

ॐ

History of Quaker Faith and Practice: 1650–1808

Robynne Rogers Healey

Periodising Quaker history is a challenge. The sect's apocalyptic origins set against the backdrop of the seventeenth-century English Civil Wars (1642–51) and Interregnum (1649–60), its survival and growth in the wake of the Restoration (1660) and persecution, its evolution to respectability following the Glorious Revolution (1688), and its continued expansion throughout the Atlantic world in the eighteenth century suggest a periodisation aligned with time-honoured political events. Certainly, as will be evident in this chapter, political affairs strongly shaped the contours of Quaker history. They cannot be ignored. Nevertheless, historians have identified less-conventional moments that significantly influenced Quaker theology and the expression of the faith among the sect's followers. James Nayler's Christ-like procession into Bristol (1656), *The Testimony of the Brethren* (1666), the loss of leading Friends in the 1690s, and internal reformation beginning in the mid-eighteenth century are all signposts that mark one Quaker period apart from others. This chapter examines the first 150 years of Quaker history. While it relies on chronological divisions of origins to 1660 (the Lamb's War), 1660 to 1680s (the Restoration), and the long eighteenth century (commonly called the 'Quietist' period), there is overlap between the periods, rather than sharp breaks. And while there was change in expression or practice of the faith, there was also continuity. The Inward Light, revelation, spiritual equality, Quaker witness (also called ethics or 'testimonies'), and group governance through discernment persisted through all three periods, and remain common to Friends today (Dandelion 2008).

ORIGINS AND THE LAMB'S WAR

The late 1640s, when Quakerism first emerged, was a turbulent period in English history. It was, in the words of one observer, 'the world turn'd upside down' (Taylor 1647). It seems likely that, despite occurrences of the plague, the population nearly doubled in the century before 1650, rising from 2.77 million in 1541 to 5.23 million in 1651 (Wrigley and Schofield 1989, 528). For a predominantly agricultural population, land enclosures and amalgamations had created dispossessed groups. Famines devastated northern populations in 1597 and 1623; these were followed by a poor harvest in 1630 and failed harvests in 1647, 1648, and 1649 (Appleby 1978, 109–55). The Civil Wars destroyed crops and animals at the same time mobile armies required food supplies to be delivered at a moment's notice (Thirsk 1990, 128). The economically powerful benefitted from rising prices, but for the majority, poverty, unemployment, and vagrancy were commonplace. With no king on the throne, these years were both uncertain and full of possibility. Restrictions on speech, printing, and modes of worship were lifted (Moore 2000, 3). Debates on politics and religion were easily disseminated in inexpensive pamphlets. As a result, political and religious factions, such as the Levellers, Fifth Monarchists, Diggers, Ranters and Muggletonians, thrived alongside 'separated' churches of Independents and Baptists (Barbour and Frost 1988, 14–20; Moore 2000, 4–5). Within these groups, and sometimes distinct from them, were 'Seekers' – those who sought, but had not found, what today might be called an 'authentic' faith experience (Gwyn 2015, 14). Those who viewed social structures as the root of injustice, and political action as its solution, found a home among the radical sects listed previously. Those who saw pride and ambition as the source of injustice, and spiritual regeneration as its remedy, found a new vision of human society in Quakerism, a religious movement that began to spread across the north of England beginning with George Fox's profound experiences of the divine (Ingle 1994, 49–50).

Moore (2002, 5) reminds us that 'there are no contemporary records of Quaker beginnings', leaving us to rely on early pages in George Fox's (1952) *Journal*, an autobiography composed in the 1670s. Ingle (1994, 3) identifies Fox as the 'founder' of Quakerism, but most scholars consider him 'the leading personality' (Moore 2013, 15) alongside other early Friends who 'for a period brought as strong a message as Fox' (Barbour and Frost 1988, 25). (James Nayler, Margaret Fell, Edward Burrough, Francis Howgill, Richard Hubberthorne, Richard Farnsworth, and William Dewsbury were all respected early leaders.) One record, included late in the *Journal*, gives the following account: 'The Truth sprang up first, in Leicestershire in 1644, in Warwickshire in 1645, in Nottinghamshire in 1646, in Derbyshire in 1647, and in the adjacent counties in 1648, 49, and 1650' (Fox 1952, 709). If these dates are correct, Moore contends that 'proto-Quaker groups existed in the East Midlands before there is any clear record of them, and possibly before the first preaching of George Fox' (Moore 2000, 5). Despite multiple influential preachers in the movement's earliest years, by 1655–56 Friends themselves recognised Fox as pre-eminent (Moore 2000, 30).

Fox was born in 1624 to a Puritan family in Fenny Drayton, Leicestershire County. He believed himself a pious, serious child (Fox 1952, 1). In 1643 he set off on a faith pilgrimage of sorts. Travelling, he found himself 'tempted almost to despair' (Fox 1952, 4), a state that continued for some years, despite his seeking counsel from both clerical and lay people whom he considered 'miserable comforters' (Fox 1952, 6). In either 1646 or 1647, travelling through Leicestershire, Fox encountered 'a tender people, and a very tender woman' (Fox 1952, 9), Elizabeth Hooton, a former Baptist, distinguished as 'the first Quaker' and Fox's 'first disciple' (Barbour and Frost 1988, 331). An influential and dedicated Quaker, Hooton was the first woman to travel in Quaker ministry. Shortly after this encounter, Fox had his watershed experience, recalling:

> And when all my hopes in them and in all men were gone, so that I had nothing outwardly to help me, nor could tell what to do, then, Oh then, I heard a voice which said, 'There is one, even Christ Jesus, that can speak to thy condition', and when I heard it my heart did leap for joy. Then the Lord did let me see why there was none upon the earth that could speak to my condition, namely, that I might give him all the glory ... that Jesus Christ might have the pre-eminence, who enlightens, and gives grace, and faith, and power ... And I knew this experimentally. (Fox 1952, 11)

Gwyn refers to this moment as 'Fox's epistemological break' (Gwyn 2015, 17). The experience of revelation was key. Pondering this, Fox equated his experience to those of the authors of biblical texts: 'These things I did not see by the help of man, nor by the letter, though they are written in the letter, but I saw them in the light of the Lord Jesus Christ, and by his immediate Spirt and power, as did the holy men of God, by whom the Holy Scriptures were written' (Fox 1952, 34).

The Inward Light was fundamental to Fox's theology. Its transformative power was universal in that it dwelt in all people; any who turned to it could experience Christ's saving power; any who turned from it condemned themselves (Hinds 2015, 48–54). Another important element in Fox's theology emerged from an experience in 1648 that led him to claim that perfection, or freedom from sin, was possible (Fox 1952, 27). Good could conquer evil. Together revelation and perfection culminated in what Quakers called the 'Lamb's War', both an intensely personal experience leading to the defeat of evil within oneself and a corporate confrontation against evil in the larger world. Fox's travels from 1647 to 1650 increased the number of Friends, as he called them. Their Lamb's War theology led to militancy, alarming authorities and leading to arrests and imprisonments. It was at a 1650 trial in Derby that a justice derisively labelled Fox and his co-religionists 'Quakers' in reference to their trembling and quaking worship (Ingle 1994, 54; Moore 2013, 16).

The earliest Quakerism was charismatic in expression and apocalyptic in theology. This combination appealed to inhabitants of the north where Quaker itinerants took their message in the summer of 1652. Still referred to as the '1652 country', here the Quaker message landed on fertile ground. At least a tenth of the population was gathered into the Quaker fold; of these, approximately 10,000 or 25 percent became permanent Friends (Reay 1985, 28–29). It was an important moment for the nascent religious movement. Leaders such as James Nayler revealed sufficient skill, charisma, or inspiration to convert his trial judge (Moore 2013, 18). Margaret Fell and her family, excepting her husband Thomas Fell, a judge of Assize and member of Parliament, were convinced of Friends' principles. Thomas Fell supported and protected Quakers and the Fell home, Swarthmoor Hall, became the organisational centre of the movement. Margaret Fell became Quakers' primary administrator and fundraiser, and her gentry status opened doors to influence at critical times.

On the heels of their northern success, Quakers – male and female – journeyed forth, combatants in the Lamb's War. Usually in pairs, these 'First Publishers of Truth' or 'the Valiant Sixty'[1] spread across England, Wales, Scotland, and Ireland in 1654 with varying degrees of success. Friends established vibrant congregations throughout England, had a considerable following in Wales, a presence in Ireland among the Ulster Irish and English colonists in Dublin but had little success in Scotland. London became an important centre in the movement, even the administrative centre by the late 1650s, although the northwest retained the largest concentration of Friends (Braithwaite 1912, 78–110). In 1655 Quakers travelled to Holland and Germany as well as to the Atlantic colonies, and in 1657 a group carried the message east to the Mediterranean. Sultan Mohammed IV of Constantinople, while unconvinced, received Friends including Mary Fisher kindly. Pope Alexander VII was not as welcoming, incarcerating John Luffe and John Perrot; Luffe died in prison, possibly starving himself to death

---

[1] The term 'Valiant Sixty' is an early twentieth-century term given to the pairs of evangelist Quakers of 1654. Fox initially recorded that there were seventy ministers, the same number of disciples Jesus sent out in Luke 10:1. That number was changed to sixty in the first published edition of Fox's *Journal* in 1694 to avoid the direct comparison that might provoke anti-Quaker reactions.

(Carroll 2010, 4). These early leaders took seriously Fox's exhortation to 'let your lives preach' (Hinds 2015, 55) and most practiced an intensely embodied theology that, paradoxically, expanded the movement by attracting new followers from all walks of life at the same time that it heightened opposition to, and persecution of, Friends.

Fuelling both expansion and opposition was Quakers' use of the press, an important weapon in the Lamb's War. Without controls on printing during the Interregnum, Quakers took to the written word to develop, spread, and defend their faith; to encourage organisation and discipline; to draw together a scattered network of meetings and travelling ministers; and to participate in political life (Peters 2005; Hagglund 2015; Landes 2015, 107–25). They were prolific writers, publishing some thirty-six titles in 1653, sixty in 1654, and between eighty and ninety per year from 1655 to 1658 (Moore 2013, 20). Their opponents were equally as profuse; more than 300 anti-Quaker titles appeared in the 1650s (Moore 2013, 22). Women authored some early tracts, though the number of female authors does not reflect their presence in the movement (Peters 2005, 129). Nonetheless, Quakers' defence of women's spiritual equality and their right to preach was a reflection of a practice in which Quaker women were already actively engaged (Peters 2005, 150).

The Quaker movement faced a significant crisis in 1656 when James Nayler, considered almost equal in leadership to Fox, and some supporters, led by Martha Simmons, processed into Bristol recreating Christ's entry into Jerusalem. Much has been written about the motivations of Nayler and the women who encouraged or supported this pageant, and space does not allow for further examination (Bittle 1986; Damrosch 1996; Massey 1999; Smith 2007; Neelon 2009). Most recently, Spencer suggests Nayler's actions were a kind of 'performance theology', reflecting his belief in Christ's 'immanent, cosmic presence, alive and at work universally' (Spencer 2015, 64–65). Local Friends were not supportive. Authorities were horrified and arrested the party on a charge of blasphemy. The case was sufficiently notorious to be tried by Parliament, which condemned Nayler to pillorying, flogging, boring of the tongue, branding, and imprisonment. These events, transpiring while Fox was incarcerated, were a turning point for Quakerism. Nayler spent the rest of his days, until his death in 1660, reconciling himself to Friends. Fox, mindful of the damage to Friends' reputation, took firmer hold of leadership and increasingly emphasised unity and order, marking the beginning of Quakers' 'metamorphosis from early enthusiasm to later soberness' (Moore 2000, 46). Quaker pamphlets generally shifted from apocalyptic proclamations to apologetics (Moore 2013, 24). And Quaker worship featured much less 'threshing'.

The Nayler affair highlighted the need for stronger organisation and regulation of individual members. Quakers had not been without organisation to that point; the need for discipline and care of the poor and persecuted emerged alongside the movement itself. Even so, believing they were living in an unfolding end time, church organisation had been designed to meet the needs of the moment, not the long term. Local meetings for worship sometimes gathered in a 'General Meeting', and 'Monthly Meetings' for business were established. Particularly important was the regulation of sexual behaviour, given early scandals and Friends' desire to regulate civil marriage themselves, distinct from magistrates. The word 'overseer' first appears in marriage regulations pointing to a hierarchy of church government between Fox and Fell and the local meetings (Moore 2000, 136). The strongest evidence for changes in church government is in the 1656 Epistle from the Elders of Balby (Barclay 1841, 277–82). Highly prescriptive, its twenty clauses articulate directions for meeting arrangements; personal life from birth to burial; ministry; relations within the meeting, within the family, and with the state; and conduct in business. That same year men Friends established a regular business meeting in London; a women's meeting to manage care of the poor began shortly afterwards. In 1657 and 1658 Quaker headquarters moved from Swarthmoor to London, and a clerk, Ellis Hookes, was appointed to manage meeting business (Moore 2000, 140). About the same time Fox directed Friends to send records of persecution to London for documentation. The elaborate hierarchy of Meetings was still to come, but a network of meetings linked to a strong central organisation in London was in place by 1658, ensuring stability during the difficult years ahead.

Oliver Cromwell died in 1658. His son, Richard, succeeded him but was unable to maintain order and the country descended into chaos, leading Quakers to wonder if God's kingdom was nigh. Feeling God on their side, Friends, especially Edward Burrough, churned out political commentary at a rate of several pamphlets each week (Moore 2000, 168). Hope faded in 1659 as persecution of the sects, especially Quakers, increased. By December 1659 the London men's meeting was advising Quakers to stay clear of politics (Moore 2000, 174). It was a confusing time. The Commonwealth fell; the exiled Charles Stuart outlined his terms for the restoration of the monarchy in the Declaration of Breda (4 April 1660); the Convention Parliament accepted the Declaration; and, in May 1660, King Charles II was proclaimed lawful monarch.

RESTORATION QUAKERISM

The Declaration of Breda promised a degree of religious toleration, but the religious settlement proved remarkably intolerant. Anglican clerics, deprived of their livings in the 1650s, retaliated against the sects. Quakers were especially suspect and the clergy accused them of blasphemy (Manning 2009). Conservative Anglicans 'now securely entrenched' in the Cavalier Parliament 'wielded their magisterial powers' (Greaves 1992, 240). Where prosecutions had been relatively light in 1660, they increased drastically in 1661. Between the two years, prosecutions escalated: in London and Middlesex from 19 to 338; in Bristol from 'few to none' to 186; in Durham and Northumberland from 6 to 108; and in Cumberland from 48 to 106 (Greaves 1992, 240–41). Quakers were not the only disaffected group. In January 1661 a small mob of Fifth Monarchists, led by Thomas Venner, took to the streets of London in armed insurrection aimed at overthrowing king and Parliament. This was not Venner's first attempt at rebellion; he had led a failed uprising in 1657 (Shilston 2012, 59). He did not get a third chance. The uprising was crushed and Venner along with thirteen associates were hanged, drawn, and quartered (Greaves 1986, 49–57; Shilston 2012, 60). A legislative program of religious intolerance (the Clarendon Code) and the brutal suppression of the sects followed. Quakers, suspected of involvement in the uprising, declared their innocence and allegiance to the Crown, and issued their 1661 *Declaration ... Against all Sedition, Plotters, and Fighters* (Fox 1660) often considered the first statement of the Peace Testimony. Their assertions fell on deaf ears, and the promise of religious freedom went unrealised.

The Clarendon Code (1661–65) and the Quaker Act (1662) were punitive laws used to persecute dissenters between 1660 and 1689. Non-compliance made Quakers vulnerable to the seizure of their property, hostility, arrest, and imprisonment. Quakers engendered antagonism and distrust for more than their refusal to pay tithes and swear allegiance to the king (Ayoub 2005, 45–63); Davies maintains their 'aggressive proselytizing and disregard for communal norms earned them a reputation as God's awkward squad' (Davies 2000, 30). Even their deportment was deemed offensive (Davies 2000, 45–63). Persecution took many forms, carefully recorded in the Great Book of Sufferings. Prison was particularly grim. Insalubrious conditions led to illness and death; 11,000 Quakers were imprisoned during Charles II's reign (Dandelion 2008, 16); as many as 450 Quakers died there, including a number of important leaders (Allen 2013, 32). Those not killed by detention suffered ill health from the experience. Friends did not avoid persecution, nor did they seek it out. Nevertheless, persecution led to a theology of suffering in which faith and persecution reinforced each other, and suffering was central to Quaker identity (Ayoub 2005, 48–49; Miller 2005, 71). Always active agents, Quakers became adept in the law and used it to contest persecution. And the central organisation in London provided legal advice to members at the same time that it vigorously lobbied Parliament and the courts for religious liberty and relief from persecution (Hunt 1961; Greaves 2001).

Outwardly Friends addressed allegations of fanaticism and sedition; inwardly Fox and other leaders strengthened structure and order. Survival, in the midst of persecution, depended on adapting to the political climate. In the 1660s Fox developed a hierarchical arrangement of meetings for worship and business with London Yearly Meeting as the centre of guidance and discipline (Allen 2013, 35–36). Business meetings implemented the instructions first issued at Balby in 1656. In 1660 Friends determined the annual General Assembly should be in London; this Meeting convened in May 1661 but met irregularly until 1668.

Intended to strengthen unity among its widespread disciples, centralisation tested it. John Perrot, returned from Rome in 1661, opposed what he saw as imperatives that stifled the Light and forced the conscience (Martin 2003, 9; Pestana 2015, 182–83). Perrot criticised prearranged meetings and the Quaker tradition of removing hats in prayer. He published his opinions without clearing them with the Quaker leadership. In view of fierce persecution, with memories of the damage caused by Nayler's 'leadings', Perrot's position became a flashpoint in part because it challenged Foxian centralisation and order. Friends censured Perrot in 1662 and dissociated themselves from him. Despite his voluntary exile to Barbados, he continued to share his schismatic beliefs, causing challenges for Quakers abroad (Worrall 1980, 29–30; Gragg 2009, 45–48). Furthermore, in London, Isaac Pennington (Cambridge-educated, former Puritan theologian and leading Friend) was sympathetic to Perrot. Careful persuasion brought him to submit to Fox's leadership (Moore 2000, 200–203; Keiser 2015, 198). Some mechanism for preventing division seemed necessary. In May 1666 Richard Farnworth and ten other London leaders delivered the solution in *The Testimony of the Brethren* (Barclay 1841, 318–24). It stressed that controlling the activities and publications of those 'out of unity with the body of Friends' was necessary to Quakerism's integrity.

Between 1666 and 1668 Fox overhauled the meeting structure in what he called 'Gospel Order'. Monthly Meetings within counties were organised into Quarterly Meetings that selected Yearly Meeting representatives who carried forward issues that could not be resolved at the local or regional level.

Particular Meetings (Preparative Meetings in North America) were the smallest unit, similar to local congregations; they reported to Monthly Meetings. Yearly Meetings were also organised in Ireland, Scotland, Wales, and in North American colonies where Friends had a presence (New England Yearly Meeting, initially called Rhode Island Yearly Meeting, first met in 1661). Colonies such as Barbados without a Yearly Meeting were still part of a 'well-ordered' structure (Gragg 2009, 54). In 1673 the Second Day Morning Meeting was formed to oversee Quaker publishing and manage the itinerant ministry. It 'gradually became responsible for the outward face of Quakerism' (Landes 2015, 25). In 1676 the Meeting for Sufferings was created to record sufferings, lobby government, and handle finances (Landes 2015, 29–32). These two administrative meetings managed the Society's affairs when Yearly Meeting was not in session. In 1679 the London Yearly Meeting (LYM) requested that local meetings respond to a set of Queries and Advices to assess the spiritual wellbeing of its meetings. The system of business meetings now handled both the behaviour and needs of its members (Barbour and Frost 1988, 68). Women played an important role in this new order, although not without question. It has already been established that women were critical in Fox's religious experiences and in the foundation and survival of the Society (see also Trevett 1991, 2000; Gill 2005). Where women's meetings had been established, they managed charitable work, as with the Box Meeting (Bacon 1986, 20–21; Landes 2015, 33). During Fox's re-ordering of meetings, he urged Friends to establish women's meetings parallel to men's meetings at every level (Larson 1999, 31). Some found this too innovative, and it was the source of controversy for many years (Martin 2003, 11).

The decision to impose uniformity of practice was challenged. Particularly suspect were women's meetings to which men might have to submit in pursuit of marriage clearance (Martin 2003, 14). The Wilkinson-Story Controversy surfaced in the early 1670s when John Wilkinson and John Story of the Preston Patrick Meeting in Westmoreland disputed these actions and the authority of London to set policy for the entire Society in what they called 'Foxonian-Unity' (Martin 2003, 12). Their meeting separated from the main body of Quakers, but they stirred up displeasure and factions (Worrall 1980, 64–65; Martin 2003, 12–15). Epistles from London in both 1673 and 1675 exhorted Friends to submit to the will of their 'brothers' and tried to ward off the crisis developing by the 'disorderly proceedings of some professing the truth' (Ingle 1994, 258).

Quaker missionary efforts continued after the Restoration with the greatest success in Britain's Atlantic colonies (Allen 2007b; Juterczenka 2007). The transatlantic network of Quaker meetings became so successful that scholars have referred to it as the Quaker Atlantic (Healey 2011; Landes 2015, ch. 6). The Barbadian mission thrived early and, prior to the migration to Pennsylvania, 'Barbados had more Quakers than any other English colony' (Gragg 2009, 1). Fox visited for three months in 1671–72 as did other ministers; between 1655 and 1720, more than seventy 'public Friends' visited the island (Gragg 2009, 57). While the Quaker population on Barbados increased in the 1670s and 1680s, it declined beginning in the 1690s. Emigration to Pennsylvania was a significant factor in this decline (Gragg 2009, 143–44).

Thus, prior to the establishment of Pennsylvania in 1681, in the face of brutal persecution, even execution, Friends had established a presence in the American colonies, but they retained hopes for a Quaker colony (Worrall 1980, 3–25; Pestana 1993, Carroll 2010). When the king granted William Penn the colony of Pennsylvania, Quakers had their opportunity for 'The Holy Experiment'. Around the time Penn received his charter, Friends had secured part ownership of West Jersey and had purchased East Jersey (Allen 2013, 40). Settlement of these areas dovetailed with settlement of Pennsylvania. The promise of religious freedom, coupled with social and economic factors in Britain, drew many Quakers to Pennsylvania, so many in fact that the declining size of some British meetings caused concern. One Welsh Quaker feared depletion of the community would 'hasten [his] hoary head to the grave', and the Yearly Meeting clerk attributed 'runnings into Pensilvania' as 'a cause of great weakening (if not total decayinge) of some meetings' (Allen 2004, 42). Pennsylvania Quakers replicated Fox's hierarchical structure of meetings and held the first session of the Philadelphia Yearly Meeting (PYM) in the fall of 1681. Travelling ministers and correspondence maintained a strong transatlantic connection between the American Meetings and London Yearly Meeting. Even so PYM, like New England Yearly Meeting, was technically independent (Hamm 2003, 28).

Commerce followed closely on the heels of migration and was important together with travelling ministers and the printed word, in reinforcing expanding transatlantic Quaker networks (Winchester 1991; Landes 2015, 37–63, 84–106). Overseas trade was risky; a good reputation and a strong network were critical. Friends' reputation for honesty in business and their use of fixed prices and 'just weights and measures' (Freeman 2013, 422) contributed to their early business success. In spite of the business-related hurdles they faced because of the oath (they could not prosecute business interests in court), they were able to leverage Quaker networks and a number became remarkably successful even before their mastery of commerce and industry in the eighteenth century (Nash 1986, 337–62; Roberts 2004, 183–84; Landes 2015, 97–101).

THE LONG EIGHTEENTH CENTURY

A confluence of factors in the late seventeenth century altered the political and religious climate for Quakers and the nature of Quakerism itself. The 1680s were unsettled years with the death of Charles II in 1685, the accession of James II, and his subsequent deposition in 1688 by William and Mary in the Glorious Revolution. The 1689 Toleration Act granted limited rights to non-conformists and suspended the harshest elements of the Restoration settlement. Dissenters could worship unmolested in registered places of worship, but they could neither attend universities nor hold political office, and the Church of England remained the established church supported by the tithes of all subjects.

Where Quakers had held out hope for the imminent eschaton in the unstable years pre-Restoration, they now fixed their sights on survival as a separated, peculiar people. This was not an altogether new development. The introspective theology Robert Barclay outlined in his *Apology* (1678) had been formed in the context of persecution and debate (Pyper 2015). What emerged was a 'meantime', not an end time, theology (Dandelion 2010), a 'theology for the eschaton deferred' (Healey 2013). During the Restoration Quakers had achieved some level of accommodation with mainstream society through local interactions and well-developed lobbying efforts (Horle 1988; Davies 2000; Miller 2005; Allen 2007a). Even so, there remained considerable suspicion about the orthodoxy of Quakers' theology and their inclusion in toleration. During this fragile period, a number of prominent Friends died. Fox's death, and the end of his charismatic leadership, in 1691 was a particular loss. Barclay's death in 1690 and Stephen Crisp's in 1692 were also felt keenly. At the same time Penn was embattled. Considered a traitor by the Crown because of his close relationship with James II, Penn lost his colony between 1691 and 1693 and lived in perilous uncertainty for a number of years.

Another internal disagreement compounded conditions. Whereas previous quarrels had been focussed on organisational changes, the Keithian Controversy began as a theological dispute then became coloured by politics (Birkel 2015a, 264). George Keith, the Quaker at the centre of the argument, was not a marginal Friend. Originally from the Aberdeen Meeting, he had worked in ministry alongside Robert Barclay, George Fox, William Penn, and George Whitehead before emigrating to East

Jersey in 1684 as surveyor-general. Originally viewed as one of the Society's 'best systematic theologians' (Barbour and Frost 1988, 79), Friends now remember him as 'the great apostate' (Birkel 2015a, 256). In 1689 Keith relocated to Philadelphia where he was shocked by (what he considered) Quakers' biblical illiteracy and unorthodox commitment to the incarnation and the physical Christ. Early Quakers had not been united on these issues, nor did they feel a unified position was necessary. After all, their Inward Light was the same Light that inspired Scripture. Keith recommended a number of reforms in 'Gospel Order Improved', including the necessity of a written creed (Butler 1974, 435–37). This did not sit well with non-creedal Friends who resisted any limitation of the power of the Light to a set of formal statements. Acrimony ensued, driven by Keith's view that Quakers' rejection of his reforms was proof of their heretical beliefs, and magnified by Keith's 'high opinion of himself' (Martin 2003, 17) and his 'acerbic manner' (Birkel 2015a, 264). PYM disowned him in 1692, 'not for doctrinal matters but for his divisiveness' (Birkel 2015a, 265). There was no quick resolution to this conflict. Keith published his version of events (Keith 1692; Keith and Budd 1692). Attempts to silence him through a defamation trial failed. Charity was in short supply on both sides (Butler 1974, 440–52).

In 1694 both parties sought redress in London, although the fallout of the dispute had preceded them with reprints of Keith's works being published in London in 1693. The extent and significance of transatlantic networks is evident in the reverberations of this conflict throughout the Quaker Atlantic. Given the political context, the dispute became grounds for a schism. LYM disowned Keith in 1695, again for his manner not his beliefs, although the differences were theological (Martin 2003, 15–18). For years thereafter, Keith exposed, through public meetings and written denuncia-tions, what he saw as the heresies of Quakerism, particularly those of George Whitehead, William Penn, and the late Robert Barclay (Keith 1696, 1697, 1698, 1700, 1701).

Keith was not the only person accusing Quakers of heresy and blasphemy. Apostates including Francis Bugg joined Keith and other clergy in launching another series of attacks on Friends who found themselves in the untenable position of defending the Christian orthodoxy of their faith and their inclu-sion in the Toleration Act. George Whitehead, one of the few remaining Valiant Sixty and a recognised leader of LYM after Fox's death, acted as one of the Society's chief defenders. His perspectives in a renewed pamphlet war must be understood in this light. *The Christian Doctrine* (1693), issued as a response to Keith and his American supporters, appears creedal, but Whitehead (1697, 156) denied this. Even though his theology was

Christological, he refused to confine grace to Scripture or to set Scripture in opposition to the Light, believing any attempt to do so limited the 'precious mystery' at the heart of Christianity.

Endless conflict did not alter Quakers' theological commitment to the Inward Light and revelation. It did, however, deepen their commitment to Quietist theology, predominant enough in this era that the long eighteenth century has been dubbed the 'Quietist period' (Braithwaite 1919; Jones 1921; Healey 2013). Quietism is associated with elimination of human will, or 'creaturely activity', through silent introspection and separation from the unholy world. It looked significantly different from the ecstatic faith of the Lamb's War. But eighteenth-century Quakerism was diverse; rationalism (moderate Quakerism that navigated the space between reason and revelation) and evangelicalism (more focussed on the atonement of the historic Christ and the supremacy of Scripture) were held in tension with eighteenth-century Quietism (Healey, forthcoming). Moreover, Quietism was paradoxical. Spiritual withdrawal from the world was coupled with the impetus to social reform. Dandelion (2010) contends that eighteenth-century Quakers created a dualistic world in which their mysticism remained separate from the world they worked to reform. Kershner (2013, 23) suggests that apocalyptic sentiments shaped John Woolman's Quietist theology 'suggestive of broader tropes in Quaker history'. Certainly, Whitehead, attributed with deepening the descent into Quietism (Punshon 1984; Barbour and Frost 1988) practiced a dualistic theology. At the same time he called for retreat from the world, he led the charge in the theological debates of the 1690s. While Quakers became more rigid about regulating behaviour (orthopraxy), Quietism distinguished between unholy (secular) and holy (spiritual) battles, shunning the former and fighting the latter (Healey 2015).

Eighteenth-century Quakerism became more organised, bureaucratised, and hierarchical in an expansion of Gospel Order and sectarianism. Consider membership. Until significant transatlantic migration began in the late seventeenth century, local meetings recognised who belonged and who did not. Colonial meetings, swelling with newly arrived immigrants, could not be certain. After 1700 they requested that LYM and its constituent meetings issue certificates to emigrating Friends, testifying to their standing in the Society, their ability to marry, and their credit status (Butler 1978, 28–29). Poor relief, a benefit of membership, was another concern. Reliably identifying members and determining the Meeting responsible for poor relief costs in cases of relocation compelled stricter classification. LYM first defined membership, and birthright membership, in a 1737 minute on 'Removals and Settlements', which dictated that children and wives of members were to be counted. While the practice of identifying children of members as members had been the convention, it had not yet been codified. This change expanded the ranks of nominal Friends who were Quaker by birth not by choice, affecting the spiritual vitality of the Society (Jones 1921, 108–10). The focus on uniformity of practice is apparent in the codification and collection of Advices, Queries, and rules of discipline. New England Yearly Meeting replaced the advices of Fox and other visitors with a formal Discipline in 1708 (Worrall 1980). The Philadelphia Yearly Meeting approved its first Discipline in 1704; this was subsequently lengthened and more carefully arranged in 1719 (Butler 1978; Bronner 1986). The London Yearly Meeting issued copies of Christian and brotherly advices, called The Book of Extracts, in 1738 (Punshon 1984, 137). The consistency of testimonies eased migration back and forth across the Atlantic, as Friends adjusted easily to new Meetings (Bronner 1986). Still, local contexts in a transatlantic world shaped expressions of Quakerism. In 1783 *The Book of Extracts* became the first officially printed Discipline (Jones 1921, 143); the American Yearly Meetings printed their Disciplines shortly thereafter (Barbour and Frost 1988, 108). Before mass printing, Disciplines were not updated consistently. Nonetheless, Yearly Meetings expected that discipline would be enforced.

Changes in the Discipline's testimonies over the eighteenth century reflect the Quietist paradox of sectarianism and humanitarianism. Plainness of speech, apparel, and decoration began as a renunciation of principles considered incompatible with true Christianity (Frost 2003, 17). Ideally, turning away from vanity in all things oriented Friends to a worshipful posture and were visible signs of godliness (Frost 2003; Lapsansky 2013). Eighteenth-century plainness became more circumscribed and subject to discipline. Defining plainness has always been imprecise; Quakers chose to stipulate what was *not* plain. Even the size of buttonholes was prescribed and, over the century, plain style became a drab, uniform costume (Frost 2003). First-generation Friend Margaret Fell Fox questioned the wisdom of this in 1698: 'for they can soon get into an outward garb, to be all alike outwardly, but this will not make them true Christians' (Barbour and Roberts 2004, 566). Eighteenth-century plainness functioned as a hedge keeping Quakers distinct from the world. Operating hand-in-hand with plainness was endogamy; Quakers were only to marry one another. These ideals were easier to dictate than achieve, and the epistolary correspondence of this period is rife with grievances against wrongdoers. Friends aimed to remedy this mid-century by launching an internal reformation. Beginning in 1755 in Philadelphia, enforcement of the Discipline became a priority to restore the 'primitive beauty and purity of the Church' (Marietta 2007, 54). Cases of discipline and disownment escalated. Between

1750 and 1790, PYM disowned 50 percent of its birthright members (Levy 1988, 16). The attention on endogamy and premarital sex (Marietta 2007, 3–31) shifted the emphasis to the family as the focus of purity and the hope for its future (Vann 1969; Frost 1973; Levy 1988; Marietta 2007), although allegiance to the faith superseded loyalty to the family (Forbes 1982; Mack 2003). LYM followed a similar reform beginning in 1760 (Punshon 1984, 142–44).

Separation from the world did not translate to keeping out of worldly affairs. Eighteenth-century Quakers expanded their mercantile interests, some accumulating great fortunes in the process (Walvin 1997). Business practices, particularly injunctions against debt, and expansive networks supported success (Tolles 1948; Winchester 1991; Landes 2015). Undoubtedly, legislation such as the Navigation Acts favoured Atlantic trade, and an expanding empire multiplied mercantile opportunities. But Quakers, shut out of universities, professions, and the civil service, were innovative and entrepreneurial. They participated in every area of imperial industry and commerce, including the trade in African slaves and goods produced by slaves (Soderlund 1985). The Darby family revolutionised iron production, paving the way for British industrialisation (Raistrick 1953, 122–46; Labouchere 1988, 1993). And Quaker families dominated the eighteenth-century iron industry (Walvin 1997, 88), demonstrating that endogamy produced dynastic mercantile and banking families (Pratt 1985, 77, 89; Price 1986; Walvin 1997, 70–72). Quaker families were also involved in steel refining (Roberts 2004, 182–83). Members of the Pease family were pioneers in the woollen industry, transitioning their business from domestic to factory production; the nineteenth-century Peases would pioneer railways (Kirby 1984). Wealth needed to be invested, leading Quakers into banking; the Barclay, Fox, Gurney, Lloyd, and Pease families were all banking families. The nineteenth century also includes many well-known success stories (Roberts 2004). American Friends gained profit in commerce. For instance, while Quakers were only one-seventh of the Philadelphia population in 1769, they comprised half of those who paid more than £100 a year in tax (Tolles 1948, 49). Interaction with the market and commercial success challenged Quietist ideals of a separated life, leading to anxiety and internal conflict (Tolles 1948; Walvin 1997). Friends dealt with this in multiple ways. Some left their faith. Some remained in the faith but did not follow the Discipline; by the end of the century, Friends themselves distinguished between plain Friends who observed regulations and gay Friends who did not. Some, including John Woolman, an extremely devout Friend, abandoned business entirely (Plank 2012; Kershner 2013). More standard was developing methods to traverse separate spiritual and temporal domains (Dandelion 2010). To this end, plainness functioned as a protective barrier, permitting Friends to venture into commercial life while maintaining their distance from it. Quakers also navigated this tension through philanthropy and benevolence, which made profit permissible as long as it was gained honestly and included care of those in distress (Freeman 2013, 423). Quaker business practices, systemised in the eighteenth-century consumer and manufacturing revolutions, have been termed 'ethical capitalism' and 'Quakernomics' (King 2014).

Quaker testimonies on slavery and war were clarified in this period, in large part the result of political, social, and economic circumstances in the Atlantic world. Beyond plainness, it is for these testimonies that Quakerism is most well known. Friends' position on slavery and abolition was complex and is complicated by popular portrayals of Quakers as proponents of racial equality and abolition from the sect's genesis. Cazden (2013) outlines events and interpretations. Eighteenth-century Quaker commercial accomplishments depended, in no small part, on the products of slave labour (sugar plantations in the West Indies and farms and mercantile enterprise in the British North American colonies) and the trade in slaves. Discomfort with slave holding and slaves' living conditions occasioned LYM to issue an infrequent minute to regulate Friends' practices. Colonial attempts to limit the trade eventually compelled LYM to articulate the Society's position on slavery, although LYM originally refused to use its powerful lobby (which, in 1722, had succeeded in finally achieving an Affirmation Act acceptable to most Quakers) to support the Pennsylvania anti-import campaign. And, even though LYM advised PYM in 1727 that the traffic in slaves was inconsistent with Friends' principles, this advice was not circulated to British meetings until 1750 when it was included in *The Book of Extracts*. An official shift occurred mid-century, coinciding with the Seven Years' War and the Quaker reformation. In 1754 PYM published John Woolman's pamphlet, *Some Considerations on the Keeping of Negroes*, and in 1758 LYM printed an epistle condemning the trade and any involvement in it. Until later in the century, however, Quakers focussed on renouncing slave holding and distancing themselves from the trade instead of abolishing it. Yet, anti-slavery sentiments advanced on both sides of the Atlantic as a result of the distribution of abolitionists' messages, like those of Anthony Benezet, and the formation of anti-slavery societies. Attention shifted to legislation banning the trade. In 1787 LYM's anti-slavery committee joined forces with non-Quakers such as William Wilberforce and Thomas Clarkson in a persistent highly organised campaign of petitions, boycotts, and lobbying that eventually resulted in the 1807 'Act for the Abolition of the Slave Trade'. Friends' individual and corporate efforts entrenched anti-slavery activism as a central component of Quaker identity and witness.

The Peace Testimony, like abolitionism, was complicated and is often misunderstood (Weddle 2001). Early Quakers had participated in the English Civil Wars and, despite Friends' declaration of peaceable principles to Charles II in 1660, behaviour did not always translate directly from a statement of belief. Again, Friends' mercantile interests in the British Atlantic compelled a clear stance. Armed conflict was commonplace in the long eighteenth century, with more than half of the period being dominated by wars of empire or revolution. Could ships be armed defensively? Could one protect one's home or property? Was it permissible to profit from privateer-ing? What about trading in military wares? The response was neither imme-diately evident nor consistently interpreted throughout the Quaker Atlantic. It was not until mid-century that Friends contemplated the social impact of violence. Late seventeenth-century reflections on Quakers' involvement in war focussed inward on injury to the soul and damage to Quakers' reputation (London Yearly Meeting 1806, 56). By 1744 the focus was outward: war was equated with 'injustice, barbarity, and bloodshed', and those involved in any way were to be disowned (London Yearly Meeting 1783, 254). Pennsylvania Quakers in the Assembly were divided in the war crisis of 1755, between those who supported a defensive war tax and those who did not. Most Quakers withdrew from the Assembly in 1756, influenced by the Quaker reformation (Hamm 2003, 32). In the American Revolution, the American Yearly Meetings adopted a position of strict neutrality; the extent to which this was followed, and its impact on Friends, depended on a number of factors (Mekeel 1996; Specht 2010). Despite strong connections to Britain, most American Quakers came to terms with their new government. A few true Loyalists returned to England, and some Friends sought free land in Upper Canada, but they were not politically motivated (Dorland 1968; Healey 2006). By the French Revolutionary Wars of the 1790s, abhorrence for war, war-related activities, or even discussion of war was complete (London Yearly Meeting 1806, 378). Pacifism had become a defining feature of Quakerism.

Quakerism at the turn of the nineteenth century appeared to be unrelated to the Quakerism of the mid-seventeenth century. The movement had become a highly organised sect, visibly and practically distinct from main-stream society. Ecstatic worship had given way to intense silence. Sectarianism reduced numbers. Some Quakers found disciplinary dictates too rigid and left; others were removed in a reformation intended to return Quakerism to its origins. The impact of this exclusive group exceeded the limits dictated by its size. For the faithful, a version of the Lamb's War (the battle against evil in oneself and in the world) continued. The resulting humanitarianism impelled by ongoing commitment to the Inward Light, revelation, spiritual equality, and Quaker witness effected immense social change. Acrimonious nineteenth-century schisms were on the horizon. Conflict first emerged in the late 1790s when Irish Friend Abraham Shackleton and American Friend Hannah Barnard questioned the accuracy of an Old Testament passage in which God commanded the ancient Israelites to exterminate their enemies. Both were disowned by their respective meetings for challenging the accuracy of Scripture (Hamm 2013, 63–64). Until this point, however, the bounds of Quaker orthodoxy were generous even if the limits of orthopraxy were not.

SUGGESTED FURTHER READING

Allen, R.C. and Moore, R.A. (forthcoming) *The Quakers 1656–1723: The Evolution of an Alternative Community*, State Park: Penn State University Press.
Angell, S.W. and Dandelion, P. (eds.) (2015) *Early Quakers and Their Theological Thought, 1647–1723*, Cambridge: Cambridge University Press.
Braithwaite, W.C. (1912) *The Beginnings of Quakerism*, London: Macmillan and Co.
Braithwaite, W.C. (1919) *The Second Period of Quakerism*, London: Macmillan and Co.
Davies, A. (2000) *The Quakers in English Society, 1655–1725*, Oxford: Oxford University Press.
Jones, R.M. (1921) *The Later Periods of Quakerism*, London: Macmillan and Co.
Marietta, J.D. (2007) *The Reformation of American Quakerism, 1748–1783*, Philadelphia: University of Pennsylvania Press.
Moore, R.A. (2000) *The Light in Their Consciences: Early Quakers in Britain, 1646–1666*, University Park: Pennsylvania State University Press.
Soderlund, J.R. (1985) *Quakers & Slavery: A Divided Spirit*, Princeton, NJ: Princeton University Press.
Weddle, M.B. (2001) *Walking in the Way of Peace: Quaker Pacifism in the Seventeenth Century*, Oxford: Oxford University Press.

∞

Conflict and Transformation, 1808–1920

Thomas D. Hamm and Isaac Barnes May

In its first issue of the twentieth century, the *Friends' Intelligencer* greeted the new era with words that Friends of all persuasions probably endorsed. "The world never needed true Quakerism more than now," wrote editor Howard M. Jenkins, "For in fact true Quakerism is that which the world, when it pauses to think, recognizes as the ideal of the age in which we live – a realization in actual life of sincerity, integrity, simplicity, and brotherly kindness" (Jenkins 1901, 6).

While all Friends would have agreed on the world's need for Quakerism, that was probably all that would have united them. Over the course of the nineteenth century, Quakerism had been transformed. A united body in 1808, Friends had split into three branches by 1860. In 1808, Friends adhered to a lifestyle that served as a "hedge" against "the world," a distinctive spirituality, and a unique form of worship. By 1920, that unity had disappeared.

This diversity reflected different choices that Friends had made. Facing intellectual, cultural, and economic changes, some Friends had responded through acculturation, moving closer to the dominant trends in their larger societies. Thus by 1920, the overwhelming majority of Friends had given up the distinctive dress and speech that characterized them a century earlier. Most Friends had become much more open to organization – they now boasted denominational agencies such as the Five Years Meeting, the Woman Friends Missionary Union, and Friends General Conference. Once opposed to higher education, they now conducted colleges and universities. A World Conference of Friends, which sought to embrace all varieties of Friends in 1920, would have been inconceivable to Friends in 1808.

While change was characteristic of Friends, so was striking diversity. By 1920, a majority of the world's Friends worshiped in a programmed setting, with pastors. Their theology ranged from Protestant fundamentalism to modernist liberalism. Friends who held to older ways of unprogrammed worship were equally diverse in their theology. All these groups had radically different understandings of the meaning of the historic peace testimony of the movement. Schisms had rent Quakerism asunder, and labels such as Hicksite, Orthodox, Wilburite, Gurneyite, and Conservative were required to denote its branches.

ROOTS OF DIVERSITY

In the 1820s and 1830s, Friends in North America and the British Isles experienced schisms. The one in North America, the Hicksite Separation, was unprecedented. The one in England, the Beaconite split, was symptomatic of tensions that would continue to affect Friends.

The Hicksite Separation took its name from the Long Island Friend Elias Hicks (1748–1830). Recorded a minister in 1777, Hicks had traveled widely among American Friends. By 1820, Hicks was voicing views that some Friends judged to be affirmations of traditional Quakerism, but that others considered dangerous, even atheistic (Forbush 1956, 3–202; Ingle 1986, 3–121).

Hicks was not a systematic theologian. But at times he had denied the Virgin Birth, implying that Jesus was the son of Joseph. Jesus had become the Christ, the Son of God, because he was the only person who had ever lived in perfect obedience to the Inward Light. Hicks always professed high regard for the Bible, but he criticized other Protestants for making the Bible, rather than the Inward Light, the primary rule of faith and practice. Without divine guidance, the Bible could be abused, and it often was. In an especially provocative 1818 statement, Hicks argued that the Scriptures had been "the cause of four-fold more harm than good to Christendom" (Hicks 1834, 44; see also Hamm 2003, 40–41). In contemporary Quakerism, Hicks saw evidence of widespread declension. Too many Friends had become worldly, growing closer to non-Quakers through their ties in reform and humanitarian groups that were dominated by "hirelings," professional clergy (Ingle 1986, 38–61, 81–95).

The Friends that Hicks critiqued viewed the situation differently. They became known as Orthodox Friends. They affirmed the divinity of Christ in terms of the Virgin Birth and Trinitarianism. And while they agreed with Hicks that the Bible should not be exalted above the Holy Spirit that had given it, his criticisms horrified them (Hamm 1988, 16–17).

Open conflict first emerged in Philadelphia. An attempt to silence Hicks during a visit there in December 1822 convinced Hicksites that Hicks was the victim of a campaign of vilification. Over the next four years, conflict became open and bitter. By 1825, a Philadelphia printer, Marcus T. C. Gould, was taking down Hicks's sermons in shorthand and then publishing them. This allowed the Hicksite message to reach Friends who had never heard his preaching (Ingle 1986, 96–180).

The first split came in Philadelphia Yearly Meeting in April 1827, when Hicksites concluded that they could no longer expect fair treatment from Orthodox leaders. So they held a conference to "reorganize" the Yearly Meeting. As monthly and quarterly meetings decided with which body they would affiliate, the separation divided the entire Yearly Meeting. It then spread to other Yearly Meetings. Hicksites were the majority, about two to one, in Philadelphia Yearly Meeting. Majorities in New York and Baltimore also sided with the Hicksites, and in Ohio Yearly Meeting, the division was almost equal. New England, North Carolina, and Virginia were Orthodox without significant divisions, while Indiana Yearly Meeting was Orthodox by a margin of about four to one. London and Dublin Yearly Meetings strongly supported the Orthodox. English ministers such as Ann Jones, Anna Brathwaite, and Thomas Shillitoe, traveling in the United States, led in condemning Hicks (Ingle 1986, 183–246).

Orthodox Friends saw the issues as theological: Hicksites were at best confused about the essentials of Christian faith, at worst deluded by the devil. Hicksites highlighted issues of authority, viewing the Orthodox as determined to hold onto power at all costs. Philadelphia Yearly Meeting has received the most study. Contemporaries noted that Hicksites dominated the rural meetings, while Orthodox Friends were the majority in the city. In 1967, Robert W. Doherty, analyzing Philadelphia Yearly Meeting, framed the split sociologically, concluding that Orthodox were wealthier than Hicksites, apparently adjusting better to the changing American economy. Hicksites, not liking the new world, hunkered down in traditionalism. How applicable Doherty's analysis is to other Yearly Meetings is unclear. More recently, H. Larry Ingle has argued that Hicksites saw themselves as reformers, restoring a primitive Quakerism eroded by Orthodox innovation (Ingle 1986, 38–61).

Hicksite and Orthodox Friends drew different conclusions from the separation. Orthodox blamed it partly on a lack of knowledge of the Scriptures, partly on failure to act decisively against Hicksite errors. Thus, their response to future dissent would be swift condemnation and disownments. Hicksites, prizing liberty of conscience, blamed intolerance and worldliness. Both prescriptions would prove faulty over the next twenty-five years (Hamm 1988, 19–20).

THE SECOND WAVE OF SEPARATIONS

Hicksites emerged from the 1820s united only by disagreement with the Orthodox. Most were conservatives opposed to innovation. An articulate minority were genuine religious liberals who felt kinship with Unitarians and social radicals such as Robert Dale Owen. The limits of Hicksite tolerance were revealed when leaders in Wilmington and Philadelphia disowned a few dissenters who had openly allied themselves with Owenite labor radicalism (Ingle 1984, 127–37).

By the late 1830s, new tensions had emerged over the involvement of Hicksites such as Lucretia Mott of Philadelphia in radical reform movements, most notably nonresistance and abolition. Nonresistants argued that Christians should repudiate human governments based on force but should instead work to usher in the Government of God on earth. Abolitionists, including thousands of evangelicals in the North, called for the immediate abolition of slavery. Hicksite reformers saw both movements as extensions of traditional Quaker testimonies. But most Hicksites feared such ties. Philadelphia Yearly Meeting spoke for them in 1830 when it told its members: "If we, as a society … mingle with other professors in what is called religious concerns … our individuality, as a people, will be lost, and our excellent testimonies … will fall to the ground" (Philadelphia Yearly Meeting 1830, 7–8). Critics especially feared the leadership of paid clergy, "hirelings" who did not wait for divine direction and did good works for pay (Philadelphia Yearly Meeting 1830, 7–8; Hamm 1994, 557–69).

These disagreements caused a wave of separations beginning in 1843. Reformers in New York, the Delaware Valley, Ohio, Indiana, Illinois, and Michigan separated to form Yearly Meetings of what they called Congregational or Progressive Friends. Not only did they embrace every imaginable reform, from nonresistance to abolition to temperance to women's rights, but to give the utmost liberty to individual conscience, they abolished almost all of the requisitions of the Discipline and declined to appoint elders or record ministers. These bodies were generally short lived. Many gravitated toward spiritualism. Other Hicksites who sympathized with reform, such as Lucretia Mott, refused to separate, but found themselves marginalized by the 1850s (Hamm 2013, 68–69).

Orthodox Friends faced different tensions. By the 1830s, many, perhaps a majority, particularly in the British Isles, defined themselves as evangelicals, emphasizing the importance of a definite conversion experience and salvation through faith in the Blood of Christ shed on the Cross. The embodiment of this vision was the English minister Joseph John Gurney (1788–1847).

Gurney advocated a self-conscious Quaker evangelicalism. One facet was joining non-Quaker evangelicals in humanitarian and reform work. Gurney argued that Friends flirted with error in elevating the Inward Light above the light found in the Bible. Comparing the former with the latter, he said that it was like comparing the light of the moon with that of the sun. Gurney also asserted that Friends misunderstood the relationship between justification and sanctification. Justification was a state of being acceptable to God, or saved; sanctification was holiness. Traditionally, Friends had argued that the two were inseparable, that one could not be justified without being sanctified as well. But Gurney separated the two, making sanctification subsequent to justification. By 1860, "Gurneyite" had become the common label for evangelical Quakers in North America (Hamm 1988, 20–22, 55–56; Spencer 2007, 140–43). Some evangelical Friends believed that Gurney had not gone far enough. They found their leader in Isaac Crewdson (1780–1844), a Friend from Manchester, England. In 1835, he published *A Beacon to the Society of Friends*, which repudiated entirely the idea of the Inward Light or the possibility of revelation other than through the Bible. When London Yearly Meeting tried to silence him, he and his followers withdrew (Jones 1921, I, 490–92, 505–8; Isichei 1970, 45–53).

Not all Friends in London Yearly Meeting, or Orthodox Friends in North America, embraced the rising evangelicalism. Quietists remained influential; Thomas Shillitoe, for example, pronounced Gurney "an Episcopalian, not a Quaker." Gurney faced fierce opposition when he traveled in North America in 1837. Orthodox Quietists dominated Philadelphia and Ohio Yearly Meetings and gave Gurney a cold shoulder. The most visible critic of Gurney, however, was John Wilbur (1774–1856), a minister from Rhode Island. His opposition was so caustic that the leaders of New England Yearly Meeting forced his disownment. Wilbur's supporters responded by forming their own Yearly Meeting. Small separations in New York and Baltimore Yearly Meetings, and a major one in Ohio Yearly Meeting, followed. Orthodox Friends in Philadelphia preserved unity only cutting off all correspondence with other Yearly Meetings (Swift 1962, 183–84, 213–14; Hamm 1988, 28–34).

By 1860, Quaker paths were clearly divergent. A majority of the world's Friends had moved closer to the larger evangelical Protestant culture of North America and the British Isles. They had embraced institutions from that culture, most notably colleges and Sunday schools. They were comfortable with politics, although almost always as Republicans in the United States and Liberals in the United Kingdom. Friends such as the poet John Greenleaf Whittier in the United States and the parliamentarian John Bright in England had become public figures in ways that would have been inconceivable a century earlier. Some Friends, both Hicksite and Wilburite, remained skeptical of the larger world. But the latter would steadily decline in numbers, while the former would take their cues, social and theological, from liberals including Lucretia Mott.

THE CIVIL WAR

"The hand of the Lord seems now to be brought heavily upon us, and when the Lord's judgments are in the earth, the inhabitants of the world learn righteousness." So the Meeting for Sufferings of Baltimore Yearly Meeting Hicksite recorded in the fall of 1861, as the United States found itself embroiled in civil war (Address 1861, 499).

Friends of all types united in seeing the Confederacy as at war, not just with the United States government, but with God and justice, founded on slavery and seditious rebellion. But, as Yearly Meetings uniformly admonished their members, that did not justify taking up arms or departing from the historic testimony against war (Brock 1990, 166–83).

Some Friends were willing to suffer for their commitment to peace. The Lincoln administration, sensitive to the strong Republican sympathies of Friends, generally released drafted Friends who objected to bearing arms. The Confederacy was less sympathetic. Many young Friends in Virginia and North Carolina fled north to stay out of the Confederate army. Others, forced into Confederate service, became notorious for refusing to cooperate; at least one died (Brock 1990, 166–83).

While very few Friends served the Confederacy, hundreds, perhaps thousands, went into the Union army. Antislavery idealism motivated some; others were doubtless young birthright Friends with tenuous Quaker commitments. Significantly, many Monthly Meetings did not take action against soldier members as offenders against the Discipline (Brock 1990, 179–83).

The war had three profound effects on Gurneyite and Hicksite Friends. One was the work among former slaves in the South. Leading Friends urged it as a way that Friends could render service during the national crisis. Yearly Meetings formed associations to raise money and coordinate efforts, and hundreds of Friends went south to teach in schools, work in hospitals and orphanages, and provide relief to the destitute (Selleck 1995). Another result was the effective end of the Peace Testimony as a matter of Discipline. Although some Monthly Meetings did review the membership of Quaker soldiers after the war, after 1865 pacifism became largely a matter of individual conscience. Yearly meetings retained strong peace statements in their books of Discipline, but enforcement ceased. Finally, the war encouraged some Friends to launch organized work outside of the regular business structure to advance peace generally and understandings of the Quaker testimony among members specifically. In 1866, Gurneyite Yearly Meetings formed the Peace Association of Friends in America (Hamm 1988, 68–69; 2000, 31–34).

HICKSITE QUAKERISM TRANSFORMED

In 1860, traditionalists appeared to have the upper hand in the Hicksite Yearly Meetings. Yet within two decades, Hicksites would have aligned themselves firmly with liberal Protestantism and accommodated themselves to the larger American culture. By 1900, they had softened the Discipline so that most of the old reasons for disownment, such as marriage out of meeting or deviating from plainness, were no longer in place. Ties with non-Quakers in reform and humanitarian causes were normal. The opening of Swarthmore College in 1869, the Hicksite embrace of higher education, was evidence of a revolution in attitudes.

The roots of this transformation are complex. Change in leadership played a part, as quietist stalwarts such as Benjamin Ferris in Philadelphia Yearly Meeting, John T. Plummer in Indiana, and Rachel Hicks in New York died in the 1860s and 1870s. Older leaders such as Samuel M. Janney in Baltimore Yearly Meeting, John J. Cornell in Genesee, and Jane Johnson in Philadelphia were of more moderate views. And new leaders emerged whose liberalism was clear. They included Jonathan W. and Hannah A. Plummer in the newly formed Illinois Yearly Meeting; Howard M. Jenkins, who became editor of the main Hicksite periodical, the *Friends' Intelligencer,* in 1885; and Henry W. Wilbur and Jane Rushmore, who would be the first paid employees of Friends General Conference after 1900. Cultural change was also a source of the transformation of Hicksite Quakerism. By the 1850s, observers noted how Hicksites were increasingly reading the same books and periodicals as their non-Quaker neighbors, following developments in literature, politics, education, and reform (Haines 2000, 7–8; Hamm 2000, 21–23).

Hicksite liberalism had several foundations: commitment to freedom of thought, antipathy toward evangelical theology, a sense of commonality with other liberal Protestants, and an emphasis on continuing and progressive revelation. Most of all, it exalted the Inner Light.

Hicksites agreed that belief in the Inner Light was "the bedrock of Quakerism." They defined it in various ways. Typical was John J. Cornell, who described the Inner Light as "that attribute of God through which he conveys to man's spiritual nature, otherwise known as his soul, or immortal part, such evidences of Himself, His Laws and directions as are necessary for man's guidance while in this life." Inseparable from the Inner Light was continuing revelation. "Truth is progressive, ever growing, ever assuming new forms," preached one minister in Philadelphia Yearly Meeting in 1876. Progressive revelation made it easier for most Hicksites to accommodate the findings of critical Biblical scholarship that agitated other denominations after 1870 (Hamm 2000, 25–26).

Hicksites had scant regard for doctrines that most Protestants considered fundamental to Christianity. They refused to make the Bible the ultimate religious authority. As one put it, if Jesus "had intended to teach the world his religion from a book, he, himself, would have written that book, and would have laid it down as the first fundamental principle of his religion." They avowed their belief in the divinity of Christ, but in ways that horrified Orthodox Friends. Jesus had become divine, the Christ, because he was the only human being who had ever lived who was perfectly obedient to the Inner Light, "the embodiment of all goodness; a perfect example of right living." Hicksites exalted liberty of conscience: no Friend should be cast out for doctrinal views (Hamm 2000, 26–28; 2002, 189–90).

Evidence of how far Hicksites had come was abundant by the 1890s. One sign was the founding of the Friends Union for Philanthropic Labor (FUPL) in 1882. Originally formed for consultation on humanitarian concerns, by 1893 all of the Hicksite Yearly Meetings had joined. Another was the widespread embrace by Hicksites of First Day Schools, clearly modeled on evangelical Sunday schools. For this reason many Hicksites regarded them with suspicion, but as they developed their own teaching materials, and as it became clear that they had given new life to a number of meetings, opposition faded. Another was the appearance of Young Friends Associations. In the 1890s, these groups began holding conferences in conjunction with the FUPL; in 1900, the establishment of Friends General Conference (FGC) formalized this. The Yearly Meetings were clear, however, that they remained autonomous, and that FGC existed for purely advisory purposes (Haines 2000, 3–7; Hamm 2000, 32–34).

The number of Hicksite Friends declined between 1828 and 1900. At the beginning of the twentieth century, they numbered about 22,000, about half of them in Philadelphia Yearly Meeting. But they were convinced that they had laid the foundations for revitalization, and that the larger religious world was moving their way (Hamm 2000, 18, 31–34).

THE REVIVAL

If Hicksites changed in important ways, the changes among Gurneyites after 1870 were revolutionary. A wave of revivals transformed worship and life. By 1900, pastors, music, and a programmed order of worship not much different from other Protestant denominations had taken hold. "You cannot understand it here," Barnabas C. Hobbs, the clerk of Western Yearly Meeting, told London Yearly Meeting in 1878. "No one can without seeing it. Our meetings were shaken as by a vast whirlwind" (Hamm 1988, 90).

In the 1860s, a new generation of leaders had emerged among American Gurneyites. They constituted a renewal movement, committed to modernizing Quaker faith and practice without sacrificing distinctiveness. Their reform program, which had made considerable progress by 1870, ranged from ending disownment for marrying out of meeting, to relaxing the restrictions of the plain life, to improving Quaker preaching, to promoting higher education. (Many were connected with Haverford and Earlham, the two colleges Gurneyites opened before 1860.) They were committed to a Quakerism, however, that differed from that of other Protestants in its emphases on women's ministry, pacifism, humanitarian work, and unprogrammed worship. By the late 1860s, they had found their vehicle in what they called general meetings, occasions that alternated sessions of worship with lectures on Quaker beliefs (Hamm 1988, 71–72).

In the 1870s, however, a revival movement pushed aside the reformers. The revivalists aimed at nothing less than a revolution. They were young ministers, such as David B. Updegraff in Ohio Yearly Meeting and John Henry Douglas and Esther Frame in Indiana, who were part of the interdenominational Holiness movement. They preached second-experience sanctification. In contrast to the renewal advocates who saw sanctification as a gradual attainment, they argued that it was the fruit of an instantaneous act of faith. Active in general meetings, by 1875, they had seized control and transformed them. Impatient with traditional Quakerism, they pushed aside old ways in the interest of aggressive soul saving (Hamm 1988, 72–92).

By 1900, the revival had transformed the Gurneyite Yearly Meetings in North America. Some conservatives in Western, Iowa, Kansas, and North Carolina Yearly Meetings could not abide the innovations and separated, eventually making common cause with the older Wilburite bodies. The plain life passed away, as revivalists scored it as "dead works." Music became part of worship. Perhaps the most radical innovation was the introduction of a pastoral system of ministry. The revival brought in large numbers of converts who were unaccustomed to traditional Quaker worship and often drifted away. So meetings made arrangements with individual ministers to provide regular preaching and assume other pastoral duties. All of the Gurneyite Yearly Meetings had embraced it by 1900, although opposition remained widespread in Baltimore Yearly Meeting (Hamm 1988, 86–87, 124–30).

The revivals produced a new wave of separations in the Gurneyite Western, Iowa, Kansas, and North Carolina Yearly Meetings, as Friends who could not accept the innovations left to uphold old ways of worship. These Conservative Friends, as they became known, eventually made common cause with the older Wilburite bodies (Hamm 1988, 92–94, 99–102).

Most of the older renewal movement's leaders had mixed feelings about the revival. Some, such as Allen Jay, embraced it and tried to moderate it. Others, including Charles and Rhoda Coffin and Barnabas C. Hobbs, came to have doubts. A few, most notably Joel Bean in Iowa, became open critics. Collectively, they formed a moderate party that retained positions of leadership in the Gurneyite Yearly Meetings (Hamm 1988, 111–20).

That leadership was critical when a new and divisive issue appeared. Holiness Friends tended to understand the Bible as inerrant, and some found it impossible to reconcile their conception of the text with traditional Quaker prohibitions on outward rituals such as water baptism and communion. So some underwent baptism themselves, and others advocated "toleration" of what Friends called "the ordinances." The controversy split the revivalists, as all of the Gurneyite Yearly Meetings except Ohio reaffirmed earlier rulings that participating in these ordinances disqualified Friends from serving as ministers or elders (Hamm 1988, 130–37).

Ohio Yearly Meeting's embrace of toleration led to a conference of the Gurneyite Yearly Meetings in Richmond, Indiana, in October 1887. Ironically, the delegates decided that Yearly Meetings' actions had resolved the ordinance issue. The most important product of the conference was the Declaration of Faith, designed as a common statement to unite Gurneyites. While deeply evangelical, it was not the work of revivalists, but of Joseph Bevan Braithwaite, probably the most influential minister in London Yearly Meeting (Minear 1987; Hamm 1988, 137–38).

In concluding sessions of the conference, Kansas Friend William Nicholson made a proposal that would lead to the formation of the Five Years Meeting, the most ambitious attempt to create a national Quaker organization in the United States. Nicholson proposed a triennial conference of Yearly Meetings with ultimate authority over all of its members. Friends moved cautiously but did agree to conferences in Indianapolis in 1892 and 1897. The latter authorized drafting a Uniform Discipline that, by 1901, had been accepted by all of the Gurneyite Yearly Meetings except Ohio to form the Five Years Meeting of Friends in America (now Friends United Meeting). Advocates hoped that it would become a force for unity, bringing the combined weight of the society to bear on deviations. Instead, it became the center of new conflicts between older holiness Friends and emerging modernists led by Rufus M. Jones (Hamm 1988, 138; Hinshaw 2013, 93–97).

BRITISH QUAKERISM IN TRANSITION

In the middle of the nineteenth century, as American Quakers contended with the growing crisis over slavery, their coreligionists in Britain were preoccupied with numerical decline. English and Welsh Quakers had reason to be worried, as their membership fell more than 30 percent between 1800 and 1860. A principal reason for this precipitous drop was Quaker endogamy, only allowing marriage to other Quakers. Because up to a third of marriages were outside the group, expulsions were frequent (Isichei 1970, 112–17, 146).

Yet as British Friends became increasingly evangelical, they embraced the legitimacy of other Protestant denominations, and hence they were more open to the idea of allowing Quakers to intermarry. A turning point was an essay by John Stephenson Rowntree, a young Friend, entitled *Quakerism Past and Present*. Rowntree called for radical reforms to improve ministry among Friends and declared the existing prohibitions on marrying non-Quakers were "an act of suicide" (Kennedy 2001, 40–42). In 1859, London Yearly Meeting finally eliminated the prohibition.

The "hedge" of plain language and plain dress also began to be optional among British Friends. Yet there were clear limits to change. In Manchester, a confrontation erupted between a faction of young Friends who wanted to move Quakerism toward theological liberalism and the dominant evangelical Quaker leaders. By the 1860s, liberals in Manchester rallied behind David Duncan, a local merchant. Evangelical Friends were horrified that many of his followers inclined toward Unitarian beliefs and that they sympathized with the Hicksites. These young Friends in turn accused the evangelical faction of neglecting the writings of early Friends and disregarding the doctrine of the Inward Light, which they saw as fundamental to Quakerism (Isichei 1970, 28–32, 38; Kennedy 2001, 50–77).

Duncan was disowned in 1871 at the behest of a London Yearly Meeting Committee presided over by Joseph Bevan Braithwaite. Barely a month later, Duncan died of smallpox, and his followers coalesced in a schismatic group dubbed the Free Friends, who persisted for a generation before many of its members became Anglicans or Unitarians. Yet the conflict between liberals and evangelicals within the rest of British Quakerism was not resolved, but simply simmering (Kennedy 2001, 50–82).

The upheaval in Manchester among Quakers was merely one expression of larger theological debates that were occurring about the future of Protestantism. Duncan first rose to prominence giving lectures that spoke favorably about *Essay and Reviews*, a work by several Anglican authors that had already elicited controversy for suggesting the Bible, despite its purported Divine inspiration, should be analyzed like any other book. Elizabeth Isichei, a scholar of Victorian era Quakerism, has observed that the notion that a church should be united by goodwill rather than enforced belief in theological dogma, held by the Manchester liberal Friends, presaged the German theologian Adolf von Harnack's advocacy of the same policy three decades later (Isichei 1970, 28–32; see also Kennedy 2001, 50–57).

In 1884, controversy again flared up among British Friends with the publication of *A Reasonable Faith*. The authors of the book, who hoped to remain anonymous, provided a concise statement of theological liberalism. They suggested that there was no contradiction between the use of reason and faith, attempted to rebut biblical inerrancy, and denounced the idea of Jesus's death being a substitutionary atonement for humanity's sins (Kennedy 2001, 102–11; Dandelion 2007, 117–19). Despite causing a public outcry, these views rapidly won new adherents.

By the end of the nineteenth century, liberal theological views like Duncan's had ceased to be a disownable offense and were becoming dominant in London Yearly Meeting. In 1895, LYM held a conference in Manchester to discuss a myriad of topics. Evolution, historical criticism of the Bible, and social activism were all freely debated. The Manchester Conference is often cited as a watershed moment where modernist thought and liberal theological views won out over evangelicalism and became the norm within British Quakerism (Punshon 1984, 210–12).

EMBRACING MODERNISM

The changes that the Manchester Conference portended were transatlantic, affecting American Hicksites and Gurneyites as well as their British coreligionists. Liberal Quakers were becoming a significant force within the denomination. In Britain this movement coalesced around John Wilhelm Rowntree, a charismatic young businessman. In the United States, faculty at various Quaker colleges, and particularly Haverford philosophy professor Rufus Jones, led it. Liberal members of the Five Year Meeting such as Jones were willing to work with Hicksites and developed collegial relationships with individuals such as Jesse H. Holmes, a Swarthmore professor and head of the National Federation of Religious Liberals. Religious liberalism seemed to offer a vision for the future of Quakerism that might heal the wounds of the past century.

Both liberal British and American Quakers were concerned that Quakerism's lack of trained clergy might lead Friends to ignore modern developments in science and biblical studies. They also worried about the influence of the Bible schools created by Holiness Friends. In 1900, Rowntree organized a program called the Summer School to provide two weeks of education in religious and historical topics for British Quakers. Jones spoke at the first meeting of the Summer School and worked with the British Friends to set up an American version of the program at Haverford. The success of the Summer Schools spurred British Friends to create Woodbrooke, a permanent center for Quaker religious study (Kennedy 2001, 171–96).

Denominational history also became a particularly important avenue for these liberal Quakers to ground their identity, both to justify their theology and to cast it as an inevitable religious development. The most important of these efforts was a collaboration of a number of Quakers, including Rowntree, William Charles Braithwaite, and Jones, on a series of volumes that outlined the history of Quakerism. Usually referred to as the "Rowntree history series," in honor of Rowntree, who died while it was being planned, the series sought, in the words of its planners, to "present early Quakerism as to commend it to the modern mind" (Southern 2011, 21). It also endeavored to portray the Religious Society of Friends as being a mystical tradition. In his popular and prolific writings, Jones further developed the idea that Quaker religious practice was a kind of mysticism rooted in direct encounter with the divine. In books such as *Mystical Religion* and *Social Law in the Spiritual World*, Jones drew heavily from Transcendentalist thought, European mystics including Jacob Boehme, and the writings of William James to portray Quakerism as a new kind of mysticism open to everyone. As Jones explained, it was "a fresh movement essentially aiming to realize a universal religion of the spirit" (Dorrien 2003, 365; see also Southern 2011).

Jones would also have a profound influence outside Quakerism. Theologian Georgia Harkness extolled him as "America's greatest exponent of mysticism." He was a key mentor to Baptist minister and civil rights leader Howard Thurman and idolized by another acclaimed minister, Harry Emerson Fosdick, who declared that "[Jones's] work opened a new era in my life and thought" (Hedstrom 2004, p. 3; see also Dorrien 2003, 364–71). *The Christian Century*, the most respected periodical of American mainline

Protestantism, even referred to the Christianity that it advocated (in contrast to neo-orthodoxy) as "the religion of Rufus Jones" (Hume 1933).

Jones and the liberals were not without their critics, however. Though religious liberalism had become the dominant view in Britain by the turn of the century, it was still hotly debated in America. Many Quaker evangelicals were avid participants in the emergence of fundamentalism in the United States. These Friends launched attacks on the *American Friend*, which Jones edited from 1894 to 1908, and tried to make the Richmond Declaration of Faith the standard of Quaker orthodoxy. They exerted pressure on Quaker colleges not to teach historical criticism of the Bible and evolution. At Earlham College, a Yearly Meeting committee investigated charges that the college was teaching heresy. Ultimately Earlham was not condemned as a result of the influence of the liberal faction. Evangelical Friends generally had greater success in creating their own educational institutions, rather than exerting control of existing ones (Hamm 1997, 103–39; 1988, 146–72).

As the twentieth century began, new divisions defined Quakerism. The old distinction between Hicksites and Gurneyites still mattered, but these were perhaps overshadowed by an increasingly polarized rivalry between religious liberals and evangelicals. Some of this was simply a relabeling of the existing splits. Most of the Hicksites in FGC became religious liberals, while those associated with the Five Year Meeting, with numerous important exceptions, became evangelicals or mainliners in their theology. At issue were more contemporary debates about the place of reason, science, and the Bible in modern faith.

MISSIONS AND THE SPREAD OF QUAKERISM

Evangelical Quakers were not solely occupied by their conflict with liberal Quakers. After 1860, Gurneyite Quakers in the United States and Friends in Britain embraced missionary work at home and abroad. American Friends initially followed the model of traditional traveling ministry. When Eli and Sybil Jones, the first American Quaker foreign missionaries, went to Liberia in 1851, their trip lasted only six months. English Friends began active foreign missions work in the 1860s in India and Madagascar. These missions were intended to be permanent; to support them financially, British Friends founded the Friends Foreign Mission Association in 1870. By the 1870s, American missions were following the British model, and a number of American Yearly Meetings supported missionaries abroad. Quaker missionaries worked in Mexico, Syria, Jamaica, Japan, China, Palestine, Cuba, Madagascar, and India, among other nations, before the century's end (Jones 1946).

The most important mission field for shaping the future direction of Quakerism was Kenya. In 1902, three Friends, Willis Hotchkiss, Arthur Chilson, and Edgar Hole, arrived in what was then British East Africa to establish the Friends Africa Industrial Mission. They began their work at Kaimosi, in the west of Kenya, intent on both evangelizing and industrial development. They saw inculcating an American lifestyle as inseparable from conversion to Christianity. During the next several years, the mission expanded, and they set up a network of primary schools, began offering medical services, and translated the New Testament into Luragoli (Rasmussen 1995, 39–44).

The mission made many converts among the Luyia peoples in the region. Initially the American missionaries, skeptical of the leadership ability of native Africans, administered the missions and the newly established churches By the late 1910s, however, African Quakerism achieved a degree of independence when existing churches were organized in five Monthly Meetings (Rasmussen 1995, 56–57) The establishment of a Yearly Meeting, and full autonomy, came in 1946.

Not all mission work was done abroad. Because of Quakers' reputation as having historically good relations with American Indians, President Ulysses S. Grant sought their help as part of his "Peace Policy" of 1869. Under this plan, religious groups appointed Bureau of Indian Affairs agents, with each denomination assigned to a specific area. Gurneyites had jurisdiction over Kansas and Oklahoma, while Hicksites took charge of Indian affairs in Nebraska. Quakers ended their work for the government in 1879, but they continued to set up meetings and evangelize among a number of groups, including the Osage, Seneca, Wyandot, Otoe, Quapaw, Modocs, Kickapoo, and Shawnee (Jones 1946, 87–104). These missionary efforts led to Gurneyites founding a few Indian congregations in Oklahoma.

British Quakers also tried to evangelize domestically. In the 1870s, many admired revivalists including Dwight L. Moody lamented that Friends did not have their own evangelists. In particular, Quaker evangelicals hoped that revivals could reach the poor, a group for whom Quakerism generally held little appeal. Wealthy Quaker evangelicals employed young men as paid Home Missioners, who conducted revivals, assisted new converts, and provided ministry and pastoral care. Critics alleged that this was tantamount to setting up a pastoral system. London Yearly Meeting created a Home Mission Committee in 1882 to manage the movement, though even at its height the number of paid Home Missioners rarely exceeded fifty (Isichei 1970, 99–100; Kennedy 2001, 122–32).

British Quakers also attempted to evangelize the working class through First Day Schools. These resembled the Sunday schools of other religious groups, but Quakers found a particular niche in teaching adult students. In 1847, they created the Friends First Day School Association to help support an expanding number of schools. Initially the schools primarily taught reading and some basic religious concepts, but by the 1880s, as a result of rising literacy, many of the adult First Day School programs resembled church services with a Quaker teacher filling the role of a minister. Though more than 35,000 students attended these schools by 1890 (almost double the number of Quakers in Britain), only a few of these students would become full-fledged members of the Religious Society of Friends (Isichei 1970, 261–75).

The missionaries' work that Friends began in the nineteenth century would not appreciably add to the numbers of the Religious Society of Friends, in England or in America. However, the great success of Quakerism in Africa would eventually shift the group's numerical center from its Anglo-American heritage.

WORLD WAR I

The factors that altered Quakerism were not purely internal to the Religious Society of Friends. World War I also challenged Quakers to determine what their historic peace testimony meant in the modern world. Yearly meetings in Britain and the United States officially held firm to the belief that Quakers were obligated to reject all war. In practice, however, Quakers were divided by the conflict. Many felt the tug of patriotism and were conflicted about their loyalties. Among American Quaker men eligible for military service, perhaps two-thirds volunteered or accepted their conscription, receiving no punishment from their meetings for their choice. Others opted to become conscientious objectors, either going to prison or performing alternative service (Hamm et al. 2000, 45–71).

Some American Quakers were caught up in the war frenzy. A group of 120 prominent Hicksites signed a statement declaring their loyalty to the president and mocking pacifists as "those who would stand idly by quoting some isolated passage of scripture while an insane man murdered him, ravished his wife, bayoneted his babies and crucified his friends." Swarthmore College established a military training program for its students. Haverford College ousted an eminent professor, biblical scholar Henry J. Cadbury, because he was too outspoken against the war (Brock and Young 1999, 31).

Others Quakers objected to the conflict and sought some way to help humanity during the carnage. In Britain, the Friends War Victim Committee (FWVC) was created to provide aid and labor for relief work in France. In 1917, American Quakers from FGC and the Five Years Meeting came together to create their own relief agency, the American Friends Service Committee (AFSC), with Jones as its chair. The AFSC provided a place for conscience objectors to serve their alternative service, helping to reconstruct Britain and France. After the war's conclusion, the AFSC would provide food aid to Germany, a program that fed a million children a day at its peak (Barbour and Frost 1988, 249–53).

Among Quakers who objected to the conflict on religious grounds, there were differences over the degree to which they should resist their government's war efforts. In Britain many older Friends backed the approach of the Friends Ambulance Unit, which employed conscientious objectors to do medical work both domestically and in war-ravaged Europe. Though they could not support the war, these Friends still believed it was important to serve in a way that helped their nation. The more radically inclined British-run Friends Service Committee (FSC), established in 1915, believed that Quakers had an obligation actively to resist the war. The committee's acting chair, Edith Ellis, suggested that the only authentic conscientious objectors were those who chose to go to prison rather than to do alternative service. The FSC successfully pressured London Yearly Meeting not to negotiate with the government for the release or preferential treatment of Quaker draft resisters held in prison unless all conscientious objectors, regardless of religion, were treated in the same way (Kennedy 1996, 194–98). Although small in numbers, the Friends Service Committee was pivotal in advancing the idea that the Quaker Peace Testimony required an effort to end conflict, not just nonparticipation as a combatant.

The war gave Quakers a sense of unity. After the conflict, in British Quaker circles former war resisters were usually held in the highest regard. The situation in the United States was more complex. Many Quakers believed that the peace testimony had an enduring value, and they hoped that this would be something that could unite them despite their disparate theology. The different branches of the Religious Society of Friends could also join together in service work. The AFSC in particular provided a shared organization and a shared mission for a community of Quakers who hoped that rebuilding Europe from the rubble, feeding the hungry, and caring for the sick could be more important than their considerable divides. But the most fundamentalist Friends worried that an emphasis on service detracted from the more vital work of saving souls.

MANY BRANCHES OF QUAKERISM

From these shared principles, Friends nurtured hope that they shared more than a name with their coreligionists. In 1920, British and American Quakers from all branches met together at the first All-Friends Conference in Devonshire House in London, a gathering devoted to the goal of reconciling the divisions among Friends and discussing plans to create world peace. Nine hundred and thirty-six delegates, including Jones, attended the proceedings (Kennedy 2001, 406).

The goals were lofty and most of them were not achieved. The notion of the conference being all inclusive of different kinds of Quakers rang hollow because it notably failed to include the growing number of Quakers outside England and America. No lasting unity was achieved between the differing branches of Quakerism, and British and American Friends bitterly debated whether Quaker beliefs necessarily led toward socialism. Perhaps the only lasting concrete result was widespread agreement among British Friends and many Americans on the importance of the Peace Testimony (Kennedy 2001, 404–14).

Whatever its achievements, the mere existence of the All-Friends conference is a testament to both continuity and change within Quakerism. At the start of the nineteenth century, when there had been a united Religious Society of Friends, there was no need to envision Quakers from different parts of the world coming together at once on equal footing. A hundred years later, the All-Friends conference showed the divisions that had emerged, but it also demonstrated the abiding hope among the branches of Quakerism that they shared more than a historical ancestry. All the participants thought of themselves as Friends and hoped to reach reconciliation. They all valued their faith, but there was still fierce debate about what exactly that faith meant.

SUGGESTED FURTHER READING

Hamm, Thomas D. (1988) *The Transformation of American Quakerism: Orthodox Friends, 1800–1907*. Bloomington: Indiana University Press.

Ingle, H. Larry. (1986) *Quakers in Conflict: The Hicksite Reformation*. Knoxville: University of Tennessee Press.

Isichei, Elizabeth. (1970) *Victorian Quakers*. Oxford: Oxford University Press.

Kennedy, T. C. (2001) *British Quakerism, 1860–1920: The Transformation of a Religious Community*. Oxford: Oxford University Press.

Southern, Alice. (2011) "The Rowntree History Series and the Growth of Liberal Quakerism." *Quaker Studies* 16, no. 1: 7–73.

3

∾

Global Quakerism 1920–2015

Timothy Burdick and Pink Dandelion

INTRODUCTION

The story of global Quakerism during the twentieth-century is one of theological unity and division, but it is simultaneously also a story of how the Society of Friends, collectively as a whole, has brought its witness to bear upon humanity in ways that echo the historical truth of social testimonies. New bitter theological debates arose during the century producing a more organic schism, while century-old wounds were healed bringing together again meetings long divided. Two world wars renewed a call to peacemaking and humanitarianism among all persuasions of Friends resulting in a Nobel Peace Prize, but little common ground could be found on what theology constituted grounds for outreach and service in the first place. The Global South experienced phenomenal growth and now holds the future promise for Friends as the number of adherents in traditional British and US strongholds wane. As discussed in this chapter, the somewhat complicated story of global Quakerism today is largely a reflection of both the successes and the struggles within the Religious Society of Friends rather than one of external pressures.

MAJOR MOVEMENTS AT THE START OF THE TWENTIETH CENTURY

Five Years Meeting

The twentieth century started out with a mild spirit of unification and cooperation among American Friends. Despite the Society having already experienced two major schisms in the nineteenth century, and despite growing tensions between revivalist and moderate evangelical Quakers at the end of that same century, by 1902, all Gurneyite Yearly Meetings

throughout North America, except Canada and Ohio, endorsed the formation of a national headship (Five Years Meeting – FYM) along with its
respective Uniform Discipline (*Minutes of FYM 1902*, 9–12).[1] FYM was
initially successful at bridging the gap between emerging modernist
Quakers and evangelical Friends, and in 1912, it successfully took over
publication of the *American Friend*. Under the leadership of modernist
Quakers such as Walter Woodward (hired in 1917 as first permanent general
secretary and *American Friend* editor) and Rufus Jones (who served as chair
of the powerful Business Committee), FYM mostly focused on national
publications and collaborative missionary projects (the American Friends
Board of Foreign Missions soon became the official 'division' for FYM
missions). While FYM made some progress improving unification among
Gurneyite Friends, it was not as strong as hoped for. It became largely a
delegate body, with its attendees lacking the ability to make binding decisions for their respective YMs.

Additionally, debates soon began over how FYM incorporated historical
statements of faith; most notably the tacit endorsement implied within the
Uniform Discipline towards the Richmond Declaration of Faith and George
Fox's Letter to the Governor of Barbadoes [*sic*]. Both documents were refer-
enced rather than endorsed. The conflict on this issue came to a head in 1912
when three evangelical-leaning YMs (Western, Kansas and California) all sent
in resolutions to FYM requesting that these documents be incorporated as part
and parcel of the Uniform Discipline. In response, the Business Committee,
chaired by Jones, elected to put forth a minute that 'approved these documents',
rather than incorporating them. But the minute also clarified that such historical
documents were 'not to be regarded as constituting a creed' (*Stenographer's
Report of FYM 1912*, 120). This compromise left both sides unsatisfied. By the
time of the Great War, these theological debates within FYM became far more
polarized and were exacerbated by a spirit of intra-denominational separation
sweeping through American Protestantism at the time.

Friends General Conference

Liberal Quakerism emerged in parallel with modernist impulses within
Gurneyite Quakerism while clearly centred on an unprogrammed form of

---

[1] Including New England, New York, Baltimore, North Carolina, Indiana, Western, Iowa,
Kansas, Wilmington, Oregon and California Yearly Meetings. Canada YM joined FYM in
1907. Ohio rejected the Uniform Discipline because it was insufficiently evangelical. North
Carolina Yearly Meeting divided over the introduction of the Uniform Discipline and a
Conservative Yearly Meeting was formed in 1903.

worship. For many daughters and sons of Evangelical Friends, such as Jones and John Wilhelm Rowntree, this combination of modernist thought and unprogrammed worship created the underpinning for a reclamation of original Quaker charisms while harnessing modern thought and the ability for Quakers to be more wholly engaged in wider society, freed from the constraints of 'the peculiarities' of earlier times. In its unprogrammed form, and with a strong emphasis on experiential over scriptural authority, it laid claim to a heritage stretching back to George Fox. Liberal Friends also built a theology on the idea of 'being open to new Light' and a strong sense of continuing revelation, giving this form of Quakerism the possibility of remaining unattached to any particular text or part of its own tradition. Liberal Quakerism emerged as a dominant theological stance in unprogrammed Gurneyite Yearly Meetings in Britain and other parts of Europe; parts of the former British Empire such as Australia, New Zealand and South Africa; and in former Hicksite Yearly Meetings in North America. These Hicksite Yearly Meetings in 1900 formed their own umbrella organisation, akin to Five Years Meeting but without its authority, called Friends General Conference (FGC) to create events, educational materials and publications to nurture the Liberal faithful. Liberal Quakerism evolved in its own unique way through the twentieth century and yet maintained coherence.

Conservative Quakerism

Conservative Friends emerged as a distinct grouping composed of Wilburite and anti-pastoral elements from the nineteenth century and the group in North Carolina in 1903 that left Five Years Meeting over the adoption of the Uniform Discipline. A reunification process took place in Philadelphia and New York, between Hicksite and Gurneyite Yearly Meetings in the 1950s; consolidation occurred in Baltimore in the 1960s; in New England between Wilburite and Gurneyite Yearly Meetings (as well as Cambridge Monthly Meeting and the Connecticut Valley Association) in the 1940s; and Hicksite, Gurneyite and Conservative Friends in Canada in the 1950s, reducing the number of Conservative Yearly Meetings. The different roots of each group's conservatism have given the three remaining Conservative Yearly Meetings (Ohio, Iowa North Carolina) different characters, and they vary in the degree of how conservative their political and theological outlooks are, while each seeks to conserve a Christocentric tradition of Quakerism founded on expectant still and silent waiting. Where Conservative Meetings have represented the only unprogrammed form of Quakerism in an area, they have tended to attract Friends who would otherwise attend Liberal Meetings, and this has affected the theological character of meetings in Iowa and North Carolina YMs.

TENSIONS WITHIN MAJORITY QUAKERISM: THE FIRST HALF OF THE CENTURY

Jean Miller Schmidt's work, *Souls or the Social Order: The Two-Party System in American Protestantism* (1991), identifies an important schism developing within Protestant Christianity at the beginning of the twentieth century, between social gospelers and conservative evangelists. On one hand, says Schmidt, were those evangelicals who thought the primary role of the church was to push for individual regeneration of souls and that the elimination of sin was humanity's greatest need. In contrast, there were those adherents of the social gospel, who had an ever-expanding view of the concept of evangelism, which included all activities that might bring people in touch with organised Christianity. By the time of the Great War, the growing tension between these two factions is recognized in academia today as the fundamentalist–modernist debates (Marsden 2006/1980). Although these debates are often cast in scholarship as impacting mostly mainline denominations, research has validated that the Religious Society of Friends was no less influenced by them, and that FYM became one epicentre of such conflicts (Burdick 2013).

Starting in 1919, both Kansas Yearly Meeting (KYM) and Oregon Yearly Meeting (OYM) considered propositions submitted from their constituent Quarterly Meetings requesting their respective Yearly Meeting to withdraw from FYM (*OYM Minutes 1919*, m. 89, p. 33; *KYM Minutes 1919*, m. 18b, p. 6). During the next two years, each YM debated the propositions, with each avoiding separation by instead agreeing to first submit formal protests to FYM before withdrawing outright. The specific demands primarily focused on the following: (1) that the Board of Publication of FYM renew its evangelical, Bible-based emphasis on curriculum and Sunday school material, (2) that the editor of *American Friend* (Woodward) discontinue his disproportionate selection of articles dealing with social and political issues, and (3) that all missionaries selected for work will come from educational institutions known to value the sacredness of Scripture (*Oregon YM 1920*, m. 35, pp. 16–17).[2]

Likewise, starting in 1921, three other YMs (California, Western and Indiana) all considered formally requesting that FYM elevate the Richmond Declaration of Faith and George Fox's Letter to the Governor of Barbados to become definitive statements of faith, and that FYM eliminate

---

[2] These are the specific requests of OYM, but similar demands were made from KYM.

the Uniform Discipline proviso, 'But they are not to be regarded as constituting a creed' (*CYM Minutes 1921*, m. 37, p. 23; *WYM Minutes 1922*, m. 48, pp.
26–27; *IYM Minutes 1921*, m. 12, pp. 10–11).[3] By the time the 1922 sessions of
Five Years Meeting arrived, both sides were deeply ossified. Jones, however,
presented a conciliatory resolution passed by the Business Committee: 'since
the clause which was adopted ten years ago stating that these declarations of
faith are not to be regarded as constituting a creed has been widely misunderstood in at least two directions, *it is our judgment that this clause should now
be eliminated*' (*Minutes of FYM 1922*, 119).[4]

Initially this action was a momentous occasion for American Quakerism
and conflicts were abated for a season. In the end, however, the elimination
of a one-sentence clause to a document of faith did not prove sufficient gain
for some. Instead FYM began to organically disband. Starting in 1924, a two-
year exodus from Indiana Yearly Meeting and Western Yearly Meeting
occurred because some Friends perceived FYM (and its leaders) to be
unsound on issues of orthodoxy. This led to the formation of Central
Yearly Meeting (Hamm 2009, 4). In 1926, after two more years of internal
debate and discernment, Oregon Yearly Meeting became the first full YM to
separate from FYM (*Oregon YM 1926*, m. 11, pp. 5–10). In California Yearly
Meeting, in 1931, a large group of Friends in Huntington Park Monthly
Meeting submitted a proposal to the Yearly Meeting requesting withdrawal
from FYM (*California YM 1931*).[5] Although California YM did not separate
from FYM at this time, several hundred Friends left the YM. In Kansas
Yearly Meeting, in 1936, multiple Quarterly Meetings sent in requests that
their Yearly Meeting sever ties with FYM. The proposal was postponed for
one year and then approved in 1937 (*Kansas YM 1937*, m. 6 & 46, pp. 6–7 & 31).
Despite the promising start of unification among Gurneyite Friends in 1902,
within three decades it was fractured into two distinct groups, much like the
rest of Protestant America.

DIFFERENT KINDS OF MISSION

Evangelical Mission

Foreign mission for Quakers had begun in 1866, but the Kenyan mission of
1902 heralded the start of a century of global expansion for Quakerism.

---

[3] Both California and Western YMs approved the proposals, while Indiana did not.
[4] Emphasis added.
[5] The proposal was also supported by resolutions from Bell, Montebello, Earlham and San
Diego Monthly Meetings.

Local Quaker groups were established in Africa, Central and South America and in Asia; eventually they were allowed to form their own indigenous Yearly Meetings. Evangelised Quakers were themselves evangelical, and prompted by the Great Commission in Matthew 25, Evangelical Quakerism has necessarily placed mission work as a high priority and its numerical growth has far outstripped the results of Liberal and Conservative outreach. Today, programmed Quakerism represents about 90 percent of global Quakerism.

Peace and Relief Work

For unprogrammed Friends and alongside the mission work of Gurneyite Friends, peace and social justice work has remained a high priority for Quakers everywhere. Service replaced the concept of mission for many unprogrammed Friends and their mission committees became service ones in the 1920s.

AMERICAN FRIENDS SERVICE COMMITTEE

The American Friends Service Committee (AFSC) was originally formed by concerned Quakers in response to World War I (Jones 1920, 8). Following Quakers in Britain, who had already established the Friends War Victims Relief Committee in the 1870s and the unofficial Friends Ambulance Unit in 1914, AFSC was to be the pragmatic expression of the faith for the Religious Society of Friends, offering humanitarian relief within a spiritual framework. Jones was selected to serve as chair of the board (*AFSC Board Minutes* 1917).

The work of the AFSC originally centred on three primary tasks. The first task was to acquire legal conscientious objector (CO) status for Friends. The second task was to engage in reconstruction and relief efforts in war-torn Europe. And the third task was to convince Friends in America of the need for such an organisation. Despite long-standing anti-war practices, since the American Civil War, Friends in America had reinterpreted their peace testimony to include a broader scope of acceptable viewpoints. Initially AFSC was successful at accomplishing all three goals. Although the Five Years Meeting was debating issues of orthodoxy in the early 1920s, in those early years of reconstruction work, AFSC was able to pull together diverse Friends under a common umbrella of humanitarianism (Jones 1920, 3).

In 1925, the AFSC officially terminated its World War I emergency services and began a discussion lasting several years on what its own purpose ought to be in the future (*AFSC Annual Report* 1923, 19). By the end of the 'roaring twenties', the Great Depression brought a sudden increase of requests to AFSC for domestic services. Under the guidance of new leaders such as Henry Cadbury (chair of the board) and Clarence Pickett (executive secretary), AFSC instituted several domestic relief programmes, a first of its kind re-education programme and homesteaded many with its subsistence-living programme (Pickett 1953). While this was good humanitarian practice, it created certain political strains. Fair or not, a growing majority of the public at the time blamed the ongoing depression on the failed policies of Republican (and Quaker) President Herbert Hoover. When the Democratic Party got Franklin Roosevelt into the White House, the president turned to AFSC for advice on how to resolve the crisis (Miller 1999, 129). This newfound visibility led to great success for AFSC and a massive infusion of funds over the next several decades (Pickett 1953). By World War II, AFSC was able to successfully negotiate to be the lead agency to handle all US federal programs for conscientious objectors throughout the war. In 1947, AFSC and the Friend Service Council of Britain were jointly awarded the Nobel Peace Prize for their respective ongoing commitment to humanitarianism.

With the AFSC's emphasis on a more democratic ideology and the focus on domestic 'social' programmes, several YMs in America eventually withdrew their support from the AFSC over soteriological concern – as they believed that the organisation no longer supported salvific-based service projects as its core mission. Although temporarily abated by the pragmatic necessities of World War II – evangelical-leaning YMs still needed to work with the AFSC for their respective COs – by the middle of the twentieth century, the same dividing lines that had split Five Years Meeting created similar divisions in AFSC.

In 1943, AFSC's ongoing opposition to the draft and the possibility of universal military training led to the formation of the Friends Committee for National Legislation (FCNL), the first religious lobbyist organisation to undertake political activity on behalf of Quaker concerns. Known for its integrity and honesty as a lobbying firm, FCNL has worked over the past seventy-plus years on issues related to ending war and violence, establishing inclusivity and equity for all and environmental protections (http://fcnl.org/). Although FCNL today does not claim to speak for all Quakers, its representative board has constituents from various YMs and Quaker organisation (Hamm 2003, 181).

QUAKERISM AS A GLOBAL FAITH

The Quaker mission in Africa dates back to 1902 when three student missionaries were sent to Kenya on behalf of the American Friends Board of Foreign Missions. The initial work largely focused on evangelism within an evangelical-based theology. By 1945, the East Africa Yearly Meeting was created, and by 1971 a Friends World Committee for Consultation (FWCC) Africa section was established with office headquarters in Nairobi (www.fwccafrica.org/about/ history). Working in countries throughout Africa that have struggled through past civil wars, gender inequality and cultural genocide, Quakers there have been able to highlight reconciliation theology as a core message in their Christian ethic. As of 2012, it was estimated that there are around 196,000 Quakers in all of Africa (representing 52 percent of the worldwide population of Friends), with predominantly 146,300 of that whole centralised in Kenya (FWCC 2012, map). Most African YMs consider their theology to be more evangelical. As a result of their numerical hegemony within Friends United Meeting (FUM, the successor to Five Years Meeting), YMs in Kenya have pushed for renewed discussions to make the Richmond Declaration of Faith a definitive statement of faith (Hamm 2009, 7).

The work in Central America has established the largest number of Quaker converts in Guatemala. Composed of early twentieth-century mission outreach of American YMs, today there are an estimated 19,620 Friends in the country, with three YMs (FWCC 2012, map). Smaller efforts have made inroads to establish Quaker Monthly Meetings, educational centres or peace programmes in Honduras, Mexico, El Salvador, Cuba, Jamaica and Costa Rica. In South America, Bolivia has become an epicentre for the Religious Society of Friends with an estimated 22,300 members (FWCC 2012, map). The initial mission work in Bolivia was to members of the indigenous Aymara people, and still to this day, they represent the largest cultural group within the YM. Through Bolivian YM and other mission ventures, work has spread to Peru and to indigenous communities in Argentina. There are also a small number of Quakers in Colombia. Although there are some unprogrammed meetings throughout Latin America, much like the African experience, the version of Quakerism found in Central and South America is predominantly programmed in their ecclesiology and evangelical in their theology. Given the historical emphasis towards serving marginalised indigenous populations in South America – and particularly in trying to improve their access to education, health care and basic necessities – social justice and a realised gospel ministry have come to the forefront in their faith and practice.

Mission to Asia began in 1866 but for the most part is a more recent phenomenon. Quakerism is now clearly a global faith.

FRIEND WORLD COMMITTEE FOR CONSULTATION

While some bodies of Friends were experiencing fragmentation throughout the first half of the twentieth century, other groups were working to bring intra-denominational fellowship and promotion among Quakers. In 1920 in London, British Friends sponsored an All Friends Conference, the first official gathering of Quakers from around the world. In the 1930s, AFSC's Fellowship Committee sponsored a series of conferences open to all Friends, resulting in a call for the formation of an official worldwide body to promote the Society's interests. In 1937, at the Second World Conference of Friends held in Swarthmore, Pennsylvania, approval was given for the permanent establishment of an international organization to help transcend past divisions, and to encourage cooperation among Friends. As a result, the new Friends World Committee for Consultation (FWCC) was formalised; its primary purpose continues to be 'to act in a consultative capacity to promote better understanding among Friends the world over' (http://fwcc.world/about-fwcc).

Today the FWCC is an international organisation, primarily focused on bringing Friends together through service projects, spiritual renewal and community building. Likewise, the organisation functions as a central clearinghouse for news related to Quaker happenings and international peace-keeping. FWCC has General Consultative Status to the United Nations as a non-government organization (NGO) and is responsible for the two Quaker UN Offices (QUNO), in Geneva and New York City. The QUNO office in New York focuses on 'building coalitions to bring little-noticed conflicts and issues to the attention of the governments at the Security Council and General Assembly'. The QUNO office in Geneva 'works with UN agencies and related organizations such as the International Organization for Migration and the World Trade Organization to bring to them the voices of the under-represented governments and groups'. FWCC also 'has named a volunteer representative to serve on the non-governmental organization committee within UNICEF' (http://fwcc.world/about-fwcc/quaker-united-nations-work/). Today, the FWCC world headquarters are in London, and there are four autonomous sectional offices (Africa, Asia-West Pacific, Americas and Europe and the Middle East).

Despite the widespread collaboration that has been initiated through the efforts of FWCC, not all Friends have been enamoured with their work and some Evangelical Yearly Meetings in particular are not members, preferring to build alliances with other Evangelical bodies rather than Quaker ones.

ASSOCIATION OF EVANGELICAL FRIENDS

By the 1940s, there were four independent staunchly evangelical Gurneyite Yearly Meetings in America: Ohio (which never joined FYM in the first place because FYM was perceived to be insufficiently evangelical), Central, Oregon and Kansas. Towards the middle of the twentieth century, these four independent meetings, along with factions of evangelical-leaning meetings and individuals within other YMs, sought a greater identity and collaboration with one another around the evangelical mantra. In June 1947, a conference of evangelical Friends was held in Colorado Springs. More than 150 Quakers gathered, with nine Yearly Meetings represented. In addition to the four independent YMs, attendees also came from California YM, Indiana YM, Iowa YM, Nebraska YM and Western YM. The conference marked a significant turning point in evangelical Quakerism, as many of the attendees and presenters called for a renewal of evangelical thought, based on a positive outlook, as well as seeking to create a sense of unity among like-minded Friends to replace past divisiveness and isolation (Roberts 1975).

Out of this conference a loose conglomerate of like-minded evangelical Quakers eventually formed the Association of Evangelical Friends (AEF), which marked the first official ongoing collaboration across evangelical YMs in America. By 1956, an official constitution for the AEF was developed (*Report of Fourth Triennial Conference of Evangelical Friends* 1956, 44–48). By 1959, an official organ (*Concern*) was being published (edited by Arthur Roberts). The leaders of the AEF sought to reshape the evangelical apologetic within the Society to one that was far more world engaging. Paralleling developments in the National Association of Evangelicals (formed in 1942) and their efforts to bring Protestant Christianity out of the clutches of fundamentalist separatists, AEF fashioned itself as a progressive orthodox Quaker organisation. Thus, by the 1959 AEF conference, Everett Cattell articulated the culmination of a subtle but significant shift within the evangelical wing of the Society. Recognising that past divisions within the Society were a tragedy, he suggested the following: (1) that liberals recognise evangelicals as a legitimate and important part of the church and the Quaker movement and (2) that evangelicals recognize that liberals who have not denied Christ and who claim Him as Saviour are to be accepted as Christians (Cattell 1959).

For the next twenty-three years from 1947, the Association of Evangelical Friends provided the leadership and bureaucratic structure necessary to restate the evangelical position among Friends and to become a rallying point for the evangelical movement. Roberts sees the ongoing history of the association as 'the ascendency of a center party among Quakers and a shift away from the strong polarities of the 1920s and 1930s' (Roberts 1975, 1). However, during the ensuing second half of the century, cooperation between evangelical and modernist Friends waned, somewhat due to evangelical Quakers' perception that modernist Friends were moving away from a Christocentric foundation.

FRIENDS UNITED MEETING

In the years 1960 to 1970, Five Years Meeting officially moved from a delegate to a representative form of government (1960), altered meeting frequency to every three years (1963), changed its name to Friends United Meeting (1965), and created a new organisational structure (1970). Although these changes were primarily pragmatic, their impetus can be found in other changes already unfolding that were largely ecumenical in nature. Echoing a similar spirit within evangelical Quakerism, and within Protestantism in general at the mid-century point, Friends United Meeting (FUM) shifted towards broader ecumenical collaboration and unity. The first such change was in Friends United Meeting's relationship to the World Council of Churches (WCC) and the National Council of Churches (NCC). By mid-century, in the hopes of collaborating on issues related to missions, peace and social questions, FUM initiated active membership in both organisations (*Minutes of FYM 1940*, m. 48, pp. 53-53; *1950*, m. 24, pp. 35-36).[6]

In addition to seeking ecumenical alliance with the WCC and the NCC, -an intra-denominational reunification movement also began that started within some Gurneyite and Hicksite YMs, as mentioned earlier, that impacted Friends United Meeting. Partly due to declining membership and partly to the ending of past theological divisions, in the middle of the twentieth century, YMs in New England, New York, Philadelphia, Canada and Baltimore were able to unite or consolidate. Thus as a result, Monthly Meetings that were previously associated with either associated Hicksite or Orthodox Friends were now merged. Likewise, in the 1960s the newly formed Southeastern YM elected for dual

---

[6] Technically, FYM elected to join the World Council of Churches in 1940, but due to a decade of provisional planning somewhat slowed by the onset of world war, 1950 is nominally when active participation in that organisation began. That same year, FYM officially joined the National Council of Churches.

affiliation in FGC and FUM (Hamm 2009, 5). As expected, a new theologically tolerant and more socially liberal FUM began to emerge.

The impact of these intra-denominational reunifications and ecumenical collaborations renewed strains for some evangelical YMs and resulted in another round of organic division within American Quakerism. In 1954, Nebraska Yearly Meeting adopted a resolution with respect to FUM, citing almost all the same concerns of Oregon and Kansas YMs from several decades before, and with the additional concern over FUM's membership in the WCC and NCC. By 1957, Nebraska Yearly Meeting, in the process of changing its name to Rocky Mountain Yearly Meeting, elected to intentionally create an organic division, allowing each Monthly Meeting to decide independently which entity to align with (*Nebraska YM 1956*, m. 83, pp. 36–37; *Nebraska YM 1957*, m. 16–22, pp. 9–12).

Likewise many evangelical Friends looked at the internal unifications with grave concern over the impact these changes would have on FUM. By default, the unification brought Hicksite Friends into FUM, which for evangelicals renewed their concerns regarding the inroads of theological secularism. Cattell decried this change as insensitive to the evangelical position: 'To the evangelical this is still a life and death matter and the evangelical cannot understand the callousness with which actions of the sort are forced upon him without consultation and without appreciation of his position' (1959, 13). Particularly with FUM now operating as a representative body, the perception of the impact of these changes renewed old debates and increased suspicion from evangelicals of FUM's ability to speak for what was left of Gurneyite unity in the second half of the twentieth century.

While today, in the twenty-first century, FUM is perceived to have reaffirmed its Christian identity, for much of the remainder of the twentieth century, it was charged with shifting towards pluralism. In an effort to decrease tensions, in the 1990s, FUM's general secretary proposed a realignment in which Monthly Meetings dually associated with FUM and FGC would cease their FUM membership, while pastoral meetings would join together with likeminded evangelical Friends. The proposal was not successful, as many moderate Friends were unwilling to commit to either polarity and viewed Friends United Meeting as a middle ground where all Quakers could share a common communion (Hamm 2009).

EVANGELICAL FRIENDS ALLIANCE

The Evangelical Friends Alliance was officially formed in 1963, but its inception went through the AEF. The AEF Steering Committee reported during a 1954 business meeting that it had received several requests for 'a more definite or permanent form of organization' (Dillon 1963, 2). Up to this point, AEF conferences had been primarily voluntary, non-representative gatherings, meant to serve as, 'a catalytic agent for the yearly meetings and their groupings as already organized' (Roberts 1975, 2). Some Friends, however, sought a more definitive (and official) form of administration that could speak for the voice of evangelical Friends (Dillon 1963, 2). This issue may not have been so pressing but for the aforementioned developments during the second half of the twentieth century in Friends United Meeting, which led to increasing alarm from evangelical Friends over what they perceived to be tolerant attitudes towards theological liberalism and secular modernism. Likewise, disagreements on social issues such as homosexuality and same-sex unions began to take centre stage within FUM sessions.

Similarly so, over the second half of the century, the American Friends Service Committee adopted what moderate and evangelical Friends labelled 'militant' and 'extreme leftist' policies (Hamm 2003, 176). After WWII, many new workers came to the AFSC not drawn by the organisation's historic religiosity, but for the humanitarian recognition the agency received (Lewy 1988, 27–55). While AFSC continued to support the historic Quaker statement 'that of God in everyone' within its mission statement, new leadership, including Lewis Hoskins, began to suggest this historic statement was 'non-theological, more psychological' (Hoskins 1950, personal communication). Such trends were a constant point of frustration for evangelical Friends. Increasingly, evangelicals called for the creation of an alternative administrative structure for evangelical service opportunities and polity development to take the place of AFSC and FUM.

In 1963, four independent Yearly Meetings (Kansas, Ohio, Rocky Mountain and Oregon – previously calling themselves KORO) formed the Evangelical Friends Alliance (EFA), an official entity representing the evangelical voice. In many ways (some of which were unintended), the EFA became a supra–Yearly Meeting, the evangelical equivalent to Friends United Meeting. Quickly, the EFA started working towards developing new mission fields and resumed publication of the *Evangelical Friend*. One of the unforeseen consequences of having two organisations (AEF and EFA) representing evangelical Quakers was a moderate power struggle between the two entities. Jack Willcuts (1963, 5–7) claimed that, in this largely unspoken competition between the two entities, the EFA came to represent the expression of the YM leaders (superintendents and clerks), while the AEF came to serve the lay leaders. Although both AEF and EFA existed side by side for some years, primarily due to a sense that its purpose had been fulfilled and because of unspoken competition between the two entities, the Administrative Council of the AEF laid down the organisation in 1970, leaving EFA to provide both ongoing structure and inspiration for the larger movement. In 1989, EFA became Evangelical Friends International (EFI) – a worldwide conglomerate of evangelical Quakers, now working under the title Evangelical Friends Church International (EFCI), with an international office in the United States and regional offices in North America, Asia, Africa, Europe and Latin America.

In 1993, Southwest Yearly Meeting (formerly California YM) left FUM for EFCI over tense disagreements on social and theological issues. In 1996, Iowa YM almost left FUM as well (also citing concern over FUM's affiliation with the World Council of Churches and National Council of Churches), but in the end, left it to each of its Monthly Meetings to decide to align with EFCI or FUM (*Iowa YM Minutes 1996*, pp. 11–19, 22–25). Thus today in the twentyfirst century there remains a bifurcation within Gurneyite Quakerism.

In 1978 the Evangelical Friends Mission (EFM) was formed to be the cooperative mission arm of EFCI. Today, EFM sees its primary goal in missions to 'fuel a worldwide movement of people who seek first the kingdom of God, planting churches that live and die to carry out the Great Commission in the spirit of the Great Commandment'.[7] EFM has been at the forefront of more recent mission work to Southeast Asia and central Europe. EFCI mission is also strong in central and southern America. EFM currently has evangelistic and humanitarian mission projects underway in locales around the world.

LIBERAL QUAKERISM

Based in and on spiritual experience alone, Liberal Quakerism has avoided the doctrinal disputes and schisms that characterised Gurneyite Quakerism in the twentieth century. However, it has also developed a theological diversity that moved it away from a purely Christian frame of reference and most recently has accommodated and included humanist elements. Doctrinally then, Liberal Quakerism represents a major shift in the scope of Quaker theology. Unity has been founded instead on a dedication to the forms of Quakerism, particularly the way of worship[8] and manner of conducting business (also through worship and without votes) (Dandelion 2007, 136–39). Issues of *how Quakers are to be Quaker* have emerged as dominant

---

[7] EFM Mission Statement. Approved May 2014 by EFM Board. Located at www.friendsmission.com/about-efm/mission-statement. Accessed March 30, 2016.

[8] Although worship became shorter in the twentieth-century, it is now normally an hour long.

in a group in which theology is downplayed. The books of discipline of Liberal Yearly Meetings have become less and less doctrinally prescriptive and more descriptive of spiritual experience and outlook. In most Liberal Yearly Meetings, the relegation of doctrine has become a mistrust of it. These liberal-Liberal or 'permissive Liberal' Friends have embraced diversity as an appropriate expression of the mystery of God and have become very cautious about any definite doctrinal claims. Rather than being uncertain of some of the church's certainties, Liberal Quakerism can today be characterised as being certain of the uncertainty of theological claims. All theological statements are personal, partial or provisional: they are 'towards' or 'perhaps' kinds of statements, with another element of coherence coming through this certainty about theological uncertainty, what can be described as an ortho-credence, a particular way of holding beliefs (Dandelion 2007, 152). However, this does not delimit theological disputes. In the 1980s, Liberal Friends struggled with the question of whether Christian belief was essential to modern Quakerism; in the early twenty first century, debates between non-theists and other Friends have raised the question of belief in God, and the language of shared statements made by Quakers (see Chapter 15, this volume, by Dan Randazzo).

As well as representing a declining percentage of global Quakerism given the mission success of programmed Friends, absolute numbers of Liberal Friends have declined through the twentieth century in line with general secularising trends in the Global North (Dandelion 2008, 113). At the same time, Liberal Quakers have continued to start off new local and Yearly Meetings such as Pacific, North Pacific, Southern Appalachian. In Britain, there are more local Meetings than there have ever been and 90 percent of Quakers there have converted in as adults (British Quaker Survey 2013). Liberal Quakers are also highly active in peace and social justice work through agencies such as AFSC and FCNL in North America and through Yearly Meeting staff departments elsewhere. Liberal Friends have made up for a numerical decline with ample resources and Britain Yearly Meeting maintains an annual budget of around £12 m.

THE GLOBAL SOUTH AND REVERSE MISSION

While the history of Quakerism in the past century has been one of ongoing processes of bifurcation and realignment, it has also been one of the phenomenal success of mission work and the creation of global Quaker communion beyond any scale imagined in the century before. Quakerism existed outside of North America and the British Isles only among small isolated groups of Quakers in mainland Europe and parts of the British Empire, until mission success in Africa, Asia and Central and South America throughout the twentieth century shifted the numerical balance of Quakerism away from the Global North.

In the twenty-first century, numerically now more Quakers are in locales identified as the Global South than in traditional strongholds such as Britain and the United States. Kenya today has more Quakers than any other country in the world, while Bolivia has quietly risen to third – after Kenya and the United States, respectively (FWCC 2012, map). Mission in the second half of the twentieth century has proved fertile for the new Quaker communities in Nepal, Taiwan, the Philippines and among the Roma people in Central Europe. Future anticipated growth models suggest this trend will continue. While these newer Yearly Meetings are typically allied to either EFCI or FUM, we can expect, and can already see, the phenomenon of reverse mission, whereby missionaries come from the once-colonised locales to help reinvigorate the spiritual life of the Yearly Meetings of their parent missionaries. From an evangelical perspective, Liberal Quakerism in its pluralist mode appears to have lost touch with its Christian roots. FUM can appear to be too broad a communion. Attitudes to homosexuality, themselves divisive within US YMs, also creates the impetus for mission work in the Global North. Only the scarcity of resources and linguistic differences hamper the new majority Quakerism, now in the Global South, from greater influence in the Global North.

THE FUTURE OF FRIENDS

The future of global Quakerism is uncertain. Some scholars cite studies to predict the eventual demise of all organised religions in Britain and the United States, and Quakers certainly have some solid evidence mimicking those trends. To what extent these 'peculiar people', who have seldom enjoyed numerical strength, can continue to be a divergent witness against the injustices of the world may hold the answer to that. Most would agree that the Global South (not to be understood as a unified entity itself) is the promise and potential for future growth among Friends, though they often lack the finances and resources of the Global North. The diverse theology of Quakers from around the world, particularly as it relates to defining what constitutes orthodoxy, continues to be a point of tension. Joint opportunities are being created for expressing a Quaker witness through service projects, often using what unity remains in the historical Quaker Testimonies as an impetus. But simultaneously, new schisms have occurred due to some YMs inability to discern their corporate ethic on social issues, frequently centred on how the Society should respond to gays and lesbians in fellowship. More than a few have suggested that Friends are united in history and nomenclature only, and that it would be best to proceed into the future as separate entities. Others strive for unity in places where such work is difficult and often with little fruit to bear. If such ventures are to see more success, the models for reconciliation and mediation provided by Friends in Africa may help Quakers worldwide discern their path forward intra-denominationally, while what unity remains within the Religious Society of Friends' commitments to peace and justice may be the necessary starting places for those discussions.

SUGGESTED FURTHER READING

Burdick, Timothy J. (2013) 'Neo-Evangelical Identity within American Religious Society of Friends (Quakers): Oregon Yearly Meeting, 1919–1947'. Unpublished Doctoral Thesis, University of Birmingham, accessible via http://etheses.bham.ac.uk/4152/.

Dandelion, Pink. (2008) *The Quakers: A Very Short Introduction*, Oxford: Oxford University Press.

Dandelion, Pink. (2007) *Introduction to Quakerism*, Cambridge: Cambridge University Press.

Frost, J. William. (2013) 'Modernist and Liberal Quakers 1887–2010' in *The Oxford Handbook of Quaker Studies*, ed. by Stephen W. Angell and Pink Dandelion, Oxford: Oxford University Press, pp. 78–92.

Hamm, Thomas D. (2003) *The Quakers in America*, Columbia Contemporary American Religion Series. New York: Columbia University Press.

Hinshaw, Gregory P. (2013) 'Five Years Meeting and Friends United Meeting, 1887–2010', in *The Oxford Handbook of Quaker Studies*, ed. by Stephen W. Angell and Pink Dandelion, Oxford: Oxford University Press, pp. 93–107.

Roberts, A.O. (2013) 'Evangelical Friends, 1887–2010', in *The Oxford Handbook of Quaker Studies*, ed. by Stephen W. Angell and Pink Dandelion, Oxford: Oxford University Press, pp. 108–25.

PART II

∾

EXPRESSIONS OF QUAKER FAITH

4

❧

Literature

Nancy Jiwon Cho

> How many Plays did Jesus Christ and his Apostles recreate themselves at? What Poets, Romances, Comedies, and the like, did the Apostles and Saints make, or use to pass away their Time withal? I know they bid all *redeem their Time, to avoid foolish Talking, vain Jesting, profane Babblings, and fabulous Stories.*   William Penn, *No Cross, No Crown* (1669)

> God is in all beauty, not only in the natural beauty of earth and sky, but in all fitness of language and rhythm, whether it describe a heavenly vision or a street fight, a Hamlet or a Falstaff, a philosophy or a joke.
> Caroline C. Graveson (1937) included in
> *Quaker Faith and Practice* (2013)

As the polar attitudes in the epigraphs – taken from two defining works about Quaker thinking and practice – evidence, Friends' attitudes to literary works have altered substantially from the inception of the movement to the present day. Although the pace of acceptance has varied among the different traditions that emerged after the schisms of the nineteenth century, there have been considerable shifts among Quakers towards a revised view of the arts. Thus, while early Friends believed that writing should be simple and honest – and, consequently, that artful genres were at best frivolous and at worst diabolical – many Quakers today believe that God is immanent in all forms of human expression. Accordingly, Quaker writers in recent decades have written novels, ghost stories, murder mysteries, science fiction and experimental poetry – all literary forms that earlier Friends would have denounced as deceitful, profane or vain. At the same time, some Quaker groups have remained cautious in their literary engagement with a minority

The author would like to thank the Farmington Institute for supporting her Visiting Fellowship at Harris Manchester College, University of Oxford, where this chapter was completed.

retaining the historical prohibition of the arts. As such, multiple positions
exist among Quakers today regarding imaginative literature.

Although several illuminating studies on Quaker writing have now been
published – especially on the seventeenth-century texts of the First Publishers
of Truth and Quakers' uses of print culture (Wright 1932; Corns and
Loewenstein 1995; Peters 2005; Hagglund 2013, 2015) – less critical attention
has been given to Friends' changing opinions about the value of imaginative
literature, specifically poetry, fiction and drama. As Hood has observed,
creative writing has historically been problematic for Friends because
'[s]ome fundamental friction seems to lie between the Quaker testimonies of
simplicity and integrity and the metaphoric, imaginative, carnivalesque spirit
that so deeply informs artistic expression' (Hood 2016, 2). This chapter seeks
to examine Quakers' changing and varied opinions about the spiritual and
moral goodliness of imaginative writing –in terms of both writing and reading
creative texts – in the context of internal religious ideas and praxis and
external literary theories and trends. The present chapter is limited to an
examination of literary attitudes and practice among British and American
Friends only, but it is hoped that further studies will evaluate this subject more
widely and in greater depth.

EARLY QUAKERS AND LITERARY PRODUCTION

From the early years of the movement, leading Quakers recognised the
power of the written word. Viewed as akin to preaching God's word
(Hagglund 2015, 32) – as Edward Burrough prophesied, 'This is the day of
thy Visitation, O Nation wherein the Lord speaks to thee by the mouth of his
Servants in word and writing' (Burrough 1672, 12) – writing was primarily
understood by early Friends as a practical mechanism for communicating
with adherents and the wider public rather than as a devotional instrument
or divinely bestowed generative talent.

Perceiving that writing could be a tool for the forging of the fledgling
movement's identity, Quakers started publishing their messages in tracts,
broadsheets and books in 1652 (Peters 1995, 1, 8). As the movement expanded
and zealous adherents inscribed their messages in rhetorical language, leading Friends called for the regulation of circulating works recognising that
injudicious content could lead to the Society's misrepresentation and dis-
repute. In 1653, George Fox cautioned Friends to 'write nothing but as you
are moved by the and from the Lord, lest there be presumption, rashnesse,
hastinesse, or pride and lightnesse in your spirits . . . Let none print any but
what they can eternally witnesse' (Fox 1653, 48). Unsurprisingly, given

leaders' emphasis on solemnity and truth, seventeenth-century Friends eschewed genres of dubious sobriety and veracity, such as 'satire, light verse, and drama' (Wright 1932, 9), and privileged nonfictional prose, such as proclamations, epistles, disputes, appeals for toleration, testimonies and journals instead.

In this context, in the early years of the Society, there was little Quaker creative writing. For instance, prior to 1660, 'there was practically no Quaker verse printed' (Moore 2005, 5). When used, it was often as a prophetic rather than artistic medium. For instance, 'A Declaration of Life and Power in Me' (1659) – a 115-line versification of the Scriptures describing Christ's character placed at the beginning of *Certain Papers Given Forth in the Spirit of Truth which Witness against the Wisdom of the World and Unrighteousness of Men* ... (1659) by Thomas Stubbs, a member of the 'Valiant Sixty' – does not aim for formal refinement; its lines do not keep to a regular metrical scheme or rhyme. This practice is comparable with the Puritan tradition of privileging truth and artlessness; for instance, the American *Bay Psalm Book* (1640) stated, 'If ... the verses are not always smooth and elegant as some may desire or expect, let them consider that God's Altar needs not our polishings', because 'Conscience rather than Elegance' and 'fidelity rather than poetry' are more highly esteemed by God ('Preface', *Bay Psalm Book* 1640). Stubbs's final line, 'Moved and written from the Spirit of the Lord by *Thomas* Stubbs called a Quaker' indicates that verse was being used to articulate the Holy Spirit working through him rather than literary ability. As prophetic writers in other eras, such as William Blake and Joanna Southcott, have done, Stubbs used the elevated language of verse to communicate divine revelation poured through the lowly mortal (see Balfour 2002; Cho and Niblett 2016).

From 1660 to 1666, there was a brief flowering of Quaker poetry when many publications included verse (Moore 2005). Much of the poetry was apocalyptic in its warnings to sinners – especially persecutors of Friends – but some works were also directed at Quakers, such as verses for pastoral encouragement at Meetings (Moore 2005, 9). This phenomenon may have been inspired by John Perrot's poetry written while imprisoned in Rome by the Inquisition; his verse was included in pamphlet accounts of his sufferings published between 1660 and 1661 and in a forty-six-page book of poems entitled *A Sea of the Seed's Sufferings, Through which Runs A River of Rich Rejoycing* (1661) (Moore 2005, 7). Viewed as a disruptive force by leaders, Perrot was eventually denounced by Quaker orthodoxy, which Moore suggests may account for the waning of Quaker poetry in the later 1660s, if verse became identified with Perrotism (Moore 2005, 8–9).

One poet influenced by Perrot was his associate Katherine Evans, who, along with Sarah Cheevers, was imprisoned in Malta by the Inquisition from 1659 to 1663. Their co-authored *A True Account of the Great Tryals and Cruel Sufferings* (1663) includes a number of 'victorious Hymns and Songs, and Praises, all in Verse' by Evans (Evans and Cheevers 2003/1663, 140–46). These works are unexpected given that Quaker worship is characterised by silence, and vernacular hymnody and was at an incipient stage at this time (see Watson 1997, chaps. 5 and 6; Clarke 2011). In fact, they offer a useful reminder that 'silence is not an end in itself but a framework providing a range of activities that is believed to be incited by the present Christ' (Johns 2013, 267). Certainly, the hymns aim to articulate divine indwelling in the persecuted women and verbalise the women's steadfast Quaker faith to readers; for instance, one hymn, which is said to have been composed after rejecting an offer for release if the women kissed the cross (Robinson 1715, 75–76), testifies to their Protestant faith in Christ's atonement:

> The Cross of Christ doth operate
> Through every vein and vital part,
> The heart and reins to cleanse from sin,
> Of them that's exercis'd therein.
>
> (Evans and Cheevers 2003, 145 ll. 45–48)

Evans and Cheevers, like other Quaker women, were enabled to participate in Friends' textual ministry by two factors: Fox's radical teaching that the Inner Light was equally available to both sexes and the scriptural authorisation of two texts, Paul's proclamation 'there is neither male nor female; for ye all are one in Christ Jesus' (Galatian 3:28) and Joel's prophecy (2:28–29), quoted in the Book of Acts 2:17, that 'in the last days . . . your daughters shall prophesy . . . And also . . . upon the handmaids in those days will I pour out my spirit.' Empowered by these beliefs, female Friends authored around 20 percent of all published seventeenth-century women's writings in Britain (Crawford 1985, 213).

In late-Stuart Britain, 'fiction' signified artifice ('That which is fashioned or framed; a device, a fabric'), lies ('Feigning, counterfeiting; deceit, dissimulation, pretence') and morally dubious fantasy ('The action of "feigning" or inventing imaginary incidents, states of things, etc., whether for the purpose of deception or otherwise') (*OED Online* 2016). As the opening question of Fox's creedal *A Catechisme for Children* (1658) affirms, the speaking of truth was of primary importance to Friends, 'Is any lie of the truth?' and his answer, 'No, for the Truth checks and reproves the Lyar, and he is not of Truth, 1 John 2.21' (Fox 1658, A1). Within this culture, 'telling stories that never happened was considered untruthful' (Hood 2016, 2) and, therefore, sinful. Indeed, the first systematic account of Quaker practices, William Penn's *No Cross, No Crown* (1682, vehemently rejected all literary forms that require artifice or invention. Progressing from Theophylact's rejection of 'all Lyes', Penn privileged plainness – in contrast with contemporary Restoration baroque – and upheld Gregory's rejection of 'fables, old-wive's tales . . . *Plays, Poetry* and *Romances* of the times' (Penn 1682, 505–6) deeming such fictitious genres dangerous in tempting readers away from spiritual improvement and useful work. In fact, anxiety about the deceit of fiction was commonplace in the period (see Loveman 2008).

Early Modern Protestants especially distrusted drama, because it was aligned with papist ceremony and ritualism. For instance, Puritan William Prynne (1600–69) published a thousand-page attack on the evils of theatre entitled *Histriomastix* in 1633 (Johnson and Savidge 2009, 34), and *A Short View of the Immorality and Profaneness of the English Stage* (1698) by Jeremy Collier (1650–1726), bishop of the nonjuring (refusing to sear allegiance to the Crown) Church of England, also ferociously attacked Restoration Drama. For Quakers, the pleasures of drama were viewed as spiritually treacherous in subverting 'their goal of simplicity . . . to turn away from "worldly" distractions, and to situate themselves in a deeply worshipful posture, with distracting influences kept to a minimum in order to receive Divine messages' (Lapsansky 2013, 335). As such, George Fox was 'moved to cry out against all sorts of music, and against the mountebanks playing tricks on their stages; for they burthened the pure life, and stirred up the people's vanity' (quoted in Graves 1996, 240). At this time, Quakers were also beginning to regulate congruity between internal spiritual purity and external visual aesthetics (Homan 2013, 497), and flamboyant Restoration pageantry was manifestly inconsistent with emerging Quaker plainness. Indeed, in the early eighteenth century, the largely Quaker Philadelphia governing assembly consistently legislated prohibitions against the theatre, which were often subsequently repealed by the British Parliament (see Johnson and Burling 2001).

Unlike his stances on fiction and drama, Penn's disdain for poetry was not characteristic of British Reformed Christianity. In 1667, John Milton had published *Paradise Lost*, and George Herbert's *The Temple* (1633) had gone into nine editions by the same year. Yet, as Elizabeth Gray Vining has quipped, Penn 'felt strongly [enough] about poets . . . to bring up in support of his disapproval all the philosophical big guns that he could muster' (Vining 1960, 97). For instance, he cited Petrus Bellonius [Pierre Belon]'s declaration that 'it was not lawful for a Christian to study Poesie' (Penn 1682, 513). As Vining clarifies, for Penn, 'poetry was effeminate; it was a time-waster; it corrupted the youth by causing their thoughts to dwell too much on love . . . it was frivolous. Worst of all, so many of the poets were also playwrights' (Vining 1960, 98). In its conscious artistry and aural pleasures, Penn perceived poetry as a threat to Quaker religion. However, not all Quakers shared Penn's disdain, for Friends including Margaret Fell, Thomas Ellwood, Lilias Skene and Mary Mollineux published verse during the Restoration. For instance, Ellwood – most famous for his belief that he inspired Milton's *Paradise Regain'd* (1671) – inscribed his Quaker theology into poems on 'Divine Worship', 'Inward Peace' and 'On Worship', and he published an epic poem near the end of his life – *Davideis: The Life of David King of Israel: A Sacred Poem in Five Books* (1712).

Severe religious intolerance during the Restoration also impacted Quaker literary production. Friends suffered the greatest religious persecution during this period with as many as 450 Friends dying in prison (Allen 2013, 32). As 'intemperate, inaccurate, repetitive works could discredit Friends' (Hall 1992, 60) and add to discrimination, the compulsion to protect the Society's reputation reinforced the need for literary restraint. Seeking to curb injurious immoderation that could lead to accusations of 'fanaticism, sedition, or worse' (Allen 2013, 35), Fox and other leaders established an official body for regulating Quaker publications. Thus, in 1672, responsibility for monitoring the Society's publications was assigned to ten Quakers (Hagglund 2013, 483), and, in the following year, the Second Day Morning Meeting was established with the aims of responding to criticism and scrutinising Quaker-authored works (Wright 1932, 97). No text was to be published by a Friend without the committee's approval. The effect of censorship, as Wright has determined, was the conservatising of the Society's literary output; as Friends 'became cautious about circulating records of visions, prophecies, lamentations, healings, and fasts' (Wright 1932, 98), publication of ecstatic writings went into sharp decline from this period. Thus, at a historical moment when Quakers were starting 'to codify some of the nuance of a "simple" approach to religious posture' (Lapsansky 2013, 336) – for instance, by imposing plain dress – Quaker writings also pursued simplicity, truth and emotional composure over artistry, imagination and fervour.

LITERATURE IN THE LONG EIGHTEENTH CENTURY

The long eighteenth century, which has traditionally been understood as the period of Quaker quietism, coincides with the period of the rise or emergence of the novel in English literary history. Despite the fact that this new genre was gaining classic generic status in the Anglophone world (see

Moretti 2006), fiction continued to be eschewed by Friends throughout the eighteenth century. As Hood elucidates, for Quakers, 'the central problem' with imaginative literary genres 'lies in the base falsity of representation' (Hood 2016, 3).

One surprising exception in the proscription against fiction was Stephen Crisp (1628–92)'s *A Short History of a Long Travel from Babylon to Bethel*, which was published posthumously in 1711. Inspired by John Bunyan's *Pilgrim's Progress* (1678), it belongs to the pilgrimage tale, 'a small but distinct subgenre of devotional literature' (Cook 2000, 186). Crisp's use of Bunyan's crude allegorical form – an 'honest fiction' distinguishable from deception by its implausibility (Gallagher 2006, 338) – may have been a factor in its eventual publication. Crisp's narrative is also imbued with Quaker beliefs and practices. Theological differences from Bunyan include the protagonist's rejection of human direction, his following of a 'Light' and rejection of a false house that represents ritualist and hierarchical churches, 'the orders . . . were most about meats and drinks, and about rules for electing of officers to rule the house of God' (Crisp 1777, 15). Crisp's is also the only pilgrimage tale 'written from the point of view of the narrator's sojourn at his destination, and . . . in the first person, symbolic of the spiritual fulfillment Quakers found within themselves in their mortal life' (Cook 2000, 189). The overtly Quaker content must have contributed to the Morning Meeting's belated authorisation of the fictional text, and it went into at least ten editions throughout the eighteenth century. However, it did not instigate further publications of Quaker fiction.

Friends' withdrawal as a peculiar people during the eighteenth century has been understood as an impact of Robert Barclay's idea of a single 'Day of Visitation' (Barclay 1827, 157) – meaning a single opportunity for salvation – replacing Early Friends' belief in a continuous 'day' (Dandelion 2007, 55). Required to remain unsullied by the world to ensure salvation, Friends re-enforced the regulation of print in their first published books of discipline. As the *Revised Discipline of the Yearly Meeting of Friends, held in Baltimore . . .* (1794) cautioned, any Friends who published without approval were to be 'dealt with as disorderly' (*Revised Discipline* 1794, 8), meaning they risked expulsion. This peril was clarified in the 1806 revision, which advised that any Friend found publishing unsuitable books should 'be testified against' (*Old Discipline* 1999, 231), a phrase synonymous with 'disowned' in Quaker discourse (*Old Discipline* 1999, 412). Such fearful consequences must have restrained Friends in their literary activities.

Early published books of discipline also denounced the reading of imaginative literature. The 1802 book of discipline of British Friends reproduced advice from 1764 that every Friend, 'under a consideration of the hurtful tendency of reading plays, romances, and novels, and other pernicious books . . . discourage and suppress the same' (*Extracts from the Minutes and Advices* 1806, 11–12). Similar warnings were also reproduced in contemporaneous American books of discipline (see Philadelphia 1806, 18; New England 1809, 146; Baltimore 1806, 231–32; New York 1810, 401; Virginia 1814, 440 in *Old Discipline* 1999). Perhaps because poetry was not specifically proscribed in books of discipline, the earliest Quaker adherents to seriously and successfully pursue creative writing were poets.

Eighteenth-century Quaker thinking and practice are imbued in the verse of Bernard Barton (1784–1849), who was known as 'the Quaker Poet'. For instance, 'The Spiritual Law' echoes primitive Quaker theology:

> Say not the LAW DIVINE
> Is hidden from thee, or afar removed;
> That Law within would shine,
> If there its glorious light were sought and loved.
>
> (Barton 1859, 346)

Other works reflect contemporary Quakers' engagement with social justice; as Healey has elucidated, eighteenth-century Friends' 'abnormal degree of introspection' and sectarianism paradoxically led to 'a rediscovery of the beckoning social tasks of humanity' (see also Jones 1921, 314, in Healey 2013, 59). *The Convict's Appeal* (1818), for instance, protests against capital punishment:

> Ye who profess the Christian name,
> Since vested in your hands,
> A Christian nation's laws to frame,
> Do what your faith commands.'
>
> (Barton 1818, 15)

This poem – written in the same year that London Yearly Meeting was pressing the case for the abolition of the death penalty in its Epistles – is an example of Quaker literary engagement with the politics of compassion, human rights and penal reform as exemplified in the work of Elizabeth Fry (1780–1845) (see Nellis and Waugh 2013, 377–91). In fact, such practice dovetailed with the contemporary poetics of British Romanticism; for instance, William Blake and William Wordsworth envisaged poets as having prophetic roles protesting against sociopolitical abuses (see Balfour 2002), and Percy Bysshe Shelley famously asserted in *A Defence of Poetry* (1821) that, 'poets are the unacknowledged legislators of the world' (Shelley 1840, 57). Directly engaging with first-generation Romantic poets including Charles Lamb and Robert Southey (see Lucas 1893, 74–114, 165–66), Barton's poetry concurred with their ideals.

Frustratingly for Barton, Friends remained suspicious of his verse despite its inherent Quakerism. As he recalled in a letter, one Quaker minister, upon meeting the poet, asked, *"What, art thou the Versifying Man?" On my replying … that I was called such, he looked at me again, I thought "more in sorrow than in anger," and observed, "Ah! That's a thing quite out of my way"'* (Barton 1850, 47). Perhaps in response to such close-mindedness, Barton wrote a vindication entitled 'The Quaker Poet. Verses on Seeing Myself so Designated' in which he makes a canny case for Quaker poetry by upholding the Society's literary values. Turning the Society's arguments for restraint to his advantage, he argues that, 'Chast'ning each soft emotion; / And, from fanaticism free', the Quaker poet can produce verse removed of 'The fervour of devotion!' (Barton 1822, 1773 ll. 78–80). Here, Barton may have been criticising the rise of Evangelical verse; for instance, popular hymns, such as William Cowper (1731–1801)'s 'There is a Fountain Filled with Blood' (1772) and Augustus Montague Toplady (1740–78)'s 'Rock of Ages' (1775) could rouse powerful emotion among singers and readers. Barton presented a crucial role for the Quaker poet as a promoter of the Society's values and a defender from erroneous enthusiasm.

THE MULTIPLE POSITIONS OF THE NINETEENTH CENTURY

Attitudes to literature became more complex in the nineteenth century after a number of internal schisms led to the development of divergent traditions of Quakerism. The most significant schisms were, in 1828, a Hicksite (liberal)/Orthodox separation, and, in 1854, a Wilbur (conservative)/Gurney (evangelical) separation. All groups of Quakers underwent great changes in the nineteenth century (see Hamm 2013), but at different paces; consequently, multiple Quaker stances regarding the arts began to coexist.

Realist fiction was among the greatest achievements of nineteenth-century Anglophone literature. Yet, despite the novel's increasing generic respectability in this period, Quakers from all groups continued to problematise fiction for much of the century. Gallagher has suggested that, as a new understanding of 'fiction' as imaginative narration with invented characters and episodes became prevalent in mainly the eighteenth century, the older meaning of '"deceit, dissimulation, pretense" became obsolete' (Gallagher 2006, 338). However, the earlier usage prevailed for Friends, and they rarely used the form. Charles Brockden Brown had published *Arthur Mervyn*, a novel shaped by his formative Quakerism, in 1799, but, as it was of the type 'created by Friends but not necessarily *about* Quaker topics' (Lapsansky 2003, 9), it did not revise entrenched Quaker antipathy to the form. Later, Sarah Strickney Ellis, who had been a Quaker before marriage, attempted to produce 'wholesome' fiction highlighting 'the value of the Quaker way – and the value of literature for reinforcing it' in *Friends at their Own Fireside* (1858) (Lapsansky 2003, 10, 9). Yet, as the most popular and influential novels of the period were not written with this impulse, fiction remained incompatible with many Friends' ethical standards.

Nineteenth-century Quaker antipathy to fiction can be illuminated by the case of Amelia Opie. Prior to her 1825 convincement, Opie had published six novels and four short story collections as well as poetry. Her *The Father and the Daughter* (1801), in particular, had been 'a cultural phenomenon', which remained 'a familiar contour on the literary landscape' for at least thirty years (Opie, King, and Pierce 2003, 11). However, upon conversion, she abandoned writing fiction pressured by Friends including Joseph John Gurney, the 'great exemplar of Quaker evangelicalism' (Hamm 2013, 70). She turned, instead, to devotional poetry and didactic writing, producing works such as *Illustrations of Lying, In All Its Branches* (1825), which publicly reversed her position from proponent of fiction to champion of truth. Some twenty years after her convincement, however, she republished her fiction against the advice of Friends.

Although her first biographer, Cecilia Lucy Brightwell, asserted that Opie 'experienced no regrets' in relinquishing fiction, archival analysis has demonstrated that Brightwell's hastily produced *Memorials of the Life of Amelia Opie* (1854) is unreliable (Cosgrave 2013, 61). Indeed, sources omitted from the biography reveal that Opie disagreed with Quaker arguments against fiction two decades after her convincement. When her novels were republished (first in America in 1838, and then in Britain in 1845–47), Opie faced disapproval from Friends. In a letter to Gurney dated 23 February 1844, she defended her decision, stating, 'I *never* thought that *works of fiction* were never to be read – on the contrary, I believe simple moral tales the very best mode of instructing the young & *the poor* – *else why* do the pious of all sects and beliefs, spread *tracts* in stories over the world – and *why* did the blessed Saviour teach in parables?' (Quoted in MacGregor 1844, 121). Gurney was not persuaded by Opie, for he asserted in his *Thoughts on Habit and Discipline* (1844), which he republished in subsequent editions before his death, that 'there is nothing more likely to unfit a young person for the duties and even the pleasures of the common life, than the habit of living, by means of the novel reading, in the highly painted scenes of an ideal world' (Gurney 1845,

87–88). Instead, he advised, 'The best and most harmless method of cultivating the imagination in children, is to bring them to an acquaintance with the most eminent and exceptional poets ... [John] Milton, [Edward] Young, [James] Montgomery, and above all [William] Cowper' (Gurney 1845, 203–4). Here, Gurney diverged significantly from earlier advices in encouraging children's creative thinking through literature at all, but he sanctioned only poetry. His privileging of verse is integrally linked to his theological stance, for all the poets he recommended are literary lions of British Evangelicalism. For Evangelicals, the 'notion of "apostolic community" was ... interpreted ... as fidelity to the teaching of the apostles as set out in scripture, rather than in historical or institutional terms, as fidelity to a specific ecclesial structure or community' (McGrath 2015, 320). The exemplary poetry of non-Quaker Pan-Evangelicals, as well as the scriptural precedent of Hebrew verse, authorised the reading and composition of poetry.

In fact, at this time, the most famous Quaker poet in history was rising as a literary and political figure. Conservative Friend John Greenleaf Whittier (1807–92) was not only one of the most published American poets of his era but 'arguably the most important Quaker writer of his time' (Jolliff 2007, 153). Today, his abolitionist poetry is taught regularly in American schools and his signature poem, *Snow-Bound* (1865), 'stands as the definitive statement of the popular American conception of rural life during the 1800s' (Jolliff 2007, 153). In Britain, 'Dear Lord and Father of Mankind' – a hymn excerpted from his 'The Brewing of Soma' (1872) – is a national favourite that is 'consistently among the top three in the BBC *Songs of Praise* polls' (Jones 2010, 8). As the work of a conservative Friend, this hymn is notable for its quietist message:

> Breathe through the hearts of our desire
> Thy coolness and Thy balm;
> Let sense be numb, let flesh retire;
> Speak through the earthquake, wind, and fire,
> O still, small voice of calm!'
>
> (Whittier 1873, 374)

Whittier's Quaker theology in the hymn can be elucidated by the larger poem, which is a protest against artificially stimulated religious enthusiasm. The titular 'Soma' refers to a hallucinogenic drug mentioned in the Vedic hymns (the ancient Scriptures of the Hindu prophet Vashishta), which Brahmin priests drink for ritual purposes. For Whittier, the artificial fervour stimulated by drugs and ceremonies – which he perceived as analogous with nineteenth-century churches' use of music and rituals – represents the worst of religion (Brown 2006, 231). By denouncing false religious enthusiasm,

Whittier, here, fulfils Bernard Barton's vision of the Quaker poet as regulator for truth and peace. Also like Barton, Whittier engaged in social activism through his poetry, and his abolitionist works are still renowned. He was not the only Friend to use poetry in the fight against slavery, however. As B. Lundy notes in her memoir of the poet, Quaker Elizabeth Margaret Chandler was 'the first American female author that ever made this subject the theme of her active exertions' (Chandler 1836, 12–13).

Although Whittier's poetry is not as critically celebrated today as in his own time, his religious verse has endured, as Jolliff attests, 'because of the spirituality it inflects, the faith revealed in his poems demonstrates an increasing complexity, yet it consistently addresses its audience in language convivial with Christian orthodoxy, a language that is simple but never simplistic, carefully crafted but never contrived' (Jolliff 2007, 186). Certainly his clarity and transparency seem to be the hard-earned results of the poet's exertion to articulate his ideas within the acceptable bounds of Quaker moral aesthetics. Although the subtlety of Whittier's verse forms have been undervalued as 'predictable' with 'little that is edgy, off-colour or challenging' (Webb 2013, 14), his formal regularity should also be understood as tied with his religion; as Blair has argued, 'when Victorian poetry speaks of faith, it tends to do so in steady and regular rhythms . . . This also holds true of other aspects of poetic form, such as the conventionality or otherwise of poetic language, verse form, and genre, all of which are more "regular" (and regulated) in the poetry of faith' (Blair 2012, 1). The celebrated example of Whittier's ethical verse set a powerful precedent among Friends of all traditions in overruling historical concerns about the frivolities and uselessness of verse.

In fact, by mid-century, neglect of the arts was identified as a significant factor in the decline of the number of Friends. In 1858, Joseph Stevenson Rowntree won a British essay contest on reasons for the Society's waning membership in which he asserted that 'to ignore the love of the beautiful in art or song, was not merely to throw away a weapon of remarkable potency in awakening religious sensibilities, but also to curtail the basis on which the Society rested, and to contract that narrow road which the Christian must tread on his heavenward journey' (Rowntree 1859, 48). In the decades that followed, all Quaker traditions in Britain and America underwent reforms; however, the speed of change and responses to different literary genres varied.

Fiction remained a problematic form for conservatives in the final decades of the nineteenth century. A tract entitled 'On Fiction Reading' (c.1881/2) published by the conservative Tract Association of Friends in Philadelphia echoed a contemporaneous addition to the conservative Philadelphia Friends' 1881 book of discipline that, 'In a day when pernicious publications and vain and corrupting amusements are multiplying, and presenting strong attractions to young and old, we believe the rightly disciplined and exercised parent, will feel the need of restraining the children from access to them' (*Old Discipline* 1999, 18). The Society's traditional fears about the immorality of fiction may have been exacerbated by *fin-de-siècle* anxiety about social degeneracy, as discussed in Max Nordau's *Degeneration* (1993/1892); certainly, the negative consequences of reading fiction discussed in the tract include insanity, suicide, divorces, theft, timewasting, restlessness and shortened attention spans.

One contemporaneous lecture, *An Address on Some Growing Evils of the Day, Especially Demoralizing Literature and Art, from the Representatives of the Religious Society of Friends for Pennsylvania, New Jersey, and Delaware* (1882) problematizes realist fiction especially – the subgenre associated with some of the most celebrated nineteenth-century novels, such as those by George Eliot and Elizabeth Gaskell. The argument is that 'novels which most attract cultivated and refined natures, where the fascination consists in graphic representation of human nature in its dealings with not unnatural, but unreal circumstances and characters', rouse readers' emotions and sympathies for ineffectual, ruinous ends: 'The sympathy which can have no outlet either in effort or prayer for the relief of actual suffering or thankfulness for actual happiness, tends to react and become morbid, or may grow as fictitious as the imagined occasions which have called it forth' (An Address 1882, 10). Thus, even seemingly moral novels were proscribed by conservative Quakers at the end of the nineteenth century.

At the turn of the century, British Friends were moving to a stance of liberal Quakerism and starting to consider creativity differently. In 1894, physician and social reformer Thomas Hodgkin – himself a poet – asserted that Friends had been 'too Puritan, almost Manichean, in our attitude towards Art' at the British Quaker 'Manchester Conference' of 1895 (cited in Greenwood 1978). A year later, Evelyn Noble Armitage extended Hodgkin's reassessment of the arts in her anthology dedicated to him, *Quaker Poets of Great Britain and Ireland* (1896), when she articulated a fully liberal theology that 'God reveals himself thro' every avenue of nature and life' (Armitage 1896, 5).

Armitage's collection is also significant for its sizeable representation of women writers. Twenty-six of the sixty-five poets are female, and all but one are nineteenth-century personages. The substantial contribution of women to this volume of religious verse accords with the wider authorship of nineteenth-century devotional poetry. This trend is partly attributable to

Tractarian John Keble's influential theory of poetry as 'the handmaid of Piety' and as 'a kind of medicine divinely bestowed upon man' (Keble 1912, 22, 484). His ideas, which rendered writing poetry comparable with the traditional female roles of nursing, tending and nurturing, authorised women's verse writing (see Francis 2004; Mason 2004). Indeed, many of the female-authored poems in Armitage's collections are conventional Victorian women's religious poetry – ostensibly devotional rather than expository and conforming with mainstream gender ideology. Elfrida Mary Crowley (1863–92)'s 'Transformation', for instance, offers intimate meditation rather than public proclamation utilising the language of love and feminine imagery:

> Dear love, an' thou wert here,
> Flowers would blossom and birds would sing,–
> Brown leaves, shrivelled and severe,
> At this fall o' the year
> Would don the tender green of the spring!
> Dear love, an' thou wert here.

(Armitage 1896, 71–72)

Such overtly feminine inscriptions are very different from the ecstatic discourses of early female Friends previously examined in Quaker studies (see Hobby 1995; Mack 1992; Gill 2005).

SOME TWENTIETH-CENTURY INNOVATIONS

In the twentieth century, women writers were instrumental as pioneers of Quaker fiction and in establishing the genre's distinct patterns. At mid-century, two contemporary Americans – birthright evangelical Jessamyn West and convinced liberal Elizabeth Gray Vining – were among the earliest successful Quaker writers of fiction. Significantly, both women produced novels in which Quaker history was envisaged as part of America's nation making. West's *The Friendly Persuasion* (1945), set in the nineteenth-century Midwest, contains heartwarming stories about the Quaker Birdwell family. The chapters revolve around characters' engagement with traditional Quaker practices and beliefs, such as the prohibition against music and use of historical language. The release of a Hollywood movie based on the novel starring Gary Cooper in 1956 and the printing of a new edition in 2003 suggest that the peculiar experience of Quaker pioneers resonates with American imaginings of the Old West. In Vining's *The Virginia Exiles* (1955), Quaker history provides the circumstances for the development of an imaginary young man into a noble American hero. Starting from the history of the banishment of eighteen Philadelphian Friends in 1777 to Winchester, Virginia, for the offense of being 'inimical to the cause of America' (Gilpin 1848, 71) in their neutrality and pacifism during the American Revolutionary War, Vining narrates the progress of the exiles. In the end, Caleb Middleton Jr decides to pursue his medical vocation by becoming an apprentice to an army surgeon so that he can 'harmonize with both my inclination and my conscience' (Vining 1955, 314). Although the formula of historical novels memorialising Friends' experiences and values set a pattern for Quaker fiction, such works have been problematised for their 'domesticating and often nostalgic Quakerism', which 'provides a zone of safety, a place of refuge from reality, a backward-looking and normalizing reassurance against fear and certainty' (Reynolds 2016, 83, 85). Instead of unrealistic and idealised depictions of Friends, Reynolds advocates the creation of a Quaker fiction that engages with real struggle, challenges and failures.

One contemporary Quaker writer who has engaged with Friends' failures is Chuck Fager. His murder mysteries and ghost stories are marked by his liberal reflections and satirical commentary on Quaker history and current sociopolitical issues. For instance, 'Old Plain Peter, The Ghost of Elders Past', the opening tale in *Fire in the Valley, Quaker Ghost Stories* (1992), tells of how the ghost of a legalist nineteenth-century Elder alters his religious views through an enriching encounter with a twentieth-century boy. After witnessing the ten-year-old playing sport, reading about dinosaurs, enjoying nature and listening to music, Old Plain Peter announces, 'I'm beginning to see that there may be more ways to be plain than I imagined' (Fager 1992, 32). Fager's liberal Quaker stance is, here, manifest by Old Peter's enlarged view of holiness. The second story 'Mount Pleasant and the Ghosts of Quaker Fighting' critiques the Hicksite separation of 1827–28. Devastatingly, Fager imagines the denunciation of non-Quaker neighbours, 'Just imagine, they said to each other, the Quakers keep telling us that God wants people to love each other, and that's why they won't fight in wars. But now here they are, about to have a battle among themselves' (Fager 1992, 38). In these works, the ghost story is not used to stimulate fear or suspense but to encourage ethical reflections. Significantly, as a liberal Friend, Fager not only probes individual consciences but also encourages critical rumination on Quaker practices and beliefs that have caused injury or restricted human freedoms.

Quakers also ventured into other fictional subgenres in the late twentieth century. Liberal Friend Joan Slonczweski's *A Door into Ocean* (1986) is a science fiction novel that displays the author's commitment to varied Quaker values including environmentalism, pacifism and gender egalitarianism. Questioned about the significance of her Quaker faith to her fiction, Slonczewski answered, 'I have been shaped by the Quaker example of listening and relating to that of God in everyone and every creature. In my books, wherever people resolve differences by intersecting seemingly irre-concilable views – that comes directly out of what I've seen among Quakers' (Schellenberg and Switzer 1998). As Higgins concludes in his detailed exam-ination of the novel, 'Aesthetically and narratively, *A Door into Ocean* is a "vied with" attempt at appropriating a religious ideology to demonstrate enacted ways in which embraced Quaker values have and can achieve satisfying closure, settled consensus, and non-violent social action' (Higgins 2016, 99). Thus, during the belligerent period of the Cold War, Slonczweksi used science fiction – a subgenre previously unused by Friends – for established Quaker ends, for ethical critique and to make Quaker witness.

THE MINISTRY OF THE ARTS

In recent decades, a new critical discussion has been emerging about the affinities between Quaker unprogrammed worship – in which the supplicant expectantly awaits God's revelation – and the experience of writing poetry (Johns 2013, 260–73). The most public exploration has been a BBC Radio 4 programme called 'Listen to Them Breathing' broadcast on 30 August 2011 presented by Sibyl Ruth, which examined the interconnections between writing poetry and Quaker worship. On the programme, Philip Gross theorised that 'What happens in Meeting is not in the first instance about creating words. It's about holding a space with each other and I find more and more that I am thinking of a poem as a thing made out of words and silence' (quoted in Ruth 2011). In 2013, he explored such ideas further with Laurence Lerner in a conversation that was published in *Quaker Studies*; in the same year, *Friends Quarterly* produced a special issue on the subject of 'Poetry and Quakerism' (*Friends Quarterly* 2013 (40, 3)). Repeatedly in these discussions, Quaker poets have reflected that 'At the heart of writing poetry is that same kind of listening [as at Meeting for Worship]' (Gross and Lerner 2012, 114).

Drama has similarly been re-evaluated in the liberal tradition. After a gradual process of accommodation, Friends actively embraced drama after 1960 (Graves 1996, 245). The 1925 London Yearly Meeting understood drama as an art 'by which performers and spectators alike may gain a truer insight into human life, a deeper appreciation of its meaning, and wider sympathy with mankind' (quoted in Graves 1996, 243). Moreover, as with poetry,

Quakers in recent decades have recognised affinities between the creative processes involved in drama and Quaker practice. In 'The Paradox of Quaker Theatre', Liberal Quaker actor Benjamin Lloyd discusses his endeavour 'to explore the divine/creative connection in a theatrical context' (Lloyd 2007, 219). Explaining that a Quaker worshipper's impulse to vocal ministry through '"a divine nudge" or "inner movement" is also present in moments of powerful acting' (Lloyd 2007, 220), Lloyd describes a project in which a mixed group of Quakers, seekers and agnostic actors, was invited to use theatrical performance as a spiritual exercise. Developed out of engagement with the avant-garde theories of Konstantin Stanislavsky about the 'inner, invisible, and spiritual' aspects of acting (1948, quoted in Lloyd 2007, 220) and Jerzy Grotowski about responding to contemporary theatre's loss of the 'sacred and ritual function' (quoted in Lloyd 2007, 221), Lloyd suggests in the twenty-first century that drama may be a medium for enabling engagement with the divine. Tamara Underiner has also explored what a Quaker theatrical practice might look like and suggested the 'intertwined history of performance' between the theatre and Quakerism might offer new insights for understanding 'much Quaker practice as both performance and performative [for instance, the enactment of corporeal prophetic signs and the attiring of plain clothes], its speech acts plain but powerful' (Underiner 2012, 111). Thus, drama, viewed for so long as irreverent, has also been reappraised by liberals as a literary mode that might, in fact, facilitate connections with the divine and enable greater understanding about Quaker modes of being.

FINAL REFLECTIONS

Although many Friends today hold revised views about the value of the creative arts, some remain highly suspicious about their spiritual dangers. For instance, at the time of this publication, Union Bible College – a Holiness Quaker institution in Westfield, Indiana, affiliated with Central Yearly Meeting – states in its catalog that students must refrain from 'degrading forms of art, music, drama, and literature' (ubca.org/academics/catalog/html). The college is strictly conservative (cinema attendance, dancing and the viewing of television are banned, and female students are not permitted to cut their hair for the duration of their enrolment); in this context, it seems probable that even a work infused with Quaker ideas such as Slonczweski's *A Door into Ocean* would be prohibited on campus for its depiction of invented alien worlds and lesbian relationships.

To readers unfamiliar with Quaker history, the epigraphs that started this chapter could have intimated a straightforward history of progress from prohibition to license in Friends' thinking about literature. As demonstrated, the situation in the twenty-first century is more complex. Most Quakers today hold a revised view about the value of literature compared to historical Friends, but the extent of their modified thinking will differ by tradition; there are still relatively few Quaker creative writers compared to those from other denominational traditions (such as Anglicanism or Roman Catholicism). The greatest acceptance and experimentation have been among Liberals, but their views are not representative of all Friends. Even among less strict Quakers than those at Union Bible College, a belief in the need for caution persists; for instance, the conservative Ohio Yearly Meeting's 2014 book of discipline advises members to 'encourage your children to appreciate the best in literature and the arts, which is consistent with our Christian faith. By this, all your lives may be enriched and the youth with tastes thus early formed may henceforth instinctively choose the beautiful and good' (www.ohioyearlymeeting.org/documents/discipline, 28–29) suggesting that go(o)d cannot be found indiscriminately in all verbal expressions. At the same time, read another way, this advice also acknowledges that literature can be sanctified. Here, as the 'Afterward, With Questions' to Hood's edited collection of essays *Quakers and Literature* (2016) profitably suggests, we find evidence that 'contemporary Friends valuably express some of the traits of . . . early Quaker literary-critical DNA, at least in so far as we evince a serious bent towards locating where disciplined spiritual growth and practical engagement for social change might come through encounters with imaginative literature' (Hood 2016, 166). Indeed, even Penn – famous for his prohibition against the arts – reflected elsewhere in *No Cross, No Crown*:

> *What a World should we have, if every Body for Fear of transgressing, should Mew himself up within four Walls!* No such Matter; the Perfection of Christian Life extends to every honest Labour or Traffick used among Men . . . True Godliness does not turn Men out of the World, but enables them to live better in it, and excites their Endeavours to mend it, *Not hide their Candle under a Bushel, but set it upon a Table, in a Candlestick.* (Penn 1682, 61)

This statement, strikingly similar in content to Graveson's twentieth-century view that every human endeavour might reveal God, is highly applicable to the history of Quakers and imaginative writing, for, throughout their literary history, Friends have sought to privilege writings that uphold personal integrity, social responsibility and justice. Unable to take creative writing for granted, Friends have always interrogated the intricate relationship between literature and religion. Until recently, their discussion has been primarily an internal debate. However, with the religious turn of literary studies in recent decades (in which scholars have gained rich insights investigating the role of religion in literary culture), Quakers' debates about the arts have a new audience. Indeed, as recent Quaker poets' and actors' publications about the correspondences between their creative praxis and unprogrammed worship attest, the twenty-first century may be an unparalleled moment in Quaker history when Friends – who so long suspicious of the arts – are testifying profound new insights about the ethical and spiritual dimensions of imaginative literature to the world.

SUGGESTED FURTHER READING

Gross, P. and Lerner, L. (2012) 'Talking in All, A Conversation on Poetry and Quakerism Between Philip Gross and Laurence Lerner', *Quaker Studies* 17:1, 110–30.

Hagglund, B. (2013) 'Quakers and Print Culture', in *The Oxford Handbook of Quaker Studies*, ed. by S. Angell and P. Dandelion, Oxford: Oxford University Press, pp. 477–91.

Hood, J. (ed.) (2016) *Quakers and Literature*, Longmeadow, MA: Friends Association for Higher Education.

Wright, L. (1932) *The Literary Life of the Early Friends, 1650–1725*, New York: Columbia University Press.

5

~

Social Justice and Sustainability

Katherine Murray

O Lord, if it is all the same to Thee, Give us a little more light and a little less noise. Abraham Lincoln (Bassuk 1987, 3)

Perhaps no greater area of consideration in a Quaker's life and practice today exists beyond concern for right action in response to social inequities and injustice. Long a voice for the voiceless and an advocate for the oppressed, Friends have a tradition of seeking to right perceived wrongs and bring light to situations – interpersonal, familial, and societal – that demonstrate imbalances in power and the overlooking or denial of the sacred center, "that of God," in everyone.

Among Friends, action on behalf of social justice arises not from outward pressure for societal change but from an inward leading, a pressure within, that calls Friends into "right relationship" with the issue needing more Light, whether that is racism, oppression, abuse of power, food inequity, the need for restorative justice, exploitation of the planet, or other pressing and worthy contemporary concerns.

The process of discerning right action among Friends can be varied and laborious, as Quakers individually and corporately seek to discern and find unity on the correct, reverential action they feel led to take in response to a particular concern of the day. The important step of "discernment," and the equally important step of taking action, along with all the deep listening and "threshing" that occurs along the way is a vital and time-proven part of Quaker process.

This chapter explores some of the roots of Quaker response and action to social needs and shines a light on major Friends organizations seeking to respond in right relationship to the concerning social issues calling for Light in the world today.

FROM THE SEED: REVERENCE AND RIGHT ORDER

From the earliest seeds of Quakerism, planted by George Fox in a social soil that was ripe for change, Friends have felt compelled to change the world in which they live by seeking to be true to principles of fairness, equality, and right order they found within, taught by "Christ the Inward Teacher." Deep in the energy of George Fox's transformative encounter with the Christ Within outside of Coventry in 1647 was the belief that Christ teaches every heart and that the inward leadings of the individual Christ-like action and transformation of the outer world follow from this encounter.

This vital call is thus part and parcel of a Divine-human relationship that invites, if not demands, soulful response. Simply receiving a teaching is not enough when there is a need for Light in the world. Friends have a perhaps unique call-to-action in the belief that the leading of spirit calls for personal response, unfettered by liturgical expectations, creeds, or church hierarchy. In hearing George Fox preach in 1652, Margaret Fell said,

> And then he went on, and opened the Scriptures, and said, "the Scriptures were the prophets' words, and Christ's and the apostles' words, and what, as they spoke, they enjoyed and possessed, and had it from the Lord": and said, "then what had any to do with the Scriptures, but as they came to the Spirit that gave them forth? You will say, *Christ saith this, and the apostles say this; but what canst thou say?* Art thou a child of Light, and has thou walked in the Light, and what thou speakest, is it inwardly from God?" (Garman et al. 1996, 235)

By listening for the Inward Teacher and then acting as so led in response to this deep leading, Friends pushed against the social order by refusing to remove hats and recognize social strata, by using "plain language" with all people, by standing against the politicized and power-oppressing movement of Presbyterianism in their time (Jones 2009, 7–8). In the preamble to Robert Barclay's *Apology*, he shared the Friends' reasoning behind resistant to doffing one's hat: "Taking one's hat off to another person, bowing or cringing, and other similar foolish and superstitious formalities which accompany them, should be forsaken. All of these were invented to feed man's pride through the vain pomp and glory of this world" (Cooper 1990, 100). Although this might seem a small change on the interpersonal level, Friends' refusal to participate in this common social custom was a painful thorn in the paw of a powerful and aggressive oligarchy. As such, it planted the seeds of a social reform movement, causing those caught in it to question their resistance or support as part of the response and allegiances of their own souls.

As a result of such small but spirit-led actions, Friends were persecuted, spent years in prison, often losing much – even their lives – for their dedication to the principle of right action that led them to seek, hear, and act on Truth.

EXAMPLES OF SOCIAL JUSTICE AMONG FRIENDS

In the late 1700s, Friends were drawn toward organized social impact when Quaker Hannah Mills was committed to York Asylum in York, England. Her family requested that Quakers in York visit Hannah, but they were turned away and she died shortly thereafter. As a result, Friends founded their own asylum, feeling that "a familiar, Quaker environment would be conducive to a cure" ("The York Retreat" 2016). Not long after, a group of Philadelphia Friends, led toward action by the belief that there is that of God in every person, raised their concern for the treatment and care of the mentally ill and founded the Friends' Asylum for the Relief of Persons Deprived of the Use of their Reason. At the asylum, their approach of "moral treatment" sought to restore the dignity and sense of worth to individuals compromised by mental illness. This response to mental illness was the crest of a wave that would lead to widespread reform in the ethical treatment of the mentally ill.

Another well-known example of the movement of inward truth to outward action occurred in the life of thirty-three-year-old John Woolman, a Quaker and clerk who wrote out the will and testament of customers who came to him for assistance. Woolman had been feeling a growing inward sense of concern about the issue of slavery in his region, and when a customer for whom he was writing a will wanted to give a Negro slave as property to someone else, Woolman was unable to proceed. Here was the reckoning, the meeting of the inner sense with the outer action, and Woolman discovered that as difficult as it was, following the inward leading was the right thing to do:

> About this time, a person at some distance lying sick, his brother came to me to write his will. I knew he had slaves; and asking his brother, was told he intended to leave them as slaves to his children. As writing is a profitable employ, and as offending sober people was disagreeable to my inclination, I was straitened in my mind; but as I looked to the Lord, he inclined my heart to his testimony. I told the man, that I believed the practice of continuing slavery to this people was not right, and had a scruple in my mind against doing writings of that kind: that though many in our Society kept them as slaves, still I was not easy to be concerned in it; and desired to be excused from going to write the will. I spake to him in the fear of the Lord; and he

made no reply to what I said, but went away: he also had some concern in the practice; and I thought he was displeased with me. In this case I had a fresh confirmation, that acting contrary to present outward interest, from a motive of Divine love, and in regard to truth and righteousness, and thereby incurring the resentments of people, opens the way to a treasure better than silver, and to a friendship exceeding the friendship of men. (Woolman 1883, 46)

As the seed of equality for all took root, Quakers in the United States acted from an intention to support, edify, and speak truth to President Abraham Lincoln as he struggled with the overwhelming issue of emancipation of slaves and the burden of leading the country through Civil War. In Daniel Bassuk's Pendle Hill Pamphlet, *Abraham Lincoln and the Quakers* (1987), he shared the many efforts and actions of spirit-led Friends to support if not sway the president as he sought to discern the way to Truth in the catastrophic conflict. Lincoln was said to have Quaker predecessors and was well versed in the manner of Friends and as noted in the epigraph at the outset of this chapter, he felt a helpmate in the movement toward discernment was "a little more light and a little less noise." In response to a letter from the Quakers of Rhode Island, Lincoln wrote in 1692:

Engaged, as I am, in a great war, I fear it will be difficult for the world to understand how fully I appreciate the principles of peace, inculcated in this letter, and everywhere, by the Society of Friends. Grateful to the good people you represent for their prayers in behalf of our common country, I look forward hopefully to an early end of war, and return of peace. Your obliged friend, A. Lincoln. (Bassuk 1987, 9)

As D. Elton Trueblood says in *The People Called Quakers*, the secret of Quakerism, if there is one, lies in the close and constant marriage between religious experience and social concern" (Trueblood 1966, 256). He continues to offer a rationale for the continuing growth and deepening of Quaker social action:

It is not surprising, in view of the determination to hold the spiritual and the social in one context, that the concept of mission has been both deepened and enlarged during the last century of Quaker experience. Over and over we have said that mission is not something added to the nature of a Christian society but is intrinsic to it. The Church of Christ, when it understands itself and its relationship to its Lord, does not *have* a mission; it *is* mission. (Trueblood 1966, 256–57)

Elizabeth Fry, a Quaker born toward the end of the eighteenth century in the United Kingdom, opened the way for English prison reform at a time when few women were advocating for social reforms in the public sphere. Fry was inspired toward advocacy after she heard a message by Quaker William Savery and felt a concern for the poor, the imprisoned, and the sick. She began doing what she could – collecting food and clothing for those without, visiting the infirm in her town, and teaching poor children to read.

At the prompting of a friend, Fry visited a nearby women's prison and was horrified by the conditions she found there. Her book, *Prisons in Scotland and the North of England* (1819), shared stories of the imprisoned and called for a change in conditions (Gurney and Fry 1819). She invited nobility to come and visit the prisons to see the conditions for themselves. Overtime she made impacts on daily provisions, education, childcare, and more. She also worked to help the homeless and established a nightly shelter in downtown London. At one point, Fry established a training school for nurses that served as an inspiration for Florence Nightingale, and nurses from Fry's school accompanied Nightingale when she served soldiers in the Crimean War.

CONTEMPORARY SOCIAL JUSTICE CONCERNS

The actions of Friends on behalf of the social concerns of the world expanded in the late nineteenth century. Quakers moved to respond to the great relief needs brought about by periods of war. Trueblood tells the story of Quaker relief work organized in October 1870 to bind up the sufferings of those affected by the Franco-Prussian War, resulting in the Friends War Victims Fund (Trueblood 1966, 257). This effort provided the pattern for the organization of the Friends War Victims Relief Committee in 1914, just after the start of World War I. Quakers in Britain started the Friends Ambulance Unit to provide assistance to those injured in the war, provided by Friends who were not themselves led to fight. These early organizing efforts led directly to many of the active Friends organizations working on behalf of social justice needs today.

American Friends Service Committee (AFSC)

The American Friends Service Committee (AFSC) has been working for peace since 1917, providing relief, support, and peace building through a variety of nonviolent efforts. Early on, in World War I, those who conscientiously objected to war but wanted to serve nonetheless staffed AFSC. Workers drove ambulances, cared for the wounded, delivered food to children in Germany, and more. After the war was over, AFSC continued by assisting distressed Appalachian mining communities whose members serve in World War II; aiding civilians on both sides of the Vietnam War; establishing economic programs in Asia, Africa, and Latin America; providing support to the US civil rights movement and desegregation; working with oppressed communities including Native Americans, immigrants, prisoners, low-income families, and more.

For their efforts in World War II, the AFSC was jointly awarded (along with the British Friends Service Council or what is now called Quaker Peace and Social Witness) the Nobel Peace Prize in 1947. In the award presentation, Gunnar Jahn, chair of the Nobel Committee, said:

> The Quakers have shown us that it is possible to carry into action something which is deeply rooted in the minds of many: sympathy with others; the desire to help others … without regard to nationality or race; feelings which, when carried into deeds, must provide the foundations of a lasting peace. For this reason, they are today worthy of receiving Nobel's Peace Prize. (AFSC and the Nobel Peace Prize n.d.)

The mission of AFSC is "a Quaker organization devoted to service, development, and peace programs throughout the world. Our work is based on the belief in the worth of every person, and faith in the power of love to overcome violence and injustice" (AFSC and the Nobel Peace Prize n.d.). Consistently working in conflict zones throughout the world, AFSC has served to support those in the wake of natural disasters, humanitarian crises, and oppressive conditions.

Through the years, some Friends have taken issue with the work of AFSC, feeling that the group had left its Quaker roots in favor of a more active engagement in social issues (see Chapter 3, this volume, by Burdick and Dandelion). In recent years, AFSC has worked to reaffirm its Quaker connections and dedication to Quaker testimonies, and it has been working to repair and represent Friends more intentionally and directly in their continuing social justice work.

AFSC has a vibrant social media network and an effective voice for the faces of social injustice the world over. Its website (www.afsc.org) includes a set of compelling blogs on a variety of pressing social justice issues, including building peace, immigrant rights, addressing prisons, just economies, and ending discrimination. For example, the Acting in Faith blog (www.afsc.org/blogs/acting-in-faith) explores how Friends' faith and testimonies interact with needs for justice in the contemporary world.

Friends Committee on National Legislation (FCNL)

The Friends Committee on National Legislation (FCNL) was founded in 1943 by Friends as a lobbying organization that would advocate for peace, social and economic justice, sound stewardship of the environment, and ethical and humane governmental practices. Quaker testimonies of peace, simplicity, equality, and integrity are central to the issues that FCNL undertakes.

The organization grew out of a Friends committee known as the Friends War Problems Committee, which sought to lobby against universal conscription into armed services. Today's FCNL bases its advocacy on the policy statement "The World We Seek" (http://fcnl.org/about/govern/policy). The four primary visions offered in the policy statement follow:

> We seek a world free of war and the threat of war.
> We seek a society with equity and justice for all.
> We seek a community where every person's potential may be fulfilled.
> We seek an earth restored.

Key issues targeted by FCNL efforts include advancing peace building, reducing military spending, promoting nuclear disarmament, supporting solutions to climate disruption, increasing integrity in political fundraising, addressing poverty and income inequality, reducing mass incarceration, promoting advocacy for Native American issues, and promoting fair and humane immigration policies.

FCNL has an extensive network that continues to expand. Many Monthly and Yearly Meetings have FCNL committees that meet regularly and participate in efforts in Washington, DC, and elsewhere. FCNL has a Visiting Friends practice that sends Quakers to interested meetings to talk more about current work and faithful action. FCNL contacts are Friends within Monthly Meetings who keep their local meetings informed about the work and needs of FCNL.

Quaker United Nations Office (QUNO)

The Quaker United Nations Office (QUNO) offers a Quaker presence at the United Nations, having consultative status, which means they can facilitate dialogue, raise issues, and express concerns but have no legislative power. QUNO has offices in Quaker Houses in New York and Geneva, Switzerland; quiet, supportive conversation goes on among UN diplomats, staff, and other non-governmental partners in these places, helping to foster relationships and explore perspectives out of the public eye.

QUNO believes the strength of its work lies "in our long-term persistence" (QUNO n.d.). Issues central to QUNOs mission of "working for a more peaceful and just world" include peace building and prevention of violent conflict, human impacts of climate change, human rights and refugees, peace and disarmament, and food and sustainability.

QUNO works often in an informal, off-the-record role, facilitating thoughtful ongoing discussion of issues affecting civil societies throughout the world. In this way, QUNO furthers the cause of peace building and diplomacy, creating a safe and reverent space for leaders to engage in meaningful exchanges and come to a better understanding of global and societal issues. In one current example, QUNO is facilitating dialogue among the leaders of Myanmar and UN staff and diplomats to assist in building lasting peace and establishing violence prevention efforts. QUNO's approach is to include all voices and welcome the cultural expertise of those in the region. This respectful approach leads toward thoughtful reconciliation and leadership where the gifts and views of all are a valued part of the continuing discussion.

ECO-JUSTICE AND DEEP CARE OF ALL LIFE

Before the turn of the twenty-first century, Quakers were concerned about the issue of climate change and advocating at the local meeting level for spirit-led change in Friends' relationships with nature. In the years since, concern has grown, leading Quaker meetings and organizations to a unified sense that climate change is real, the earth is showing signs of distress, and species are suffering great and sometimes sweeping losses, with some edging closer to extinction each day.

Friends are now aware that not only is reverent and immediate care needed for the planet but that environmental issues are not be separate from Quaker testimonies of peace, justice, and equality. The case can be made that the industrialized nations of the world are the biggest and most extensive contributors to CO_2 emissions, and the actions of those countries seriously threaten smaller and more vulnerable nations. Earth care is no longer a problem that is "out there" in the future somewhere. It is here, now, asking for Friends to listen for and discern their leadings and act accordingly.

In 2016, Native Americans from a number of tribes and people of all ethnicities – as well as professional organizers, including a group from Black Lives Matter in Minnesota – gathered at Standing Rock, a Sioux reservation in North Dakota, in peaceful protest at the site, trying to block construction of the Dakota Access pipeline that cuts through native lands. The tribes gathered called for a spiritual deepening and an understanding of the relationship with the land; the protest spotlighted violations of early treaties that have spanned decades. Quakers participated in the protest at many levels, including nonviolent protest training, daily support, prayerful consideration, and leading efforts in local meetings to raise awareness of the issue and contact elected officials with minutes of concern.

Friends have a long history of advocating for justice on Native American issues. In 1868, Friends of the Yearly Meeting for the Friends of Iowa convened a Committee on Indian Concerns, which was joined by several other Yearly Meetings, and drafted a letter of request asking Congress to allow their members to be part of the forming of relationships among agents and tribes.

This kinship of spirit and advocacy appears in an experience John Woolman related in his *Journal*, in which the spiritual commune of all gathered in love made it unnecessary for interpreters to translate his words into tribal language:

> On the evening of the 18th I was at their meeting, where pure gospel love was felt, to the tendering of some of our hearts. The interpreters endeavored to acquaint the people with what I said, in short sentences, but found some difficulty, as none of them were quite perfect in the English and Delaware tongues, so they helped one another, and we labored along, Divine love attending.
>
> Afterwards, feeling my mind covered with the spirit of prayer, I told the interpreters that I found it in my heart to pray to God, and believed, if I prayed aright, he would hear me; and I expressed my willingness for them to omit interpreting; so our meeting ended with a degree of Divine love. Before the people went out, I observed Papunehang . . . speaking to one of the interpreters, and I was afterwards told that he said in substance as follows: "I love to feel where words come from." (Woolman 1883, 146–47)

Seeking the clarity of right order and standing with those who suffer oppression and injustice are common leadings among individual Friends and Friends organizations. Individual meetings feel led to address issues in unique and compelling ways that may lead them toward peaceful protesting, committee action, intercessory prayer, divestment of resources, and more.

Several Quaker organizations have helped Friends organize their efforts and respond to their concerns. This section offers an overview of Earth Quaker Action Team, Quaker Earthcare Witness, and the FCNL focus on climate change.

Earth Quaker Action Team (EQAT)

Stirred by a concern for the protection of their local environment and as a call to eco-justice to PNC Bank (which is a historically Quaker bank), Friends at Philadelphia Yearly Meeting organized in 2009 an organization known as Earth Quaker Action Team, or EQAT. The group follows Friends practices and uses nonviolent direct action methods to protest and challenge actions and involvements that are harmful to both the environment and their fellow citizens. They intentionally confront "the people who benefit from the current energy system" (EQAT). Using the method of nonviolent direct action enables protestors to challenge existing power structures and shine a light on injustice, while remaining in alignment with Friends testimonies of peace and justice.

In 2010, EQAT launched its first direct action campaign, designed to pressure PNC Bank into withdrawing its financial support from companies that were performing mountaintop removal coal mining. After five years of direct action practices – during which time more than 500 mountains were destroyed and countless lives affected – PNC agreed to change its investment policy.

As part of the direct action, EQAT Friends stage sit-ins, stand-ins, marches, worship in public places, and even at times go to jail. The mission of EQAT is "Earth Quaker Action Team is a grassroots, nonviolent action group including Quakers and people of diverse beliefs, who join with millions of people around the world fighting for a just and sustainable economy."

In 2015, EQAT launched its second campaign – Power Local Green Jobs – asking utility companies to step up and create green jobs to benefit poorer communities and communities of color by committing to use locally generated solar power for electricity.

Quaker Earthcare Witness (QEW)

Quaker Earthcare Witness, formerly known as Friends Committee for Unity with Nature, started after a small group of Friends gathered for six days at the Friends General Conference Gathering at Oberlin College in Ohio, considering questions of how best to live in harmony with nature. What emerged from that rich time was a sense that there was a need for Friends to provide a witness to the sacredness of creation and to demonstrate right relationship with the earth.

The Quaker Earthcare Vision and Witness statement says,

The purpose of Quaker Earthcare Witness is to search and to help others to search for that life which affirms the unity of all creation. To apply and to help others apply Friends' practice to live in deep communion with all life spirit. To be guided by and to help others to be guided by the Light within us to participate in the healing of the earth. To provide resources, networking, and support to yearly and monthly meetings of the Religious Society of Friends, and to others of whatever persuasion; to help them in their search for effective ways to reach the above objectives. To provide a reflective and energetic forum that will strengthen and deepen that spiritual unity with nature which values the integrity, diversity, and continuity of life on earth. (QEW, Quaker Earthcare Vision and Witness, 2016)

QEW members believe that right relationship with the planet is a vital part of working toward peace and justice for all, and increasingly QEW has gotten involved in social efforts to educate, inform, inspire, and advocate for right action on a variety of social issues connected to an ecologically sustainable worldview. Key concerns in QEW's approach include the following:

- The innate interrelatedness of all life, the overbalance of population, and concerns about unchecked CO_2 from developed countries
- The profound and rich complexity of the web of life that is being damaged by climate change
- The disproportionate effect of the actions of human beings, especially those caused by overconsumption, materialism, greed, and exploitation
- The unpredictability of the effect of our actions on the environment and the impact that could displace or damage vulnerable populations
- The need for caution and modesty of action ("walking gently") and a change from a human-centric view of life to a systemic, sustainable model. (QEW, Quaker Earthcare Vision and Witness, 2016)

Quaker Earthcare Witness publishes a bimonthly journal called *BeFriending Creation* (www.quakerearthcare.org/befriending-creation), focusing on stories of earth care advocacy, inspiring leadings and statements from Quaker meetings, opportunities for involvement, and more. QEW has an active website where articles and events are posted, as well as a business site (open for all Friends to join) where ongoing discussions occur on various environmental topics. Quaker Earthcare Witness awards mini-grants to Quaker meetings and organizations interested in doing earth-friendly projects at the Monthly or Yearly Meeting or community level. QEW mini-grants have been given internationally, assisting meetings in designing and creating rain capture projects, organic gardens, sustainable orchards, urban gardens; installing low-flow toilets;

and a tree planting project (in Bolivia), an energy efficiency project, food preservation, and more.

Friends Committee on National Legislation: Climate Change

In recent years, the actions of FCNL toward increasing awareness of the needs of the planet (especially as they relate to lobbying the US Congress) have become a larger focus of the organization. FCNL urges Congress to embrace a "new moral, bipartisan and cooperative spirit" in matters with an environmental impact. FCNL is often at the forefront of Quaker legislative efforts and brings together diverse groups and views to find a common ground.

For example, in April 2016, FCNL brought together 121 religious organizations and traditions – which represented tens of millions of Americans – and delivered a letter to Congress asking the body to allocate $750 million in 2017 to the Green Climate Fund (GCF), which dedicates half of its holdings to help nations vulnerable to climate change to make the adaptations they need to survive (http://fcnl.org/issues/energy/121_religious_communities_urge_congress_to_support_the_green_fund/).

Friends World Committee for Consultation

The Friends World Committee for Consultation (http://fwcc.world/) was started in 1937 by the Second World Conference of Friends to serve to increase the understanding of Quakers throughout the world. In 1948, the FWCC was given "consultative" status with the United Nations and has continues to work with the Quaker United Nations Office and maintain offices in Geneva and New York.

The primary office for FWCC is in London, England, and the mission of the organization continues to be to nurture fellowship among all Friends everywhere in the world. Today Quakers from seventy-five nations are part of FWCC, and the organization has four sections: Africa, the Americas, Asia and the West Pacific, and Europe and the Middle East.

Because climate change is clearly a global concern, FWCC has been a leading voice among Friends to address the deepening needs of our planet and the concern for all life. At the FWCC World Conference in April 2012, those gathered at Kabarak University near Nakuru, Kenya, approved the Kabarak Call for Peace and Ecojustice and circulated it among Yearly Meetings worldwide. The compelling statement called for Friends to realign their concern for the earth with the clear stream of their faith:

We are called to see what love can do: to love our neighbor as ourselves, to aid the widow and orphan, to comfort the afflicted and afflict the comfortable, to appeal to consciences and bind the wounds.

We are called to teach our children right relationship, to live in harmony with each other and all living beings in the earth, waters and sky of our Creator, who asks, "Where were you when I laid the foundations of the world?" (Job 38:4)

We are called to do justice to all and walk humbly with our God, to cooperate lovingly with all who share our hopes for the future of the earth.

We are called to be patterns and examples in a 21st century campaign for peace and ecojustice, as difficult and decisive as the 18th and 19th century drive to abolish slavery. (FWCC 2012)

At the FWCC World Conference in Pisac, Peru, in 2016, a minute building on the Kabarak Call was proposed, seasoned, and approved. The resulting document, *Living Sustainably and Sustaining Life on Earth*, was shared with Quakers worldwide (http://fwcc.world/fwcc-news/living-sustainably-and-sustaining-life-on-earth-the-minute-from-the-plenary). The statement includes a call to action for individuals and meetings and asks Yearly Meetings to do the following:

Initiate at least two concrete actions on sustainability within the next 12 months. These may build on existing projects of individuals or monthly meetings or they may be new initiatives. We ask that they encourage Young Friends to play key roles. We ask that meetings minute the progress and results, so as to share them with FWCC and Quaker meetings.

Support individuals and groups in their meetings who feel called to take action on sustainability.

Support the work done by Quaker organisations such as the Quaker United Nations Office and the Quaker Council for European Affairs to ensure that international agreements and their implementation support sustainability. (FWCC, Living Sustainably and Sustaining Life on Earth – The Minute from the Plenary, 2016)

Monthly and Yearly Meeting Actions

Although Friends participate at a national level with the organizations mentioned earlier, a considerable amount of action is being taken on the part of local Monthly and Yearly Meetings around the world. The Monthly Meeting is a fertile seedbed for new leadings about a shared concern for the environment; many meetings then organize committees or subcommittees, under the care of Ministry and Council for Peace and Social Justice, to discern leadings and propose actions toward better stewardship of their land and resources. In 2011, Britain Yearly Meeting committed itself to becoming a low-carbon community.

Friends' meetings have been led to start community gardens, do away with paper products, establish rain capture gardens, reduce ineffective electrical lighting, add solar panels, and more. At the Yearly Meeting level, Quakers have been educating Monthly Meetings about our responsibility for steward-ship, offering training for energy efficient practices, and in some cases supporting energy audits and matching funds for building renovations.

At this local level, Friends who share a leading can explore what they feel called to address in their own specific landscape, addressing a unique envir-onmental need. Although this may seem a different form of advocacy than an organized effort waged at a higher framework, it is at this day-to-day responsive level that Friends can feel most in congruence with the spiritual calling to respond to the stirring of their concern.

TOWARD A LIVED SUSTAINABILITY

Although the modern world seems to present today's Friends with a complex and ever-tightening web of social and environmental issues, the center of Quaker process still holds. Hundreds of years of the faith and practices of Friends offer a reliable witness to a path of discernment that leads to inward light, no matter what the outer circumstances might be.

In his book, *A Sustainable Life: Quaker Faith and Practice in the Renewal of Creation*, Douglas Gwyn encourages Friends to return to the stillness of their roots, to settle and be nourished by the deepest movement of spirit (2014b). Gwyn offers that sustainability means living from a place of peace and light at the deepest level, radiating outward the concentric rings of Friends' influence in the world. This approach, says Gwyn, moves Friends toward wholeness for the world on all levels, not simply into specialized factions of Quakers siloed in different issues. Sustainable living is healing for all. Gywn states, "The horizon of destiny revealed in the last half-century is the urgent need for the human race to find a sustainable balance with the resources and life systems of the earth. But that destiny will not be reached without a just, equitable, and peaceful society among humans" (Gwyn 2014b, 24–25).

Gwyn uses the image of a wheel with sixteen spokes to illustrate sixteen energies present in Friends' practice that can move humanity toward sus-tainability. The sixteen energies occur along eight axes, composed of pairs of qualities: *light* and *seed*, *worship* and *ministry*, *personal integrity* and *discernment, peace* and *nonviolent action,* and *simplicity* and *sustainability.* Gwyn calls Friends back to familiar Quaker process and invites them to listen once again to Friends' voices that have shaped the tradition and given evidence to the presence of the Light.

In *Renewable: One Woman's Search for Simplicity, Faithfulness, and Hope,* Eileen Flanagan (2015) begins her work with the moment she handcuffed herself to the White House fence in her first committed act of civil disobedience, before discussing the volunteerism and social concern that cooled as Flanagan settled into a life in suburbia with her husband, two children, and large home. Flanagan discusses her struggle as she worked to reconcile her image of herself as a middle-aged, suburban mother with the image of the engaged, socially concerned Peace Corps volunteer in Botswana many years prior. The seeds of sustainability began to grow as Flanagan considered how simplicity and sustainability could be goals in her life in US culture as well:

> Even so, we did have choices. The size of our house was within our control, obviously, as well as the temperature we set our thermostat, though we had no individual control over the process that produced the gas that heated our home. Similarly, we chose what kind of food to eat and where to buy it, but our options were shaped by farm policies that favored big agribusiness, which used a lot of fuel to produce and transport food. Given this tension, I wondered, how guilty should I feel about my carbon footprint, which was much lower than the U.S. average, but much higher than the global average? (Flanagan 2015, 107)

The story is an inspiring one of the inner and outer workings of spirit in an individual Friend's life, stirring concerns, opening ways, allowing for further discernment and action aligned with the compass of principle. The path toward sustainability – singularly and communally – is not without darkness, anxiety, and temptation to despair, but Friends are invited, or perhaps compelled, to turn toward the Light again and again, seeking the wisdom and promise of the Inward Teacher.

Ruah Swennerfelt, a Friend in the northeastern United States and a proponent of the Transition movement, has written *Rising to the Challenge: The Transition Movement and People of Faith.* In her book, Swennerfelt shares the origin of the Transition movement, tells of how she got involved, explores how the Transition movement fits into a faithful world view, and offers a collection of stories about Transition communities that are thriving in very different parts of the world. Swennerfelt's own path toward sustainability includes considerable peace and justice activism, which led to several jail terms resulting from her protest of the US government policy of sending arms to El

Salvador. Her path led her to a world conference of Friends in Honduras, where she picked up a QEW publication with a compelling quote: "There's no peace without a planet." Swennerfelt writes,

> That simple statement changed my life. I began to see how all social and ecological issues are interconnected, and that to continue to work for peace I also needed to work for a healthy planet ... The other part of my experience of continuing revelation was personal – examining my own ecological footprint and making significant efforts to reduce it. (Swennerfelt 2016, 1)

Swennerfelt served as the general secretary of Quaker Earthcare Witness for a number of years, as she worked to minimize her dependence on natural resources and worked to live a more sustainable life. These inward concerns led her to learn more about permaculture ideals, which led to involvement in earth activism efforts and then to the Transition movement:

> As a Quaker, I have to ask whether I can possibly live out the Quaker Testimonies of simplicity, peace, integrity, community, equality, and sustainability without acting in the world where there is a need. I bring my Quaker faith into my work with Transition, without always naming it. I was especially drawn by the movement's emphasis on Inner Transition. Real change springs from the heart, though I recognize that the effort to change the laws and regulations is also important. (Swennerfelt 2016, 5)

In terms of what the Transition movement can offer Friends, Swennerfelt says,

> The global Transition movement represents one of the most promising ways of engaging people and local communities to take the far-reaching actions that are required to mitigate the effects of peak oil, climate change and the economic crisis. Furthermore, these relocation efforts are designed to result in a life that is more fulfilling, more socially connected, and more equitable than the one we have today. Indeed, the Transition movement offers us the opportunity to foster communities that are much more closely allied with Friends' historic testimonies on simplicity, peace, integrity, community, and equality. (Swennerfelt 2016)

FRIENDS' RESPONSE TO RISING CONCERNS

In light of Friends' tradition, the movement of Spirit, and the needs of the world around them – as individuals, families, meetings, and more – how will Friends continue to respond to the call for action amid the ills and hurts of contemporary society? In his book *On Listening to Another*, Quaker Douglas Steere evoked Kierkegaard's metaphor in the book *Purity of Heart* as one suggestion:

> The natural way to listen to such a (devotional) message, Kierkegaard suggests, is to consider oneself as seated in the audience and the one giving them message as an actor on the stage. The listener is therefore quite free as a member of the audience to criticize both the content of the message and the art, or the lack of it, in the one who delivers the message. But Kierkegaard insists that this is not the right way to listen. And until it is reversed, the exercise of listening is likely to have little result, no matter how habitually it is practiced. To listen correctly, we must radically shift the poles. Now it is not the deliverer of the message who is performing before me, but I myself am on the stage speaking the part. Now there is only a single listener in the audience. That listener is God. But where in this altered scene has the deliverer of the message been placed? In the wings, where he belongs. He has no more than the role of the prompter on the old Danish stage who stood in the wings and spoke over the actor's lines in a low voice so that if the actor missed them at any point, he could recover them with this assistance.
>
> There is no deeper spiritual insight in Kierkegaard's writings than this vision of a man placed squarely before God, the Listener, and he continually returns to it in his works. Finally we shall be alone with God and there will be no hurry. Finally there will be no crowd to hide in, no favourable comparisons with others to draw about us like a protective coat, no more self-deception. (Steere 1943, 199–200)

Being true to Friends' inward leadings – in all matters but perhaps particularly in concerns of social conscience – requires a continuing openness to self-honesty, vulnerability, and revelation. Friends are called to diverse needs in diverse ways; one Friend may be a contemplative, led to pray and hold efforts in the Light; another may be led toward peaceable action of a more public sort. In unity of Spirit, Friends can understand the uniquely tender and sacred call to be the speaker on the stage, responding to the stirring of Spirit within each heart. In so doing, there lies the hope that individually, corporately, and for the alleviation of suffering throughout the world, Friends enact their soul's response to Fox's question, "What canst thou say?"

SUGGESTED FURTHER READING

Flanagan, E. (2015). *Renewable: One Woman's Search for Simplicity, Faithfulness, and Hope*, Berkeley, CA: She Writes Press.

Gwyn, D. (2014b). *A Sustainable Life: Quaker Faith and Practice in the Renewal of Creation*, Philadelphia, PA: FGC Quakerpress.

Swennerfelt, R. (2016). *Rising to the Challenge: The Transition Movement and People of Faith*, Albany, CA: QIF Focus Books.

Trueblood, D. E. (1966). *The People Called Quakers*, New York: Harper & Row.

Woolman, J. (1883/1774). *A Journal of John Woolman*, Philadelphia: Friends Books.

6

ॐ

Seeking Peace: Quakers Respond to War

Elaine Bishop and Jiseok Jung

The Quaker peace 'testimony' (QPT) is regarded by many as one of the central, historic and uniting features of Quakerism. Yet for much of its history, this testimony was not a testimony *for peace* but a testimony *against war*.

After exploring the concept of 'testimony', this chapter surveys the history of QPT. It reflects on our scholarship charting five twentieth-century shifts that have changed the testimony significantly. The chapter explores challenges of defining peace, reflecting on the need for some definition to facilitate effective witnessing to the testimony. It uses an original model, developed by Bishop, on how modern QPT is of two sorts, 'war abolishing' and 'conflict-transforming'. Finally it describes some current expressions of QPT, including examples from the authors' countries, Canada and Korea, illustrating the analysis and shifts described, and closes with some challenges as Friends maintain their witness for peace into the future.

TESTIMONY IN FRIENDS' TRADITIONS

Testimony has been an important concept throughout Quaker history. George Fox used the term to describe the witness of early Friends who opened shops contrary to national practice on holy and fast days. The term was used in the 1661 statement on QPT to the king. That statement, described as 'our testimony to the whole world' (Fox 1952, 399), articulated Friends' refusal to fight or participate in violent civil strife.

The word 'testimony' means *witness*. Testimony is a consistent body of words about faith in action, not only what Quakers say, but what they do and how they live individually and corporately (Cave and Morley 2000, 26–27). Testimony 'is about the Life that we allow to come through us' (Dandelion 2014, 22).

Testimony is a way of putting belief into action, which accumulates into a corporate expression of shared faith. Testimony takes place in a historical context. In British Quakerism, the meaning of testimony was so well known that it was not defined in the Discipline until 1995. Prior to that, the entire Discipline could be described as being about testimony with a variety of behaviours being described as 'testimonies'.

The testimonies, articulations of Quaker faith applied to specific spheres of life, offer ways of living testimony. Historically, some articulated ways to live beliefs about equality and simplicity, including plainness in dress and speech. Others called for behaviour that contradicted social practices of the time including refusing to use common names for days of the week and months of the year, refusing to take oaths, opposition to slavery and opposition to paying tithes (London Yearly Meeting 1834). Cooper (2001, 129) defines these as *social* testimonies, stating that *spiritual* testimonies of the soul, like belief in the sacred nature of all creation, form the bases for the social testimonies.

Testimonies arise from worship. Over time testimonies need to be reaffirmed by Quaker bodies, and rearticulated to resonate with the times, coming from the same Spirit, yet challenging new generations and different cultures to find ways of living that are congruent with testimony. Testimonies are a form of communication, publically proclaiming a vision of the way the world could be, and consequently how individuals should live (Cave and Morley 2000, 31). Ultimately, testimonies are about God, a declaration about the nature of God as expressed in wider society and in the daily lives of Quakers.

Six characteristics of testimonies follow:

- They are integral to Quaker faith, not optional.
- They come from spiritual convincement, from within.
- They are at their deepest level positive, even when expressed in apparently negative ways, such as a testimony against something.
- They are absolute, not conditional or contextual; their basic nature does not change although the behaviour expressing them may.
- They are to be lived in daily life.
- They are a means of engaging with the world, not withdrawing or separating from it. (Peace Testimony Subgroup 1993, 16–17)

Currently the generally accepted testimonies are equality, integrity, simplicity and peace. Some Quaker meetings add community. Yearly Meetings also may recognise testimonies out of their own corporate life such as testimonies to justice by Canadian Yearly Meeting (CYM) (2011, 123–35).

Many Yearly Meetings now are acknowledging a testimony to the earth or unity with creation (CYM 2011, 135–40). The 'Kabarak Call for Peace and Ecojustice', issued by the Friends World Conference in Kenya 2012, advocates earth care as a way to unite traditional Friends' testimonies, including QPT. Friends present dedicated themselves to renewed relationships with the earth in response to climate change, calling on Friends everywhere to be patterns and examples in the twenty-first century.

A growing secularisation in some Quakers' traditions has resulted in some dilution of ways in which testimonies have been fundamental to Quakerism. It has been suggested that testimonies relate to the Quaker past rather than being a crucial aspect of the current spiritual life of the Society (Cave and Morley 2000, 56–61). Yet others experience the testimonies as expressions of the core of Quakerism that identify Quakers as distinct people (Dandelion 1996, 22).

HISTORY OF QUAKER PEACE TESTIMONY

The Quaker testimony against war and for peace goes back to the origins of Quakerism. Fox refused to take up arms in the English Civil War, stating that early in his life he had 'come into the covenant of peace which was before wars and strifes were'. In 1651, when offered a commission in the Commonwealth army, Fox chose imprisonment rather than accept, responding that 'I lived in the virtue of that life and power that took away the occasion of all wars, and I knew from whence all wars did rise, from the lust according to James doctrine' (Fox 1952, 65).

It is helpful, when thinking about the origins of QPT to remember the context surrounding Fox and early Quakers. Quakerism began during the English Civil War. Perceived as a conflict between Parliament and the king, different understandings of Protestantism that conflicted with the established church were significant factors in the conflict. The New Model Army (NMA), a people's army whose members perceived themselves as engaged in a holy war advocating religious toleration and social and economic reforms such as the end of feudalism, served the parliamentary, Protestant side led by Oliver Cromwell. Fox, whose ideas resonated with those of the NMA, was occasionally identified with it (Ingle 1994, 3, 38, 39, 45).

Not all early Quakers were pacifists. Some, when converted, were soldiers of the NMA. The effectiveness of Quakers' proselytising amongst members of the NMA resulted in Quaker converts being expelled from the army. Their testimony to equality was seen as making them unfit for military service (Brock 1990, 11–12).

The first formal statement of the QPT was issued in 1661 by twelve Friends, including Fox, to the king at the time of the Fifth Monarchy uprising, a small uprising of radicals looking to overthrow the king and replace him with a government led by Christ (see Chapter 1, this volume, by Robynne Rogers Healey). It drew upon a statement written some months earlier by Margaret Fell (Ross 1996, 128). The statement articulated Friends' refusal to fight with outward weapons. It was firmly based on early Quaker Christian theology: 'the spirit of Christ which leads us into all Truth will never move us to fight and war against any man with outward weapons, neither for the kingdom of Christ, nor for the kingdoms of this world'. The statement cites many biblical references from both the Old and New Testaments (Fox 1952, xxix, 398–403).

TESTIMONY AGAINST WAR IN THE EIGHTEENTH AND NINETEENTH CENTURIES

After its early periods, Quakerism moved into an extended period of withdrawal from the world, followed by the Evangelical period. During this time, the testimony against war (TAW) was a significant aspect of the behavioural rules of the Society. The TAW focused on individual members and behaviours articulated in the Books of Discipline including the Advices and the Queries. The Disciplines acted to enforce behaviour, listing expected and proscribed activities. Elders were empowered to enforce behaviour, having options for disciplining offenders. In the eighteenth century, fighting Quakers were disowned. The 'Free Quakers' who fought on the American side during the War of Independence formed their own short-lived meetings for those breaching the TAW (Brock 1990, 153).

Bearing arms, fighting, talking about war, making loans or accepting profit from war, arming or carrying guns on ships, hiring substitutes for militia training, providing transport for any military purpose, and using armed men to protect property were amongst the behaviours forbidden to Friends during the nineteenth century. Behaviours that were demanded included keeping a peaceful demeanour, fulfilling the evangelical promise to learn war no more, being prepared to suffer for the testimony, fulfilling the example of Christ to respond to evil with love, being faithful to the historic testimony, and watching the behaviour of other members. Meetings were exhorted to deal with members in breach, including disowning them. Queries consistently asked whether Friends were being faithful to maintaining this Christian TAW (London Yearly Meeting 1802, 1822, 1861, 1883).

The American Civil War created particular dilemmas for Quakers in both the US North and South. Some Quakers formerly had been enslavers. Quakers contributed significantly to the movement to end enslavement and were surrounded by a war being fought for its abolition. This caused deep divisions. Many Quakers remained non-combatants, often providing humanitarian aid to mitigate the suffering that the war brought to both sides. Some served in the war, believing that their goal of the abolition of enslavement was more important than maintaining the TAW (McDaniel and Julye 2009, 141–52). After the war, meetings were encouraged to welcome 'delinquents' back (Brock 1968, 273–399). Few meetings disciplined members who paid governments' fees for war-related activities in this context (Brock 1990, 166–83).

Throughout this period, the basis for TAW continued to be the Christian foundation of Quaker faith. Books of Discipline used phrases such as 'fulfilling the evangelical promise to learn war no more' and following Christ's example. The British Peace Society, founded by Quakers in 1816, condemned war as contrary to Christianity (Isichei 1970, 220).

TWENTIETH-CENTURY TESTIMONIES

The twentieth century offered significant challenges to Quakers worldwide with this testimony. During World War I (WWI), Yearly Meetings upheld the TAW with many individual Friends witnessing to it. British Friends strongly opposed the use of force as a solution to the conflict. They also held that it was right for Friends to devotedly serve their nation albeit advocating a firm adherence to pacifism ('To Men and Women of Goodwill' 1914). Yet many, including graduates of Friends' schools, joined the military. One-third of military-age British Quakers enlisted (London Yearly Meeting (LYM) 1923, 231–32). Some, but not all, Monthly Meetings disciplined and disowned members who supported the war (Kennedy 2001, 301). British Quakers maintained their opposition to conscription ('A Note on Conscription' 1915). They helped found anti-war organizations working for conscientious objectors (COs): the Non-conscription Fellowship and the Fellowship of Reconciliation, both in 1915 (Barbour and Frost 1988, 248).

CONSCIENTIOUS OBJECTION AND ALTERNATIVE SERVICE

Conscientious objection became representative of the TAW as it moved into the twentieth century. The British government made provision for exemption for COs for both religious and civil liberties objections (Brock and Young 1999, 15). The Militia Act allowed members of any recognised religion fundamentally opposed to all war to be recognized as COs (Braithwaite 1995, 135). London Yearly Meeting (LYM) encouraged young Quakers to stand before military tribunals to claim that status.

COs were classified into three types: non-combatant, service under the military in non-combat roles; alternative service, service in other organisations performing work of social value; and absolute, those opposing any contribution to war. Absolute objectors claimed unconditional exemption on the basis of their belief in Jesus Christ the Prince of Peace being superior to the state's law. They were willing to accept all kinds of suffering resulting from their objection, including harsh imprisonment (Rae 1970, 89).

Quakers undertaking alternative service aimed to express loyalties to both Christ and their countries. Friends created a number of organisations that provided relief to those suffering from war. These provided opportunities for alternative service. Activities included medical care, providing food, and reconstruction work including agriculture.

In 1914, the Friends Ambulance Unit (FAU) was developed in Britain. FAU offered COs alternative service, including medical care of those wounded in battle. The FAU expanded as needs grew, developing both Home and Foreign Services. The Home Service operated hospitals. The Foreign Service provided medical services and civilian relief (FAU WWI). The FAU operated in WWs I and II, and from 1946 to 1959 offering medical, mechanical and administrative service in more than twenty-five countries (The Rowntree Society; Socknat 1987, 54, 252–55). Being seen as too close to war efforts, it was not officially endorsed by some Friends organisations (Brinton 2002, 208).

After the United States joined WWI in 1917, American Quakers were challenged. They faced a lack of legal CO protection and fervent patriotic support for the war (Brock and Young 1999, 29; Frost 1992, 11). American Yearly Meetings reaffirmed the TAW and rejected conscription. Individual Quakers followed the leading of their consciences (Walton 1917, 324). The fighting Quaker tradition reappeared with many American Quakers serving in combat (Barbour and Frost 1988, 251).

The American Friends Service Committee (AFSC) was formed in 1917. It provided relief and reconstruction programs. In some countries including Canada, many Friends still were rural farmers; so young Friends received exemptions from military service to continue farming. These Friends financially supported Friends' relief and reconstruction organisations (Dorland 1968, 332).

ALL FRIENDS PEACE CONFERENCE

The large numbers of Quakers who served in the military during WWI disturbed Friends around the world. To address this, a Conference of All Friends was held in London, England, in 1920. Impetus for the conference arose from New York Yearly Meeting's 1915 approach to LYM to assist with joint work for peace, and LYM's proposal in 1916 to hold such a post-war conference. It was believed that Friends around the world needed an opportunity to explore the nature, basis and application of Friends' historic TAW. This was the first world gathering of Friends (Kennedy 2001, 404–7). Almost a thousand participants attended. Although the majority were British and American, Friends attended from Australia, Canada, China, Europe, India, Jamaica, Japan, New Zealand, South Africa and Syria (Conference of All Friends 1920)

Seven commissions in each of Britain and the United States prepared papers examining aspects of QPT. The term 'Quaker peace testimony' was used although much of the content of the papers reflected the TAW (Bishop 2004, 127). Although the conference failed to bring about world peace, as some had hoped, it affirmed QPT as a fundamental Quaker Christian truth for the Society (Kennedy 2001, 413).

CONTINUING THE TWENTIETH CENTURY

Wars and conflicts throughout the twentieth century offered Quakers opportunities to extend and broaden their witness to QPT. Quaker peace and service organisations continued work on relief and reconstruction in response to various wars.

In 1932, influential American theologian Reinhold Niebuhr, formerly a pacifist, shocked the pacifist world. He argued that only individuals could express Christian love, that human sinfulness compromised institutions and systems, which at best, only could achieve justice. Niebuhr proposed accepting a dualism between individuals and groups, allowing that coercive violence was acceptable to achieve justice. Consequently, Niebuhr perceived QPT as naïve optimism about human nature (Chernus n.d.; Niebuhr 1932, 43–54). Nevertheless, Quakers continued their commitment to pacifism, focusing on love, little affected by this theological disagreement (Appelbaum 2009, 50–51).

During World War II, American Quaker COs worked for the Civilian Public Service, performing work of national importance including forestry, soil conservation, fish and wildlife preservation, staffing state mental hospitals and volunteering for scientific research and agricultural projects (Knohe 1941–1946). In 1939, a number of British Friends helped establish the 'No Conscription League' (Braithwaite 1939). From 1939 through 1943, Scattergood Friends School in Iowa served as a hostel for refugees fleeing war in Europe (Scattergood Friends School 2016). In 1947, Friends' relief and peace work was recognised when the Quakers, represented by AFSC and British Friends Service Council, received the Nobel Peace Prize (Jahn 1947).

Quakers actively opposed the Vietnam War. In the United States, AFSC conducted an anti-draft campaign, and the Friends Committee on National Legislation lobbied Congress in efforts to abolish the draft (Walker 1968, 97–99). Canadian Friends Service Committee (CFSC) sent medical aid to all three parts of Vietnam. American Quakers opposing the war sent donations to CFSC and marched on fifty post offices when the US Post Office banned parcels and letters addressed to CFSC. Quakers visited Vietnam during the war (Stieren 1998, 26–30). American, British and Canadian Quakers helped American COs flee to other countries including Canada and Sweden (SCPC 1970–1999). Friends' witness, at times, resulted in hostile attention: during the Vietnam War, the Des Moines Valley Friends Meetinghouse, including the building housing the regional AFSC office, was bombed. Friends from across Iowa worked together to remove the debris and repair the buildings.

With the establishment of the United Nations (UN) in 1948, Friends extended their work for peace under the auspices of the Friends World Committee for Consultation, which, in 1948, was recognised by the UN as a non-governmental organisation. At the UN, Friends addressed a variety of issues including social and economic justice, disarmament and decolonisation. This work included quiet diplomacy with UN representatives (Bailey 1993, 101–12). Other Friends were involved in international conciliation (Yarrow 1978). Quaker service organisations in different countries continued to be involved in sustainable development, relief, disarmament and reconciliation work at home and abroad. In 1973, British Quakers played a lead role in establishing of the Bradford School of Peace Studies, the first university peace education program (Rogers 2011). Quaker peacemaker Adam Curle was its first director.

Throughout the twentieth century, Quakers' early witness to refusing to pay for war transformed into movements of war tax resistance in various countries. Some Quaker meetings created personnel policies to enable their employees to divert to relief or peace work the percentage of their countries' taxes that would pay for military expenses (CYM 2016, 2)

Changes in Books of Discipline reflected this broadening of QPT. LYM's 1922 revision advocated living free from materials things. Its 1925 revision included sections on poverty, instructing children in peace principles, disarmament, supporting the League of Nations, supporting international courts of justice, and participating in the Friends International Service. The 1960 revision included advocating non-violent resistance, realising more fully the fundamental character of the QPT, removing enmity between countries, working for liberty in political and economic life, personal visits to communist countries, being sensitive to all oppression, and striving to end injustice and the unequal distribution of the earth's produce.

The 1995 Britain Yearly Meeting (BYM), formerly LYM, revision, *Quaker Faith & Practice*, was broader still. There are sections on peace, peace education and peace testimony, conscientious objection, disarmament and relief work. Relief work includes sections on the FAU, poverty and Quaker Peace and Service, BYM's peace and service arm. The chapter 'Living Faithfully Today' includes a section about conflict and conflict resolution. A chapter on QPT includes entries on the history of the testimony, statements by individual Friends and Quaker organisations, experiences of witness to QPT and dilemmas of the pacifist stand. Practical expressions of QPT described include public protest, relief of suffering, reconciliation and mediation, disarmament, building international institutions for peace and social justice, and the right sharing of world resources.

FIVE SHIFTS IN QUAKER PEACE TESTIMONY

An analysis of the historical sweep of the Quaker testimonies against war and for peace identifies five significant shifts. These are complex and have significant consequences.

1   From Testimony against War to Quaker Peace Testimony

The shift initially appears as a change of the name and then expands to a change in content. TAW is clear – Friends opposed preparation for and participation in war. The corporate position of the Society was frequently articulated. The focus is against war: any behaviours that might contribute to war were proscribed. Members were expected to be willing to suffer rather than comply with government demands for behaviour defined corporately as contrary to Quaker faith.

The TAW became newly labelled as QPT in the twentieth century. The corporate commitment to the testimony and calls for consistent witness by members continued. Earlier articulated opposition to war remained and was extended with calls for disarmament and continuing opposition to conscription. This expanded as members in many Yearly Meetings were encouraged to engage in ever-growing areas of ameliorative work in situations of conflict and preventative work that addresses root causes at local, regional and international levels. There is no clear articulation of personal behaviours that members are expected to undertake to witness to this re-conceptualised testimony. The content of QPT expands vastly to include a variety of aspects of life that may contribute to peace, including social and economic justice, abolition of poverty and racial justice.

2   From a Christian-based Testimony against War to Christian, Universalist, and Non-religious-based Quaker Peace Testimony

Although some individual Quakers asserted anti-war ideas based on pragmatic and humanitarian grounds (Gregg 1990, 8–30; Kennedy 2001, 243–44; Robbins 1979, 124–40), TAW was based on an interpretation of scriptural Christian faith. QPT is based on a broad spectrum of Christian and Universalist faith as well as on non-religious ideas.

QPT continued to be seen as an expression of the Light Within, which confirmed war as contrary to the Spirit of Christ (Hirst 1972, 520), but Quakers also opposed war and carried out peacemaking through moral and other religious inspiration. Core ideas of this moral ground include the sacredness of personality and the supreme worth of life. Ideas of democracy, world federation and human affinity with one another also became grounds of QPT.

3   From a Prescriptive to a Permissive Individual Option

Another significant shift was increased tolerance towards different individual interpretations of QPT. Until the end of the nineteenth century, Quakers corporately adhered firmly to the TAW. Generally Quakers who violated the testimony were disciplined and could be disowned from membership. Twentieth-century Quakers assumed various attitudes to war. QPT was maintained as the corporate position of the Society, but individual members' free interpretation of the testimony, reflecting various attitudes to war and peace, was tolerated. Quakers maintained their testimony in various ways: conscientious objection, alternative service, relief work and political lobbying and negotiation. Yet numbers of Quakers enlisted for military service. They regarded enlisting as more important than the QPT, being called by their sense of social responsibility, fellowship and patriotic passion. They regarded their participation in war as just (Isichei 1970, 144). Not all were disciplined by their meetings. Some Friends even called those serving 'conscientious fighters' ('Friends and Enlistment' 1914, 932). These Quakers, many of them COs, saw QPT as a matter of personal conviction.

Dandelion describes this type of Quakerism as personal/institutional or popular religion. The institution maintains its orthodox position, so TAW and then QPT continue to be the corporate positions of the Society. Yet the Society tolerates personal interpretations of ways in which individuals may witness to it. Some Yearly Meetings adapted to this, no longer requiring witnessing to the testimonies as a condition for membership (Dandelion 1996, 21, 270).

4   From a Focus on Internal Individual Behaviour to External Focus on the World

Another shift is on the focal point of the testimony. The major focus of the TAW was internal to Quakerism, on the behaviour of members. Members were admonished not to participate in a variety of activities seen to contribute to war. Members were expected to moderate their behaviour in line with the corporate testimony. Monthly Meetings were expected to discipline members in breach. Members were expected to suffer consequences of their witness patiently, whether financial loss or reprisals by government. Implicitly, all of these behaviours were within the control of the Yearly Meeting.

With QPT, a major arena in which the content of the testimony is implemented shifts to the world, beyond the control of meetings. Individuals still are encouraged to witness in particular ways, such as conscientious objection, including withholding the military portion of taxes and participating in public protests. However, significant attention is focused outside the Society. Calls are made for substantive changes in economic, social and international relations. Quakers are encouraged to think about the personal implications of such changes, yet no explicit guidance is given concerning Quakers' behaviour with respect to income, activities or appropriate areas of work.

Special departments or agencies, such as AFSC and CFSC, are maintained within Quakers' corporate structures with paid staff to facilitate implementing Quaker thinking about peace and the needs of people at home and abroad. It is countries, legislatures and worldly powers that must be persuaded to change. Much of the work of living the testimony is focused on persuasion targeted outside the Society rather than internally on the personal behaviour of Quakers.

5   From a Narrow to a Broad Concept of Peace

Prior to the twentieth century, the focus on the testimony was opposition to war. The twentieth-century QPT incorporated a broadened concept of peace. Peace became something more than 'no war'. After WW II, the LYM Peace Committee issued a statement on the future of the world which included the Law of God as composed of five principles: democracy, fellowship, service, integrity and self-sacrifice (London Yearly Meeting 1945, 3–5). The broader understandings of peace are further demonstrated in BYM by the expansion of its Books of Discipline cited earlier.

UNDERSTANDING PEACE: A CHALLENGE AFFECTING QUAKERS

With the shift from a corporate TAW to a corporate QPT, Quakers worked to understand and mitigate those conditions that resulted in war. Quakers have continued to explore and elaborate their understandings of peace. In seeking the meanings of peace, it is important to recognise that the world may use the term to describe what Bishop calls 'false peace' (2004) and Curle calls unpeace (1981, 13). For example, the submission of people as a consequence of sustained bombing, if described as 'peace', is an example of false peace. So is the silence that returns to a community after a demonstration is dispersed by tear gas and truncheons. Conflicts in which solutions are imposed by the powerful against the interests of others are yet another example of false or un-peace. Understanding true meanings of peace offers Friends an ability to assess whether something described as 'peace' really is.

Quakers, corporately and individually, have wrestled with defining peace. They have called conferences, held special sessions at Yearly Meetings, written pamphlets and statements, amended Books of Discipline and worked in the field. Friends have written from experience in conflict zones (Zaru 2008), offered peace education and training (Bello

1986; Fisher et al. 2000) and offered lectures (Bailey 1993; Curle 1981) as ways of grappling with this task. Peace has been defined as a condition and as a process.

Some themes emerge of the dynamics necessary to actualise Fox's vision: 'to live in the virtue of that life and power that takes away the occasion of all wars' (Fox 1952, 65). Justice is one dynamic. Outside Quakerism many studies explore differing understandings of justice. Entries in Books of Discipline indicate that early Quakers used the concept, some linking it to peace. In the twentieth century, Friends expanded their understanding, embracing a variety of issues including economic and social justice. Frequently Friends connect two terms into a phrase, 'justice and peace', some suggesting that justice is a prerequisite for peace. True justice demands justice at both individual and structural levels. Some recognise justice as an outcome of peacemaking: dimensions in relationship united by love, implementing fair distribution, wholeness, human dignity and righteousness, a state of being just before God (Curle 1981, 101). Recognition that different cultures understand justice differently is an important insight (Ross 2006, 1)!

Human rights are another dynamic. An exploration of human rights, and the conflicts that arise in defining and implementing them, demon-strates their interconnections with justice and peace. In 1948, the UN adopted its Universal Declaration of Human Rights. Its preamble makes links between justice, peace and human rights. The declaration sets out a variety of rights inherent to all individuals because of their humanity. These include the right to life, liberty, a basic standard of living, rest, work, leisure, education, health care and freedom from slavery and torture. It recognises a variety of legal rights including presumed innocence, and rights to nationality and freedom of movement. This declaration also recognised human duties to the community. Since 1948, a variety of inter-national covenants and regional declarations have further protected human rights. In 2007, the UN approved the UN Declaration on the Rights of Indigenous Peoples (UNDRIP). Every paragraph of UNDRIP is based upon known instances of countries' violations of the human rights of Indigenous Peoples (Chandler 1998, 10).

Taking away the occasion for war requires more than righting unjust situa-tions. It requires addressing the damage done during conflict. Reconciliation, another dynamic, is a process for implementing this. Early Quakers used reconciliation. In 1870, British Quakers were advised to initiate reconciliation in interpersonal conflicts rather than waiting for another to do so. The 1925 LYM Discipline recognised reconciliation as the basis for all international

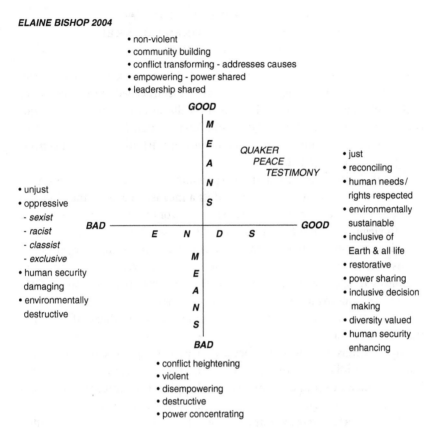

Figure 6.1 Locating Quaker Peace Testimony

service. Truth, justice and mercy were identified as being essential in building reconciliation.

Reconciliation does not come easily. It requires persistence and time. It is based on respect for a shared humanity. Reconciliation seeks restorative justice, demanding neither revenge nor impunity. Reconciliation seeks remembrance without pain, fear, bitterness or guilt, not necessarily forgiveness. It does require a willingness to coexist and to work for a peaceful resolution of continuing issues. Reconciliation requires commitment, especially from those who benefitted from the injustice (Fisher et al. 2000, 136).

Other concepts can be explored to further understand the complex ideas of peace. Figure 6.1, integrating some, is a tool that can be used to explore whether a process or condition may contribute to peace and consequently be reflective of QPT.

THE SHIFT FROM THE TESTIMONY AGAINST
WAR TO A TWO-COMPONENT QUAKER
PEACE TESTIMONY

The five shifts, combined with knowledge of current Quaker activities implementing the testimony, suggest that what is presently called the 'Quaker peace
testimony' may be understood as an umbrella testimony with two major
components: 'war-abolishing QPT' and 'conflict-transforming QPT'. This
model allows the many diverse components of QPT to be more effectively
recognised and integrated.

War-abolishing QPT is a modern expression of the TAW. It focuses on the
components of war. War is recognised as a means. Quaker witnessing and
strategies are aimed at denying to governments, or others attempting to wage
war, the legitimacy and resources needed to do so. Quaker witness includes
conscientious objection to military service or taxation for military purposes,
opposition to the arms industry including specific weapons systems, and
responses to specific threats and executions of war. War-abolishing QPT
includes responding to the immediate effects of war, particularly the needs of
refugees, internally displaced persons, the injured and others affected and
traumatised by war.

Conflict-transforming QPT focuses on addressing causation, on those
sources of conflict that result in war. The potential areas for action are
immense, including but not limited to local, regional and international issues
of justice, human rights and reconciliation. This can be described as peace
building: undertaking programmes designed to address the causes of conflict
and the grievances of the past and to promote long-term stability and justice
(Fisher et al. 2000, 13–14).

Figure 6.2 is a visual representation of the two-component QPT that helps
conceptualise the complexity and breadth of this testimony.

LIVING QUAKER PEACE TESTIMONY
IN THE TWENTY-FIRST CENTURY

What does it mean, in the twenty-first century, to live 'in the virtue of that life
and power that took away the occasion of all wars' (Fox 1952, 65)? A survey of
Quakerism around the world provides information on many challenges and
much Quaker work.

In parts of Africa, Friends are concerned about pressure on their youth
and the risk of their being recruited by terror groups such as Al-Shabaab
(Africa Section 2015, 8–9). In Europe and the Middle East, Friends face

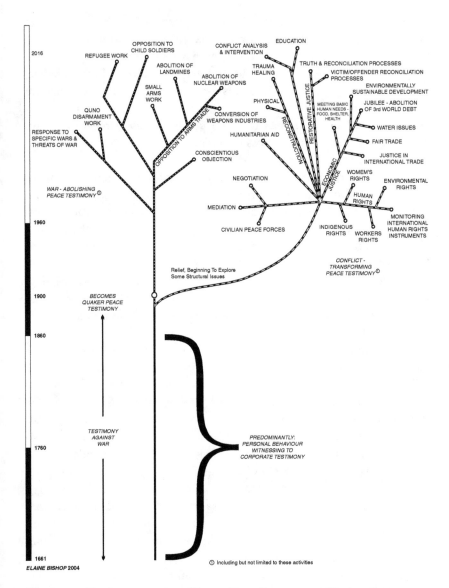

Figure 6.2 Testimony against War to Two-Component Quaker Peace
Testimony

continuing conflicts in Israel/Palestine and the Ukraine. Friends are
amongst those responding to the needs of refugees from these and
other conflicts who flood the world seeking safety and refuge. US and
British Friends face governments wanting to renew their nuclear

weapons and Trident nuclear submarine systems. Friends in post-colonial countries around the world are called to respond to ways in which the effects of racism and colonialism have blighted their countries. Friends join citizens everywhere being forced to address climate change, calls for climate justice and the needs for communities to build resilience in the face of significant climate disruption. Challenges internal to Quakerism call upon Friends to live a peace testimony regarding ways to strengthen community across different traditions of Quakerism that can lead to disconnection and conflict.

Quakers in different parts of the world have access to different resources through and with which to express QPT. The risks to which Friends are exposed by living this witness vary significantly. Friends in the Middle East, for example, face very different conditions and risks calling for the boycott, divestment and sanctions movement in Israel/Palestine than do Friends in North America.

All Friends are called to integrate the testimonies into day-to-day living. Each Quaker's life is a continuous opportunity to live QPT: in interpersonal relationships, at work, at home, in raising children, as a basis for marriage, in ways in which money is spent, in what is purchased and owned. Such personal witness becomes a grounding for Friends' corporate work against war and for peace.

There is diversity across Quaker traditions with respect to the testimony today. Quaker meetings and organisations publish statements advocating for renewal of QPT and calling on governments to transform conflict in the world. Some Yearly Meetings maintain the articulation of the Christian-based TAW in their Advices and Queries (Britain YM 1995, 13; Evangelical Friends Midwest YM 2010, 74–75; Northwest YM of Friends Church 2012, 13). Some integrate into their Queries work for peace (Northwest YM of Friends Church 2012, 13). Others address a breadth of work for peace in sections of their Disciplines (British Yearly Meeting (BYM) 1995, sec. 23, 24, 25; Canadian Yearly Meeting (CYM) 2011, 114–23). Some individual Quakers remain ignorant or questioning of this part of historic Quaker witness.

Significant numbers of Friends' organisations actively address QPT. Friends' service committees continue working nationally and internationally in Aotearoa/New Zealand, Australia, Canada, the United States and Great Britain. Friends' Peace Teams, based in the United States and Kenya, have programmes working in various African countries, Asia-West Pacific and Central and South America. In 2015, Friends United Meeting, the membership of which unites a large number of Yearly Meetings worldwide, offered an alternative gift catalogue enabling Friends to support initiatives for peace, relief and nonviolence including training teachers in Kenya to use a new peace curriculum. In the Democratic Republic of the Congo (DRC), Kinshasa Monthly Meeting has more than twenty years' experience offering peace trainings and building peace cells which offer local conflict resolution and election monitoring. In eastern DRC, local Friends provide a small hospital and trauma counselling. Canadian and UK Quakers respectively help finance this work. Quaker United Nations Offices continue work in New York and Geneva, including addressing peace building, prevention of violent conflict, the impacts of climate change, disarmament, human rights and refugee issues.

QPT IN TWENTY-FIRST-CENTURY KOREA

Quaker peace work in Korea illustrates both war-abolishing and conflict-transforming peace testimonies working together, complementing each other in response to the Korean conflict. The history of Korea Quakerism began during the Korea War (June 1950–July 1953). British Quakers conducted their war-abolishing peace testimony 'for mediation in the Korean dispute' (LYM Minutes 1949–1952, 79). Jointly with AFSC after the ceasefire, they sent Quaker doctors, nurses, social workers and physiotherapists to do humanitarian work, also expressions of war-abolishing QPT (Jung 2006, 190). A Quaker meeting started in South Korea, which Koreans attended. Ham Sokhon, Korean peace thinker nominated for the Nobel Peace Prize by AFSC, met the Quakers, was impressed by their faith and practice and became a Quaker believing that Quakerism was a religion of peace (Ham 1983, 18).

Korean Quakers work actively for peace and unification on the Korean peninsula. The 1953 ceasefire remains in effect with a demilitarised zone (DMZ) separating the two Koreas. No peace treaty has been negotiated. Korean Quakers recently participated in an anti–naval base campaign in Jejul Island, South Korea, This military port, completed in 2015, can berth twenty warships, mostly American, opposing China, creating military tension. Korean Quakers expressed their war-abolishing QPT through peace vigils, fasting, lobbying, 'three steps one bow' pilgrimage and other non-violent actions for peace, and social justice.

AFSC has been conducting humanitarian work since 1980, helping the North Korean people suffering economic difficulties and famine. Currently AFSC's peace work there aims to raise agricultural productivity, an example of conflict-transforming QPT, illustrating the fifth shift, humanitarian work.

In the 1990s, AFSC introduced to civil society in South Korea programmes of conflict resolution and conscientious objection. Young people in South Korea still go to jail for conscientious objection. There are 669 CO prisoners in South Korea, 92.7 percent of CO prisoners worldwide (UNHCR 2013). AFSC also undertakes advocacy and education in the United States regarding North Korea. It advocates for government-sponsored people-to-people exchanges on topics such as science, and agriculture, a conflict-transforming strategy that has preceded improved relations between the United States and other countries (Jasper 2016, 12, 22).

Another example of integrated war-abolishing and conflict-transforming peace testimonies is the Border Peace School (BPS). It started in 2013 in a border village south of the DMZ. The BPS aims to educate peacemakers working for peace and unification. The vision is to extend BPS to other villages south and north of the DMZ, along the border on the Korean peninsula, so that the peace schools may become peace channels between the two Korean peoples.

QUAKER PEACE TESTIMONY AND INDIGENOUS RIGHTS IN CANADA

Colonial relationships in Canada between Indigenous Peoples, formerly named Indians or native peoples, and settler peoples, those arriving from around the world and their successors (Lowman and Barker 2015, 1) are rife with injustice. From the time of contact, colonisation was used to seize Indigenous lands for settlers based on the Doctrine of Discovery, the belief that Christian countries could take Indigenous lands because the occupants were not Christian (Truth and Reconciliation Commission (TRC) 2015, 46–47, 191–95). One of the colonial strategies saw more than 150,000 children taken for forced attendance at residential schools, depriving children of family, community and identity. This broke the transmission of culture and language. Canada's Truth and Reconciliation Commission (TRC) describes this as cultural genocide (TRC 2015, 1). Some argue that it was genocide as defined by the UN Convention on the Prevention and Punishment of the Crime of Genocide (Preston and Joffe 2016, 1, 6). The TRC calls Canada to renewed relationships based on fully implementing the UN Declaration on the Rights of Indigenous Peoples, including guaranteeing equitable Indigenous access to the economic, health and other resources benefitting settler peoples (TRC 2015, 139–317).

Canadian Quaker work on Indigenous rights illustrates that conflict-transforming peace testimony requires varieties of work and may need years to accomplish. For more than fifty years, Quakers have listened to Indigenous Peoples, building significant relationships and forming strong alliances across Canada. The 1982 Canadian Yearly Meeting (CYM) stated, 'To work for peace in Canada necessitates support for native peoples in their quest for justice' (Canadian Yearly Meeting (CYM) 1982, 65). Actions taken over the years include camping between armed warriors and armed police during a park occupation; providing medical care and economic development in response to a pulp mill's mercury poisoning of a reserve river; years of attending the UN in alliance with Indigenous Peoples through the drafting, approval and implementation of UNDRIP; funding Indigenous initiated and led programs; advocacy with the Canadian government; and work with other allies including intervention in legal cases before the Supreme Court of Canada. CYM affirmed UNDRIP in 2010. In 2013, it repudiated the Doctrine of Discovery.

This work illustrates four of the shifts. It is a testimony for peace. Work addresses issues that will lead to a broadly defined peace. The major focus is on changing powers external to Quakerism. Although educating Quakers and approving minutes, this work is permissive: those Quakers led are engaged. CYM does not require specific individual Quaker behaviour of its members.

TOWARDS THE FUTURE

Friends worldwide are engaging in both war-abolishing and conflict-transforming QPT. Yet changes are taking place in the ways in which the world executes colonialism and oppression and participates in war. These create continuing challenges for Quakers to stay grounded in Spirit while living QPT in new and innovative ways that respond to changing conditions in the world.

Two challenges merit consideration:

- Creating cultures of peace: how do Quakers implement this, called for by the UN and Quaker organisations, in their countries? Characteristics of cultures of peace needing implementation include respect for individual dignity and human rights, a permanent ban on all weapons of mass destruction, eradication of poverty in the world, and a well-funded and staffed global environmental protection agency protected by both governments and civil society (Thomson 2006, 12–13).

- Terrorism: how do Quakers respond to terrorism when others, in response demand the use of armed force? Quakers in Britain issued an insightful statement after the bomb attacks in Paris in November 2015. It advocates responding to terrorism as crime, denying arms to parties in areas of conflict, applying international law equally to all conflicting parties and exporting peace rather than war. In Kenya in 2014, members of the Friends Church Peace Teams (FCPT) met with thirteen leaders of a terrorist group. The rebels asked to be included in the peace and reconciliation work of the FCPT. FCPT organised some Healing and Reconciling Our Communities workshops for the rebel group and arranged other activities, including building a small peace centre, to enable this work to continue (Zarembka 2015).

Evangelical Quaker academic Ron Mock (2004) argues that Christians must love their enemies and must ground their responses to terrorism and tyranny in love. He describes sources of terrorism in political misery leading to corrosive grievance and dehumanizing hatred that can result in belief in the myth of effective violence. Mock advocates a broad variety of strategies to address these, including implementing justice, enabling Christians to love, in the face of terrorism and tyranny.

CONCLUSION

This chapter articulates the important role of testimony in Quakerism and then offers fresh thinking about Quaker peace testimony. An understanding of war-abolishing and conflict-transforming QPTs offers an analysis that has the potential to foster broader understanding and engagement with this testimony. The history of TAW reminds Friends of the critical importance of transforming daily life to ensure that their ways of living do not contribute to war. The war-abolishing QPT work of Friends addresses the damage done by war and withdraws the social consent of Quakers to governments' perpetrating war. This makes an important contribution to addressing the deep need that the world has for the abolition of war. Friends working with conflict-transforming QPT address root causes. Jointly this work moves the Society towards achieving Fox's vision of living in the Life and power that away the occasion of all wars.

SUGGESTED FURTHER READING

Bailey S. D. (1993). *Peace Is a Process*, London: Quaker Home Service and Woodbrooke College.
Brock, P. (1990). *The Quaker Peace Testimony 1660–1914*, York: Sessions Book Trust.

Broughton, G. (2013). *Four Elements of Peacebuilding: How to Protect Nonviolently,* Toronto: Canadian Friends Service Committee. Available as a free download from http://quakerservice.ca/news-and-resources/public-statements/ scroll down to the section on Peace.

Curle, A. (1981). *True Justice: Quaker Peace Makers and Peace Making,* London: Quaker Home Service.

7

∾

Quakers and Education

Stephen W. Angell and Clare Brown

Quakers have had a profound engagement with modern education at many levels. Many Friends teach in, or are students in, state schools (or non-Quaker private schools) from primary school to university levels. Other Friends homeschool their children. But the heart of Quaker education occurs in Friends schools. The greatest number of Friends schools in the twenty-first century are in Kenya, where there are more than 1,500 primary and high schools (at least 200 of these are high schools) and many colleges (Wafula 2016, 36). The Friends Council of Education lists more than seventy member schools in the United States, and affiliate schools in eight other countries (Australia, Britain, Costa Rica, Ireland, Japan, Kenya, Lebanon, and Palestine) (friendscouncil.org). As of 2010, Quaker schools in the United States had 21,000 students, 4,500 teachers, and 1,200 trustees (McHenry 2010). In the United States, Friends (or a Friend) have founded fifteen colleges and universities, and many of these maintain some level of connection with their Quaker roots. Postgraduate religious studies with a Quaker emphasis occur at Woodbrooke in Britain, and, in the United States, at Earlham School of Religion in Indiana, George Fox University in Oregon, and other locations (Oliver, Cherry, and Cherry 2007). Pendle Hill, a Quaker center for study and contemplation near Philadelphia, has offered significant non-degree programs since 1930 (Gwyn 2014a), and Woodbrooke similarly so since 1903.

Scholars and practitioners tend to agree that Quaker schools have distinctive emphases, but they differ somewhat on what those are. According to Earlham professor Paul Lacey, Quaker schools showed "respect for each individual's uniqueness, creativity, and originality, appreciation of cultural and religious diversity, trust in others, openness to a wide range of sources for enlightenment, and an emphasis on cooperative and collaborative learning" (Hamm 2003, 112). Many commentators point to the Quaker testimonies (such as integrity, equality, simplicity, community, and peace) as formative for Quaker education (e.g., Fremon 2001). Melvin Keiser points to the importance of God within each person, often expressed by Friends as "the inward teacher," in forming Quaker ideals of education. The inward teacher "engenders courage in community; to speak one's mind and heart, however different from what has already been said; to listen with compassion to others; to be open to changing one's mind rather than defending one's initial stated position; and to engage creatively and collaboratively in achieving [a consensus]," or what Quakers have often called "a sense of the meeting" (Keiser 2014, 22).

Quaker education has not merely been interested in the growth of Quaker youth and adults, but it also has played a role in modeling innovative forms of altruism to the wider world. By the mid-nineteenth century, Friends' involvement in education often overlapped with their many other commitments to social reform movements (Isichei 1970, xix). Several Quaker philanthropists became household names in the Victorian era, such as Elizabeth Fry and Joseph Sturge. Although they are now better known for other philanthropic activities, both Fry and Sturge were involved in educational work.

Quaker education has also served as an attractive force for some administrators, teachers, and students coming as non-Friends to Friends schools, who have become "convinced Friends" after their experiences of Quaker education. Irene McHenry, surveying the heads of eighty-five Friends schools across the United States in 2010, found that nearly half were Quakers and that most had become so as a result of their experience of working in or graduating from a Friends school. Accordingly, McHenry is concerned that Quakers undervalue an important outreach function, Friends' education (2010). Friends' rich spiritual traditions offer an opportunity for all connected with Quaker education to go progressively deeper in their engagement with Quaker values in the classroom. Ayesha Imani, an experienced teacher in Philadelphia, describes encountering Thomas Kelly's *Testament of Devotion* after four years as a convinced Quaker. Kelly's writing, especially his advice not to simply "follow our Lord halfway," deeply affected Imani, both personally and professionally. She described how she asked her "students to listen to their own inner voices so they could cultivate their capacity for self-control and self-determination," and how they responded positively to this teaching (Imani 2001).

This chapter provides a broad survey of educational institutions, philosophies, and trends in schools started by Friends worldwide. It pays due attention to both practical and religious dimensions of Friends' education, with attention to how these have evolved within the different branches of Quakerism. We examine how theological learning was downplayed in the seventeenth century, while utilitarian subjects, such as history and languages, were emphasized. Several kinds of Quaker schools were founded in the eighteenth and early nineteenth centuries. We explore the nature of the "guarded and select" education that Quakers gave their own youth on both sides of the Atlantic, as well as the ways they educated the poor and African Americans, reaching out to youth from the margins of society. We also look at the effects of the Holiness revivals on Quaker education in North America and elsewhere from the late nineteenth century onward. We explicate how the religious and theological dimensions of Quaker studies have made a comeback in the twentieth and twenty-first centuries. Finally, we examine some recent controversies over the nature of contemporary Quaker education, especially as it relates to the education of the children of the wealthy and powerful.

THE SEVENTEENTH-CENTURY QUAKER EMPHASIS ON A PRACTICAL CURRICULUM

Quakerism has had a long history of evolving religious attitudes toward education. Given early Quaker hostility toward the educated clergy, it is little surprise that the first generation of Quakers was hostile toward universities. Early Quakers held firmly to the notion that every person has the right and ability to approach God, rejecting the idea that an ordained clergy must stand as an intermediary between the individual and God; no one had the special calling of priest because all were called priests (Campbell Stewart 1971, 13–14). As it was thought that all members of the Society had the potential to serve as a minister, educated adherents were needed (Kenworthy 1987, 7). Yet early Friends did not want to inculcate their children with formulaic religious notions that might only produce head-knowledge, for they believed that every individual had something of God within, and that personal experience of Divine prompting was essential for spiritual growth.

An aspect of education that particularly perturbed early Quakers was the teaching of theology in schools and universities (Greaves 1969, 23). In 1680, the Quaker botanist Thomas Lawson (1630–91) expressed a view common to Quakers when he asserted that theological knowledge might even impede spiritual awareness, if it were taught and received with earthly ambitions in mind (Lawson 1680, 42). George Fox addressed this issue in his *Primer for the Schollers and Doctors of Europe* (Fox 1659, 44–45). In this treatise, Fox argued that students would not gain spiritual understanding unless they rooted their life in the "wisdom of the Holy Ghost"; this was the one method of enquiry that would yield real truth, not just sophistries

(Angell 2003, 5). Fox did not deprecate the use of human reason but viewed it as a tool that could be rightly used only with guidance from the Inward Light.

However, early Quakers also made certain that young Quakers were exposed to Quaker beliefs about God, Christ, and the Light. Fox facilitated the process of Quaker education by coauthoring a primer for Quaker children, one that was often reprinted during the next century. His primer included a brief catechism highlighting Quakers' spiritualized understanding of Christian concepts. Quaker theologian Robert Barclay authored a catechism that was similarly much used and often reprinted during the seventeenth and eighteenth centuries (Angell 2003; Barbour and Roberts 1973, 314).

In 1668, George Fox advised Friends to teach persons of both genders "whatever things were civil and useful in creation" (Hamm 2003, 109). William Penn (1644–1718) propounded a method of education based on personal activity and observation. In *Fruits of Solitude*, he asserted, "Children had rather be making of tools and instruments of play ... than getting some rules of propriety of speech by heart" (Penn 1726, I, 820). At the same time, mid-seventeenth-century Quakers recognized the usefulness of literacy; all Friends were encouraged to study the Bible in their mother tongue, alongside approved literature. Proficiency in foreign languages was endorsed, perhaps in part because this could further the Society's missionary aims. At the end of the seventeenth century, London Yearly Meeting was encouraging schools to teach Latin and other languages (Campbell Stewart 1971, 28). The attitude to Latin was utilitarian; Friends noted that knowledge of the language facilitated intercourse between nations. Friends prioritized the acquisition of useful skills over a familiarity with classical texts (Campbell Stewart 1971, 25–26).

Physical labor was also an important feature in a number of Quaker schools. John Bellers's vision for "a college of industry," published in 1695, included a curriculum that Lacey calls "eminently practical"; Bellers suggested four hours of study and four hours of labor each day (Lacey 1998, 117).

A GUARDED AND SELECT EDUCATION

The first school begun by Quakers in North America, the William Penn Charter School, was established in 1689 to provide an education based on Quaker principles and was open to all citizens of Pennsylvania (Kashatus 1997, 14–20). Not all Quaker schools were to have the same inclusive mission regarding non-Quakers, however. In 1690, London Yearly Meeting exhorted the Quarterly and Monthly Meetings to establish more schools, in the hope this might protect children from being corrupted by the views of non-Friends (Barbour et al. 1995, 146; London Yearly Meeting 1806, 38). In 1701, London Yearly Meeting advised against schooling children with non-Friends, "whose example occasions their losing the plain language and excites them to vanity" (Campbell Stewart 1971, 32). Indeed, by the early eighteenth century, Quaker schools were particularly focused on protecting their students from pernicious influences; Friends referred to this approach as "guarded education" (Braithwaite 1919, 536). A guarded education was a caring education free of harmful spiritual influences, which, for eighteenth-century Quakers, included novels, art, music, and theater. In 1718, an Epistle from London Yearly Meeting encouraged Friends to be "diligent in providing schools" for the education of their youth so children would be taught "our holy self-denying way" to be an example of "our holy profession" (London Yearly Meeting 1858, 149). In both Britain and the United States, a number of the Quaker schools embodying this ethos were located in rural areas, partly because a country setting was thought to be healthier than the city, but also to limit interaction with non-Quakers (O'Donnell 2013, 410).

For the Quakers of the eighteenth century, plain language and plain speech were both important demonstrations of their "holy profession." It has been argued that, during this time, Quaker "peculiarities" became rather a fixation for some Friends. Distinctive dress and speech demonstrated simplicity of life but also proved loyalty to the Society (Lacey 1998, 73, 150). Yet these "peculiarities" served another important purpose; they helped sustain the Quaker way of life. Quaker schools reinforced the idea of Quaker plainness, and this may well have fostered a sense of belonging and solidarity. Without this sense of identity and commitment, young people might be drawn away by the amusements and ambitions prevalent in the wider society. In the later part of the eighteenth century, this issue particularly concerned the eminent Quaker physician John Fothergill (1712–80). Referring to the "tender minds" of children, he grieved that young Quakers were sometimes so caught up with "the customs of the world" that they no longer exhibited Quaker principles (Lettsom 1784, 10–11). In 1777, Fothergill and some associates purchased an estate in Pontefract, Yorkshire, under the aegis of London Yearly Meeting. Ackworth School was founded there in 1779 to serve members "not in affluence"; by 1781, it had 310 pupils, boys and girls, from all over the country (Campbell Stewart 1971, 49).

A similar trend could be observed among American Quakers in the eighteenth and early nineteenth centuries. Some of the most enduring Quaker schools, such as Westtown, founded in 1799, were established as "select" schools (for Quakers only, using mainly textbooks written by Quakers) and to provide a "religiously guarded education." The curricula of such schools tended to emphasize the study of the Scriptures. By the nineteenth century, the texts of Fox and Barclay had been replaced by ones written by more contemporary Quaker authors, Henry Tuke and Elisha Bates, complemented to some degree by a scientific ethos (Hole 1978, 57). Building on William Penn's recommendation (in *Some Fruits of Solitude)* that Friends engage in the study of the natural world, Quaker schools of the nineteenth century often provided instruction in science, particularly botany. The rural surroundings of many select schools facilitated this instruction. According to Helen Hole, science was generally "outstandingly taught" in Friends schools, in part because the experimental method in science was similar to the experimental method of Quaker spirituality (1978, 57). As Quakers advocated *firsthand* experience of the Divine, so scientific experimentation required *firsthand* experience of the material world (Loukes 1958, 59).

Many late nineteenth-century and early twentieth-century Quaker educators deliberated over how much to modify the "guarded education" pedagogy. During the second half of the nineteenth century, music, arts, fiction, and theater gradually entered the curricula of Quaker schools, while endeavors to maintain a strong religious and spiritual core within the curriculum met with varying degrees of success (Hole 1978, 59–71). The impulse to shield Quaker children from non-Quaker influences waned by the beginning of the twentieth century. However, when defined more broadly, guarded education is still relevant today, as proponents seek "to provide a supportive environment, good companions, and caring guardians, so young people could learn the habits which would enable them to live faithful lives in the world" (Lacey 1998, 168). According to Paul Lacey, "never has there been greater need to identify and guard what is most precious in educating the young" (Lacey 1998, 169).

THE WORLDWIDE SPREAD OF QUAKER PRIMARY AND SECONDARY EDUCATION

During the late nineteenth century, a number of Quaker schools were founded outside the United States and the UK. In 1887, Friends Girls School was founded in Tokyo, Japan (Tokyo Friends Girls Junior & Senior High), and, in the same year, Friends' School was established in Hobart, Australia. In 1889, the Girls' Training Home was established in Ramallah, with more informal work among Palestinian girls beginning two decades earlier (Ramallah Friends School). In Brummana, Lebanon, schools were founded with the help of Friends in the latter half of the nineteenth century (Brummana High School). In Ontario, Canada, West Lake Boarding School was founded in 1841 and then reestablished in 1878 as Pickering College (Garratt 1927, 303). In India, Quaker missionaries established schools in Jabalpur, Sohagpur, and Hoshangabad in the 1870s (Abbott 2012, 223; Robinson 1891, 237).

Friends established schools in other parts of the world during the twentieth and twenty-first centuries. In Guatemala, a Quaker girls' school was founded in 1908 and a boys' school opened in 1912; these schools were amalgamated and became the Friends School (Abbott 2012, 65). In the early 1900s, Quaker missionaries established schools in Bolivia; in the twenty-first century, this mission has continued through the Bolivian Quaker Education Fund (BQEF), which funds various educational ventures. A Friends school in Monteverde, Costa Rica, was established in 1951 by Friends who emigrated from the United States "in search of a non-militaristic society" (Monteverde Friends School). In Belize, convinced Friend Sadie Vernon began the Belize Continuation School in 1964, which provided an alternative education for teenage girls; the Friends Boys School was established in 1994 (Vernon 2000, 142).

After the Korean War (1950–53), Quakers helped establish schools in refugee camps in Kunsan, and the Friends Service Unit paid for Korean teachers (www.quakersintheworld.org/quakers-in-action/241). Quakers in Kenya have founded numerous primary and secondary schools, which are now funded and supervised by the Kenyan government (Rasmussen 1995, 112). Several Quaker schools in Rwanda and Mwananshuti Centre (Friends Peace House) provide vocational training to vulnerable and street children. A primary school (Samathonga School) is attached to Friends Rural Development Centre in Hlekweni, in Zimbabwe.

COLLEGE AND UNIVERSITY EDUCATION AMONG FRIENDS

Beginning in 1833, more than a dozen schools founded by Friends in the United States discerned a mission beyond secondary education and achieved status as a college, university, Bible institute or theological seminary, or some combination thereof. More Quaker higher educational institutions have been founded since 1917, especially in the Global South. The Friends Theological College in Kenya, founded in 1943 at Lugulu and later moved to Kaimosi, the Instituto Biblico de Formacion Teologica Jorge Fox, founded in 1980 in Honduras, and the Great Lakes School of Theology, founded in 1999 at Bujumbura, Burundi, are three examples of higher educational institutions established by Quakers in these regions. These colleges serve a vital role in training Quaker ministers for service in their home countries and regions. The focus of all three in preparing students for Friends' ministry are typical of Quaker schools for adults in Africa and Latin America, which often use a Bible Training School model (Abbott 2013, 555; Painter 1951, 110; Roberts 2013, 117; Welling 2013).

In England, however, Quakers have largely availed themselves of public universities. While Quakers were barred from fellowships at Oxford and Cambridge until 1871, University College London was open to them from its inception in 1826, but some Friends did not approve of a college that Thomas Arnold famously referred to as "that godless institution in Gower Street" (Campbell Stewart 1971, 57). Until well into the nineteenth century, aspiring Quaker teachers had few opportunities for advanced studies. In 1848, a Quaker teacher-training center was founded at Ackworth, known as the Flounders Institute. The course of studies at the institute was adapted to the examination requirements of University College London in 1858. In the twenty-first century, the academic study of Quakerism can be pursued at a postgraduate level at the Woodbrooke Quaker Study Centre, which offers masters' and doctoral degrees in Quaker studies, in partnership with the University of Birmingham and, in terms of its online programs, the University of Lancaster.

In the United States, the timing of the establishment of Quaker higher education was, according to Thomas Hamm, highly purposeful. Orthodox Friends founded most early Quaker colleges in the immediate aftermath of the Separation of 1827–28 (see Chapter 2, this volume, by Hamm and May). Orthodox Friends "were convinced that ignorance – ignorance of the Bible and the doctrines of early Friends – lay at the root of the schism" (Hamm 2007, 45). Some Friends hoped that better schooling might set all this aright. However, while Friends often proved adept at the fundraising, marketing, and other tasks that accompany the operation of a successful college or university, the mere opening of such an institution provoked a variety of other difficult questions that had to be addressed before setting up a curriculum or marketing their educational wares.

Foremost among these questions was, what should be the goals of Quaker higher education? This question had several kinds of answers. Some Quaker colleges perceived the need for a common religious doctrine embraced by faculty and students alike. For example, George Fox University and Malone University require faculty and students to agree to a common statement of faith. Other Quaker colleges see their Quaker mission more in terms of outward actions, students and faculty providing service to a broader community, for example, or adhering to Quaker testimonies of peace, simplicity, integrity, equality, temperance, and so forth. A third approach, perhaps stemming from the common statement by Friends that the core of their religious witness is to testify to Truth, finds the central purpose of Quaker higher education to fall in searching for that truth through the most rigorous disciplines in the sciences, social sciences, or humanities, and in reasoned and mutually respectful discourse. While these three emphases are not mutually exclusive – indeed, some Quaker colleges and universities would claim to achieve all three – Quaker institutions often prioritize one of these emphases above the others.

During the first half of the nineteenth century, many of these American Quaker colleges and universities were envisaged as "select" or "guarded" institutions that would primarily serve Friends. For a variety of reasons, no Quaker college or university would suggest that it has such a goal in the twenty-first century. One very practical reason is the marked decline in the number of Quaker students, faculty, and administrators in the colleges and universities founded by Friends. In the twenty-first century, many of these institutions have a student body that is less than 5 percent Quaker. In one of these universities, Friends University in Wichita, Kansas, the Quaker presence on the faculty has been described as "minimal" (Holmes 2007, 235); while there are more Quaker professors at other Quaker colleges and universities, in virtually all such institutions they constitute a small minority of the faculty. Various consequences flow from this. It is difficult for Quaker colleges to expect strong adherence to Quaker testimonies under such circumstances. Thus many colleges have loosened their prohibitions against the consumption of alcohol on campus, which also has coincided with declining emphasis of the temperance testimony among the Yearly Meetings that sponsor the college or provide most Quaker students. In more Evangelical institutions, the adherence to a guarded Quaker education has been replaced by the goal of living a good Christian life, beyond denominational identity.

At various times during the twentieth century, Quaker colleges faced numerous challenges, from within and without, over the peace testimony, especially during World Wars I and II and the Vietnam conflict. For some, antiwar actions were "an affront to those who had been drafted to fight" (Hodges, O'Donnell, and Oliver 2003, 514). In some cases, this led to a de-emphasis of the peace testimony on campus. On other campuses, this led to the establishment of Peace Studies programs so those students most interested in pursuing peace could find a suitable major, while other students and faculty could channel their efforts elsewhere.

HOLINESS REVIVALISM, MODERNISM, AND THE
EVOLUTION OF QUAKER COLLEGES

While Orthodox Quakers founded most Quaker colleges in the United States, this group suffered many internal tensions and divisions from the mid-nineteenth century onward that perforce affected the kind of education offered by Quaker colleges. None of these tensions was more important than the Holiness revivalism that swept through many Gurneyite Quaker meetings in the last third of the nineteenth century. This revivalism also aroused significant opposition among Gurneyites, and colleges often found themselves aligning with the revivalist or anti-revivalist position. In the aftermath of these momentous events, as we have seen elsewhere in this volume, many Quaker meetings decided to hire pastors.

By 1915, Haverford (Pennsylvania), Guilford (North Carolina), Earlham (Indiana), and Whittier (California) had all aligned themselves, or were in the process of aligning themselves, with the anti-revivalist position, and the religion departments at each institution were dominated by modernists who supported historical critical studies of the Bible. When a religion department was established at Whittier early in the twentieth century, it was with the understanding that "religion was to be primarily an object of study, not a creed to be adopted" (Kiley and Fairbanks 2007, 192). In such states as Indiana and Kansas, tensions existed between the Holiness Christian theology espoused by most Friends churches and the curricula of such institutions as Earlham, Whittier, and Friends University, curricula perceived by most local Friends as overly focused on "the social gospel and new scholarship" (Holmes 2007, 229). These institutions were thus subject to sharp attacks by local Friends of the Holiness persuasion (Hamm 2010).

As was the case with Quaker secondary schools, Quaker colleges were often outstanding in their science scholarship and education. This was certainly the case at Earlham, where biology professor Joseph Moore, an early Midwest advocate of evolution, dominated science education for the half century prior to his death in 1905 (Hamm 2007, 47). In 1920, Earlham faculty was charged with heresy by ministers of Indiana and Western Yearly Meetings for being "unsound" for their teaching of evolution, but an investigation exonerated the faculty of all charges.

Even without directly receiving ministerial training, in the wake of the recent growth of pastoral Quakerism, many Quaker college graduates used their education to go into ministry. A 1912 survey found that fifty-three alumni of Earlham were serving as ministers. Quaker colleges that had been in existence a shorter time than Earlham had lesser numbers of alumni in ministry:

William Penn College counted 34; Friends University, founded in 1898, could boast of only 11 (Hamm 2010). As the twentieth century progressed, however, Quaker options for ministerial and religious education increased markedly, both in variety and number.

By way of contrast, doctrinal orthodoxy became a dominant factor at such Quaker colleges as Cleveland Bible Institute (later Malone University) in Ohio, Haviland Bible Training School (now Barclay College) in Kansas, Union Seminary in Indiana, and the Training School for Christian Workers (later Azusa Pacific University) in California. Bible colleges, which typically had minimal requirements for admission, provided intensely practical training in ministry with the Bible as the central text, and they were low cost and not unique to the Friends' church (Hamm 2010). The Cleveland Bible College and the Training School for Christian Workers placed especial emphasis on the training of Christian missionaries. The first three Quaker missionaries bound for Kenya in 1902 hailed from the Cleveland Bible Institute. By its thirtieth anniversary, celebrated in 1930, the Training School for Christian Workers recognized 104 of its students who had served as missionaries in 14 countries or mission fields (Welling 2013).

J. Walter and Emma Malone, founders of the Cleveland Bible College, championed social reform work and "practical Christianity." The Malones condemned war, capital punishment, and abortion and strongly supported women's leadership and calls to ministry, including women's preaching. The college founded by the Malones, and other similar institutions, eventually incorporated many aspects of the liberal arts model into their courses. Yet several of these founders' emphases, such as the Malones' social stances, became unfashionable over time in Holiness Christian churches and consequently were downplayed or denied outright by the Malones' successors (Oliver 2007, 219). Pacific College (later George Fox University) in Oregon and William Penn College (in Iowa) wended a middle way through the early twentieth century, but in each case, college presidents perceived to be too friendly toward modernism were forced out in the 1940s. In Oregon, the Portland Bible Institute served for a time as a more fundamentalist alternative to Pacific (Burdick 2013). A 1957 survey of 185 Quaker pastors found that the largest number, 29, had graduated from the Cleveland Bible College; Earlham followed in second place, and William Penn College was third (Cooper 1985, 3–4).

EDUCATING STUDENTS ON THE MARGINS

Quaker concerns for education were not limited to fellow Quakers but often reached to those on the margins of society. At the beginning, these concerns were often intensely practical. It was hoped that education might help the poor avoid lives of crime and escape the vicious cycle of poverty. Additionally, Epistles from Yearly Meeting reminded Friends of their "Christian duty" to "exert their charitable assistance" to impoverished members of society (London Yearly Meeting 1818, 169, 198, 383). While Quakers believed in spiritual equality, this did not translate, at least in the early years of the movement, into a belief in a thoroughgoing social equality. Thus, the education that affluent Quakers planned and provided for the poor did not usually meet the standards of the education they would have expected for their own youth. The British Friends' Educational Society put the point this way in 1839: "The end object of instructing the poor should be to afford them the knowledge requisite to the due performance of the duties of their situations in life" (O'Donnell 2013, 406).

An early plan for affordable education directed toward the less affluent was produced by John Bellers (1654–1725), an English educational theorist (Lacey 1998, 113). One of Bellers's overriding concerns was the provision of education for the poor and the disabled. In 1695, he published *Proposals for Raising a College of Industry of All Useful Trades and Husbandry*, in which he argued that the huge disparity between the rich and poor was a moral issue that should not be ignored. While many of his contemporaries essentially accepted the utility of poverty, Bellers argued that useful, affordable schooling would greatly improve the material lives of the needy (Valenze 2006, 121; Lacey 1998, 114). Indeed, the Religious Society of Friends had sought to provide schooling for the children of poor members from early in its history; for example, in 1674, London Friends founded a school for the children of poor Friends, with free tuition furnished for all who were sponsored by their Monthly Meeting (O'Donnell 2013, 408). Friends' concern for educating the poor would eventually extend beyond the boundaries of their own sect, however.

By the mid-nineteenth century, a number of prominent British Quakers were involved in ventures that sought to help disadvantaged groups who lacked educational opportunities. This work could perhaps be regarded as an example of the "self-critical" philanthropy of that era; those who subscribed to this view of charity were "expected to give generously of their time and resources and to have a sustained personal involvement in their work" (Himmelfarb 1997, 52). Indeed, some Friends did not simply give money to charitable causes; they were interested in the projects themselves and gave of their time (Campbell Stewart 1971, 54). Personal interaction with the disadvantaged often heightened the Friends' sense of social responsibility. For example, in 1817, Elizabeth Fry (1780–1845) met a woman in Newgate Prison who had been sentenced to death for killing her child; later she wrote in her diary, "The whole affair has been truly afflicting to me; to see what poor mortals may be driven to." That same year, Fry founded the Association for the Improvement of the Female Prisoners in Newgate, which established a school, and provided materials so the prisoners could sew, knit, and make goods to sell (Corder 1853, 213).

Historian Alex Tyrrell has argued that the Friends First Day School Association was one of the most successful forms of working-class adult education during the nineteenth century (Tyrrell 1987, 154–55). The association was launched in December 1847 to coordinate the work of a number of schools that were already serving several towns. These schools were modeled on a Birmingham scheme instigated by the Quaker reformer Joseph Sturge (1793–1859). Sturge's idea for the first school had been inspired by his 1842 visit to a Sunday school run by a fellow Quaker, Samuel Fox, in Nottingham. Three years later, he persuaded some of the young Quakers of the Bull Street Meeting to organize a similar school in Birmingham for the working-class youths and young men of the town. A Quaker businessman, William White (1820–1900), was largely responsible for the expansion of the Adult School movement in Birmingham. A bookseller and printer, White became a teacher in 1848, a position he retained for more than fifty years (Rae 1903, 347). The movement was particularly strong in York; by 1905, there were 13 adult schools in the city with 2,648 members (Watts 2015, 187). Joseph Rowntree II (1836–1925), the Quaker philanthropist and chocolatier, was a teacher in the first adult school in York.

In his history of adult education in Great Britain, Thomas Kelly reports 29,000 students attended Quaker adult schools by the end of nineteenth century (Kelly 1992, 204; Aldrich et al. 2013, 213). In numerous towns and cities, the Society's adult schools helped shape local community life, and many Quaker teachers were deeply impacted by their work. Through close and regular interaction with their students, teachers were exposed to pertinent social and political issues, such as homelessness, inadequate housing conditions, prostitution, alcoholism, and mental health disorders (Chrystal 2013, 34). William White's experience as an teacher in an adult school informed his work as chairman of the Improvement Committee that cleared a section of the Birmingham slums in 1876. George Cadbury's (1839–1922) model village in Bournville was largely the outcome of his encounters with students who lived in those crowded and unsanitary back-to-backs (Masterman 1920, 76). In a speech written for a conference of the Society of Friends, the Quaker philanthropist Elizabeth Taylor Cadbury (1858–1951) declared: "Probably our Adult Classes have saved our Society; they have enlarged our views and now we must solve the problem – why are we more successful in our Adult Schools than in our Meetings for Worship?" (Wolfson Centre for Archival Research, MS466/1/1/10/1/5).

In the United States, Quakers engaged in several notable efforts to educate African Americans. Typically, prior to the mid-twentieth century, most Quaker schools for African Americans were segregated. (There were a few exceptions in the Midwest.) Of these schools, two were especially noteworthy, the Institute for Colored Youth (ICY), founded in Philadelphia in 1837, which survives today as Cheyney University, and Southland College, founded in 1864 near Helena, Arkansas, and closed in 1925. In both colleges, religious instruction was highly valued. The standard of education at ICY was seen to be equal to that received by whites, and a recent study has concluded that the "Institute was an important step in advancing academic opportunities for African Americans" (Genovese 2015, 249, 251). As the more vocationally oriented "industrial education" philosophy of Booker T. Washington became fashionable around 1900, the curriculum of Southland College shifted from more academic pursuits toward industrial education (Kennedy 2009, 114). The high success rate of ICY graduates points to the great impact of Quaker educational endeavors for African Americans in Philadelphia (Genovese 2015, 253).

In the mid-twentieth century, two Quaker schools in Continental Europe served as a place of refuge for children who lacked access to educational opportunities. German Quakers provided the impetus for the foundation of a school for children whose families faced persecution in Nazi Germany. As a result of this vision, Quaker School Eerde was established near Ommen in Holland in 1934 (Lichti 2008, 192; Schmitt 1997, 75–84, 129–33, 199–202). During its operation, pupils received an education that would have been denied them by Nazi racial decrees. After the Greek Civil War, Friends helped establish the Girls' Domestic Training School in Salonika, Greece, as a refuge for young Greek women. This school was unique in Greece; no other institution provided such a practical and comprehensive program for young women at this time (Marder 1979, 378–81). In addition to reading, writing, and arithmetic, the students were taught farming skills, home economics, childcare, gardening, and simple animal husbandry.

During the mid-to-late twentieth century in the United States, there was a shift away from racially segregated teaching patterns toward a more thoroughgoing racial equality in Quaker education at all levels. There has also been a great strengthening of the "equality" testimony, galvanized by the concern to increase diversity in racial backgrounds and other student characteristics on Quaker campuses. Until the mid-twentieth century, most East Coast Quaker schools excluded African American students. The board of Sidwell Friends School in Washington, DC, voted to integrate in 1956, but it took 11years for the first African American students to graduate from Sidwell, in 1967 (Zug 2009, 42–44). Haverford did not hire its first African American faculty member, sociologist Ira Reid, until 1946, and its first black student born in the United States, Paul Moses, graduated in 1951. A black student from Jamaica had previously graduated from Haverford in 1926 (Szi 2015). No African American students attended Swarthmore prior to 1943 (Densmore 2007), nor did any attend Guilford College, in Greensboro, North Carolina, until 1963. Gwen Erickson has pointed out that "Guilford was by no means a leader" in racial integration, even in its region, the South (2007, 36). The same can be said of many other Quaker schools. In the Midwest and the West, the situation for African Americans attending Quaker colleges was slightly different. There generally was no bar against their attendance of Quaker colleges in those regions, and Earlham College (in Indiana) and Whittier (in California) admitted African American students in the nineteenth century. Of Earlham, however, one scholar writes that until the mid-twentieth century, African American students were "few in number and often faced petty harassment" (Hamm 2007, 54). In general, the drive to admit more African American students coincided with the civil rights movement, and often its later stages; for example, African American students put pressure on a receptive Haverford College to increase minority enrollment during the early 1970s (Szi 2015; Peterson 2007, 16).

QUAKER SEMINARIES AND OTHER ADULT RELIGIOUS EDUCATIONAL ENDEAVORS

Other models of Quaker adult religious education followed the introduction of Bible colleges. With the backing of industrialist George Cadbury, John Wilhelm Rowntree, and others, the Woodbrooke Settlement for Religious and Social Study was established in Birmingham, England, in 1903, for the purposes of studying Quaker approaches to the Bible, to social service, and to the history and current practices of Friends. After Rufus Jones determined that he should continue his work in America and decline the offer of becoming the first director of Woodbrooke, the erudite, evangelical, and mystical J. Rendel Harris accepted the position (Hamm 2010). The Woodbrooke model was attractive to liberal American Friends, especially on the East Coast, and led to similar types of institutions being established there, most notably, Pendle Hill in Wallingford, Pennsylvania, a Quaker adult education center that offered various non-degree and non-credit forms of instruction in Biblical studies, Quakerism, and other aspects of religion. British Friend Henry Hodgkin became the first director but died soon after Pendle Hill's founding in 1930. Howard and Anna Brinton provided Quaker leadership for decades. According to Douglas Gwyn's study of Pendle Hill, the work of the Brintons and others implicitly focused on "Personalism," a form of liberal Christian theology based on the claims that the greatest reality is personality, both divine and human, and that the loving personality of Jesus is a guide to this reality (2014a).

In terms of Quaker adult religious education, the foundation of theological seminaries has been a recent innovation. Since the inception of the pastoral system among Friends, these had been feared by some who keenly felt the import of the early Quaker admonition that being trained at Oxford or Cambridge did not make someone fit to be a minister. In 1887, Mary S. Thomas of Baltimore Yearly Meeting warned the Conference of Friends in Richmond, Indiana, that if they gave approval to the pastoral system, Friends would "find the theological seminary at the end of it." Thomas was correct, but it took nearly three-quarters of a century for her prophecy to come true (General Conference of Friends 1887, 254). Some Friends in the first half of the twentieth century dreamed of a Quaker seminary, but Friends' geographic dispersion and doctrinal disagreements made the fulfillment of such a dream difficult. Quakers who desired the kind of ministerial training that would be provided by seminary education went to a plethora of other schools. Finally, in 1960, with the leadership of Landrum Bolling, then Earlham College president, Wilmer Cooper, who would become the founding dean of the new seminary, and numerous other persons, the first Quaker theological seminary, the Earlham School of Religion (ESR), was founded, granting degrees in masters of arts and masters of ministry (the latter being the equivalent of a masters of divinity degree in other seminaries). In 1985, after a quarter-century of operation, Bolling reflected on the success of this venture, writing that ESR "drew more students than once we thought would ever be possible ... and our graduates went to serve in more different kinds of Quaker communities and institutions than we had any right to hope for" (Cooper 1985, xiv).

Subsequently, in 1996, George Fox University would merge with Western Evangelical Seminary, which had previously been a Wesleyan Holiness seminary, bringing a second theological seminary under Quaker higher education administration. By the twenty-first century, various other Quaker educational institutions, in addition to Earlham and George Fox, would offer masters' degrees in different aspects of training for religious ministry and service.

QUAKER PRIMARY AND SECONDARY EDUCATION,
"SELECT" TAKES ON A DIFFERENT MEANING

Quaker education has always had to balance the ideal and the practical, and its most persistent practical challenge has invariably been how it can be paid for. As early as 1695, there were reports that tuition income from Quaker students was insufficient to pay a living wage to the teachers in Friends schools, a pattern often replicated since then (Lacey 1998; 87). The early nineteenth-century Lancastrian system issued, first and foremost, from the need for inexpensive education for the poor. With the help of student monitors, a single teacher could instruct hundreds of students; other supposed benefits of that system came as an afterthought (Lacey 1998, 128–29). The inability of many Quaker families to pay the expense of Quaker education remains a pressing issue even in the twenty-first century. In 1978, Helen Hole noted that the training of Quaker teachers and their subsequent employment will always be an expensive proposition, and she advocated that the Religious Society of Friends "rearrange its priorities" in order to generously support Quaker education (Hole 1978, 125). The kind of cost cutting that the Lancastrian system entailed is no longer seen as acceptable; yet, for many reasons, the expense of Quaker education has grown even greater.

For reasons of expense, as well as a shifting conception of their mission, Friends schools are no longer "select" in the previous sense of the word, not even if they retain the word "select" in their names. That is, Friends schools increasingly educate non-Friends, who are often best able to bear the significant expense of private education. The reverse proposition is also true. Increasing numbers of Quaker children are educated in state schools, or in homeschooling. A 1996 survey of American Friends schools showed that of the student body of the average Friends school, 6 percent were Quaker students. On average, the faculty of these schools was 15 to 20 percent Quaker (Hamm 2003, 114).

Some of these schools, however, have become "select" in quite another sense of the word, as they have become highly sought-after places for the children of American political and economic elites to gain a private education with refined, but not overly religious, values. Three children of US presidents, Chelsea Clinton in the 1990s and Malia and Sasha Obama beginning in 2009, have attended Sidwell Friends School in Washington, DC, as well as the children of many other prominent persons in the United States. It would be fair to see Friends schools such as Sidwell as among the most elite educational institutions in the United States.

Reflecting on such developments, H. Larry Ingle, a Quaker and scholar of Quakerism, who taught in public universities, is one who has decried these recent trends in the strongest terms. He laments that Quakers "scrounge and dig and borrow and beg to build endowments to maintain buildings and pay teachers to teach other people's children, mostly children of the rich and famous." Quaker schools, like other private schools, serve mainly as a means for elite status to be passed on from generation to generation. Consequently, Ingle regards "Friends schools as a major liability, essentially refuges for children of the well-off and the well-to-do of whatever religious faith or none" (Ingle 2010, 14).

A vigorous rejoinder to arguments such as Ingle's has been made by journalist, Friend, and graduate of Quaker institutions Brenda Beadenkopf, who notes the importance of teaching Quaker testimonies at Sidwell even to those who do not belong to the Society of Friends. Beadenkopf believes "'that of God' in Malia and Sasha [Obama] will be treasured and kept safe at Sidwell Friends, as many graduates of Friends schools can attest" (2010, 39). She explains that her "standout take-away experience" of Quaker education was that of the "overwhelming and awesome, non-judgmental acceptance youngsters feel in the open arms of loving Friends, teachers, and students" (2010, 39). Contemporary Quaker schools might define and demonstrate "Quakerliness" in different ways, but all prioritize various forms of social action and maintain a reflective ethos, in both the classroom and community. Paul Lacey, quoting Thomas Farquhar, former head of Westtown School, calls this "worship across the curriculum" (Lacey 1998, 11).

CONCLUSION

Throughout Quaker history, Quaker schools have been a major way for Friends and non-Friends alike to encounter Quaker beliefs, practices, and testimonies. Quaker education has made its mark in many ways. At times, it is the worship and spirituality found in Quaker schools that has been most notable. Schools associated with the Society of Friends often place a high value on a student's "inner life," and ample space is given for silence and reflection. At other times, Quaker values and testimonies have served as an attracting force, as many Quaker schools have chosen as their guiding principles such aims as equality, peaceableness, integrity, and service. Like other private religious schools, Quaker schools and colleges often have a strong academic reputation, but their close attention to other dimensions of human development often makes them attractive to Friends and non-Friends alike. At the same time, Quaker schools have faced challenges over the years, often related to the need for greater inclusion of low-income families and racial minorities. Yet overall, it seems likely that a strong demand for Quaker educational institutions will continue, and that the endeavor to define the purposes of Quaker education will persist, as scholars and practitioners continue to push and pull toward (or away from) the many ideals that can be embodied in Quaker schools.

SUGGESTED FURTHER READING

Campbell Stewart, W. A. (1971). *Quakers and Education as Seen in Their Schools in England*, London: Kennikat Press.

Hole, Helen G. (1978). *Things Civil and Useful, a Personal View of Quaker Education*, Richmond, IN: Friends United Press.

Lacey, Paul A. (1998). *Growing into Goodness, Essays on Quaker Education*, Wallingford, PA: Pendle Hill Publications and Friends Council on Education.

Oliver, John W., Jr., Charles L. Cherry, and Caroline Cherry. (2007). *Founded by Friends, the Quaker Heritage of Fifteen American Colleges and Universities*, Lanham, MD: Scarecrow Press.

Painter, Levinus King. (1966). *The Hill of Vision, the Story of the Quaker Movement in East Africa, 1902–1965*, East Africa Yearly Meeting of Friends.

The Changing World of Quaker Material Culture

Emma Jones Lapsansky

"Quakers? They're all dead, aren't they?" That question arises surprisingly often, as modern audiences, their ideas shaped by images of seventeenth-century Pennsylvania founder William Penn (and perhaps by those of nineteenth-century abolitionist/peace activist Lucretia Mott) associate "Quakers" with distinctive drab clothing, with archaic language that includes "thee" and "thou," and with somber morality. If people who "dress funny" and "talk funny" are not obvious in the modern world, does that mean that Quakers – and Quakerism – are dead? In fact, the evolution of the Quaker religion, through time and geography, has left Quakers quite alive, though, in many ways, the modern-day hybrid religion is much transformed from its English roots. Beginning with the foundations of Quakerism, and moving through its diaspora out of seventeenth-century rural England, this chapter explores aspects of the origins of Quakers' thinking about how day-to-day choices of objects and behaviors might best reflect their theology. The guiding concepts of what founding Friends spoke of as "plain" or "unostentatious" have remained an important touchstone of Quakers' vocabulary and identity for more than three centuries. Over time, however, the language, interpretations, and implications of those concepts have been shaped and reshaped by region, culture, and circumstance. Situating the beginnings of Quaker thought in an international context, we examine distinctive ideas, speech, clothing, building design, and other markers of what Quakers called "outward" customs, as a way of reflecting their "inward" religious commitment.

QUAKERS IN THE EARLY MODERN WESTERN WORLD: THE PLAIN LIFE

The emergence of the Religious Society of Friends (Quakers) coincided with significant markers of a modernizing Western world – including an embryonic market economy in the Atlantic world, and the dissemination of democratizing ideas heralded by England's John Locke and other Enlightenment thinkers such as Dutch philosopher Baruch Spinoza, and France's Rene Descartes. Increasingly powerful technologies and international economies allowed Europeans to move about the globe, creating new fortunes. Simultaneously, as Enlightenment sensibilities challenged entrenched symbols of hierarchy and authority, Quakers added their unique voice to a chorus of modernists, insisting that what William Penn called "true religion" should reflect "equality" and "natural rights," should resist arbitrary obeisance to authorities, and should strip away the "needless" things of the physical world. Early Quakers contended that all souls were equal before God, and – dismissing the worldly authority of titles and credentials – they maintained that formal training for clergy was unnecessary. Other manifestations of this resistance to established norms and authority included Quakers' refusal to acknowledge some of what traditionally had been material symbols of power, wealth, and social status. Clothing that announced one's social standing, the use of deferential language and postures when addressing one's social "betters," and architecture and decorative arts that announced one's high status in the economic pyramid were among the norms that Quakers shunned, in their efforts to strip away "worldly" paraphernalia. Friends argued that by jettisoning such "outward things," they could facilitate a direct intimacy with God, and a "True," unfettered devotion to, and practice of, Christianity. In Quakers' theology, neither the robes and castles of kings nor the vestments and cathedrals of clergy should be allowed to distract one from that "True" and direct connection between human beings and Divine Power (Frost 2003, 18–20).

In 1686, British Quaker Joan Vokins explained the practice of these values to her children: "Be careful and take heed that you do not stain the testimony of [religious] Truth that you have received, by wearing needless things and following the world's fashions in your clothing and attire, but remember how I have bred you up." Vokins had "bred her children up" to follow guidelines that were also voiced by her contemporary Robert Barclay, who cautioned his compatriots not to "adorn themselves in the use of their clothes as to beset them with things having no real use or necessity, but merely for ornament sake, to gratify a vain, proud, and ostentatious mind." On his deathbed in 1704, another Quaker warned his family to "be careful that you follow not the vanities of the age in pride and ostentation," but rather "keep plain in your habits and houses" (i.e., clothing, speech, homes, and worship buildings) (Lapsansky-Werner and Verplanck 2003).

Thus there developed an insiders' vocabulary, codifying the objectives within Friends' communities. "Vanity," "pride," "ostentation," and "ornament" were to be avoided. The "needless things" dictated by "the world's fashions" should be shunned. "Useful" things and "necessities" should be embraced. But how to translate these objectives into the practices of daily life? What did – and does – it mean to "keep plain" in "habits and houses"? These questions have bedeviled Quakers for more than three centuries, for Quakers have had an easier time defining what does *not* meet their ethical principles and values than interpreting what constitutes the acceptable acquisitions and behaviors. There was – and is – also the risk of allowing ritualized or prescribed choices to *substitute* for those values. Vokins's comrades quickly pointed out some of those risks: "It's a dangerous thing," wrote Margaret Fell in the 1680s, "to lead Friends much into the [definition and] observance of outward things ... For they can get into an outward garb, but this will not make them into true Christians" (Fox 1710, 535). Over succeeding centuries, Friends' communities have endeavored to define, and to be mindful of, the dynamic relationship between "outward garb" and true Christianity, sometimes establishing committees to discern and to discipline behaviors that were inconsistent with the "plain" life.

In the pursuit of a "True" Christianity, early Friends took some of their inspiration from language and imagery they gleaned from their interpretations of biblical passages – especially from Paul's admonitions in the New Testament – which explained that Christ "has come to teach his people himself." According to Quaker theology, Christ intended to draw together a cadre of "peculiar people, zealous of good works" (Letter to Titus 1–2). Since those good works included dissolving distinctions between aristocrats and commoners, and emphasizing the equal of human souls, Quakers opted for "plain" language that refused to acknowledge social distinctions (hence, the avoidance of the use of the formal "you" and "your" when addressing one's social "betters," in favor of using the informal "thee," "thou," and "thy" for everyone). Rejecting the custom of "hat honor" (e.g., deferential doffing of one's hat when greeting someone of higher social status) was yet another manifestation of "plain-ness." Defying traditional sumptuary laws and customs that obliged one to dress in keeping with his/her "station" in society, Friends – sometimes even wealthy ones – advocated a modesty, humility, and frugality in clothing fabric, color, and design that eventually evolved into a formulaic costume of unadorned, often undyed, garb. In the Bible such a life was described as "sober" and "temperate" (Titus 1). And Friends made a virtue of the fact that, in the early years of their movement, they worshiped outdoors or in members' homes. Then, when official gathering places were erected, they were purposely limited to restrained scale and design to demonstrate Friends' nonconformity with what they viewed as the excesses of their day – including the ornate architecture that arose from the rebuilding of London's churches and public buildings in the wake of the Restoration and the destructive fire of 1666 (Frost 2003, 21–23).

The goals of "True Christianity" also included what, in modern times, might be described as an "environmentalist" perspective. For example, Quaker tradition soon came to look down on wasteful or ostentatious use of natural resources, as evidenced by Penn's complaint that the "very trimming [on the clothing] of the vain would clothe the naked" (Frost 2003, 20). According to this logic, the creation, promotion, and consumption of worldly things that used up more than minimal time, energy, or natural resources should be avoided, lest people of means take up more than their "fair share" of the finite resources of time and materials. But even in this guideline, there was ambiguity, as at least one Quaker thinker suggested that it was acceptable for a wealthy Quaker to define "plain" more lavishly than for a Quaker of lesser means (Barclay 2002). By the twentieth century, as the gap widened between wealthy and deprived nations and communities, this concept would be expressed as "liv[ing] simply, so that others may simply live" (www.quakersintheworld.org/quakers-in-action/134).

George Fox, William Penn, and others of the idealistic seventeenth-century Quakers who shaped this theology against the backdrop of their shared English culture and vocabulary assumed that words such as "needful" and "ostentation" would be easily understood. However, as Friends fanned out across the world and encountered places and peoples far from their English moorings, it became more difficult to define and to maintain a consistent meaning and practice of "plain," "needful," or "ostentatious." Clothing, architecture, interior design, and language were all undergoing critical changes during the era when the Religious Society of Friends was developing its ideas and its communities; yet Quakers aimed to distinguish themselves in each of these manifestations of culture. Lacking specificity in the guidelines for "plain," "simple," or "needless," the concept often came to be associated with "nonconformist," and Quaker orthodoxy often came to be defined as whatever was out of fashion. It is clear, however, that by the end of the eighteenth century, the terms "plain" and "simple" were often used to describe Quakers' uniqueness, not only by Friends themselves but also by non-Friends describing Quaker culture. For example, a 1784 narrative by French commentator St. John de Crevecoeur includes a reference to Quaker "simplicity" (Justice 1905, 41–63).

The concept of simplicity or "plain-ness" was – and is – intended to help Quakers maintain a disciplined life, free from distractions, and designed to create the setting for an intense and focused inward religious experience. But the discourse about what constituted plain and simple, enjoined as early as the seventeenth century, was not only designed to help Friends *themselves* find salvation. William Penn was concerned that not only Quaker communities but society as a whole was impoverished, because in making luxury goods, workers' energies were deflected from making, or doing, such "needful" things as attending to prayer or attending to the physical and spiritual health of both Quakers and non-Quakers. Thus, from earliest times, some common aspects of daily practice (e.g., music or gambling) were forbidden, or severely limited, by Quaker faith and practice. Through the eighteenth century, fiction, theater, music, portraiture, decorative home furnishings, and other manifestations of the "fine arts" were viewed with suspicion in Quaker communities. Such indulgences – "un-needful" in the view of many Friends – absorbed energies that should be better deployed. For some – but by no means all – Friends, abstinence also carried an implied critique of the emerging international market economy in general, which, they believed, excited the passions and fueled an acquisitiveness that was – in the words of eighteenth-century Quaker stalwart John Woolman – "unquiet" (Kett 2014, 60). Scholars continue to explore when and how the language, concept, and practice of plain-ness and simplicity have developed over time. There is evidence that some mid-nineteenth-century British Friends considered the possibility that plain-ness might be mostly an inner state of being, even as some Quakers in America insisted that a distinctive style of dress was a necessary component of simplicity (Collins 1996, 277–288; 2000, 121–139; Homan 2013).

CLOTHING AND TEXTILES

Textile historian Adriene Hood maintains that in the eighteenth-century Atlantic world, fabric was so labor intensive that it not only represented a sizable household investment but also helped usher in modern capitalist consumer culture. In the seventeenth century, acquiring and processing flax (linen), hemp, cotton, and animal skins had been time consuming. In addition, tools, time, and skill for spinning, weaving, dyeing, and sewing were in short supply. Hence, most clothing was of coarse fabric and monotonous design: for all but a privileged minority, it was crude, colorless, drab, and sparse. For the wealthy and or urban households, however, textiles might be imported, and the wealthy might display their privilege through the higher quality and perhaps varied design and coloring of French or Asian products, which contrasted sharply with the utilitarian home-spun materials procured and processed locally by those of lesser means (Hood 1996, 56–66). In England, royalty and nobles could thus advertise their status through ostentatious clothing, which often involved superfluous fabric displayed as elaborate collars, ruffles, and billowing skirts. Part of the commitment to matching one's outward behavior and appearances to one's inward simplicity, therefore, involved even well-to-do Quakers sometimes choosing to eschew fine linens and imported silks in favor of less-refined fabric and unadorned construction (Frost 2003, 15).

The choice to forgo elaborate clothing was not just about solidarity with the poor. As eighteenth-century techniques increased the availability of cotton, some Quakers became uneasy about the connection between textile production and various forms of exploitative labor (Walvin 2014, 170–71). American Quaker John Woolman refused to wear dyed clothing and wrote passionately about his concern over the health risks to workers who produced and worked with the toxic chemicals needed to create colored fabrics (Plank 2012, 87). Woolman, who spent many years of his life in England, was also among a cadre of outspoken British and American Quakers who were troubled by the connection between cotton and slave labor. So, too, were they concerned about the exploitation behind the sugar that had become the *sine qua non* of the stylish cups of tea that arrived from Asia to grace the tables of Britain's wealthy households. And Woolman cautioned against the use of precious metals and gems for household items or personal adornment. All of these, he argued, were examples of the privileged living a life of luxury at the expense of the lives of workers whose health was impaired by laboring to produce these "vanities of the age."

However, as eighteenth-century technology and capitalism spread unaccustomed wealth around the Atlantic rim, Quakers, surrounded by an ever-broadening array of consumer goods, sought to align their identity and their plain-ness proscriptions in the light of the new realities. For many wealthy Friends – especially in the New World – "simplicity" increasingly translated into what one historian has described as "of the best sort, but plain," which described a taste for goods of very high-quality (and often expensive) materials and skilled craft work, but devoid of such "useless and superfluous things [as] striped or flower'd stuffs" (Tolles 1963, 126).

The complexities were legion as Atlantic rim capitalism and consumerism grew increasingly robust. Friends' commitments to a simple level of consumption ironically were complicated by the disjunction between two high-minded facets of Quaker faith: (1) an emphasis on hard work, meticulous skilled craft, and scrupulously ethical business practices and (2) an equally important emphasis on frugality/simplicity. The result was a prosperity and surplus capital that severely strained Friends' self-restraint. Thus, as Frederick Tolles described it, many Friends were soon numbered among the wealthiest residents of their communities; one result was some Friends making seeming compromises by purchasing high-quality, but somber, consumer goods: "Of the best sort – but plain," sometimes became the index of simplicity (Tolles 1963, 123). Thus, eighteenth-century affluent Friends began to interpret plain and needful in ways that allowed them to take pleasure in the luxuries that could be procured with their rising wealth.

For many Friends, however, the nineteenth century saw the return to coarse fabrics, lifeless colors, and unadorned styling, as more Quakers – especially in America – adopting reform causes, came to associate elaborate textile production (cotton, indigo, ochre) with oppressive working conditions (Kraak 2000, 51–63). In her article "The Language of Clothes," fashion historian Alison Lurie has argued that clothing – how many layers, how many changes of clothing for specific events or times of day, as well as what body shape fashion caters to – have, for many centuries, been indicators of a person's status and/or philosophical posture within his or her culture or society (2000, 62). Whereas early Quakers sought to make confrontational statements about this reality, and to position themselves to organize their lives and their households to avoid having their identity be categorized by outward things, the mid-nineteenth century sometimes saw Quaker plain dress and behaviors evolve into a readily identifiable "uniform" – drab colors and a distinctive bonnet for women, collarless dark coat for men. Such an image of Quakers' dress was widely circulated in treatises, fiction, and caricatures, composed by Quakers and non-Quakers alike (Backhouse 1833; Ellis 1858; Lippard 1845; Gurney 1860). The 1850s American antislavery novel *Uncle Tom's Cabin* portrayed a stern, austerely clad Quaker: benign, moralistic, nonconformist, and aloof from the prevailing styles of the era. This novel, translated into numerous languages, was soon distributed worldwide. Similarly, a late-nineteenth-century popular American "dime novel" series featured "Old Broadbrim," a Quaker detective who reinforced this stereotype, and a number of twentieth-century British and American films cemented these images (Stowe 1852; Rathborne 1902; Butterworth 2015).

In the twentieth century, as clothing became relatively inexpensive, Friends distinctive sartorial tastes became less obvious. Still, many Quakers, continuing to view their choice of clothing as a measure of their disregard for outward things, tended to steer away from high-fashion trends, expensive fabrics, and clothing produced under exploitative conditions (e.g., see www.quakerjane .com/spirit.friends/plain_dress-.html;
www.quakerjane.com/spirit.friends/plain_dress-plainquakers.html)

ARCHITECTURE AND DECORATIVE ARTS

Interpreting and embodying the slippery concepts of "plain" and "simple" in architecture presented yet another set of challenges. Unlike clothing, a structure built as a house of worship was both permanent (or planned to be so!) and visible to passers-by. What would Quakers want their worship houses to say about them, in the present and in the future?

In addition, unlike a structure designed to reflect the tastes or interpretation of one individual, or even one family, the design of a worship house reflects a shared and negotiated vision of a community. And there were other constraints for early meetinghouses – the availability of building materials, the skills and limitations of local builders, as well as the dictates of such variables as climate, function, and practicality.

Early Quaker founders – who preferred to proselytize in public spaces – left little guidance. When pressed, George Fox recommended that existing buildings, such as a barn, might be renovated to serve the needs of indoor worship. Raising the building a few inches off the cold or damp ground would be more "wholesome," Fox suggested, and a sturdy slate roof, plastered walls, and a porch would add to the practicality and longevity of the structure (LaVoie 2003, 158). No steeple or imagery, no ornate windows, no pulpit, no architectural features – such as a pulpit, a baptistery, or a nave – should detract from the direct connection to the Divine by defining worship ritual, sacraments, or authority. Fox also recommended that local materials and local builders should be used to contain costs. Thus, early meetinghouses, subject to the limitations of the builders' experience, often resembled stripped-down adaptations of British rural parish churches, which, as scholar Roger Homan has noted, were the prototypes of "a ubiquitous character before there was a style." This "character" – first defined less by "surface of style" and more by "depth of spirit" – soon became something of a formula, as clothing had done (Homan 2013, 493). Nevertheless, the pattern of Friends' meeting – a worship service that included both men and women in one room, then the retiring of the women to separate, smaller quarters to carry out the "business" of the women's subdivision – dictated the practical layout of early Quaker meetinghouses (LaVoie 2003, 159–62). Even as Friends' communities spread across the North Atlantic and into the South Pacific, the tradition of a square meeting room long remained a norm, with a smaller room attached, and large windows throughout to let in natural light.

Several modern Friends buildings, conceived, constructed, and/or renovated in the late twentieth century, suggest the persistence of the vaguely defined but enduring commitment to simplicity, even as Quaker liturgy has evolved over time and geography (Homan 2013, 501–3). For example, the Friends Meeting of San Antonio, Texas, describes its sleek modern building as embodying "a quiet, contemplative setting for meditative worship ... inspired by the functional and simple spaces of early meetinghouses ... [of] extremely durable, low-maintenance material derived from recycled paper – a modern, sustainable interpretation of vernacular design" (www .sanantonioquakers.org/meetinghouse/meetinghouse.htm). Though the San Antonio, Texas, meetinghouse has continued the tradition of avoiding a steeple, the Friends Church of North Olmsted Ohio (founded in 1968) does have a belfry, and in Bolivia, home to more than 17 percent of the world's Quakers, meetinghouses range from very spare to quite ornate, depending upon location and availability of local materials.

As important as the meetinghouse conception and design were – and are – the *process* by which meetinghouses were conceived and constructed was equally important. The process involves a community decision-making procedure, wherein a committee consisting of members of the meeting either erect the building themselves or choose a builder with whom they work closely to ensure that the community's goals are met. Even as older buildings are modernized, the goal of remaining true to traditional guidelines is an important aspect of the project. In the early twenty-first century, when England's Doncaster (Balby) Meeting renovated its three-century-old building, the community kept a watchful eye over the old traditions that dictated a spare and serviceable design (www .doncasterquakers.org.uk/node/7).

Domestic architecture for Quakers – their homes, barns, and workplaces – was, from the earliest times, governed by the same principles of serviceability-over-adornment that informed public spaces. As architectural historian Bernard Herman has described them, Quaker homes were often "characterized by their durability," even as "Quaker builders drew on and shaped the broader architectural aesthetic of the [era and] region [in which they worked]" (Herman 2003, 189, 201). However, argues Herman, Quakers early established an enduring tradition of homes that were "furnished and refurnished in the context of the material culture of worldliness." While early Friends may have adhered to principles, Herman argues, "if early Quakers were 'plain', they were clearly not self-effacing" (Herman 2003, 201). As modern interpreters struggle to identify and define a consistent "style" that is "Quakerly," they are stymied by the diversity that characterizes what various Quaker architects, cabinet makers, and interior designers define as "plain."

RELIGIOUS LITURGY, RITUAL, AND AUTHORITY

Quakerism, born in the confrontation between Catholic and emerging Protestant cultures, which identified its worship houses and ecclesiastical leaders through visual and ritualistic symbols, has – over several centuries – remained in conversation with the surrounding realities. Whereas early Quakers turned their backs on what they saw as outward religious indicators, preferring instead to "wait in silence" for divine inspiration to lead any member of their gathered group to disseminate God's word, some modern Friends construct worship spaces to support baptism, holy communion, chants and anthems, and worship services led by formally educated clergy focusing on prepared services and liturgy (Johns 2013, 261–73).

The decision-making process – often called by Friends "Meeting for Worship with attention to Business" – is, for many Quakers, the keystone of Quaker theology and community life. In 1963, Thomas S. Brown described it thus: "The basis upon which we hold . . . [Quaker] . . . meetings for business . . . is that this is God's world, that God has unfinished business for us to do, and that it is possible for us to ascertain God's will for us in this world" (Brown 1963, 5). Created in the context of the moral equality of each member of the Quaker community, business meetings aim (with mixed success) to operate as if the Divine voice may speak through anyone present. Traditionally, no formal "rules of order" govern business meeting procedures. Instead, Brown describes a "period of worship prior to the undertaking of business . . . long enough to permit Friends to put aside the heat and tumult of the day's anxieties and to enter into the quietness that comes from trust in God and in God's concern for the affairs of men and women" (Brown 1963, 6). Thus is simplicity factored into the decision making of most Quaker communities, from constructing a budget, to choices about community programs and building design, to questions of disciplining an errant member (Johns 2013, 266).

However, an important aspect of Quaker theology is the idea of "continuing revelation": the belief that religious "truth" is continually being revealed over time. Hence, the day-to-day practice of simplicity has been repeatedly evaluated, as technology, the market economy, geographic attenuation from British customs, and encounters with worldwide cultures remain in dialogue with – and repeatedly push against – the lifestyle that early Quakers had sought to create. For example, as Britain colonized the Americas, and Friends crossed the Atlantic in that diaspora, joining their compatriots in slavery and the African slave trade, Quakers found themselves struggling with the question not only of whether bondage implied violence toward the enslaved but also with the implications of whether slavery encouraged excess and arrogance among slave*holders*. Similarly, as luxury consumer goods – tea, fine furniture, ornate architectural detailing, and carriages – became more accessible, some Quakers readjusted their plain-ness barometers to deem such items acceptable, as long as they were manufactured in the context of high ethical standards.

By the end of the eighteenth century, there arose an idealized notion of the "simple Quaker," ever-patient, ever-kind, ever a model of Christian virtue. Codified as early as 1806 by Thomas Clarkson's romanticized *Portraiture of Quakerism* (Clarkson 1806), this imagery endured as the scaffolding for literary narratives such as Harriet Beecher Stowe's *Uncle Tom's Cabin*. However, as Quakerism entered the twentieth century, it also entered parts of the world far distant – both geographically and culturally – from the setting of its roots. In the American West, in Africa, Asia, and South America, plainness and simplicity merged with the norms of local residents, to embrace a more complex and diverse tradition (Homan 2013, 502). Certainly, with very few exceptions (e.g., Conservative or "Primitive" Friends, mostly in the American Midwest and Britain) (Taber 2010, 3; https://plainquakers.org/), the visually identifiable version of simpleQuaker clothing and design might be considered to be dead. But founding Friends of the seventeenth century, as well as the diverse varieties of twenty-first-century Friends would surely argue that Quakers are indeed alive, and pursuing the spirit of founding Friends' values – the concept of "continuing revelation," which holds that "true" religion holds firm to its central values, while remaining in continued conversation with the world its adherents inhabit. Gradually, by the end of the twentieth century, most Friends' communities and educational institutions have incorporated fine arts, music, and literature into their daily lives, even as slogans such as "right sharing of world resources" and "live simply, so that others may simply live" are peppered onto many a Quaker conversation and publication. Environmental conservation and a focus on consumer products that do not defile the earth nor contradict social justice are among the causes that continue to focus some of the Quaker energy for simplicity.

SUGGESTED FURTHER READING

Boucher, Jack, Joseph Elliott, Catherine C. Lavoie. (2001). *Friends Meeting Houses, Philadelphia Yearly Meeting*, Washington, D.C.: U.S. Dept. of the Interior, National Park Service, Historic American Buildings Survey.
Butler, David M. (1999). *The Quaker Meeting Houses of Britain: An Account of the Some 1,300 Meeting Houses and 900 Burial Grounds in England, Wales and Scotland, from*

the Start of the Movement in 1652 to the Present Time; and Research Guide to Sources,
London: Friends Historical Society.

Eisenbarth, Erin. (2002). *Plain and Peculiar: A Case Study of Nineteenth-Century Quaker Clothing*, Newark: University of Delaware Press.

Nicholson, Frederick James. (1968). *Quakers and the Arts: A Survey of Attitudes of British Friends to the Creative Arts from the Seventeenth to the Twentieth Century*, London: Friends Home Service Committee.

Tolles, Frederick B. (1963). *Meeting House and Counting House: The Quaker Merchants of Colonial Philadelphia, 1682–1763*, New York: Norton.

PART III

REGIONAL STUDIES

9

༼

Quakers in North America

Stephen W. Angell and John Connell

Quakerism in North America is lively and quite varied, divided into three main branches and some smaller ones. At times, it has shown its fractiousness, but there have also been movements during the past century toward Quaker unity, and the interplay between unity and fractiousness has been complex and ongoing. This chapter takes the approach of profiling each of the three largest branches, starting with Friends General Conference, the most liberal branch, and proceeding to Friends United Meeting, which serves a mixed group of Quaker liberals and evangelicals, and then to the Evangelical Friends Church International, a clear voice for Evangelical Friends. See the chapters earlier in this volume by Hamm and May (Chapter 2), and also by Burdick and Dandelion (Chapter 3), for the schismatic origins of these branches. Western Yearly Meeting, composed of meetings affiliated with Friends United Meeting located in Western Indiana and Illinois, is the subject of a case study for this chapter.

FRIENDS GENERAL CONFERENCE

Friends General Conference (FGC) is an organization of Liberal Quakers who practice mostly unprogrammed worship. Rooted in the Hicksite branch of Quakers, it was founded in 1900 as an amalgamation of four Quaker organizations: the conferences of the First Day School Associations, the Union for Philanthropic Labor, the Friends Religious Conference, and the Friends Education Conference, all of which had been founded between 1868 and 1894 (Abbott et al. 2003, 110). As it has evolved, Friends General Conference disclaims any authority over its subscriber Yearly Meetings; instead, it sees its mission as sharing resources; bolstering Quaker practices and processes; and organizing occasions, such as an annual gathering, at which Friends may gather for mutual enrichment. Originally, Friends General Conference was concentrated in the Northeast United States and the adjacent Canadian pro-vince of Ontario. Seven Yearly Meetings (Philadelphia, New York, Baltimore, Genesee (western New York and Canada), Ohio, Indiana, and Illinois) were charter members of FGC. However, these Yearly Meetings were of unequal size: most of the approximately 18,000 Friends who belonged to one of these Yearly Meetings were members of Philadelphia Yearly Meeting (11,270, or 62 percent). Another quarter belonged to Baltimore or New York Yearly Meetings. Less than 10 percent of these Friends belonged to the three small Yearly Meetings west of the Appalachian Mountains (Ohio, Indiana – now Ohio Valley, and Illinois). In 1902, FGC had no members whatsoever in the American South, or in the trans-Mississippi West.

Over the next 115 years, FGC grew modestly and unevenly in members, and markedly in geographical spread. In 1982, sometime after its five largest Yearly Meetings had united with their Orthodox counterparts, the total membership of FGC had grown to 38,118; since then it has subsided in numbers to about 30,000. Its largest Yearly Meeting, Philadelphia, gained thousands of members in 1955 by uniting with Philadelphia Yearly Meeting (Orthodox). In 1962, the united Philadelphia Yearly Meeting had 17,657 members, but by 2007, it had declined in membership by one-third, to 11,681. By 2016, fifteen Yearly Meetings were affiliated with FGC, including four in the South (Piedmont, Southern Appalachian, South Central, and Southeastern), three Yearly Meetings in the Midwest and Mountain West (Lake Erie, Northern, and Intermountain), and an Alaska General Conference. These eight Yearly Meetings are all fairly small, but together they have more than 5,400 members, or more than one-sixth of the total membership of Friends General Conference (Barbour and Frost 1994, 234–36; FWCC 2007). Two liberal unprogrammed Yearly Meetings, Pacific and North Pacific Yearly Meetings, encompassing the states of California, Oregon, and Washington, deliberately remain independent of Friends General Conference, although similar in faith and practice, because of practicalities attending to the great geographic dis-tance from East Coast Liberal Quakers, and, more profoundly, a desire not to reinforce divisions among Friends by affiliating with any one of the branches that divided North American Quakerism (Abbott et al. 2003, 142).

The geographical and numerical growth in Liberal Quakerism embodied by Friends General Conference has come through a movement that has been called the "New Meetings Movement." Betsy Cazden has called this move-ment a "reinvention of Quakerism," similar in significance to the Holiness revivals in the American Midwest in the late nineteenth century, and the missions outreach to Africans and Latin Americans chronicled in Chapters 10 and 11 in this volume (Cazden 1997, 1). Throughout the twentieth century, new meetings, liberal in doctrine and flexible in practice, grew up in numerous cities and towns throughout the United States and Canada, often places where universities played a large role in local culture. A high proportion of their members were college professors. During the mid-twentieth century, many of the members had been conscientious objectors during America's wars or military veterans who were led to pacifism because of the killing that they witnessed during their time of service. Many of these new Quakers gravitated to the liberal theology of Rufus Jones and other modernist Quakers, whose writings were published in abundance during that era. While FGC Friends formally avoided "evangelization" or "proselytization," they did heartily approve of "Advancement" and "Outreach," which were promoted through an FGC Advancement Committee and served much the same purpose of attracting more members that evangelization served among Orthodox branches of Friends (Hansen 2008, 42).

The vast majority of members of FGC meetings in the early twenty-first century are white professionals. Few members are people of color, in FGC or in any branch of North American Friends. African Americans have at times been attracted by Quakers' "understanding toward humanity" and "the quiet informal atmosphere" of their worship services, according to Vera Green, an African American Quaker anthropologist (Weaver et al. 2011, 235). Yet white Quakers did not uniformly hold that understanding attitude, and African American Quakers sometimes suffered from passive and active forms of discrimination in their own religious home. Barrington Dunbar, an African American Quaker social worker, wrote, "The Black members of the Society of Friends do not amount to more than a handful of convinced Friends ... Maintaining our identity among Quakers who preach non-violence, but yet by their complicity and silence support the violence of the status quo, presents a problem" (Weaver et al. 2011, 132). In 1990, a Fellowship of Friends of African Descent was formed under the FGC umbrella, offering a variety of workshops and other programs for African American Friends (McDaniel and Julye 2009, 382–86).

A century ago, Friends General Conference mostly embodied a modernist liberal theological stance, similar in many respects to the theology of some Orthodox Friends, including the prolific writings of Rufus Jones on mysticism and Christian spirituality. The views of Progressive Friends, a left-wing offshoot of Hicksite Friends founded in the 1840s and 1850s, but ending formal existence with the dissolution of the Longwood (Pennsylvania) Meeting in the 1940s, found increasing currency among the Friends of Friends General Conference, especially through the writings of Jesse Holmes, a philosophy professor at Swarthmore College. According to Holmes, the "Society of

Friends commonly called Quakers" subscribes to no creed but is based on "a common purpose" grounded in ethics: "Right – is that which serves the end of a human society based on good will to all men; wrong – is that which hinders or thwarts that end" (Stern 1992, 22). From this starting point, Holmes derived Quaker pacifism, and also a socialist approach to economic issues. God is a "unifying influence which makes men long for a brotherly world," "the Chief Imperative of human existence," or "the Christ within." Holmes concluded that Quakers "have a faith which we believe may properly be called a Christian faith, which has nothing to fear from science." His pamphlet, *To the Scientifically Minded*, from which these quotations have been drawn, could be found at many FGC meetings through the 1950s (Stern 1992, 23). Holmes apparently believed in a Jesus who was human but not divine, "a great prophet and teacher, whose moral principles were too seldom obeyed or practiced by capitalistic followers of Mammon" (Wahl 1979, 308).

In the late twentieth century and early twenty-first century, the humanist theological tendencies evident in Holmes's writing have blossomed and diversified among FGC Friends, many of whom who have espoused universalist ideas, meaning the idea that the divine can be found in some way in all of the world's great religions, not just Christianity, or nontheism, a variety of Quaker theology that downplays or eliminates any notion of the Divine. (See Chapter 15, this volume, by Randazzo.) With the continuing presence of some, more orthodox Christian Quakers within FGC Quakerism, the FGC theological spectrum is wide.

FRIENDS UNITED MEETING

Friends United Meeting (FUM), formerly Five Years Meeting (FYM), is the broadest among the branches of world Friends. It incorporates a range of Friends from liberal unprogrammed Friends, mostly on the East Coast of North America, to Evangelical Friends who worship in programmed meetings. Because of its diversity, it has sometimes been thought of as a "big tent," but more commonly, it has suffered from strain because of diverse views on issues such as biblical authority. It was founded as Five Years Meeting in 1902, two years after FGC. It was designed as an umbrella organization for all Friends who became Orthodox in the Great Separation of the previous century, and it provided, and provides, a mechanism for those Friends to conduct business together, including coordination of missions and (until 1945) a joint book of discipline (Faith and Practice) that its Yearly Meetings would share. Since 1945, the Yearly

Meetings in FUM/FYM have had their own separate books of discipline (Abbott et al. 2003, 116–17).

Unlike FGC, FUM has a worldwide presence. It encompasses meetings in the Caribbean, Central America, and Africa, but the life and thought of those meetings are covered in other chapters and hence are passed over here. As of 2017, there are twelve Yearly Meetings in North America that are affiliated with FUM. Four are united, or dually affiliated, meetings located mainly on the East Coast: Baltimore, New York, New England, and Canadian Yearly Meetings. Two are associations that have recently separated from more evangelical Yearly Meetings but have opted to maintain their FUM affiliation: the Western Association of the Religious Society of Friends (with meetings in California) and the New Association of Friends (with meetings currently in Indiana, Ohio, and Michigan). Six are long-established Yearly Meetings, more than a century old, almost exclusively pastoral and programmed; most, but to varying degrees, share an evangelical Christian witness: North Carolina, Wilmington, Indiana, Western, Iowa, and Great Plains Yearly Meetings.

FUM Yearly Meetings in North Carolina and the Midwest have been declining in membership, in part because the largely rural meetings have suffered from the decline of the North American farming economy. The five largest Yearly Meetings in FUM in 1902 (Indiana, Iowa, North Carolina, Western, and Wilmington) had a combined total of 58,679 members; by 2007, they had a total of 22,293, a decline of 62 percent. They suffered substantial further losses from 2007 to 2017. The three largest dually affiliated meetings have also suffered declines, but not to the extent of the pastoral Yearly Meetings with a single affiliation. The three largest East Coast Orthodox Yearly Meetings that affiliated with FYM (Baltimore, New England, and New York) had a combined total of 9,019 members in 1902. In mid-century, these Yearly Meetings added about 5,000 members as a result of uniting with other Yearly Meetings. In 2007, these three meetings had a combined total of 12,392 meetings, about a 12 percent decline from their mid-century membership totals, accounting for all branches of Friends (Barbour and Frost 1994, 234–36; FWCC 2007).

Because of its diversity, FUM has had a large degree of internal dissension from the start. A good portion of the disagreement has related to the status of certain doctrinal statements agreed to when the organization was founded. The most important of these is the Richmond Declaration of Faith (RDF) of 1887 (see Chapter 2, this volume). The Richmond Declaration reaffirmed traditional Quaker views of the inward sacraments and the peace testimony, and it based these on strongly evangelical views of

God, Christ, and biblical authority (General Conference of Friends 1887, 24–43). Subsequently, its views of God and biblical authority have generally garnered more attention among Orthodox Friends than its reaffirmations of Quaker distinctives.

The more liberal meetings historically have objected to giving this declaration any particular or special status. In 1912, a session of FYM stated that the RDF was not to be regarded as a creed; this upset the more evangelical meetings, so in 1922, another FYM session rescinded the statement from the session ten years earlier, without, however, giving any definitive new proclamation on its status (Barbour and Frost 1994, 240). Essentially the same disagreement arose in a 1987 FUM meeting. As a consequence, some of the more evangelically oriented Yearly Meetings saw FUM as insufficiently committed to biblical authority and other principles of orthodox Christianity. The commitment of some of the more liberal Yearly Meetings to the social gospel espoused by the American Friends Service Committee further exacerbated these divisions. In addition, the degree to which Quaker identity itself is important to FUM Friends differs. Some mostly rural Friends churches, seeing their Christian identity as important, but not their Quaker identity, have resolved to become independent and shed their Quaker affiliations; the Friends Church in Clinton Corners, New York, is an example of this (Barbour et al. 1995, 230). In 2001, John Punshon, professor of Quaker studies at Earlham School of Religion, published a vigorous plea for evangelically minded Friends churches to maintain and strengthen their Quaker identity, entitled *Reasons for Hope: The Faith and Future of the Friends Church* (2001).

One result of such trends has been periodic disaffiliations by the more evangelical Yearly Meetings, with Oregon (now Northwest) relinquishing FYM affiliation in 1926; followed by Kansas (now Evangelical Friends Church Mid-America), in 1937; Rocky Mountain, in 1957; and Southwest, in 1995. In the 2010s, renewed tensions erupted among Yearly Meetings remaining in FUM, as is detailed later (Hinshaw 2013, 99, 102, 104).

Meanwhile, the mostly liberal and mostly unprogrammed meetings on the West Coast, seeing considerable similarity in worship and theology with unprogrammed Hicksites and Conservatives, began a unity movement to heal divisions from nineteenth-century separations. From the beginning of the century, this process was painstakingly nurtured over several decades. For example, in the area of Boston, Massachusetts, a pastoral Friends meeting in Roxbury, their meetinghouse sold to Congregationalists in the early twentieth century, was supplemented by an unprogrammed meeting across the Charles River in Cambridge. The two meetings held joint worship from 1926 to 1937 and participated in a wide range of mission and service projects together, with leadership from such leading Friends as D. Elton Trueblood[1] and Henry J. Cadbury. In 1937, the two groups jointly purchased a new meetinghouse and declared themselves independent of any branch of Friends; but, eight years later, in 1945, when FYM, Conservative, and FGC Friends joined in a united New England Yearly Meeting, the new Cambridge Monthly Meeting joined (Selleck 1976, 169–221). The united New England Yearly Meeting affiliated with both FYM and FGC. In 1955, the Hicksite, Orthodox, and Conservative strands of Canadian Quakers also reunited into a single Canadian Yearly Meeting (Dorland 1968, 339–47). Similar movements of unity between Hicksite and Orthodox Friends reunited, or consolidated, New York, Philadelphia, and Baltimore Yearly Meetings between 1955 and 1968. Of these five united Yearly Meetings, all except Philadelphia held dual affiliations with FUM and FGC. Philadelphia's sole connection with an umbrella organization was with FGC (Hinshaw 2013, 100–101). In the Midwestern United States, while there were no unity movements at the Yearly Meeting level, some Monthly Meetings carried dual, or multiple, affiliations with FGC, FUM, Evangelical, and Conservative Yearly Meetings, and many of their members hoped that eventual reunion would be possible in their region, too. The growth of Universalist and non-theist theologies within the dually affiliated meetings has also occasioned a great deal of unease among evangelical Christian members of FUM.

[1] One of the leading interpreters of Orthodox Quakerism of the FYM/FUM type was D. Elton Trueblood (1900–94), professor-at-large at Earlham College from 1946 until his retirement in 1966. He was personally acquainted with several US presidents, including fellow Quakers Herbert Hoover and Richard Nixon (Hamm 2003, 207; Abbott et al. 2003, 285–86; Trueblood 1974, 31, 47, 59; Ingle 2015, 111, 123, 154). While Trueblood lauded the vitality of the early Quaker movement, and George Fox's ability "to create a living fellowship," he cautioned against attempting to reproduce their methods in the present: "The past cannot be repeated." He urged a Quakerism that stayed faithful to Quaker ideals and was staunchly Christian at the same time. He perceived a continuum between early Friends and contemporary Orthodox Friends in giving equal emphasis to the Light of Christ and the historical Jesus, and seeing these as firmly linked. He placed particular emphasis on the importance of a Quaker orientation toward ministry that incorporated both a "universal ministry" and a "specialized ministry," with a major purpose of the specialized ministry being to equip, or build up, all Quakers to be useful ministers. He spoke positively about both silent, waiting worship and programmed worship, seeing an important place for both methods within the Society of Friends. Trueblood was realistic about the small numbers of Quakers in the world, and although he urged an evangelical approach to Christianity, he was certain that the Quaker movement would never grow in membership such that it would rival larger Christian denominations. But he saw a definite place for a Christian Quaker movement that would act as a leaven for a larger Christianity, highlighting issues such as peace to which all Christians would need to attend. Consequently, he saw Quakers as an "order" in the universal Christian church, similar to the role that Jesuits play in the Catholic Church: "Quakerism is at its best when it is passionately loyal to the Church Universal, yet fully aware that it is not by any means identical with that grand totality" (Trueblood 1966, 19, 38, 117, 282–83).

Since the 1970s, theological differences have sometimes worsened internal divisions within FUM, especially in regard to methods of biblical interpretation as applied to lesbian, gay, bisexual and transgender (LGBT) issues. In 2008, West Richmond Meeting, then part of Indiana Yearly Meeting, declared after a lengthy period of discernment that it welcomed and affirmed LGBT persons. The Ministry and Oversight Committee within Indiana Yearly Meeting sought to persuade West Richmond Friends to reconsider this decision, finding it to be opposed to a 1981 minute approved by the Yearly Meeting, but West Richmond Friends reaffirmed the results of their discernment. The result was a "reconfiguration" process in which those meetings that supported the right of West Richmond Friends to come to such a discernment (even though it conflicted with the beliefs of most Indiana Yearly Meeting Friends and an existing Yearly Meeting minute) were asked to form their own Yearly Meeting and to leave Indiana Yearly Meeting. They would be permitted to retain their own meetinghouses, and provision would be made for a division of Yearly Meeting assets. Eventually, in a process finalized in 2013, fifteen Monthly Meetings in Indiana, Michigan, and Ohio agreed to join West Richmond Meeting in a new Yearly Meeting, named the "New Association of Friends." The fifteen meetings did not agree on LGBT issues but did agree that the Yearly Meeting did not have the authority to overrule a congregation like West Richmond on such matters (Angell 2011, 2014). A similar range of issues has subsequently convulsed North Carolina Yearly Meeting. As of 2016, twenty of the Monthly Meetings in North Carolina Yearly Meeting, all but one evangelical, have departed from the Yearly Meeting to become independent or to pursue other Yearly Meeting affiliations. The remainder of the Yearly Meeting, still divided between liberals and evangelicals, as of 2017 seemed likely to forgo a complete separation. North Carolina Yearly Meeting would remain a single Yearly Meeting in order to hold property, but otherwise two associations would be formed for worship, fellowship, and most other activities under the umbrella of North Carolina Yearly Meeting (Fager 2016b).[2]

---

[2] A similar situation with a "welcoming and affirming church," West Hills Friends, in Northwest Yearly Meeting (NWYM), part of Evangelical Friends Church International, has led the elders of NWYM, in July 2015, to "release," or expel, West Hills from the Yearly Meeting. Within a month's time, eight other congregations in NWYM appealed to the Yearly Meeting to retain West Hills. After eighteen months delay, the Administrative Council of NWYM decided on a restructuring process that, as of this writing, is intended to result in a separation into two Yearly Meetings. Similar to the 2013 Indiana Yearly Meeting separation, one will be a Yearly Meeting that will affirm existing statements on sexual ethics; the other

CASE STUDY: WESTERN YEARLY MEETING
OF FRIENDS CHURCH

Western Yearly Meeting (WYM) currently encompasses forty Quaker meetings/churches, located in western and southern Indiana, and northeastern Illinois. WYM was originally formed in 1858 by the westernmost members of a then rapidly expanding Indiana Yearly Meeting (Bill 2008, 9–12).

WYM's present state is one largely defined by the accelerating rate of decline in both congregations and members. This numerical descent appears to have a correlative relationship with several developments, both historical and contemporary, and these are briefly touched upon to give background and context to the current situation in the Yearly Meeting.

Historical Developments Affecting WYM

When the Holiness Revival Movement swept through the United States in the 1860s and 1870s, WYM – like several other Gurneyite Yearly Meetings – was powerfully transformed. The revival movement was both a cause and an effect of the Religious Society of Friends becoming less segregated from other Christian denominations over the course of the nineteenth century. The thinning of the cultural and theological "hedge" that had previously served to preserve traditional Quaker discipline, belief, and practice among Friends was greatly accelerated by the revivals (Hamm 1988, 75–120).

As a result, many innovations were embraced by the end of the nineteenth century among the majority of Quakers in WYM that reshaped their sectarian religious society into one that more closely resembled the mainstream Evangelical Christianity of the surrounding culture. Practices that had been traditionally rejected among these Friends, including hymn singing, paid ministers, prepared sermons, and altar calls, were all enthusiastically adopted. The unprogrammed silence of waiting worship that had been central to Friends meetings was mostly replaced with a programmed order of service that would characterize the gradually renamed "Friends Churches."

These liturgical innovations among Friends reflected an underlying theological evolution. The continuing redemptive process of traditional Quaker "convincement" was steadily replaced by an insistence on experiencing a more definitive evangelical conversion experience. The primary inward authority of the Light of Christ within, as interpreted through Scripture and

will be a Yearly Meeting that will allow "welcoming and affirming" churches such as West Hills and will come up with a revised Faith and Practice (Angell 2015; Fager 2017).

the experience of earlier Friends, was steadily subsumed under the primary outward authority of the Bible as interpreted through evangelical doctrine. The traditional Quaker emphasis upon spiritual renewal as manifested through right conduct was joined with an Evangelical-Protestant emphasis upon immediate salvation from sin through right belief. The inevitable tensions produced by these changes between Revivalists and more traditional Friends in Western finally boiled over, leading to a separation of the Yearly Meeting at the 1877 annual sessions. The resulting exodus of Conservative Friends to start their own Yearly Meeting made the transformation of WYM all the more rapid and comprehensive (Connell 2013).

For the metamorphosed Western Yearly Meeting of Friends' Church,[3] the revivals were largely viewed as a divine blessing that brought spiritual vitality and renewal to the Yearly Meeting. Most notably, the revivals brought in new members and led to new churches being built, with the total membership of WYM reaching its apex in 1899 at 16,179 (Roberts n.d.).

However, as WYM Friends shed the distinctive practices, theology, and culture that once marked them as an insular and sectarian religious society and adopted those of the larger Evangelical-Protestant culture, they also surrendered many hallmarks of their unique religious identity. Consequently, WYM Friends have struggled since the revivals to maintain the unique moral and spiritual particularity that once characterized earlier generations of Quakers. As is briefly discussed later, this remix of identity is likely related to WYM's inability to check the withering power of attrition since the revivals. In particular, WYM continues to experience great difficulty in retaining the children born into their religious society.

Contemporary Developments Affecting WYM

From its peak in 1899, WYM experienced a steady drop in membership throughout the twentieth century. This decline has grown more precipitous since 1970 and has continued to pick up momentum in the twenty-first century. Between 1900 and 1970, the total membership of WYM declined by 30 percent. From 1970 to 2000, it dropped a further 52 percent. And in just the first fifteen years of the new century, total membership in WYM has plummeted yet another 56 percent, to an all-time low of 2,338. Moreover, that number reflects both resident and nonresident members.

---

[3] The addition of "Church" to the name of the Yearly Meeting first appears in the 1891 version of the Book of Discipline; however, the replacement of the word "meeting" with the word "church" had already begun to be seen in the text of the 1881 version.

The number of total resident members reported in 2015 was 1,532 (WYM Statistical Report for 2015, 126–27).

The number of Friends churches in Western also shows a corresponding decline, falling from 115 individual congregations in 1898 to 40 in 2015. Here too one can observe an increased velocity to this downward trend. Between 2000 and 2008, eleven congregations were either laid down or withdrew from WYM. Another twelve have withdrawn or been laid down just since 2009. Inevitably, financial struggle has followed closely upon the heels of membership decline in an increasing number of WYM congregations. Of the forty congregations that remain in WYM, eleven have an average weekly attendance of ten or less (WYM Statistical Report for 2015, 126–27); the laying down of several of these is either in process or appears imminent.

Even the few churches in Western that remain relatively stable in terms of overall membership are nonetheless rightfully concerned about the shifting age demographics among the membership. No comprehensive data is available, but the membership of almost all congregations is clearly aging, and informal estimates place the median age of attender in many WYM congregations at well over sixty years of age. The increasing lack of young and middle-aged Friends attending is the most ominous portent of continued and accelerating decline for the Yearly Meeting.

Despite falling membership, many WYM congregations still consider their general spiritual health to be good at present, but they remain keenly aware of what these worrisome signs might mean for the future. To contextualize this membership decline further, it is helpful to mention three salient yet interrelated factors that continue to define the struggle of Friends in WYM. These factors will be briefly described under the areas of *ministry, theology*, and *identity*.

Ministry

With the adoption of a paid pastoral ministry in WYM during the 1880s, increased dependence for spiritual leadership and ministry was consolidated into the office of the pastor. Thus, the health and vitality of many congregations have grown dependent upon the individual in that office. Even with a contraction in the total number of churches – and a growing list of congregations that are now too small to support a full-time pastoral minister – WYM has long struggled to meet the demand for quality pastoral candidates.

Consequently, WYM has often drawn its pastors from not only beyond the bounds of the Yearly Meeting but also from outside Quakerism itself. This variety of religious backgrounds and educations has brought a diversity of ministry to WYM but has also resulted in a de-emphasis of traditional Quaker interpretations of Scripture, theology, and the testimonies. A few meetings have returned to being unprogrammed and non-pastoral, and these report that this development has only deepened their worship experiences and spirituality (2015 WYM State of Society Report 2016).

Theology

Friends in WYM continue to struggle with unresolved theological tension. In addition to the – at times – uneasy alliance between Quakerism and Evangelicalism, more prominent tensions have resulted from the broader culture wars. These tensions have manifested most notably in controversies over the issues of homosexuality and universal salvation. WYM has attempted to remain an inclusive Yearly Meeting, with both liberal-leaning and evangelical-leaning congregations, by so far resisting calls for a formal separation. But this disinclination to pursue an intentional separation has not prevented the splintering of the Yearly Meeting over these issues. Ten of the twelve churches that have departed from WYM since 2009 have withdrawn because of either explicit theological disagreement or a sense of disconnection with the larger Yearly Meeting.

The churches that remain in WYM embrace a diversity of theological and social views that largely reflects the influences of their pastoral ministry and surrounding culture. Many churches in rural areas tend to be generically evangelical, in which Quakerism is largely equated with Evangelical-Christian doctrine and belief. A number of these meetings remain largely uninvolved with the rest of the Yearly Meeting because of its perceived tolerance of heterodoxy.

The more liberal-leaning meetings that tend to be near urban areas equate Quakerism primarily with the testimonies, but reinterpreted through secular ideologies of social justice. While fewer in number, these liberal meetings often feel likewise alienated from the Yearly Meeting due to its perceived lack of social and theological progressiveness.

Identity

Evidence suggests that a link may exist between this difficulty among WYM Friends in coalescing around a common theological vision and distinct social identity and their membership struggles, particularly as pertaining to the retention of children born into the Yearly Meeting. A growing body of research into the reciprocal, interrelationship between religious beliefs, religious behavior, and religious community – all demonstrate the importance of forming a distinct religious identity in the binding together of religious groups (Haidt 2012; Putnam and Campbell 2010; Froese and Bader 2007). It may be that a lack of distinctiveness in identity among WYM Friends has at least some correlation to the continuing exodus of the children born into their religious society and, thus, leading to the aging and diminution of the Yearly Meeting.

Looking at just one WYM congregation as an example, 69 percent of respondents to a recent survey first came to attend a Friends Church as an adult. Of those respondents who came to Quakerism as an adult, only 30 percent were younger than age 50, and none younger than age 32. Meanwhile, when taking a closer look at the 31 percent of respondents who were birthright Friends or came to Quakerism during childhood, less than half of those were younger than age 64 (Angell and Connell, 2015–16).[4] To illustrate this example even further, consider that this same Friends Church reported ninety-five junior resident members in 1981 (Minutes, 1980–1982). However, as of 2015, only one of those ninety-five junior members remains a member of the meeting. Many other WYM churches report a similar trend where entire generations of children who have been born into WYM have disappeared as adults.

Undoubtedly a number of factors in our increasingly mobile society have contributed to this exodus of younger members. But many Friends in WYM have wondered why the religious identity as Quakers that most young WYM Friends receive has not proved to be a lasting religious identity for them as an adult. For even those youth who remained in the same area as an adult, why hasn't that identity been sufficiently distinct, appealing, and affirming to make them want to remain among Friends?

Looking Forward

Despite their diminished strength, the Friends of WYM continue to make what impact they can in the lives of their members and communities, as well as supporting the wider ministries of FUM. But as the Friends of WYM grapple with an uncertain future, the needs of an aging and diminishing faith body, internal tensions, and the struggle to manifest a distinct witness to the world of their religious experience, many WYM congregations view the future with a

[4] North American Quaker Survey, 2015–16. This was a survey of beliefs and attitudes administered to a sample of congregations in WYM. The survey sample covered nearly one-quarter of the churches in WYM and was intended to represent diversity of meeting size, geographical location, and theology present in the Yearly Meeting.

sense of prayerful seeking tinged with some anxiety. The following response by one WYM church to the Yearly Meeting on the state of its religious society would probably be echoed by many others: "We are asking ourselves, 'What is God saying to us in the 21st Century? How can our faithfulness to Jesus be more attractive and fruitful?'" (2015 WYM State of Society Report 2016).

Much of what has been stated here of Western Yearly Meeting is true of the North American portion of Friends United Meeting as a whole. Despite its membership losses and continuing strains, Friends United Meeting serves as a vital center for American Quakerism, offering important opportunities for both Christian missions and Friends' service, on the basis of obedience to the presence of Christ among them. A great deal of the future of North American Quakerism depends on the ability of FUM Friends to successfully address their challenges.

EVANGELICAL FRIENDS CHURCH INTERNATIONAL

The Evangelical Friends Alliance (its name later changed to Evangelical Friends Church International, EFCI) was founded in 1963. All of the founding Yearly Meetings had either never joined Five Years Meeting in the first place (Ohio Yearly Meeting, later Evangelical Friends Church, Eastern Region (EFCER); and Alaska Evangelical Friends Conference) or had departed from FYM/FUM (Oregon Yearly Meeting, now Northwest; Kansas Yearly Meeting, now Evangelical Friends Church–Mid America; and Rocky Mountain Yearly Meeting). Southwest Yearly Meeting, now Evangelical Friends Church–Southwest, joined EFCI in 1995. Overall, the membership numbers for all these Yearly Meetings held nearly steady from the mid-twentieth century until 2007. In 1952, the combined membership of all these Yearly Meetings, except Rocky Mountain, totaled 26,722; in 2007, the combined membership of the same five Yearly Meetings was 26,772, a net gain of 50, or 0.02 percent. These mask some very different trends among the five Yearly Meetings, however. EFCER and Northwest Yearly Meeting made substantial membership gains over this sixty-five-year period, similar to other North American Evangelical Christian Churches; their combined membership climbed from 10,743 in 1952 to 15,635 in 2007, an increase of 46 percent (Barbour and Frost 1994, 234–36; FWCC 2007). The other Yearly Meetings, such as the FUM pastoral meetings, registered membership declines over the period similar to mainline Christian churches in the United States. However, as the peak of Evangelical-Christian membership passed in the first decade of the twenty-first century, all of the EFCI Yearly Meetings appear to have registered declines from 2007 to 2012. Eastern Region declined from 9,252 to 7,987, a loss of 14 percent, while Northwest Yearly Meeting declined from 6,383 to 4,858, a loss of 24 percent.

Fundamentalism attracted some Friends whose hearts had been changed by Evangelical Holiness revivals, and objections to the modernism perceived to be rampant in FYM led in large part to the departures of these Yearly Meetings from FYM (Roberts 2013, 111–15). The road toward the Evangelical Friends Alliance had been paved by nine conferences of an Association of Evangelical Friends that had met from 1927 until 1968. An initially exclusive spirit among Evangelical Friends eventually gave way to a more welcoming spirit toward other branches of Friends, leading to a 1970 Faith and Life Conference in St. Louis and a 1977 All-Friends Conference in Wichita. As a leading evangelical Friend Everett Cattell[5] stated in 1959:

> Be very tender with each other's consciences and consult together with hearts as open to truth as they are firm in truth and as open to each other as should be true of brethren in Christ. At the same time let each be prepared to grant full freedom to the other circle to work together in such organizations as each may see fit to establish for the implementation of their concerns. (Burdick 2013, 246)

Some Evangelical Friends have played important roles in several organizations that have nurtured robust participation across the Quaker branches, such as the Quaker Theological Discussion Group and its journal, *Quaker Religious Thought*.

At times, the cooperative spirit with FUM, FGC, and other Friends has proved to be fragile, however; by 1977, significant strains had emerged. Evangelical Friends wished to confer only with other Friends who understood

---

[5] Few Evangelical Friends leaders were more widely respected than Everett Cattell (1905–81), a longtime missionary to India early in his career. Despite the small size of the Evangelical Friends community in India (or, perhaps partly because of it), Cattell was catapulted into leadership of the Christian Churches in India during the 1940s and 1950s (Stansell 2009, 187–94). His concern for Christian unity continued on his return to the United States, and to active involvement with Friends on behalf of the Evangelical Friends Church, Eastern Region. His widely read *Spirit of Holiness* found Quaker roots in the Evangelical concern for Christian holiness, but also focused on Wesleyan ones as well (Cattell 2015). In a series of speeches among Friends in the United States, he urged Christian unity, as long as it clearly advocated for "the Lordship of Christ" (Roberts 2013, 118; Cattell 1970). The drift of FGC Friends, and some Friends in FUM, toward more humanist theologies worried Cattell, and he thought realignment among Friends, with liberal Quakers and evangelical Quakers clearly separated from each other, would be preferable to "a fused disunity which would be more enervating than the status quo" (Cattell 1966, 11). However, Cattell's Holiness background was more important to him than formulating a distinctively Quaker theology. Given his deeply held ecumenical concerns, his reliance upon traditionally evangelical language (not "Quakerly" language per se) may be completely understandable (Johns 1992, 13).

themselves as Christians, and by 1977, a universalist strain of Quakerism that welcomed non-Christian forms of spirituality had begun to emerge among more liberal Friends. Even more pressing, however, were differences over homosexuality, and varying interpretations of the biblical passages seen to offer guidance on that topic. The Friends Committee for Gay Concerns had asked for exhibit space at the Wichita Conference to display their literature, and Evangelical Friends objected, and then almost pulled out of the Conference. In the end, they stayed through the conference, but this disagreement has thus far forestalled any conceivable further effort to convene another All Friends Conference in North America (Fager 2002, 1–8).

Much of evangelical thought and scholarship have continued to move away from fundamentalism. Twenty-first-century Evangelical Friends scholars have sought to work in the middle ground between liberalism and fundamentalism. As Arthur Roberts has written:

> Evangelical Friends broadened their understanding of how truth is revealed through sense, reason, and intuition. Interaction with other Quakers became more congenial. Together they sought a coherent understanding of revelation – God's word of truth spoken through the Bible, directly by the living Christ, *and* through creation. (Roberts 2013, 113)

An example of the kind of scholarship to which Roberts refers is Carole Spencer's innovative study on Quaker Holiness, *Holiness: The Soul of Quakerism*, in which she traces holiness influences from the seventeenth to the twentieth centuries, engaging in great depth theologians from all the branches of Quakerism (Spencer 2007).

In many ways, the heart of Evangelical Quakerism is its mission efforts. Those missions have borne fruit, and consequently the vast majority (78 percent) of Evangelical Quakers live outside North America (Roberts 2013, 121). While the mission efforts on other continents are covered elsewhere in this volume, a significant missionary outreach in North American to the native peoples of Alaska will receive mention here. Quakers from the Pacific Northwest carried on evangelization in both southeast and northwest Alaska, but it is only the latter that yielded a Friends Church that has endured into the twenty-first century. The first Quaker meeting for worship among the Inuits (Eskimos), a programmed one, took place in 1897 with the arrival of the first Quaker missionaries to the Kotzebue Sound region of Alaska. With the help of a steady presence of dozens of missionaries, the Friends Church there grew rapidly during the next several decades, incorporating about 60 percent of the Kotzebue Inuit by 1970, despite competition from Catholics and Seventh-Day Adventists (Roberts 1978, 365). The Friends Church largely conducted its services in the Inupiat language and utilized native pastors long before other Christian denominations did. It was known for its strictness and "legalism," forbidding smoking, drinking, gambling, and dancing; the latter prohibition occasioned conflict in 1932 between Inuit elders and Quaker missionaries, on the one hand, and secular government authorities, schoolteachers, and Inuit youth, on the other hand (Roberts 1978, 302–5). The Friends Church in Alaska preserved its teachings on spiritual baptism, undoubtedly a welcome relief in the icy Arctic (Nash 1979, 115). In cooperation with ministers from other denominations, the Quaker missionaries helped introduce reindeer into the Inuit economy and way of life. Some EFCI and FUM meetings in the early twenty-first century have inaugurated outreach programs to Hispanic American Quakers.

OTHER BRANCHES OF FRIENDS IN THE UNITED STATES

The Wilburite, or Conservative, Friends survive in 2017 in three small Yearly Meetings, Ohio, Iowa (Conservative), and North Carolina (Conservative). As explained in Chapter 14, this volume, by Michael Birkel and Deborah Shaw, these Yearly Meetings preserve the Christ-centered theology of early Friends, as well as their unprogrammed worship. They also have declined in numbers during the late twentieth and early twenty-first centuries. Ohio and Iowa, combined, had 1,843 members in 1952. By 2007, they had declined about 40 percent, to 1,097 members. An even smaller group is Central Yearly Meeting, an independent Evangelical Holiness group, which during the same time period declined from 576 to 150 members, a decline of more than 70 percent (Barbour and Frost 1994, 234–36; FWCC 2007).

One of the few groups of Friends to maintain a level membership during this period are the Independent Liberal Yearly Meetings on the West Coast (California, Oregon, and Washington state) of the United States. In 1973, Pacific Yearly Meeting, which encompassed all of these Friends, set off the Quakers in Oregon and Washington into a separate North Pacific Yearly Meeting. From 1962 until 2007, the aggregate numbers of the Friends in these Independent Liberal Yearly Meetings increased very slightly from 2,309 to 2,333, an increase of less than 1 percent (Barbour and Frost 1994, 234–36; FWCC 2007).

CONCLUSION

In general, we have sketched a picture of long-term decline among North American Friends. We have also found differing views among these Friends on the question of whether unity among Quakers is better, even when sometimes Friends disagree on certain matters of faith and practice, or whether in some cases there may be a need for continuing separation of Friends into smaller bodies where Friends would be inclined to be of like mind about the issues of most importance to them. Dialogue, unity, and further communion among disparate Friends have strong advocates in North America. This is detailed in chapters by Margery Abbott (Chapter 18) and C. Wess Daniels and Greg Woods (Chapter 17). The issue of how to attract younger generations of Friends, in order to forestall further decline, is also a pressing one, as we have identified in this chapter. On the whole, Quakers in North America do maintain considerable vitality, although it is manifested in quite varied ways.

SUGGESTED FURTHER READING

Appelbaum, Patricia. (2009). *Kingdom to Commune: Protestant Pacifist Culture between World War I and the Vietnam Era. Chapel Hill,* Chapel Hill: University of North Carolina Press.

Bacon, Margaret H. (1986). *Mothers of Feminism: The Story of Quaker Women in America,* San Francisco: Harper and Row.

Dorland, Arthur G. (1968). *The Quakers in Canada: A History,* Toronto: Ryerson Press.

Hamm, Thomas D. (2003). *The Quakers in America,* New York: Columbia University Press.

McDaniel, Donna, and Vanessa Julye. (2009). *Fit for Freedom, Not for Friendship,* Philadelphia: Quaker Press of Friends General Conference.

Roberts, Arthur O. (1978). *Tomorrow Is Growing Old: Stories of the Quakers in Alaska,* Newberg, OR: Barclay Press.

10

ᛤ

Latin American Quakerism

Ramón González Longoria and Nancy Thomas

INTRODUCTION

In one of the most exuberant expressions of worldwide Quakerism, Latin American Friends weave a lively faith that spreads from the high Andean planes of Bolivia and Peru, runs down through the mountainous and tropical regions of Central America, and then stretches into Mexico, Cuba, and Jamaica. While their expressions vary as much as their geography, certain threads run through these differences, uniting them in a colorful tapestry that does not reflect the traditional "Quaker gray" of their European and North American ancestors.[1]

In this chapter, we give a brief overview of Latin American Friends, beginning with a case study of the history of Cuban Friends. We then explore the question many have asked, "How Quaker are these churches?" We look at the evangelical threads that run through the different expressions, then focus on what makes them Quaker, and conclude with a reflection on how the cultures of Latin America add to the tapestry.

THE STORY OF CUBAN FRIENDS: A CASE STUDY

Quaker presence in Cuba dates back to 1898 when Episcopalian missionary Francisco Cala, influenced by Mexican Quakers, became a convinced Friend himself. He changed the name of the small group of churches he had formed to the Evangelical Friends Church of Cuba (Mahalah Jay 1900, letter to

---

[1] Quakers in the eighteenth century began dressing in the color gray as a testimony to simplicity, in protest of the ostentatious clothing styles of the times. While this particular custom is no longer carried out, the value of simplicity still characterizes Quakers.

Wilmington Yearly Meeting). Centered in Havana, this work was not deeply rooted and lasted only a few years. But the work of Cala's associates Arthur Dowe and Arthur and Helen Pain in western Cuba went forward, recognized by North Carolina Yearly Meeting in 1902 and partially supported by the American Friends Board of Foreign Missions (AFBFM) until 1915. This small group of Friends dissolved in 1946, after Arthur Pain's death. Again, its Quaker roots were shallow, many of the Cuban workers having come from other denominations. The few surviving meetings passed over to the Methodists and the Baptists.

The more enduring work in eastern Cuba began on November 14, 1900, with the arrival of a small band of missionaries sent by the AFBFM. These included Sylvester and May Jones, Emma Phillips, and Maria de los Santos Trevino, a Mexican Friend. They came with clear evangelical purposes: "To preach the Gospel, always preaching Christianity above denominationalism – Christ crucified, the Savior of men – and not beginning with the words or practices of the doctrines and concepts established by Friends" (Hilty 1977, 13). By 1905, they had preached in eighteen villages and organized work in seven of them.

In each mission station established, the missionaries followed the model of building a parsonage, a meetinghouse, and a school. Evangelism and education ran side by side, with even the schools exercising a form of "quiet evangelism." Heavily influenced by the Evangelical Holiness emphasis of the times, they had stated goals of eventually forming a self-sustained and self-governing national church. Yet the colonial civilizing model of mission seemed predominant, with the idea that "the Cubans need to be first elevated to a pattern of civilization, adopting the model of the culture, society and image of the missionaries" (Graves 1999, 10).

These early missionaries were all aggressive evangelists; yet they attempted from the beginning to train and incorporate national workers. Their success was limited, partly due to the low level of economic support (suffered by both expatriate and national workers) and the "Americanizing" goals of the missionaries. Most of the national workers of this period defected to the Methodists or Baptists.

In 1921, the mission, with the approval of the board, set up a Central Committee ("Junta Central") of national leaders to administer the church; with each succeeding year, the mission handed over more responsibility. The AFBFM backed out of the work in 1927, which led to the premature formation of the Cuban Yearly Meeting on April 13, 1927. Still not completely independent from the mission, the national church was far from being native and continued to perpetuate the forms and attitudes received from the pioneering missionaries, including the strict puritanical American Protestantism of the period (Hilty 1977, 106).

The work continued, gradually becoming independent of the mission, until the Cuban Revolution of 1959 when Cuban Friends, along with all other Christian groups, were forced underground. Many of the Friends' leaders went into exile and some even renounced their faith, leaving the surviving church small and hidden, isolated from contact with Friends from other parts of the world. All Friends' schools were nationalized. Yet a small surviving body of Quaker believers continued faithful, trusting in their Lord. They met as they could, developing their own leadership and slowly becoming stable. In spite of all the difficulties, this small hidden band of Quakers continued preaching the gospel as they could.

The political situation forced all Christian groups to associate and work together, which in one sense was positive. In another sense, however, this ecumenism, plus the isolation from other Friends, put Cuban Friends in danger of losing their Quaker identity.

Some twenty years after the revolution, a changing political climate enabled Cuban Friends to reestablish relationships with other Friends organizations, and this helped break the isolation and deepen Quaker roots. These included Friends United Meeting, of which they are now a part, the Friends World Committee on Consultation, Quakers in Britain, and in the New England and Southeastern Yearly Meetings.

For the past twenty years, Cuban Friends have focused on organizational changes and internal rebuilding, not emphasizing evangelism and growth. Yet in recent years, a spiritual awakening is resulting in a resurgence of house church worship services and prayer cells, with work in new places and the reopening of mission centers.

In 1994, Cuban Friends formed the Good Shepherd Bible Institute for the formation of its leaders. Since then, an extension of the Latin American Bible University of Costa Rica and the Evangelical Theological Seminary in Matanzas has offered its services to Friends. And in 2012, Cuba Yearly Meeting organized the Cuban Quaker Peace Institute, a result of workshops sponsored by the American Friends Service Committee. The institute proposes to deepen the Quaker roots of Cuban Friends and provide tools for transforming conflict into peaceful solutions. With the collaboration of professors from the Earlham School of Religion, the institute celebrated its first graduates in 2015.

Today Cuba Yearly Meeting has ten Monthly Meetings and four mission points for outreach. In all of their story, Cuban Quakers clearly see the hand of God.

OVERVIEW OF LATIN AMERICAN QUAKERS

The oldest continuous presence of Friends in Latin American began in Mexico. In 1871, Indiana Yearly Meeting sent missionaries Gulielma and Samuel Purdie who helped establish the first Monthly Meeting in the capital city in 1888, as well as meetings and schools in the northeast of the country. In 1947, Herberto Sein helped plant another meeting in Mexico City and founded the *Casa de los Amigos* (Friends House). This work eventually led to the formation of the *Reunión General de los Amigos en México* (General Meeting of Friends in Mexico) in 1958. In 1967, the Evangelical Friends Mission sent Roscoe and Tina Knight to Mexico (L. E. Fernández González in Abbott et al. 2003), and this work, known simply as Mexico Yearly Meeting, currently has meetings in and around the capital and in the states of Aguascalientes, Zacatecas, Sinaloa, and Chihuahua. Another small evangelical Yearly Meeting in the state of Coahuila with ties to the Evangelical Friends Church, Mid-America, has six meetings (Dan Cammack 2015, interview). The estimated number of Friends in Mexico is around 800 (Anderson and Anderson 2014, 130).

Quakers visited Barbados and Jamaica as early as the seventeenth century, with George Fox himself involved. While several meetings had been established by 1700, the presence of Friends today in Jamaica dates to 1881 when Iowa Yearly Meeting sent missionary Evi Sharpless. The Jamaican Yearly Meeting was formed in 1941 and today has several churches, as well as schools and homes for boys and girls. Currently around 400 Quakers form the church in Jamaica (Anderson and Anderson 2014, 130; "Quakers in Jamaica and Barbados" n.d.).

The presence of Friends in Central America began in 1901 when the Training School for Christian Workers in Southern California (today Azusa Pacific University) sent Quaker students Thomas Kelly and Clark Buckley to Guatemala. Others followed, and California Yearly Meeting of Friends soon took over the support of the work. Evangelical in nature and largely influenced by the Holiness movement in the United States, the work advanced through church planting, schools, and pastoral formation via the Berea Bible Training School. As Guatemalan Friends reached out, meetings started in Honduras and El Salvador. The work in Guatemala received recognition as a Yearly Meeting in 1970; Honduras was recognized in 1983, and El Salvador in 1989. In 1986, a group broke off from the Guatemala Yearly Meeting to form the Holiness Friends Yearly Meeting in that same country (both groups are currently linked to Evangelical Friends Church International, EFCI). Another small group of eleven Quakers families from Fairhope, Alabama, formed a community in Monteverde, Costa Rica; since 1952 that group has been sponsoring programs for alternatives to violence and a center for peace education, in addition to their meeting and school ("History of Monteverde and the Quakers" 2013). The overall number of Friends in Central America is estimated to be around 22,000, with most of those in Guatemala (Anderson and Anderson 2014, 130–35; Pickard 2014, 125–29).

Friends' presence in the Andean region began in 1919 with the arrival of missionaries from Indiana and California. The Union Bible Seminary in Westfield, Indiana (largely Quaker but open to other Holiness groups) sponsored Emma Morrow and Mattie Blount as their first missionaries to Bolivia. Florence Smith, a woman from Kansas Yearly Meeting who had arrived two years earlier as an independent missionary, met them in La Paz.

Simultaneously, Peniel Mission of California sent William Abel to La Paz. Abel, a Native American Quaker and a graduate of the Training School for Christian Workers in California, joined forces with the three Quaker women as they engaged in open-air evangelistic meetings on the streets of La Paz. Abel died of smallpox that very year, but one of his disciples, a young Bolivian named Juan Ayllón, was inspired to carry the work forward. Ayllón traveled to Guatemala for training in the Berea Bible Training School; then he returned to Bolivia in 1924 as a missionary sponsored by the Central American Friends Mission and the newly developing national Friends Church in that region.

The work of those early Friends who preached on the streets of La Paz in 1919 later developed into separate Yearly Meetings. In 1926, Central Yearly Meeting became involved in sponsoring part of the work begun by the Westfield Quakers. The work begun by Abel's disciple Juan Ayllón was turned over to the sponsorship of Oregon Yearly Meeting in 1930.

From these seeds grew all the various Yearly Meeting groupings existing in Bolivia and Peru today. As Harold Thomas notes in his overview of Andean Quakers,

> The present denominational organizations in Bolivia of the *Seminario Bíblico,* *Amigos "Central," Santidad Amigos, Estrella,* and the *Estrella de Belén* come from the mission work of the Union Bible Seminary in Westfield, Indiana (1919) and the Central Friends Yearly Meeting (1926). The *Unión Boliviana de los Amigos* and the INELA Friends in Bolivia and Peru come from the roots of Juan Ayllón ... (1924) and the Oregon Friends (1930). (Thomas 2003)

Most of these groups remain small splinters off the larger groups. Those that would count as major Yearly Meetings are the *Santidad Amigos, Amigos "Central,"* and the INELA churches (*Iglesia Nacional Evangélica de Los Amigos*) in Bolivia and Peru. Thomas estimates that Andean Friends have around 30,000 people officially on the church lists, and a larger community of 50,000 (Thomas 2014, 115–24). Most of these groups participate in EFCI. This gives an overall estimate of between 73,000 and 74,000 Quakers in Latin America.

COMMON THREADS

While the origins, history, and geography of the different Latin American Quaker groupings are complex and diverse, certain common threads run through them, in varying configurations. We identify these as the evangelical threads, the Quaker threads, and the Latin American cultural threads. We explore each of these emphases in turn, although they all weave together in the life of Latin American Quakers. Many examples come from Bolivian (INELA) Friends, but we also use narrative essays written by Friends from Guatemala, Honduras, El Salvador, and Peru, collected in the book *De encuentro a ministerio: la vida y fe de Los Amigos latinoamericanos* (Thomas 2012).

EVANGELICAL THREADS

The missionary movements that led to the Friends work in Central and South America came from the programmed, pastoral branches of Friends in Indiana, California, and Oregon and, in the case of Cuba, from the American Friends Board of Foreign Missions, a branch of the Five Years Meeting. The missionaries who served under these organizations were all heavily influenced by the American Holiness movement that formed in the mid-1880s, taking its inspiration from the Second Great Awakening in the late eighteenth century. Theologically Arminian in nature, it emphasized a conversion experience, complete sanctification, the authority of Scripture, correct doctrine, and involvement in world missions. Its appeal crossed denominational lines and included Friends.

Around the turn of the century (1900), a number of Bible training schools rose up in the wake of the Holiness movement; these focused on the preparation of consecrated Christian workers on the local and international levels. Among these in Friends circles were the Cleveland Bible College; the Union Bible Seminary in Westfield, Indiana; the Training School for Christian Workers in California (Whittier); the Berea Bible Training School in Chiquimula, Guatemala; and the Portland Bible Institute in Oregon. The first catalog of the Training School in California claimed as an institutional goal, "to inspire missionary enthusiasm; and to cultivate a passion for winning souls ... We would see this school as a hotbed of germinating missionaries."

This would have been typical of all these holiness training schools. This type of ministerial formation profoundly influenced the work of the early Quaker missionaries to Latin America.

Juan Ayllón provides a good example. This Bolivian young man, discipled under William Abel and educated in the Berea Bible Training School in Guatemala, returned to his native land in early 1924 as a missionary, dedicated to winning converts among the Aymara peoples of the highlands and forming them into Friends churches. Something of his evangelistic fervor comes through in his letters back to the supporting Guatemalan churches.

On November 14, 1924, Ayllón wrote about providentially encountering a group of Aymara Indians in the community of Tembladerani:

> On Oct. 7 we established ourselves for the first time in that place and found hungry souls. In the first meeting, after having heard the message, they sought the Lord at the altar. We told them that we were sent to those of their class, to the victims of sin, superstition and darkness, to the weary and heavy-laden ones, that they might find rest of soul. We had meetings with them six Sundays, and not a meeting passed without an altar service. We understand this is a sign of God's approval on it all ... In the six months that we have been here, we have been at the front of the battle, not only carrying the responsibility and burden on our hearts of preaching the Gospel, but also the weight of the bitter pain of so many perishing people falls upon us. (Ayllón 1924)

Ayllón passed his fervor and his theology on to the people who came into the church as a result of his labors. In addition to Bible training classes among the new believers, Ayllón always invited certain men in whom he saw leadership potential to accompany him on his evangelistic trips across the high plains and around Lake Titicaca. Soon new Friends leaders including Pedro Choque, Esteban Chipana, and Cipriano Mamani were also preaching the gospel and leading in worship services.

By the time Oregon Yearly Meeting (OYM) sent its first North American missionaries to Bolivia, the young Friends Church there had grown to a community of about eighty believers, gathering in two organized meetings and many small developing groups. The foundation laid was evangelical. The OYM missionaries carried on the same holiness emphasis in their work, and the resulting Friends Church was solidly evangelical in faith and practice. While these details are specific to the INELA, they could be replicated in all the Friends groupings in South and Central America, as well as in Cuba. This tradition has carried through to the present time.

As the church in Bolivia grew in those early years, believers who were scattered in meetings in La Paz, on the *altiplano* and in communities around

Lake Titicaca gathered once a year for the annual Easter Conference (precursor to the Yearly Meeting sessions). The main event at those gatherings was the preaching of the Holiness gospel, encouraging the believers to live lives worthy of Jesus, and to spread the good news throughout their communities and beyond. One of the earliest of several names that the church adopted was the "Evangelical Society of Bolivian Friends" (1948). Jack Willcuts, missionary in the 1940s and 1950s, observed that one of the purposes of the Bible training school on the farm at Copajira was to "inculcate" Quaker doctrine, but he also noted in a letter home that "we are not here to make Quakers but Christians" (1955). This replicates the purposes of the early missionaries to Cuba, as we have seen, who determined to base their work on the preaching of the Christian gospel of Christ, rather than the precepts of Quakerism.

The strong evangelical emphasis of the early years shows up in the Christian tones of Latin American Quakerism today. Manuel de Jesús Coronado Monroy pastors a Friends Church in Chiquimula, Guatemala. He tells the story of his childhood in a "disintegrated home." His father's alcoholism and desertion added to the poverty in which Manuel and his four siblings grew up. But through persistence and grace, Manuel managed to be accepted to the local Friends school. During his first week there, he attended a chapel service where in the strange words of the sermon he found reason to hope that his future could be better. He sensed "something special" in the school.

He got hold of a Bible, and surreptitiously went to a Friends Church service. At the end of the service, "I walked to the front, knelt down and asked the Lord to take from my shoulders this heavy burden. And the Lord, with his great power, grace and mercy, dried my tears, lifted up my anguish, and said to me, 'Don't cry anymore; from today forward, you will begin to live for me.'"

Manuel experienced an immediate change in his attitudes and habits. He became involved in the local church and began telling people what had happened to him. Several family members and street friends joined with him in this new adventure. Today he says, "The 'something special' I felt in that Friends school was Jesus. He gave me reason to live, and we will walk together the rest of my life here, and beyond" (in Thomas 2012, 11–16).

Manuel's story could be repeated, with different details and in different settings, throughout Latin American Quakerism. The common threads are personal conversion, gathering of like-minded believers into local congregations, an emphasis on Jesus as the living word of God and on the Scriptures as the written word, and the preaching of a Christocentric gospel that encourages people to live like Jesus and to carry forward his ministry in the world around them. Worship services include lively worship music, times of prayer, and a message from the Scriptures.

Latin American Friends are almost universally pastoral and programmed; in this light, they have much in common with other Friends in Asia and Africa. In Bolivia, the Yearly Meeting organization legally owns local church property, but local members use their own resources to build and maintain their church buildings. (They prefer the word "church" to the more traditionally Quaker term "meetinghouse.") In rural areas, these churches are simple structures, usually adobe, with a sign on the front clearly identifying it as an Evangelical Friends church (INELA). Urban church buildings range from simple to more elaborate, depending on the zone and the size of the congregation, but all identify openly as Christian and Quaker. Bolivian Friends pastors receive a small salary from the offerings of their members, and most need to supplement this with other work. A few urban congregations give total support to their pastor.

On the INELA Yearly Meeting level, some members of the executive council receive a minimal salary; these include the president, the secretary of evangelism, and the treasurer. Other members serve voluntarily. Decision making in the Yearly Meeting sessions is through consensus where possible, but resorting to voting for the election of officers and other issues. This organizational style is similar among most Latin American Friends, although the details vary.

QUAKER THREADS

While the evangelical threads help define the Latin American Friends tapestry, these are interspersed with Quaker threads that give it a distinctive texture. A brief look at some of the Quaker elements of the history of the church in Bolivia gives insight.

One of the first Quaker missionaries to Bolivia was, as we have seen, a Native American man, William Abel, who was born on a reservation of the Kumeyaay tribal group in San Pascual, California. Orphaned at an early age, he spent his childhood as an indentured servant, herding goats and pigs in the hills of Southern California. He decided to become a Christian in 1897 as a result of revival meetings at the Ramona Friends Church. He was discipled in that church and in his early thirties went to the Training School for Christian Workers in Whittier. He arrived in time for the opening of the first group of students in 1900, the founding date of the school.

While at the school, Abel imbibed the oliness emphasis and missionary fervor typical of the times, but he also found his Quaker values and beliefs reinforced. Although the intent from the beginning was to make this an interdenominational school, the founders were predominantly Quaker. The first chairman of the board was Irvin H. Cammack, also the superintendent of missions for California Yearly Meeting. The first classes were held in Philena Hadley's home in Whittier (Philena was the vice-president of the Yearly Meeting's Women's Foreign Missionary Society). Mary A. Hill, a Quaker from Ohio, was invited to be the first president.

One of the frequent visitors to the school was Amos Kenworthy, a Quaker leader known for his spontaneous prophetic ministry. We can imagine his influence on Abel, as the young man participated in preaching services in the different congregations in greater Los Angeles, part of his practical ministry assignment. Apparently he occasionally preached in Friends churches in California, and he spoke in the manner of Friends. In an article written several years later, Quaker missionary Dana Thomas remembers "seeing many large audiences composed of cultured, intelligent people, who were moved in a wonderful manner by this simple native. He was a true Friend, refusing to address meetings where he did not feel the Spirit's leading" (Thomas 1907, 7).

William Abel's service in Bolivia in 1919 was a ministry of sowing seeds; he died of smallpox that same year. Juan Ayllón, his disciple, is credited with actually beginning the first meeting of the Bolivian Friends Church (INELA). Ayllón, a man of mixed Aymara and Spanish blood, was drawn to Christianity through a Methodist missionary; he actually converted to Christianity in a Salvation Army church meeting; he then began attending a local Baptist Church. But in 1919 he was drawn to the street meetings held by Quakers Abel, Mattie Blount, Emma Morrow, and Florence Smith. Ayllón joined with them. Through this contact, he decided he had found his community of faith among Friends. Something about the beliefs, the practices, and the ministry focus convinced him to throw his lot in with these particular people.

After three years in the Berea Bible Training School in Guatemala, the Central American Friends Mission and national church sent him back to Bolivia to plant Friends churches among the Aymara people. Ayllón brought both his Evangelical Holiness training and his convincement as a Friend to this task.

The correspondence from missionaries between 1924 and 1940 emphasizes the evangelical focus of the work above any particular Quaker influence. But we get hints of how the Quaker beliefs and testimonies were being taught and lived out among the people. An example of this comes from the experience of the Chaco War, a conflict that devastated Bolivia and Paraguay between 1932 and 1935, affecting the indigenous populations of both countries.

The war certainly affected the young Friends movement in Bolivia, planted specifically among the Aymara peoples. The government drew its troops mainly from the lower indigenous classes; as the Friends came from this population, this put a damper on the development of the work, taking away most of the young men. In letters back to Oregon in 1933 and 1934, OYM missionary Carroll Tamplin writes that young Aymara "Indians" have no chance of exemption from military service, but that some are going as conscientious objectors, carrying guns to the front but refusing to use them. He writes of encountering three young Quaker believers in meeting just before going to the front. One of them testified to the group, "Although you see me here today with this uniform, dressed as a soldier of the government, I want to testify to you that I do not fear death nor do I want to take life. I am a soldier of Jesus Christ." In another letter Tamplin wrote that of twelve young men he had been training as Friends leaders, some entered the war as soldiers, and of these a few maintained a stand as conscientious objectors and suffered persecution as a result. Others carried out their military duties like other soldiers; still others could not "take their stand as conscientious objectors and have taken to hiding." Several were killed. This shows that there was a serious attempt to teach the Friends peace testimony, even when taking the stand proved life threatening. Among most Latin American Friends today, the peace testimony, while not a key emphasis, is slowly gaining importance among young adults, partly through the influence of contact with the wider circle of Quakers, such as the Friends World Committee on Consultation and the Bolivian Quaker Education Fund.

Missionaries in the following years taught Quaker Christian beliefs and practices, and the organization of the INELA grew along specific Quaker forms, from the Yearly Meeting structure, down to Quarterly Meetings, Monthly Meetings and outposts. Although pastoral, church government developed horizontally with the church council and Monthly Meeting carrying the final decision-making authority. Other Quaker practices that developed include the unique combination of individualism and community (where each voice has equal value in a meeting), the combination of gospel passion with compassionate service (evidenced in the Friends grade schools that rose up along with the churches), a spiritual perspective on the sacraments of baptism and communion, and an openness to the voice of the Spirit. Again, although these specifics come from Bolivia, they reflect the Quaker experience in other countries.

Bernabé Sánchez has served as a leader and teacher in the Honduran Friends Church, as well as a pastor in the San Pedro Sula meeting. His experience of becoming a Christian illustrates a Quaker focus on revelation. As a child, he grew up in a small town where animosity between Catholics and Protestants confused him. His personal search for truth is reminiscent of the young George Fox, asking questions of everyone, offending some with his intensity. One day Bernabé found a Protestant New Testament in the street and, taking it home, began to pour over it, noticing that Protestants and Catholics used some of the same words. Finally his family got hold of a Bible and began reading it aloud.

This went on for several years, and Bernabé's spiritual hunger would wax and wane, never quite satisfied. This changed when a group of Christians meeting in a home invited him, and although they used the Bible in their teachings, they focused on Jesus. That was revolutionary to Bernabé. He decided to become a follower of Jesus and found what he had been searching for. He now says, "Bible reading, going to worship services, prayer – that's all good, but it's not complete if we don't know the author of the Bible." Reverence for the written word of God but dependence on the living Word, Jesus, is a Quaker value characteristic of Latin American Friends (Thomas 2012, 37–40).

Manuela Calisaya de Alanguía is a Peruvian Quaker, married to one of the leaders of the Peruvian Friends Church and a minister in her own right. She exemplifies the spirit of loving service and generous hospitality that characterizes Latin American Quakerism. Her life also gives witness to the acknowledged value of women in ministry. She remembers a time early in her marriage when, because of her own shyness, the ideas of service and hospitality frightened her. "And yet," she says, "when God wants to use you in his ministry, he prepares you."

She tells the story of God putting into her heart the thought of opening her home through hospitality even to strangers. The idea came in the form of a sermon in her Friends Church, and it wouldn't leave her alone. That very week she says that God provided her and her husband with some extra money. And of course, soon afterward, a couple from another village arrived, asking for a place to stay while the woman sought medical care. Manuela and Noé hosted the couple and soon discovered other needs, including marriage counseling and spiritual reconciliation. Manuela experienced God using her in new ways and remembers, "It was beautiful to see God's hand touching the hearts of this couple."

The woman's physical condition was serious, and later that week, she died in the emergency room of the local clinic, leaving five children in her home village. This unexpected event was painful for Manuela and Noé, but they helped the man figure out what to do next and where to find help. Now, years later, the children are well, growing up, finding their place in life and following Jesus, partly because of their mother's brief encounter with this Quaker couple who opened their home to strangers. Manuela says, "Although years have passed, I remember this experience as if it happened yesterday. From that day until now, all the blessings we've received from God we share with all who come to our home" (Thomas 2012, 76–78). It's a small, simple story, but it exemplifies the testimony of service in daily life, common among Friends throughout Latin America.

Beginning in the 1970s, other groups from the wider Quaker community began making contact with Andean Friends. That has continued to the present time throughout Latin American Quakerism. While many organizations and Yearly Meetings have taken part, the Friends World Committee for Consultation (FWCC, Section of the Americas), Quaker Bolivia Link (QBL), and the Bolivian Quaker Education Fund (BQEF) have played especially important roles. These contacts have strengthened the sense of being part of the Quaker family and deepened the Quaker identity of Spanish- and Aymara-speaking Yearly Meetings, while not compromising their evangelical perspective.

LATIN AMERICAN CULTURAL THREADS

Quakers from other parts of the world who visit Latin America often observe that these Friends do not always look or act like Quakers. The worship seems too enthusiastic and usually lacks the element of silence. Business meetings can seem to a visitor to be too informal, perhaps even chaotic at times. Occasionally, the group votes on an issue, rather than waiting for consensus.

As one of us (Nancy) recalls:

I (Nancy) remember the first time I participated in a large FWCC conference, for the Section of the Americas. It was held in Chiquimula, Guatemala, and I formed part of the Bolivian/Peruvian delegation. I had been invited to stay on after the event for special meetings about the production of Quaker literature in Spanish. I was curious as to how Andean Friends would respond to the more formal North American Quaker forms for worship and business that I figured would predominate at the main event. I discovered that many of these men and women had previously traveled in broader Friends circles and they knew just what to do. They fit in with the formalities and behaved calmly in "appropriately Quaker" fashion. But in the special meetings, after the North American delegates had gone home and it was just a group of about fifteen Latin Americans (with a few of us gringos thrown in), the whole flavor changed. The meeting was louder, livelier, more informal and more highly participatory. The difference amused me. It also caused me to wonder: is one style more Quaker than the other? The after-sessions were definitely more Latin American!

And of course, there is not one single Latin American culture. Each country and even region brings its own unique colors and patterns. Another memory:

This time it was a Latin American Friends' pastors conference, held in Santa Cruz, Bolivia. Leaders from North, Central, and South America, as well as the Caribbean, gathered to share stories, learn from each other and worship together. Each evening, different groups would present the work of Friends from their country. One evening we listened to three presentations. The first, a dynamic young Hispanic pastor from California, used PowerPoint˙ to illustrate his highly educated and articulate introduction to the work among Spanish-speakers in the United States. A pastor from Cuba followed him, and he spoke quietly without notes, fanfare or technology, but I was impressed by the dignity and formality of his presentation. He seemed professorial, someone with whom I could discuss great literature. The Peruvian delegation made the third presentation that evening. Rather than one representative, the whole group of about ten women and men gathered on stage, conferred briefly and then arranged themselves and began to sing, accompanied by a charango and a flute. While not a polished or professional performance, they sang wholeheartedly. Then several people spoke, spontaneously sharing their gratitude at being present and for God's provision. It took more time than the other presentations, but no one seemed to care.

Again, the differences in the presentations amused me, and also warmed me. These differences reflected culture more than anything else.

While differences exist within the Latin American context, some of the cultural threads that run throughout these Friends churches include the importance of celebration, and the role of music, complete with native instruments, in expressions of spirituality. If we look at broad patterns, the intuitive, emotional side of human experience seems to predominate over the more rational, reflective aspect when people come together to worship. (Of course, many exceptions exist.) Other common threads include the importance of the extended family, in an expanding context of community. These traits, to some degree, characterize people all over the world, but the emphasis varies from one setting to another.

Another cultural aspect that contributes to the complexity of Latin American Quakerism is the presence of the indigenous peoples, especially in the Andean countries, and in Guatemala and Mexico. And in some places, a history of violence and upheaval makes its mark. One thinks especially of Cuba.

In Bolivia and Peru, the Friends church has developed almost exclusively among the Aymara people, a pre-Incan group with its own complex world view and cultural expressions. When Oregon Yearly Meeting (now Northwest Yearly Meeting) took on the work in Bolivia in 1930, it intentionally adopted indigeneity as a strategy for planting the church. In other words, the goal was to encourage the development of a Christian Friends church that would flow in Aymara forms and styles as much as possible. This partly accounts for the unique character of this community today.

Gaby Maita's experience illustrates the influence of an animistic background on contemporary Friends. Gaby grew up in Cochabamba, Bolivia; her family was neither Catholic nor Protestant but, like so much of the population, paid homage to the local gods. She remembers the regular incense offerings her parents made in the home, practices that obligated the whole family to use alcohol and cigarettes as well as the potions prescribed by the diviners. She remembers the hatred and fear her family expressed toward Christianity.

When Gaby was sixteen, she responded to the message of a street preacher and became a follower of Jesus. She says that she was immediately delivered from her alcohol addiction, not able to even stand the smell of the liquor her family sold from their home. Her conversion infuriated her parents and she suffered "punishments" at their hands for two years. Through the friendship of an older Christian woman and participation in a small church, Gaby slowly grew in her faith. In time her parents also became followers of Jesus.

Since that time Gaby and her husband Esteban Ajnota have pastored Friends churches and even served as missionaries sent from the Bolivian Friends Church to the work in Peru. She has also worked as director of the Compassion program in a Friends church in Santa Cruz. Gaby says, "Having found Jesus from within my own culture helps me understand how animism, with its particular customs, traps people. I've learned how to reach out to others in this culture with the Word of God" (Thomas 2012, 28).

Because of this animistic background, many Latin American Quakers are aware of the power of evil and do not take lightly the seriousness of being cursed. They are also open to the many ways God can communicate to his people, including dreams and visions. They tend to be more open to the supernatural realm than are their fellow Quakers to the north.

Ignacio Plata Mamani, also from Bolivia, was raised on a remote area of the where his family subsisted on sheep herding and a small crop of potatoes when the weather permitted. Animism, the belief in a spirit-filled world, permeated life in his community. He remembers one time when his mother was gravely ill, watching as the local diviner scattered the coca leaves to learn the causes of her illness. The leaves showed that the illness came from an envious neighbor, a distant relative, who had cursed his mother. His grandfather then brought in a powerful *curandero* (ritual curer) to find a way to counteract the curse. This *curandero* confirmed,

> You are surrounded on all sides by evil people who are envious of your prosperity, but the worse enemy is your relative who has, by magic and cursing, placed you in the hands of the devil so that he might bring you sickness, spoil your crops and kill off your animals. They want you to leave so they can take over your land.

The *curandero* told them to sacrifice a llama and sprinkle his blood on the neighbor's fields and then told them the ingredients of an offering to counter the curse, a strange mixture of incense, alcohol, a llama fetus, small candies, and colorful threads. His price to perform the ritual was high, but the family gathered the stuff and paid the price. Immediately after the ritual offering, the mother recovered, and the problems seemed to be over for a while.

But hardly a year passed when Ignacio's baby sister became sick, and this time the diviners and *curanderos* did not seem to be able to help. An aunt who had become a follower of Jesus learned of the situation and came to take the baby to a local evangelical church for prayer. After a week of prayers and care by the women of the church, the child recovered, and to the family it was a miracle. Moved by the recovery of the little girl and the testimonies of the believers, Ignacio's family decided to also become followers of this Jesus. The believers visited Ignacio's home to bless the family and pray for their animals and fields. That long-ago day marked a radical change in the family's life. They became part of a Friends church and they have remained faithful to this day.

Ignacio remembers learning another way to handle curses and those who place them. He moved to the city of La Paz as a young adult. One day when he was home visiting his parents, he learned that the neighbor who had cursed them years before had suffered the death of his son-in-law and was about to lose his daughter to sickness. Ignacio's father told him they planned to go and pray for the daughter. Ignacio, remembering the curse, protested, saying this man was only getting what he deserved, that he was their enemy. But the father insisted, telling his son that the way of Jesus was to forgive those who have wronged us and to love the enemy. This was a foreign gospel to Ignacio, but respect for his father won out over his protests. Together they visited this neighbor and prayed for the daughter. She recovered, and relations between the families were healed, perhaps the greater miracle. Today Ignacio is active as a Sunday school teacher in his Friends church, a husband and father to six children, and a firm believer, not only in the power of God to heal the sick but also in the importance of showing pardon and love to those around us (Thomas 2012, 58–62).

CONCLUSION

The Quaker Yearly Meetings around the world express themselves in many ways, with both common threads and unique aspects. No one group could be characterized only by the threads of "Quaker gray." The purpose of this chapter has been to portray Latin American Friends as an expression of Quakerism, a legitimate and colorful part of the worldwide family.

The origins of the Friends movement in England were highly contextual, rising out of specific problems of social and spiritual unrest. And the forms and content of the answers were also contextually specific. Much of the faith and practice, including the testimonies, although specific to seventeenth-century England, has proved true in other times and contexts and contributes to our Quaker identity cross-culturally.

The practice of following the Spirit's guidance for "here and now" is part of the Quaker DNA. Being Quaker means responding to the voice of the Spirit in ways that are both affirming of local culture and, at times, prophetically countercultural. As this chapter has demonstrated, Latin American Friends exemplify this trait of response to their context, following the Spirit's guidance in ways that are both uniquely Quaker and more broadly evangelical Christian.

As in any community of human beings, Latin American Friends have their struggles, areas in which they can grow. Yet their interweaving of evangelical Christian, Quaker, and Latin American threads adds color and vibrancy to the worldwide Quaker tapestry.

SUGGESTED FURTHER READING

Graves, Brian Christopher. (1999). *Americanizing Cuba by Cubanizing Protestantism: the Cuba mission of American Friends, 1900–1948*, Unpublished MA thesis, University of Texas in Austin.

Hilty, Hiram. (1977). *Friends in Cuba*, Richmond, IN: Friends United Press.

Nordyke, Quentin. (1972). *Animistic Aymaras and Church Growth*, Newberg, OR: The Barclay Press.

Thomas, Harold R. (2003). *Cultural Themes, Worldview Perspectives, and Christian Conversion Among Urbanizing Evangelical Aymaras*, Unpublished Ph.D. dissertation, Fuller Theological Seminary, Pasadena, CA.

Thomas, Nancy J., ed. (2012). *De Encuentro a Ministerio: La Vida y Fe de los Amigos Latinoamericanos*, La Paz, Bolivia: CALA.

11

ॡ

Quakers in Africa

George Busolo, Oscar Malande, Ann K. Riggs, and Theoneste
Sentabire

INTRODUCTION

Worship among Friends in the Global North is communal. It was among an
"assembly of God's people" during the seventeenth century that Robert
Barclay encountered the "secret power" that touched his heart. It was that
community to which he longed to be united and knit, that he might know
himself to be "perfectly redeemed" (Barclay 2002, Propositions XI § VII).

In contrast, the study of Quakerism has largely followed the more individually oriented styles typical of theological disciplines and religious studies
in the Global North. In Africa, reflection on religious faith and theology are
more often communally oriented. Agbonkhianmeghe E. Orobator writes in
Theology Brewed in an African Pot of a course he leads at Nairobi's Hekima
College titled "'Palaver Session.' This is the time when students sit in a round
hut and talk about God, faith, and their religious experience in an African
context" (Orobator 2008, xi).

The term "palaver" can have a negative connotation in English usage,
suggesting time-wasting discussion over negligible details. In African usage,
it denotes thoughtful discussion of substantive matters worthy of communal
attention.

Palaver among the authors of this chapter began when Kenyan Oscar Lugusa and Rwandan
Theoneste Sentabire met as students at Friends Theological College, Kaimosi in western Kenya
in 2007. George Busolo began his studies at the college in 2010. Ann Riggs served as principal
and senior lecturer in theology at Friends Theological College 2009–14. Busolo contributed
research into the historical and cultural background of Maragoli Friends and conducted
targeted interviews at Vozoli Village Meeting, Keveye Monthly Meeting, Chavakali Yearly
Meeting for the chapter. Sentabire and Lugusa researched and prepared drafts for sections on
Friends beliefs and practices, respectively. Riggs designed the study and prepared the final text.
All contributed to the section on community.

How is the lively oral experience of palaver to be captured in written form, making it possible to draw others into the exchange? In this chapter, Kenyan, Rwandan, and US authors share the results of their palaver of many years' duration on Quakers in Africa. The chapter begins with an introduction to the historical and cultural context of present-day African Friends and their considerable diversity even within a given region of a given country. A "thick" ethnographic description of the beliefs, practices, and community among a specific group of Friends at Vozoli Village Meeting, part of Keveye Monthly Meeting, in Chavakali Yearly Meeting, Kenya, follows. African Quakerism is everywhere inculturated and shaped by pre-missionary cultures. More modern historical events often also impact Quakerism in each place. Space does not allow for more than a few comments in the final section highlighting distinctive differences from our Chavakali Yearly Meeting example in other African areas.

CONTEXT

In 1902, when Friends Arthur Chilson and Edgar Hole arrived in western Kenya from the United States, in company with the more experienced Willis Hotchkiss, their goal was the establishment of a self-propagating, self-sustaining, native Quaker faith community. Friends Africa Industrial Mission addressed a holistic spectrum of needs: the sharing of Christian faith as understood by Friends, health care, income generation, and forms of education needed to participate in the emerging world of global modernity (American Friends Board of Foreign Missions 2007; Kimball and Kimball 2002; Painter 1966; Riggs 2014).

The mission collaborated with partner missionary bodies and the British colonial administration in building and operating schools, roads, hydroelectric power facilities, and civil administrative structures and in the creation of the civic culture that laid a foundation for the independent country of Kenya. The close relationship between Church and civic culture found in the United Kingdom in the Church of England and the Church of Scotland inevitably shaped the development and self-understanding of Friends in Kenya colony and still stands in the background of contemporary Friends life in Kenya (Riggs 2011). For instance, the more than 1,200 Quaker schools in Kenya are sponsored by local Friends bodies, but, with few exceptions, the faculties and staffs are public employees and students are studying to meet nationally mandated standards and perform in national examinations. Over time Friends in eastern Africa have brought innovations into the local cultural context, for example, changing understandings of the roles of women and girls (Angell 2006). Yet, the vivid sense of Quakers as a counter-cultural body that appears in some parts of the world does not characterize Friends in eastern Africa in the same way.

In 1946, East Africa Yearly Meeting was set up as a member Yearly Meeting of Five Years Meeting, later Friends United Meeting (FUM). Evangelization and population growth have led to the establishment of numerous Yearly Meetings in Kenya, Uganda, and Tanzania and sent offshoot missions that led to Yearly Meetings in Burundi, Rwanda, and the Democratic Republic of Congo (DRC) that belong to Evangelical Friends International.

Predecessor Quaker initiatives in Africa from Britain have had a rather different history and development. British Friends carried on a mission focused toward newly emancipated enslaved people on the island of Pemba, now part of Tanzania, from 1897 to 1963. British Quaker Joseph Sewell and American Quakers Louis and Sarah Street traveled to Madagascar in 1867. Friends in Madagascar had strong ties to other Protestant bodies there and in 1969 joined with French Reformed and Anglican groups to become the new Church of Jesus Christ in Madagascar. British and Dutch Friends have had a small presence in South Africa since 1728. Central and Southern African Yearly Meeting was set off from London Yearly Meeting in 1948. There are small meetings and worship groups in many larger cities across Africa. Today, the largest Quaker presence continues to be in the Friends United Meeting bodies of Kenya and surrounding countries.

The vision of Friends United Meeting as an international association of local jurisdictions, rather than a nationally defined body, is an ongoing conflict point in Kenya, where more than 40 percent of the world's Quakers live and worship. For a vocal minority of Kenyan Quakers, separation of Friends Church in Kenya from Friends United Meeting is a matter of postcolonial self-determination. For others, participation in the international FUM body is a significant dimension of self-identity and a valued link to a living and spiritually nourishing heritage. Kenyan, Tanzanian, and Ugandan Friends share common doctrine and Church government forms, articulated in *Faith and Practice of Friends in East Africa* (2011), although local expressions vary considerably. Friends in neighboring Rwanda, Burundi, and Democratic Republic of Congo grew out of branching divergences in theology and spirituality within the Kaimosi mission and participate in the Evangelical Friends Church International Africa Region.

Powerful negative economic and social forces press upon Friends in eastern Africa. Transparency International's corruption perception index for 2015 places Kenya, Uganda, DRC, and Burundi among the more corrupt countries in the world. Society-wide corruption has the potential to negatively impact almost every aspect of the social fabric, siphoning public funds needed for social well-being, community security, education, health care, public utilities, and infrastructure to enrich select elites. In Kenya, the gross domestic product (GDP) per capita expressed in purchasing power parity increased 50 percent in the half century after independence. India's GDP per capita, equal to Kenya's in 1964, tripled during the same period (Kandie 2015). Burundi and DRC are among the five poorest counties in the world measured by per capita purchasing power (Pasquali 2015). Yet, the vast mineral wealth of DRC has created a vicious context of ongoing violence that draws into its web numerous consumers in the richer Global North (Burgis 2015). Depleted soils and inefficient farming methods mean the average farmer across non-Saharan Africa produces one ton of grain per hectare (2.47105 acres), a yield less than half of an Indian farmer's, less than a fourth of a Chinese farmer's, and less than a fifth of an American farmer's output (World Bank 2007).

Membership in a tribe, which might be defined as an "exclusive, territorially bounded, self-conscious collectivity of people sharing a common language, history and culture," is a central organizing life principle in eastern Africa (Spear 2003, 16). Tribal competition and conflict, sometimes deadly, even genocidal, shapes the cultural landscape.

The history of the emergence of Chavakali Yearly Meeting and our focus meeting, Vozoli Village Meeting, is told in local accounts in tribal terms. The original East Africa Yearly Meeting served Friends across the internally diverse Luhya super-tribal group. In 1973, the large Bukusu group separated into Elgon Religious Society of Friends (Quakers), sometimes called Lugulu Yearly Meeting. In 1981, the Maragoli group established East Africa Yearly Meeting of Friends South at Vihiga, and in 1997, Chavakali Yearly Meeting was established from within East Africa Yearly Meeting South.

In 2016, Chavakali Yearly Meeting was composed of fifteen Monthly Meetings, made up of fifty-eight village (local) meetings. Most of the founding leaders and members of Vozoli had passed away, with only three members of the group remaining: Philip Kidake, recording clerk of the meeting; Beatrice Kekaya, meeting treasurer; and Esteri Vuguza, one of the elderly leaders of the meeting's United Society of Friends Women (USFW) group. The meeting had forty-three adult members, thirty-nine full members of the Church, and four yet to be accepted as full members. The Church had 119 young Friends, suggesting a promising meeting in the future.

Milka Njeri Kasavuli was the pastor of Vozoli in 2016. She is of the Gikuyu (Kikuyu) tribe from central Kenya, formerly a member of Presbyterian Church of East Africa. She became a Quaker by virtue of marriage to a Quaker husband of the Maragoli sub-tribe. She noted that it was a challenge at the beginning adopting the Quaker style of worship, so different from the Presbyterian style. It was also difficult to engage with the culture of the Luhya people, who seemed to vary among themselves on traditional matters, but she had learned how to respond to the challenges (Interview March 13, 2016).

The ancestral home of Maragoli people is in Maragoli land in Vihiga County, Kenya. High population density led to emigration in large numbers from the ancestral home and settlement in other farming areas and cities and larger towns across Kenya and into Tanzania. As a result, Maragoli communities can be more cosmopolitan in perspective than some more physically insular groups.

Also in 2016, Samburu Rosina Lepario served as a pastoral student (intern) from Friends Theological College at Vozoli. The Samburu people are a branch of the Maasai tribal cluster and are primarily located in the semi-arid north central area of Rift Valley province, Kenya. Tribal members are pastoralists subsisting on the milk and meat of their herds of cattle, goats, sheep, and camels. The Samburu region is prone to drought and cattle rustling, with associated violence. Lepario is the second Samburu student, and first woman, to be educated for Church leadership in the Samburu Quaker community. The Samburu believe that God created the world and everything that exists and he disappeared to heaven or "shumata." The name of God is "NKAI Eng'iro," "God who stays in mountain." Friends mission work began among the Samburu in 1995 led by Luyha Isaiah Bikokwa as an extension of the older Turkana mission. The more immanent and intimate understanding of God presented by Quaker missionaries has been particularly attractive to Samburu women.

BELIEFS

In *What Is Not Sacred? African Spirituality*, Laurent Magesa writes, "The goal of African spirituality, and African *Christian* spirituality for that matter, is the good life (John 10:10)." Incorporating language from Samuel Kobia (Kenyan theologian and ecumenist, formerly general secretary of the World Council of Churches), Magesa continues:

"Life comes where nothing had been, and everything is constantly being sublimated into something beyond the reach of time." Human participation in this process of continual "sublimation" constitutes the essence, meaning, and requirement of spirituality. The foundation of the vital force that makes universal existence possible is God . . . The cosmos is a "moral" reality in the African worldview; it is a performance or experience "nurtured . . . through the relational value of all life within the cosmos but especially by the [active] network of human relationships." (197, 195f.)

East African Friends beliefs are shaped by their daily life experience and their perception that God is at work within quotidian occurrences. Their experience of the Divine significantly impacts their beliefs in God, Jesus Christ, the Holy Spirit, the Church, theological anthropology, soteriology, and the Good Life.

Maragoli Friends believe God is a unique supernatural being. The giver and sustainer of life, God created all things. With suggestive Old Testament resonance, Maragoli Friends believe that God can act out of anger toward them if they "rebel" by neglecting God's rightful worship and is merciful and forgives them if they repent and return. Negative life events may be attributed directly to God's will and action or to the power of Satan, the Enemy, whose activities God is able to defeat and overcome. Some believe that before Maragolis settled in western Kenya, the tribe lived in what is now Saudi Arabia and were in direct contact with a Jewish community.

In the village meeting setting, the day-to-day experiences of people in the meeting are a vital communal concern. Participants share their concerns and joys. When people are sick, they ask the congregation to pray for them. When they recover from distress, they bring their joys to the fellowship. Some will thank God for positive interventions by bringing a special gift to the Church, such as food, money, live goats, or chickens. Routine successes may also be attributed to the attentive care and love of God, the giver and sustainer of life.

God is experienced interiorly by believers through daily interaction of personal devotion in prayers, singing, and working. Vozolian elder Sarah Undisa shared orally at a meeting of the United Society of Friends Women that she was sick and listless for two weeks. On a Friday night, God revealed Godself and brought to her a song in *Tsinyimbo Tsya Natsaye* (*Songs of God* Maragoli language hymnbook) number 122, which she sang in a different tune than usual. When she sang, she was well and praised God for such an instant healing (Interview March 13, 2016).

Local people understand their Trinitarian belief in God, Jesus Christ, and the Holy Spirit to be distinctly Quaker. Beatrice Kekaya notes: "we believe in God the father of Jesus Christ, God the Son and God the Holy Spirit. The God of whom our parents were taught of by Bwana Ford" (early twentieth-century US missionary Jefferson Ford) (Interview March 13, 2016). Kekaya adds that this is why Quakers do not focus on John 3:16, as the verse does not mention the Holy Spirit or the Spirit's work in the believer. Kekaya uses the name *Nyasaye* for the Triune God. *Nyasaya* is the name Maragoli people use in African Traditional Religion for the one supreme divinity.

JESUS CHRIST

Jesus Christ is viewed as mediator between Friends and God. People feel freer to address Jesus Christ as their intercessor than God himself. People think that at some point, Jesus Christ's primary role in the Divine mystery of Trinity has the particular function of intervening in our lives as a Savior, who always keeps fixing things that can endanger our lives. They believe their prayers and supplications reach to God via Jesus Christ to whom they feel much closer and perceive as forgiving to them.

HOLY SPIRIT

The Holy Spirit is the central focus of beliefs at the village meeting of Friends. People believe the work of God through Jesus Christ is carried out by the invisible power that is closest to them at every step of their life's experiences. They believe the Holy Spirit enables them to do God's will as well as shows them how to do it. The Holy Spirit guides them and empowers their resilience, enabling them to recover from the challenges they may face. They believe the purifying work of the Holy Spirit in their lives is essential to their human well-being. Seeking purification for their lives by the Holy Spirit requires timely repentance. Purification of each person is led and enabled by the Holy Spirit through prayers, worship services, fellowships, and services to the needy, among the other activities.

THE CHURCH

The Church is the community of the people of God. Although people view the Church in the first instance as the gathering (fellowship) of believers at their village meeting, they believe that the Monthly, Quarterly, and Yearly Meetings and other Christian communities around them are also Church. From their village-meeting level to the national and international levels, all people who participate in Christian communities in faith, beliefs, and actions form the global body of the Church.

People experience themselves as part of the Church while with others. They feel fellowship with God while they are with fellow believers. People gather at the Church's building expecting practical support and motivation from the wider community during the meeting. Although the village meetinghouse may not have particular signs and images, people consider it as a sacred place. People come seeking to right wrongs they may have done and to restore their relationship with God and other people. This is the place where people share their joys and concerns and believe and trust that their pleas have reached God. Some view the Church as a hospital for the needy; others see it as a place of celebration and thanksgivings for the successes of people of God. Some see the Church building as a holy place where God lives. Mzee Herbert Jumba observes that in the past, a Church was a point of unity to the community. In his view, internal conflicts have led the Church to be seen in more individualistic terms and even unable to continue "proclaiming the word of Christ" (Interview March 13, 2016).

THEOLOGICAL ANTHROPOLOGY

Friends in Africa believe that life is a sacred gift from God. The creation story of man and woman "in the image of God" is greatly cherished (Gen 1:27). They believe human beings should join in fellowship with one another as they do so for their Creator. They believe that the "woes of life" started with the first couple's failure to adhere to God's command (Gen 3). However, they believe that God in kindness and love for people initiated a special plan for restoring a happy life of fellowship with God and revealed this plan through Jesus Christ. As a result, human beings can enjoy that fellowship with God again, once they accept being led in their lives by the Holy Spirit.

Any act threatening to life is discouraged and condemned. People want to live a long life even with challenges such as poverty or incurable maladies. Humans are made up of body and soul, both of which relate to God, whose purpose is to make them live happily. Christians' destiny and survival in this world belong to God. This contrasts vividly with some African Traditional Religion (ATR) beliefs that focus on the potential malevolent spiritual power of other humans. One's life after death is predicted by one's relationship with both God and his people. In a general way, well-behaved people are believed to have a better chance to enjoy life than those who misbehave.

SOTERIOLOGY

People are viewed as having an essential need for salvation. Vozoli Friends believe salvation is a special gift from God. Through Jesus Christ's acts of mercy and love, they believe a person is given "eternal life" and becomes a permanent member of the Kingdom of God (Titus 3:5–8). By this act of grace, one is granted the abundant life, regardless of challenges experienced in this world. This gift of eternal life, which makes it possible to join in fellowship with God and his people as "children of God" (John 1:12) must be accepted. The Holy Spirit inwardly enables the reception of salvation.

Participation in outward processes of becoming an active member of the Church is also expected. Chavakali Yearly Meeting currently offers junior membership to young people between ages eight and twelve. However, the primary catechetical formation processes of new members are of long standing: "Book 1" and "Book 2." Despite the titles, the catechesis is oral. Each requires a period of three to six months of learning. In Book 1, those being trained learn doctrines as understood by Friends: God, Jesus Christ, Holy Spirit, Salvation, the Church. Successful completion leads to associate member's status and a membership card. In Book 2, practice is added to this knowledge of faith. Those who succeed are granted a full membership card, allowing them to work in different capacities within the Friends Church such as preaching, teaching, leading a committee, or being presiding clerk of various groups and meetings.

Some members express a belief that the catechetical process does not currently have an adequate impact on participants. They see some in the Church as only coming to get membership cards with a hope of having a good "send-off" when they die. This is attributed to weaknesses in the formation program: increased focus on memorization of verses, to the detriment of spiritual depth and a proper focus on "a true life of salvation."

THE GOOD LIFE

As noted earlier, in ATR the Good Life is the focus of religious spirituality. In western Kenya, this focus is carried over into Christianity, sometimes using the terminology of "abundant life." "When you go to the local village meeting," researcher Theoneste Sentabire records, "you can wonder if these people have such a life that is commonly known as 'abundant life', since there are so many challenges that surround them!":

> "Good life" for them is a simple living that makes people connect well with other creatures and their Creator. Some may be wealthier and healthier than the others but still consider their fellow members to have a "good life," since they know that sometimes people may be given what seems to be enough for them in the eyes of God. One of the paradoxes here is how members of the village meeting enjoy and praise God regardless of the challenges they are facing, as they struggle to handle them. In fact, when confronted with some of those challenges like lack of school fees for their kids, for example, they bring such a problem in the congregation as a prayer request. When answered, then many thanks go to God for solving it. While

still waiting for the answer there is still hope that God will have a way. So, one can say that the congregation at the village meeting level is a community of hope and restoration. They just want to have a "good life" that, of course, recognizes our human limitations. For them, the good life does not mean the smooth-flowing of it. They believe that once faced with life's challenges, blessed is the one who stands firm and succeeds in the face of it. They believe that being contented with what they have is enough for them to have a good life. Thus, being thankful to God for their social status is crucial. So, the Church's mandate, in this case, is to help people understand the paradoxes of life as they teach them how to work hard in order to have such a good life. If people work on their lands (shambas) and get a good harvest, they believe, is to have a good life. Success for them just means something that makes their life sustained. If not, then something wrong is happening and they need more prayers and support from the congregation.

PRACTICES

African Traditional Religion is rich in rituals and practices that mark passage through life from before birth, through birth, naming, initiation, marriage, parenthood, work, health, sickness, death, and movement through states of status as an ancestor. Life includes moments of specific religious practices of worship, prayer, sacrifice, and consultation with religious experts (Mbiti 1990, 2015) The Quakerism of Vozoli Village Meeting also marks life participation and progress with distinctive practices that incorporate elements from traditional culture, Christian Quakerism, and global modern culture. Space permits discussion of only a few: patterns of worship, prayer, and child dedication.

PATTERNS OF WORSHIP

Worship is similar to or reflective of semi-programmed worship patterns found in many Friends United Meeting settings around the world, although the "feel" and sound are often distinctly local and may vary considerably among meetings not too physically distant from one another. As elsewhere, meeting for worship and business meetings differ in some regards.

The business meeting is presided over by the presiding clerk. In our focus area, it is normally scheduled to take place on seventh day, a day before the worship meeting. If there is a pressing issue, a business session can be held after the worship meeting.

Worship meeting can be presided over by the presiding clerk and run by the recording clerk. This can cause conflict over the roles of the pastor and the clerk. There has been a longing among some Friends for the worship meeting to be presided over by the pastor, but presiding clerks are sometimes reluctant to let this happen, especially in this part of the country. The notion behind this is that the pastor is not the custodian of the affairs of the local community but has been sent to serve the local community.

At Vozoli, the meeting starts with an opening prayer from the clerk, followed by singing of two songs from hymnals in the local dialect. Praying for different needs follows and an interlude of announcements. Then there is singing to invite the pastor to read a Scriptural text and preach. After the preaching, the pastor may pray; then there is an offertory. After the giving, the meeting is closed. Prayer, announcements, Scripture reading, and preaching may be in English, Kiswahili, or the local dialect.

Other elements can occasionally be included within the worship meeting. There may be praying for a bereaved family and a kind of after-ceremony of the funeral declaring the dedicated period of mourning over and the bereaved free to go on with other duties. There could be child dedication or confirmation of members. Visitors may be asked to offer a greeting. The clerk's table in worship meetings may include subordinate presiders representing the different constituencies of the meeting: the main meeting (the meeting as whole) on the first week of a month, the youths (who can be as old as fifty) on the second week, women on the third week, and men on the fourth week.

After the worship, the leaders of the Church together with the pastor meet over a cup of tea. In other instances, after the occasional services, for example, the hosts invite members to share food together. Coming together to eat is familiar after worship; there is a sense here of a kind of small celebration. Although the explicit idea may be unknown to members, one researcher noted that this could be understood as a kind of celebration of the victory wrought at the cross by Jesus.

Historically, a strong sense of orality in the culture was grounded in elders telling stories, giving teachings and other advice to be handed down to other generations by word of mouth. When Quakerism was first introduced, there was no writing in Luhya cultures. Orality would have had a great impact in unifying communities, passing on the right knowledge and maintaining it; the privacy of handed down information was expected. The process empowered capability for a strong memory.

With modern education systems, technological changes, and the influence of westernization, the earlier focus on the storytelling of elders for handing down knowledge is diminishing. In worship meetings now, reading takes center stage. Formally, the orientation is toward expecting members to depend mostly on reading rather than on what they hear. In practice, however, there is hesitancy to fully rely on reading. Sometimes it is not easy for people to remember clearly what was read. It is storytelling that people tend to remember easily. Pastors note that for people to remember, one has to use a story for illustration.

Business meetings are presided over by the presiding clerk. The role of the pastor in most cases is to give guidance in matters of faith and practice. If members have disagreements, the pastor is expected to create and nurture harmony in the meeting and unity in decisions. Arriving at unity is first attempted through extensive consultations. If members do not arrive at unity, matters of business are suspended for further deliberations as people seek the guidance of the Spirit through prayer. Unlike some other forms of Quakerism, here the theological accent in communal decision making is on pleasing God through human harmony, rather than on unique and otherwise inaccessible knowledge of God's will for the group.

PRAYER

Praying is a central practice. Most often prayer is vocal, in continuity with the prayer style of ATR. People believe that as they speak in prayer, they are speaking directly to God. Prayers may be offered at any time. At times people believe that what they are praying for needs more attention from God, and they will request prayers from others. The pastor of the meeting or a meeting group, in particular, may be called on to play a role of mediator to God.

There is a tendency in these prayers for the use of recurring phrases such as "the blood of Jesus," "God come down," "our Father in heaven," and "in the name of Jesus." The general idea in the phrase "blood of Jesus" is a call for protection. As people pray using this phrase, there is a sense of finding security. Behind this lies the blood sacrifice of traditional religion. In pre-Christian times, Africans sacrificed blood to appease the evil spirits who were believed to cause harm. By extension, to get protection through prayer, it is thought necessary to seek the powerful blood of Jesus, sacrificed on the cross. Prayers for safety in travel frequently include a request that "the blood of Jesus" cover the travelers.

A great longing for God to meet the needs of the people directly is often overtly evident. In desperate times, people will always resort to prayers and any positive outcome in difficult circumstances is followed by an appreciation to God.

Keshas are occasional overnight prayer events. They may be organized at any time but are particularly popular at New Year's Eve and Easter. *Keshas* are designed for spiritual and emotional refreshment and renewal. Sessions feature a sequence of lively praise and worship songs, preaching and teaching on pastoral subjects, and periods of unprogrammed simultaneous personal vocal prayer. *Keshas* are often popular with youth and led by young pastors. In some areas United Society of Friends Women (USFW) groups hold popular *keshas* that also attract men and young adults. At times, this kind of prayer has not been received well by elders who see it as a worship form that has come into Friends practice from other Churches and is not a Quaker way of worship.

During pastoral visitations in homes, families come together to pray with the pastor. Most families pray together during mealtime or at the break of day. Frequently, as the day begins individuals in the family may pray aloud on their own.

CHILD DEDICATION

Parents bring children to the Church to be dedicated to God by the pastor: boys at eight weeks of age and girls at six weeks. Some claim the source of the ritual is in the Torah. Whether for this reason or some other, female pastors have been reluctant to carry out this responsibility.

The pastor is informed in advance of plans for the dedication so that preparations may be made. It is expected that the pastor is in good standing before God and meeting members at this time of dedication: the dedicator's sanctity is necessary to avoid transmission of any kind of bad luck to the child. During the preparation period, the United Society of Friends Women will visit the parents to learn the name of the child and convey this information to the pastor.

The event is announced in the meeting to all community members. After the dedication, the parents are expected to host a celebration in their home, where gifts are presented. Although some ATR settings have rituals of gift giving for newborns, these gifts are usually associated with those the Wise Men brought to Jesus at the time of his birth.

During the dedication, the pastor reads Scriptural passages, such as those connected to child dedication or Luke 18:15–17, where Jesus allows children to come to him. There is time for encouragement and teaching to the parents from the pastor and other members of the Church. There is celebratory singing after which the pastor is given the child to dedicate. The child has to be held in a given position where the head rests on the pastor's left so that when the pastor is praying he or she is able to lift up the right hand to bless the child. After the prayers, the child is handed back to the parents. At the conclusion of the service, members are invited to go to the parents' home for further celebration.

A birth certificate form is issued by the Yearly Meeting and given to the parents, confirming that the child has been dedicated. This is a legally recognized document in Kenya and may be used later for national identity card registration. Within the Church, the burial procession of a person holding a dedication card is different from that for someone without this dedication.

COMMUNITY

Every Christian community is established among people who already have cultural beliefs and practices. In Africa some elements of ATR influence understandings of Christian faith and practice. Modernity and its technological innovations directly impact almost all human communities. Even communities too isolated or impoverished to actively engage modern technologies are impacted by the environmental effects of technological change.

Each community consists of multiple webs of relationships both local and more attenuated, created and maintained through multiple means. In this section on community, we consider the weaving together of elements from African Traditional Religion, Christianity, and modernity in groups within the local meeting and relationships with wider community networks and bodies.

WEAVING TOGETHER OF ELEMENTS FROM AFRICAN TRADITIONAL RELIGION, CHRISTIANITY, AND MODERNITY

The act of people of a community coming together for a worship service is a familiar form; coming together for worship is a major component of ATR. When there is distress or any challenge that the community should address, the committee of the elders (*baraza la wazee* in Swahili) calls people in the street or rural area to come together, at a particular place or homestead, to discuss the matter and try to find the solution. Once the determined solution is successfully implemented, the *wazee* will call the group together to celebrate. The *wazee* may direct people to offer sacrifices such as goats, sheep, or cows. In the Christian setting, the community meets in the Church and upon success brings something of value, which may or may not be an animal, to the Church as a gift for thanksgiving.

In ATR, the community itself is one of the elements in which people have faith. Traditionally people talked to one another face to face. Now in a Quaker setting, communication is often in mobile phone calls and text messages and many people have access to television. People can follow sermons on TV without necessarily going to the village meeting; they can engage in videoconferences, and so on. These new technologies may limit people's previous experiences of the physical presence of others in community gatherings. On the other hand, people in the village meeting are thankful for God's provision of technological discoveries that may improve their lives. Communication technologies, modern medicine, and improved construction and farming practices are seen as contributing to the well-being of the village meeting.

There are areas of conflict over the continuing presence of some ATR practices and about incorporating changing technologies, when they are seen as contradicting or challenging substantive Christian beliefs. In Maragoli, traditional memorial services (*lovego*) are understood as deeply connected with non-Christian, non-Quaker beliefs. Friends in nearby Kakamega Yearly Meeting are no longer observing *lovego* and whoever is found practicing it is disowned. Some of the pastors in Maragoli are criticizing the practice, as well. As a result, Pastor Milka notes that the Church has decided to call the practice an anniversary party to avoid attracting opposition (Interview March 13, 2016) But underlying tension remains.

Members of the bereaved family carry out *lovego* memorials. There is always a meeting to discuss any matters of concern that might not have been attended to by the deceased when alive. If there were any debts, they would be settled. Undivided family land is subdivided. In the case of inherited tribal land, a few families are adjusting to modern sensibilities in allowing the daughters of the deceased a share.

Rituals are carried out to appease the dead. In ATR, it is believed that if the family of the bereaved does not carry out the memorial *lovego* service well, the dead will haunt them. A cow is slaughtered by the grave and the blood is spilled there. The meat of the cow is considered to be special; if family members are absent, some is preserved for them. A ritual shaving of the entire head of all family members follows. Some families incur so much expense that land is sold and educational resources for the children depleted. Both fear of the dead and the damaging of family capacity to meet the expenses of the future seem contradictory to Quaker faith to many contemporary believers.

Another area of conflict is the style of worship. The elderly members of meetings associate slow singing of songs, limited charismatic movement, and traditional sermon styles with Quaker identity. The younger generations long for electronic keyboards, public address systems, and the kinds of worship song and praise dancing familiar from praise music videos and television. Forms of dancing rooted in traditional culture and associated with certain occasions, such as weddings, funerals, and other celebratory occasions, have become connected with the meeting for worship. But other dance elements come from secular popular culture. A community's singing and dancing, created from a mix of traditional forms and contemporary forms, are part of its unique identity. When a visitor arrives, participants may feel united by dancing together with that person.

Across Africa, youth are leaving meetings without the new technologies and worship styles. Pastor Milka observes that to counter such movement, Quaker meetings have begun to invest heavily in electronic instruments and are providing room for newer forms of worship, seeking a balance that will not do away with older Quaker values (Interview March 13, 2016).

GROUPS WITHIN THE LOCAL MEETING

Within meetings, affinity groups can be powerful spiritual and social forces. United Society of Friends Women (USFW), Youth (younger adults), Quaker Men, Sunday School (children), and widows' groups are vigorously active. Some carry out extensive pastoral activities separate from the "main" meeting and may have their own pastors.

USFW participants have worship meetings to join in fellowship together in homes or in the Church between Sundays. In these meetings, participants teach one another life skills and share their problems as they pray together. The pastor of the village meeting is at liberty to come and join in fellowship with them. There are USFW business meetings, as well, where the group makes certain decisions together about its activities. USFW groups often display notable unity and resourcefulness in fundraising in village, Monthly, and Yearly Meetings and national settings.

They determine among themselves who is to represent the group during the annual Yearly Meeting conferences and national USFW prayer meetings. For child dedications, members choose among themselves two or three women to visit the parents of the child, get the name of the child, and give it to the pastor. USFW women take leading roles in the dedication ceremony such as carrying the child and presenting the baby to the pastor to be prayed for.

During funeral ceremonies, USFW members lead the singing of the burial procession. After the burial, on the third day, very early in the morning, they go to the grave, putting flowers, in preparation for prayers offered during the day at the site. The meeting's men participate during the funeral primarily by carrying the casket during the burial procession.

Funerals are a potent locus of community expression. The funeral of a respected mature person will draw several hundred participants: extended family members, childhood and initiation age-mates, coworkers, and meeting members. A daylong process of recalling and praising the life of the deceased and singing, praying, reading of Bible texts, and preaching celebrates the fulfillment of the deceased's life and reestablishes the web of community relationships reconfigured by the death.

Quaker Men have meetings in homes and in Church following the pattern of women's meetings. They rarely attract the numbers of participants and energy the USFW has achieved, however. The Quaker Men undertake fundraising for specific projects such as new Church buildings. At many times they get support from the women's group and lend support to USFW projects.

Widows in the village meeting come together to encourage and teach one another. Widows groups are encouraged to participate in income-generating projects to support themselves financially. At the special worship meetings marking Easter, the offertory is set aside to help widows who are in need.

Participation in Young Friends may continue through one's forties. Their activities are similar to those of USFW and Quaker Men. Youth prayer, preaching, and worship events are often designed with lively popular music sensibilities in mind and charismatic devotional practices such as glossolalia are accepted among younger Friends where they may not be among older generations.

Sunday school services are understood to be age-appropriate worship occasions for children. They are arranged separately during the worship meetings on Sundays. A Sunday School teacher who has been trained through workshops and seminars normally gives instruction. Sunday school children also have a chance to participate in Sunday school conferences organized at the Yearly Meeting level.

RELATIONSHIPS OF LOCAL MEETING COMMUNITY
WITH WIDER COMMUNITIES

Most participants of Vozoli Village Meeting are Luhya of the Maragoli subtribe. They and others who reside with them are expected to live peacefully together, an ideal of both ATR and Quakerism. In contrast, in some parts of the wider Quaker community and in the broader culture, substantial ethnic tension and conflict exist.

Opportunities for fellowship in wider webs of relationship lie in Monthly, Quarterly, and Yearly Meeting business tasks and prayer events. *Keshas*, pastoral teaching and preaching events, annual and triennial conferences of several days' duration attract extensive participation. National and international meetings of Friends Church in Kenya, USFW Kenya, and Friends World Committee for Consultation Africa Section are well attended.

Members are encouraged to participate in the wider world of Kenyan society affairs. A high birthrate and high incidence of AIDS means that many families include orphaned nieces and nephews. Concern among Friends for impoverished orphans means that many provide funds or direct food support for the care and education of non-relative orphans. Friends vote and participate in local citizen-based organizations focused on civic well-being or the environment. There is active participation with the wider Christian community. Friends are represented and energetically involved in the National Council of Churches in Kenya (through Friends Church in Kenya) and take an interest in the work of the World Council of Churches and All Africa Conference of Churches (through Friends United Meeting). Members strive to work together in transforming humanity and toward a better world.

CONCLUSION

Quakerism came to Africa through different channels. Eighteenth-century commercial travelers stopping in South Africa had different purposes in establishing a Quaker presence there than did British and US missionaries to Madagascar, Tanzania, and Kenya in the nineteenth and early twentieth centuries. Quakerism was received into quite different cultural and life contexts, as well. The newly freed clove workers of Pemba were imported migrant workers, not members of settled communities. Missionaries in Kenya colony were assigned regional tribal groups to evangelize by the local British authorities. The Yearly Meetings that grew up in response to missionary presence, despite many differences in specifics, display some underlying similarities to the agricultural and small-town life of the Yearly Meetings from which the early missionaries came. The meetings found in larger cities across the continent grew out of and respond to the needs of Quaker diplomats, educators, international aid workers, and international business community members on assignment from areas where Friends were longer established.

Christian theological differences have played a part in the development of different kinds of Quakerism across Africa, as well. In meetings with roots in British Quakerism, unprogrammed or open worship means silence-based worship. In other meetings, unprogrammed worship is noisy with the sound of individual oral prayer. In 1927, a charismatic revival at the mission at Kaimosi generated substantial energy and disagreement. The African Church of the Holy Spirit split off as a separate body in 1933, and Kaimosi missionaries Arthur and Edna Chilson moved to Burundi, founding the Evangelical Friends Church there in 1934.

At some point, pressures from ambient civil society impinge on the forms of the Quaker community. In Rwanda and Kenya, expectations from beyond Friends that Christians mark membership not by a Book 1 associate membership card or by infant dedication but by water baptism have been pressed upon them. In Kenya, persuasive theological explication has always been an adequate response. In Rwanda, the press to either utilize water baptism or be categorized by the society as a potentially dangerous cult has been strong enough for Friends to accept the practice. In Tanzania, the secular government controls which group is publically recognized as a legitimate Yearly Meeting, presumably due to fears of uncontrolled influx of culturally disruptive missions.

In recent decades, movement from being a "mission receiving" Church to being a "mission sending" Church has had deep meaning for some African Friends. It is experienced as a mark of maturation of their faith and structures and the strength and resourcefulness of their meetings and personnel. Missionaries from within the large Kenyan community serving needs in Congo, Tanzania, South Sudan, and now Belize have also meant a shift in how these Friends relate to the global community of Friends and the wider human community.

Modestly priced airfare and digital technology have made communication and dialogue possible across time zones and continents with an ease that was unimaginable a short time ago. New forms of contact reveal differences and contrasts in newly obvious ways. Compelling global opportunities for palaver open prospects of a new period of Quaker experience in Africa, as well as potential for a new period of global impact outward from African Quakerism.

SUGGESTED FURTHER READING

Angell, Stephen W. (2006). "Quaker Women in Kenya and Human Rights Issues," in R. Drew Smith, ed. *Freedom's Distant Shores: American Protestants and Post-Colonial Alliances with Africa*, Waco, TX: Baylor University Press, pp. 111–30.

Friends United Meeting. (2011). *Faith and Practice of Friends in East Africa*, Kisumu, Kenya: Friends United Meeting.

Kimball, Herbert and Beatrice Kimball. (2002). *Go into All the World: A Centennial Celebration of Friends in East Africa*, Richmond, IN: Friends United Meeting Press.

Painter, Levinus K. (1966). *The Hill of Vision: The Story of the Quaker Movement in East Africa 1902–1965*, Kaimosi, Kenya: East Africa Yearly Meeting.

Riggs, Ann K. (2014). "Friends in Eastern Africa," *Quaker Religious Thought* 123–24 (November): 85–92.

12

Quakers in Europe and the Middle East

Hans Eirik Aarek and Julia Hinshaw Ryberg

This chapter gives a current overview of the Quaker presence in Europe and the Middle East. The history of Quakerism in this area contains the earliest history of Quakerism itself. The origin of Quakerism took place in England. This means that the 'mother church' of Quakerism is situated in Europe. There was a Quaker presence in many areas of Europe and the Middle East from the very beginning of the movement, with missions to Ireland and continental Europe from the 1650s. The history and workings of Britain Yearly Meeting[1] (BYM) are the focus of much writing elsewhere in this volume, and this chapter focuses primarily on other meetings in Europe and the Middle East and their interaction.

RELATION TO CONTINENTAL AND NORDIC EUROPE

From the very first days of Quakerism, British Friends were eager to spread their new faith to continental Europe and the Middle East, as well as to America. Reports of Friends travelling in the ministry tell that as early as 1658, Quakers tried to meet the pope to convince him. Quakers also headed for Istanbul and Jerusalem. These expeditions often had severe consequences, such as imprisonment, torture and death. Destinations closer to Britain were more often visited. Ireland and the Netherlands had extensive contact with British Friends, and visits to Denmark and Norway also took place around 1657–59. In 1671, George Fox travelled to Germany with George Keith, William Penn and Robert Barclay. Barclay's *Apology* was translated into other European languages, as were publications by George Fox, William Penn, Samuel Fisher, William Ames, Isaac Penington, Francis Howgill and others (Bernet 2010, 25–41; Bernet 2011).

---

[1] London Yearly Meeting changed its name to Britain Yearly Meeting in 1994.

As a result of this, small Quaker groups emerged in different places in continental Europe in the seventeenth century, for example, in Germany and Holland. A Yearly Meeting (YM) was set up in Amsterdam to serve some of the European countries, but lasted only for a short time. During the eighteenth century, fewer Quakers went to continental Europe and only a few groups of Friends existed. In the nineteenth century, especially in the evangelical period from the 1850s, an increasing number of itinerant British and American Quakers visited continental Europe.

London Yearly Meeting (LYM) showed great interest in this activity and set up the Continental Committee (1790–c. 1916). Worship groups were established in several places, for example, the strong worship groups at Bad Pyrmont in Germany and at Congénies in France (Otto 1974, 184; Etten 1938), although only two YMs were founded. Norway YM was established in 1818. Denmark YM was constituted in 1875 and had its first annual gathering in 1879. Around 1900, these two meetings were considered by British Friends to be the most promising Quaker groups in Europe, with other groups decreasing in size or disappearing.

LYM offered indispensable spiritual and financial support to Friends abroad. An instrument for this was the practice of giving Friends certificates for 'travelling in the ministry' to guarantee their doctrinal soundness. Discussions about the Continental Committee's reports at the YMs are another example. British Friends also supplied literature and financed translations and publications and even printed some publications in foreign languages in England. Before 1900, non-English or non-American authors wrote very few publications.

MODERN EUROPEAN QUAKERISM DEVELOPS

A modern revival of Quakerism on the continent of Europe took place after World War I (WWI). This was a modern, liberal Quakerism, inspired by Britain and especially the influence of Woodbrooke College, Birmingham, England, which had welcomed several European students from its start in 1903. Another influence was the presence of Quaker Embassies/Centres – supported by the British Quaker Council for International Service – which from 1918 were established in some of the major European cities, such as Berlin, Paris, Geneva and Vienna, following up the Quaker Ambulance Unit work after WWI.

International conferences were organised as well. One was the All Friends Conference in London in August 1920, which gathered 936 delegates. Most of the delegates were from Britain and the United States. Of the forty-six delegates from the rest of the world, only 10 came from continental Europe. This conference was instrumental in revitalising the Quaker Peace Testimony, making it one of the pillars of European Quakerism. The other was the Young Friends International Conference of 1928 in Brussels, which gathered fifty young Friends from fifteen countries. Europe, outside the British Isles, had a share of fifteen delegates. There were signs of acknowledging and even wanting a greater Quaker fellowship in the twentieth century – a fellowship that transcended the Anglophone borders and in a way represented a return to the seventeenth-century goal of reaching out to the whole of Europe.

Some of the central European countries developed YMs soon after the establishment of Quaker Embassies/Centres: Germany in 1925, France in 1933 and Switzerland in the 1920s. The Netherlands had a special and strong connection to Woodbrooke from the very beginning, which influenced political and religious life in the country. The Woodbrooke connection was instrumental in establishing a YM in the Netherlands in 1931 (Davis 1953, 166–67), while Sweden YM (1935) emerged largely by itself with some support from LYM and American Friends.

British and American Quakers' interest in the Middle East resulted in the establishment of a school for girls in Ramallah in 1869. A boys' school appeared later. The schools have since amalgamated and are now co-educational. A worship group was established in Ramallah during the late 1800s, followed by the erection of a meetinghouse in 1910. The meetinghouse is still an active centre for Quaker activities in the area, especially in peacemaking efforts. In Lebanon, Brummana School started in 1873, and a worship group meets at the school. Since 1929, these two meetings have constituted Middle East Yearly Meeting. However, conflicts in the region make interaction between them difficult and restrict their representation at international gatherings.

International cooperation between the European YMs increased substantially after the founding of Friends World Committee for Consultation (FWCC) in 1937, followed by the formation of the Europe and Middle East[2] Section in 1938 (EMES). Both FWCC and its four geographic sections[3] were designed to be a channel of communication among Friends, helping to nurture their identity as Quakers so that they could better perform their service to the world.

---

[2] The original name was Europe and Near East Section, and it was changed to Europe and Middle East Section in the 1980s.

[3] In addition to EMES, the Section of the Americas, Africa Section and Asia West Pacific Section.

A CASE STUDY OF NORWAY IN A NORDIC CONTEXT

Now follows a focus on Norway as a case study of European Quaker life with additional insights from the other Nordic countries. The Nordic countries are regarded as a unit that shares many similar features in their political, social and cultural characteristics. In terms of religion, they all have or have had Lutheran State Churches. The development of Quakerism in these countries is interesting in that it mirrors many of the features of international and European Quaker development, while demonstrating national adaptations and peculiarities. This offers possibilities for comparisons between the Nordic neighbours and other European Quakers. Norway and Denmark YMs are the only ones in Europe to have existed through the transformation from nineteenth-century Quakerism to modern liberal twentieth-century Quakerism.

Early History

The Quaker presence in Norway dates from 1814. Contact with the Quaker faith took place onboard prison ships in Britain during the Napoleonic wars. Christopher Meidel's Danish translation of Barclay's *Apology* and contacts with British Friends resulted in the convincement to Quakerism of about twenty Norwegian and some ten Danish prisoners.

On their return home in 1814, these convinced prisoners tried to live as Quakers. The original Quaker groups in Denmark faltered after a few years, but some Quaker activities are reported during the middle of the nineteenth century, and a first YM gathering in 1879. Most of the Norwegian Friends settled in Stavanger, with a few in Christiania (Oslo). They gained some supporters but also met opposition from the authorities. The first conflict with the Norwegian authorities is reported in 1816 concerning a Quaker wedding. Normally, pastors conduct weddings among Protestant Christians. Among Quakers, the group, or meeting, is understood as marrying the couple, through the work of the Holy Spirit; there is no pastor. This would have been very controversial in Norway in 1916, and obviously some Norwegian authorities thought it to be illegal. The need for a stronger organisation was felt, and when William Allen and Stephen Grellet visited Norway in 1818, a Book of Discipline was published. The bimonthly meetings founded in Stavanger and Christiania constituted the establishment of a YM (Allen et al. 1818).

The main concerns throughout the nineteenth century were the struggle for religious freedom and acceptance as an independent church. In the first years, freedom from using church rituals in connection with infant baptism, confirmation and funerals was the main issue. Later, this also included the refusal to pay church and school taxes and to undertake military service. Young male Friends were instrumental in achieving a concession in 1902, after more than fifty years of struggle against conscription. Friends suffered punishment such as solitary prison confinement, fines and seizure of property.

Concessions were gradually made after pressure was applied. In 1826, named Quakers were permitted to live in the Stavanger area. Quaker weddings and burials were eventually accepted, but full religious freedom was not granted, even when the Dissenter Act was passed in 1845. This led to extensive emigration to America, comprising one-third of all Friends in the nineteenth century. The first emigration to the United States from Norway occurred in 1825, organised by Quakers. Danish Friends were also decimated by emigration.

In addition to struggling for religious freedom, Friends were instrumental in founding the temperance (1859) and peace (1894) movements in Norway and supporting them. Friends operated their own school in Stavanger from the 1820s until 1912 and for shorter periods also in a few places in rural areas.

The relationship to the 'mother church', LYM, was strong throughout the nineteenth century. Responses to the 'Queries' in the Book of Discipline were sent to LYM almost every year from 1841 to 1890. Reports of travel amongst Friends were published in *The Friend*. Financial support for publications and the building of Quaker meetinghouses and schools was donated by LYM. British Friends provided eldership and oversight for Friends in Norway and Denmark and in other European countries. Even though many Friends had emigrated from Norway to the United States and close personal ties existed, Quaker YMs in the United States had little influence on Norwegian Friends.

The 1860s represented a peak in the membership and activities of Norway YM, with a total of 173 recorded members in 1868. According to the 1865 census, 473 people regarded themselves as Quakers. Denmark saw a peak in its members in the 1880s; the census of 1880 reporting 117 members and the minutes of 1884 listed 60 adult members and 31 children. Several Friends of this generation were well-to-do citizens engaged in trade, shipping and politics. However, a decline in numbers was experienced in the last decades of the nineteenth century, with membership figures in Norway dropping to about 100 and in Denmark to around 70 (Norway, 1865; Membership protocol, Glimt fra Dansk 1975, 65).

The first two decades of the twentieth century saw a further decline in the membership and activities in Norway and Denmark. The Friends' School in Stavanger was closed in 1912. Many of the small rural groups disappeared and the Society had difficulties in leaving its conservative traditions and solving its internal differences.

Renewal and Enlightenment

A thorough renewal started in Norway in 1920 with the visit of the English Quaker Henry Theodore Hodgkin (1877–1933), who gave lectures in large venues in Stavanger. He was invited by Ole F. Olden (1879–1963), a radical Christian though not yet a Quaker, who was to become one of the reformers of the Religious Society of Friends in Norway. Hodgkin's visit by was followed by that of a young Norwegian Quaker who had studied at Woodbrooke and brought modern liberal Quakerism to Norway. In Denmark an evange-lical trend was prominent for a while with the ministry of Johan Marcussen (1851–1936). However, the Woodbrooke impulse manifested itself indirectly through Friends Peter Mannice's International High School, where several Quaker events took place in the 1920–30s during a critical time for Danish Quakers.

In the 1920s, a couple of lecture schools with leading British Quakers took place in Stavanger, as well as Old Woodbrookers' events in different parts of Norway. Old Woodbrookers are adult students who have studied at Woodbrooke Quaker Study Centre in Britain, who then form associations for contact, and for arranging gatherings both nationally and internationally. After 1945, Quaker lecturers would visit Norway and provided not only Stavanger Friends but also the general public with lectures on biblical, religious, ethical and international issues. The Woodbrooke influence was instrumental in forming Norwegian Quakerism in the twentieth century. The 'rebirth' of Quakerism in Norway coincided with the establishment of liberal modern YMs in several European countries.

This shows one of the central features of modern liberal Quakerism: *enlightenment*. It took different shapes in the Nordic countries. While Norway invited many foreign lecturers, Sweden had its own cultural Quaker person-alities, such as Emilia Fogelklou (1878–1972) and Elin Wägner (1882–1949). Cooperation between the countries was also attempted. A periodical, *Kvekeren*, was published in Norway beginning in 1937. This was meant to be a Nordic project but was not as successful as had been hoped, which meant that *Kvekeren* became a Norwegian periodical after WWII. Swedish Friends began to publish their own periodical in 1949.

Parallel translations of Rufus Jones's book *The Faith and Practice of the Quakers* (published in 1927) into Danish, Swedish and Norwegian in the 1940s became the benchmark of modern Quakerism in Scandinavia. When

Kvekerforlaget (Norwegian Quaker Press) was established in 1978, one of the goals was to publish Scandinavian Quaker literature as a means of strengthening regional Quaker identity and outreach.

Relief and Development Work

The interwar years also saw the beginning of relief work, which was to become one of the other features of Scandinavian Friends in the following decades. It started rather modestly with a concern for refugees, especially Jews from Central Europe. This was a joint Scandinavian project and parallel to several similar Quaker projects in Europe, materialising in the Quaker Centre in Copenhagen. Scandinavian Friends also supported relief work in Barcelona after the Spanish Civil War. When WWII broke out, local rescue work included evacuating people from Stavanger to safe places in the countryside. This was the start of Kvekerhjelp (Quaker Service Norway).

In 1946–47, Norwegian Friends took part in a project together with Danish Friends and Scandinavian rescue organisations to rebuild Finnmark in the north of Norway, which had been destroyed by the retreating German troops. British relief workers also took part, thereby promoting European cooperation. A parallel project took place in Finland, mainly initiated by American Friends, which was important for the growing Quaker group in Finland. A large-scale aid and relief project, initiated by Stavanger Friends and joined by other organisations, businesses and the general public, took place in the autumn of 1947. Thirty trucks loaded with clothes and food travelled to Hamburg in Germany to help the suffering inhabitants of the town. The concern for Germany lasted several years and was a joint venture with German Friends, both at the Berlin Quaker Centre and in the Holm-Seppensen project. Swedish and Danish Friends were also involved in this work.

The next major project was launched in the 1960s, when the situation after the war in Algeria became a concern of Norway YM. A development project in Kabylie, Algeria, was set up by Kvekerhjelp with wide public support and funding from the Norwegian Agency for Development Cooperation (NORAD). Cooperation with other European Quaker Service organisations made it a joint European project. This was the beginning of Kvekerhjelp's engagement in several projects and countries, partly in cooperation with Friends in other countries. Sweden and Denmark had a special interest in Eastern Europe. Swedish Friend Herman Backman's (1912–2011) concern in the 1950s was revived as an East-West peace conference in Stockholm in 1981. This was followed by Danish Friends and EMES with the Baltic Friends Meetings from 1984 to 2004. Over the years, Swedish and Danish Friends have had their own projects in Bangladesh, Ethiopia and Eastern Europe while also supporting Kvekerhjelp.

In 1993, Kvekerhjelp was invited to take over the administration and running of American Friends Service Committee's (AFSC) kindergartens in Gaza, and from 2006 this was extended with a programme for teachers on trauma relief. In 1998, peace-building projects after the ethnic conflicts in Burundi, Rwanda and the Democratic Republic of Congo in Central Africa became a major concern. These projects were financially supported by Norwegian governmental agencies.

Current Situation

The Religious Society of Friends in Norway in the twenty-first century is thriving. In 2016, regular meetings for worship were held in Kristiansand/ Mandal, Oslo and Stavanger. Monthly or occasional meetings were held in Bergen and Bø in Telemark. Meetings for worship or business are held regularly in Kristiansand/Mandal, Oslo and Stavanger. Most meetings also arrange midweek or other convenient gatherings for learning, discussion or participation in other activities. Some groups participate in interfaith dialogue events and in activities that foster sustainable living.

Membership grew from 129 in 1995 to 150 in 2016. Several new people also began to attend Quaker meetings after having encountered Quakerism on the Internet. Premises are owned in Oslo and Stavanger and hired at the other sites. Two historic meetinghouses, at Stakland and Røyseland, are occasionally used in the summer for meetings for worship. Several historic Quaker sites, including graveyards, are found in the Stavanger area.

By 2016, Oslo Monthly Meeting (MM) was the group with the largest membership. The YM's and Kvekerhjelp's offices were on the same floor, thus making it a Quaker Centre. Some of the rooms were hired out to Somali non-governmental organisations (NGOs), two travel agencies and an author, thereby making it a vibrant place for dialogue and fellowship. The MMs in Stavanger and Kristiansand were smaller but maintain regular meetings for worship and other activities. The Bergen group, a worship group under the care of Oslo MM, has grown in recent years. In 2016, this group consisted of six members and as many regular attenders and had found public premises for their meetings. A couple of small groups interested in contact with Friends have sprung up in different parts of Norway. A question in this connection has been how a 'virtual MM' could be developed for Friends separated geographically but wanting to foster spiritual fellowship.

Most of the new members who have joined the Quakers are adults. Only a couple of families have Quaker roots through generations. Quaker children have not usually followed their parents into membership. This may change, especially as more family-friendly policies were introduced in the 1990s. Of the 150 members in 2016, 18 were younger than age 15.

The annual YM is residential. In recent decades, Norway YM has invited young people and families with children (including grandchildren) to take part in its annual gathering and other all-age events at reduced cost. Groups of Quaker children have formed friendships across geographical divides, and teenagers have taken part in further gatherings, thereby introducing them to Quakerism and enabling them to develop a Quaker identity. After a two-year programme, one group of teenagers celebrated their journey together in a meeting for worship in which those who wished were welcomed as adult members. This can be seen as a parallel to church or humanistic confirmation, both strong traditions in Norway today.

Norway YM has a rich history; the archives are extensive and often visited by professional and lay historians. A website has resulted in a small yet steady stream of enquirers. Norwegian schools require students to work on projects in which they have to present a given faith group or denomination. The website is set up to provide information suitable for such projects. Some student groups also attend local meetings for worship and ask questions afterwards before presenting their projects in class. The Stavanger area has many organisations with a particular interest in history, and members are invited to give presentations about Quakers and Quaker history. One of them has also contributed chapters on Quakerism and Quaker history to anthologies on religious topics. Other authors and scholars have also written about Quaker history.

Nowadays Norwegian Quakers have a good reputation among other churches and relief and development organisations. Quakers are members of various umbrella organisations, some of which are ecumenical and some oriented towards peace and relief. They also work locally on environmental issues.

The annual budget is dominated by the expense of running the premises in Oslo and Stavanger. Most of the income comes from members, although the Norwegian state and local councils are legally obliged to grant money to churches and life stance organisations (organisations that have a nonreligious life stance; often they are health care organisations) on a per capita basis and equal to their contributions to the national church. In addition, a special concession offers tax reductions to religious organisations and certain NGOs, including Norway YM and Kvekerhjelp.

New thinking about ecological consciousness and stewardship in relation to nature has been a concern for Scandinavian Friends for decades. Formulating a specific Quaker thinking and spirituality on these issues has been the subject of several annual gatherings and publications. At present, a compilation of Quaker insights and experience is being developed, documenting Norwegian Quakerism today, *Tro og Liv* (Faith and Practice). In recent years, Swedish Friends have made a similar compilation. Questions of right ordering and the running of the Society have been discussed in recent years, especially in terms of discipline, structure, eldership and oversight.

The official status of the Nordic Quakers varies. In Norway and Sweden, they are recognised churches, but the groups in Finland and Denmark are too small to warrant 'church' status. As mentioned earlier, religious and life stance groups have a legal right to public financial support in Norway, which is not the case in the other Nordic countries. Swedish Friends have the option of dual membership, which is not possible in Norway.

Since 1947, the most sustainable cooperation between Nordic Friends has been the summer gatherings. After a pause of some years in the 1990s, the idea of a Nordic Quaker Gathering every three or four years emerged. The venue, theme and activities are shared, with each YM holding its business proceedings separately. The first took place in 2002. These gatherings have strengthened the ties between the Nordic YMs. They have also encouraged a Nordic Quaker identity, nurtured by the liberal social-democratic ideologies of equality, democracy and human rights in the Nordic countries.

MODERN EUROPEAN QUAKERISM

General Description

In 2016, the Europe and Middle East Section (EMES) consisted of twelve YMs, two MMs, two Recognised Meetings (RM) and fifteen Worship Groups (WG).[4] In comparison, the EMES report in 2003 included only one worship group. Europe and Middle East Young Friends (EMEYF) was established in

---

[4] Monthly Meetings in this context are independent, permanent meetings which can accept new members in countries with no YM. Recognised meetings are permanent meetings under the care and oversight of FWCC/EMES where new members will have international membership. Worship Groups (WG) are the remaining groups connected to FWCC/EMES.

The constituent YMs, MMs, RMs and WGs of FWCC/EMES are unprogrammed, with the exception of the Evangelical Friends Church in Tolna, Hungary, which is programmed. In Europe, but not officially part of EMES, there are eight Evangelical Friends groups or churches. See Table 12.1.

1984 and is an autonomous organisation within EMES for Young Friends age 18–35.

Most of the YMs have long traditions, regardless of their current size. Many of the worship groups are small and more recent. The larger YMs have more resources than the smaller groups, the latter being more dependent on overarching international organisations such as EMES.

The European Quaker landscape is changing. The traditional structures of national YMs and local MMs were predominant in the interwar period and after WWII. Since 1989, a number of small, isolated WGs have been formed in countries with no previous Quaker presence. Many of these groups have formed around individuals who have been accepted into membership through the FWCC International Membership Programme. These new meetings need international contact and care as well as new kinds of support and communication.

From around 2000, EMES has been able to intensify its service to its constituent groups. In addition to its own annual meeting, EMES arranges and encourages different kinds of cooperation, projects and gatherings, such as international family gatherings, Border Meetings, seminars, peace and service consultations and the Quaker Youth Pilgrimage. It encourages mutual understanding between Quaker groups and creates bonds of fellowship among European Quakers.

Developments and Interactions between Quaker Groups

After the fall of the Berlin Wall in 1989, small groups of unprogrammed Quakers were formed in ten of the former communist countries in Eastern Europe. Evangelical Friends are found in eight countries. In 2016, there were Quaker groups in thirty-five of the forty-eight European countries, including Britain, and four countries in the Middle East. A common trait for many of the small groups is that some of the members are often expatriate Friends from Britain or the United States. This may cause problems of language and the continuity of the group when these members move away.

Sharing worship and seeking a common witness are high priorities for Quakers. Larger gatherings of various kinds are especially important for isolated Friends and small groups. Each YM holds its own annual meeting, and the Quaker tradition of 'intervisitation' and sending representatives to one another's annual gatherings continues within Europe and the Middle East. The annual meetings are often residential gatherings with themes and interest groups in addition to the business proceedings. Both EMES and

EMEYF hold annual gatherings with a theme and business proceedings. EMEYF also arranges an annual retreat.

There is a general and growing interest in holding regional meetings. The focus of these gatherings is fellowship and sharing, rather than decision making. The joint Nordic Quaker Gathering has been mentioned in the case study. Regular Border Meetings bring together Friends from Switzerland, Germany and France. Others are held between Friends from Austria and Hungary.

The Central European Gathering has been held in different parts of the region nearly every year since 1996. At first, it was sponsored and supported by EMES but is now self-sustaining. Central European Friends, representing many worship groups and meetings, are considering establishing themselves as a body within EMES that would be able to offer formal membership.

EMES sponsored a Russian-speaking gathering in 2011, and Friends in Eastern Europe have since taken the initiative to organise something similar. All-Poland gatherings were held for three consecutive years beginning in 2013. Friends in the Iberian Peninsula are considering regional gatherings, as new worship groups are established. While EMES aims to support these initiatives, groups are encouraged to become self-sustaining. Many events also happen outside EMES auspices, for example, the annual gatherings of the YMs, the work of the Quaker Council for European Affairs (QCEA), the European branch of Quakers Uniting in Publications (QUIP) and the activities of Evangelical Friends in Europe.

Theological Diversity

The Quaker YMs, MMs and groups in EMES belong almost exclusively to the liberal unprogrammed tradition. Friends in Northern Ireland have a more evangelical theology while maintaining the tradition of unprogrammed worship. Recent years have seen more diversity, with evangelical meetings being established and other traditions making themselves known via the Internet. The resulting theological diversity of Friends can also often be seen within a tiny worship group, with some Friends identifying more than others with the evangelical programmed tradition.

Larger evangelical groups of Quakers, with a pastoral structure, are entering the Central European scene. Finding large groups of evangelical Friends in Hungary, Romania and Albania has been a surprise to many unprogrammed liberal Friends (see Table 12.1). In fact, the unprogrammed tradition now only represents about 10 percent of Friends worldwide. The number of European unprogrammed Friends outside the British Isles is now growing but is less

Table 12.1 Quaker Meetings in Europe and the Middle East

Quakers in Europe and the Middle East are grouped into Yearly Meetings, Monthly Meetings, Recognised Meetings and Worship Groups. Britain Yearly Meeting is the largest and oldest Yearly Meeting. The various meetings follow the traditional structure of Quaker bodies in Britain and the United States and Canada, with Yearly Meetings having autonomy, and Monthly Meetings able to accept members. Recognised Meetings and Worship Groups are under care and oversight of EMES/FWCC, which also deals with international membership applications. In addition, there are Evangelical Friends as a result of American EFCI mission.

UNPROGRAMMED YEARLY MEETINGS			MEMBERS ESTIMATE*		
Country – Town	First mentioned /Early contact	Established	FWCC 2012 Members	Historical Dictionary of Friends 2012 Members	FWCC 2015 includes members, attenders, children
Belgium & Luxemburg		1976	40	33	106
Denmark	1677	1875–79	30	30	30
Finland	1933–37	1992	20	25	40
France	1788/1919	1933	70	60	160
Germany and Austria	1671	1925	340	273	453
Ireland	1654	1669	1 600	1 534	1 991
Middle East (P=Palestine)	P 1869	1929	70		65
Netherlands	1653	1928–31	120	93	115
Norway	1659/1814	1818	150	125	200
Sweden	1850s	1935	100	100	130
Switzerland		1920/1947	100	100	185
United Kingdom	1647–52	1668	15 800	14 907	23 067

UNPROGRAMMED MONTHLY MEETINGS

Russia	Moscow		1996	30	13	26
Spain	Barcelona		1958	10		6

UNPROGRAMMED WORSHIP GROUPS

Czech Republic	Prague			10		12
Estonia	Tallin			10	5	6
Georgia	T'Blisi			20		10
Hungary	Budapest Recog. Meeting			?		9
Italy	Bologna – Milan			20	Bol 10	14
Latvia	Latvia Recog. Meeting			10		7
Lithuania	Kaunas Quaker Group			10		0
Malta	Friends group	1659		10		6
Poland	Poznan – Warsaw			10		12
Portugal	Portalegre			10		0
Spain	Madrid			10		3
Iceland		1861/1937?	2014/2015			2
Egypt						
Bulgaria						
Dubai						

EVANGELICAL CHURCHES/MEETINGS/GROUPS

Country /	Town	Type of group	Established	FWCC 2012	Historical Dictionary of Friends 2012	FWCC 2015 with inclusions
Albania		M/CH		380		
Croatia	Vukovar	W Gr		50		
Greece/Athens	Christian Friends Meeting	M		10		2
Hungary		Church	2005	4 000	4 000	
Ireland EFCI Mission					53	
Romania		Church		920	920	
Serbia		Church		50		
Ukraine	Kiev – Periaslav	W Gr		10		3

* As YMs, MMs and groups vary in the way they produce statistics, these figures can be regarded as tentative.

than 1 600. The general response among liberal Friends has been to cultivate their own Quaker tradition and remain open to interactions with other Quaker traditions. Despite the growth of evangelical Quaker groups in Europe, the unprogrammed liberal tradition remains the custodian of the history and tradition.

This results in a diverse Quaker landscape, which is partly intensified by the impact of the Internet and social media. However, a sense of community among Quakers is both encouraged and experienced by means of various learning opportunities, intervisitation and an understanding of the shared challenges, joys and common interests.

Britain Yearly Meeting and Woodbrooke

BYM remains the mother church and its Book of Discipline, *Quaker Faith and Practice*, is an important resource for European Quakers. Recently, several groups have begun to create their own Books of Discipline that reflect their faith and practice, while continuing to use BYM's *Faith and Practice*. There is a growing understanding that Friends in continental Europe have much to offer British Friends. Witnessing the passion of new Friends and the growth of new groups into maturity can be an inspiration to more established meetings. There is also a realisation of shared experience – there are isolated Friends and tiny or fragile meetings in Britain as well – and an acknowledgement of a common European Quaker fellowship.

Woodbrooke Quaker Study Centre in Birmingham, England, has always been a significant source of learning and inspiration for Quakers, and for those interested in Quakerism, in Europe and the Middle East. European Friends have made use of Woodbrooke's general curriculum, including longer programmes such as the two-year part-time 'Equipping for Ministry' course. Set up in 2015, the Young Adult Leadership Programme has attracted Young Friends from continental Europe. Some European Friends take part in Woodbrooke's online postgraduate programme in conjunction with Lancaster University. European Friends have also served as tutors on Woodbrooke courses. Woodbrooke on the Road, which takes learning events directly to meetings and tailors events to suit, is well used by European Friends. These have included bilingual fellowship weekends and courses for European clerks, for translators of Quaker literature into European languages and for members of tiny meetings and isolated Friends.

Significant Cultural and Political Factors

Europe has experienced many wars and conflicts; the two world wars started in Europe and it was enveloped by the Cold War. Conflicts in other parts of the world influence Europe, especially those in the Middle East and in the former Soviet states. In world conflicts, thousands of refugees flee to Europe. The special situation of Europe, with its many nationalities, languages and cultures, is a challenge for Quaker activities. The long history of wars and conflicts continually tests the peace testimony.

Political Changes

The Western European humanistic Quakerism, especially the social-democratic Nordic variety, often resonates with left-wing political standpoints. The values of equality, democracy and tolerance are at the backbone of Quakers in the West. Quaker groups that have developed in former communist countries have often been characterised by a deep longing for spiritual freedom, born from first-hand experience of a repressive regime, coupled with lack of experience in democratic, egalitarian structures and governance, and personal and collective decision making. This is a source of dynamic tension that can be both a challenge and a learning opportunity for new Quaker groups, and in interactions between new groups and the established Quaker tradition.

Church Contexts

Quakerism in continental Europe has come into being and exists in a variety of religious contexts. Some countries and areas are predominantly Lutheran, while some are predominantly Catholic or Orthodox. Others are highly secularised, even though they may have a predominant church tradition. The religious context of any area affects the spiritual journeys of those who come to Quakerism. It also influences what draws them to the Quaker way and the attitudes and responses to Quakerism from society at large. Countries with an open and active ecumenism respond to Quakers and Quakerism differently from those places where the predominant religion is pervasive. In some countries, the formal relationship to a state church affects membership in a Quaker meeting, as can be seen from the case study.

Quaker groups may find themselves in religious contexts that are traditionally focused on sin or hierarchies or with a repressed religiosity that makes witness in the world difficult. Quaker egalitarianism, a focus on the 'priesthood of all believers' and the importance of faith in action often represent something of a paradigm shift to those finding their way to Quakerism.

Eastern Europe experienced both a vacuum and a freedom after the fall of the Berlin Wall, which provided an array of spiritual possibilities. For some, Quakerism offers a new religious paradigm. The problems associated with freedom, combined with the many alternative interpretations within modern Quakerism, can easily result in fragmentation and a do-it-yourself religion. The diversity of Quaker expression that is available online makes it possible for groups to be established in a variety of Quaker traditions and coexist in same area, for example, in Poland, where meetings have profiled themselves very differently. These differing contexts affect how Quaker groups relate to issues of authority, leadership, democracy and responsibility and how the dynamics between individuals and community evolve. These dynamics require EMES to carefully consider its role in governance, attention to right ordering, guidance and pastoral care without stifling new and appropriate expressions of Quakerism.

Internal Issues

A wide variety of themes engage Quaker groups in their internal dynamics. Issues of language are crucial in a multilingual Europe. Some groups need to strike a creative balance between using English and the local language. Some groups are necessarily multilingual (e.g. Barcelona, Budapest, Finland and Switzerland). The need for interpretation, and the time it takes when meeting, is increasingly viewed as an opportunity rather than a problem, since the process of translation creates a slower tempo and allows for deeper understanding. However, it is a challenge to translate traditional Quaker terminology, especially seventeenth-century English, when there is little first-hand experience of the actual phenomena.

Outreach is an ongoing theme, with the important distinction between informing and proselytising. This is a current challenge in Russia due to the political climate. There is also a realisation that outreach and in-reach must go hand in hand when growing a meeting.

Homosexuality is one of the issues that has divided Quakers worldwide. In some meetings in the region, such as Scandinavia and Estonia, this is a non-issue, because people with varied sexual and gender orientations are accepted and integrated. In others, including Georgia, homosexuality can be a divisive issue. The evangelical Quaker churches have different views than do liberal meetings. Often, the Quaker view reflects the pervading cultural attitude in any given region. The issue has not been as divisive as in some American meetings, but it nevertheless remains a potentially contentious one.

Technology

The digital era has had a profound impact on Quakerism in the region since the 1990s. People have been able to find Quakerism on the Internet and, as has been suggested, those without any direct experience of Quakerism have been drawn to express their own version of it.

Beginning in 2007, Woodbrooke and EMES jointly sponsored a project of online study of Quakerism, available in many European languages. The *Quaker in Europe* study project has helped to make the Quaker way known and accessible. An underlying principle is that knowledge of English should not be a prerequisite for learning about Quakerism. Most Quaker groups have websites and focus on these as tools for outreach, information and inward communication in their own languages. All over the world Friends are exploring technology in communication, worship and decision making. However, these opportunities raise issues of inclusivity and equality, since not all Friends have access to the Internet or the competency or interest in technological developments.

Children and Young Friends

Many small meetings in Europe have few or no children among them. When there are larger gatherings, such as YM or Border Meeting, attempts are made to arrange a meaningful programme for children and Young Friends. This is often dependent on the existence of a critical mass of children of similar age.

Some groups, for example, Norway YM, have found ways to incorporate children as described in the case study. German YM has invested in the production of a handbook for intergenerational activities. Sweden holds a weeklong camp each summer at Svartbäcken, the Quaker Retreat Centre some 60 km to the north of Stockholm. This is a tradition that began in the early 1950s. From being a traditional children's camp with adult leaders, in the past twenty years it has become a popular intergenerational opportunity for fellowship, worship and play. Stockholm Meeting experimented for a few years with all-age worship. Singing, painting, clay modelling and candle making were done in the silence. One WG in Sweden holds meeting in members' homes. Two children (and a dog) are regular attenders.

The Quaker Youth Pilgrimage has been jointly sponsored by the Section of the Americas and EMES since the 1950s. It is now in transition as interest in global interaction grows. Representation at Britain YM's youth gatherings, Geneva Summer School from 1955 and the dispersed community that EMEYF offers are activities for young people within the region. EMEYF's attention to the Quaker business method has proved a source of inspiration for 'older' Friends.

Concluding Comments

In his book *Quakers and the Modern World*, the American Quaker William Wistar Comfort (1874–1955) writes about the importance of European Quakerism:

> If we look to the future, it may well be that the spiritual leadership of Quakerism will come from groups in northern and central Europe. In America we have the weight of numbers and of material resources, and we have the attendant weight of responsibility. But the smaller groups in Europe from Scandinavia to France possess the imagination, the faith and the spiritual vitality to do great things . . . Not ignorant of physical privation and of mental torture, they have passed through a fiery furnace without losing their loving kindness and their dynamic faith in the Eternal Goodness. They may have something of vast import to the future of Europe. (1949, 207)

After WWII, European Friends shared some of this post-war optimism of a Quakerism with its main focus on serving humanity, taking part with enthusiasm in the rebuilding of Europe after the war and engaging in peace and reconciliation work. Peace and reconciliation work is still important, often now combined with environmental and humanitarian concerns.

Europe has seen great changes in the hundred years of modern, liberal Quakerism. It has been embedded in and surrounded and marked by a modern society characterised by a growing pluralisation, differentiation, individualisation and secularisation. Quaker meetings in Europe and the Middle East have remained grounded in the modern principles of the early twentieth century and remain faithful to Quaker tradition. At the same time, Friends have been prepared to explore new ways of expressing their faith and practice.

During these 100 years, Quakers have responded to the challenges in appropriate ways: Friends Ambulance Service during the two world wars, rescuing Jews and non-Arians from Nazi countries, Quaker *Speisung* in

Germany after WWII, peace and reconciliation work in many settings, East-West contacts during the Cold War. The fall of the Berlin Wall in 1989 and the introduction of the Internet in the 1990s are two of the most important changes that have taken place in recent years and have had a decisive impact on the life of Quaker groups in Europe. The environmental and climate challenge, the militarisation of conflicts and the immigrant and refugee situation are more recent challenges. A new picture of Quaker organisation is emerging, implying new forms of networking, meeting spaces, nurturing and care.

It should not be overlooked that some YMs in Europe (i.e. Britain and France) are concerned about the decline in membership and challenged by statistical predictions of the termination of their own YM during the twenty-first century, whereas other YMs and groups experience growth, or at least status quo, and look with optimism to the future. Rapidly growing groups in Africa, Asia and South America and the development of their relations with European Friends may also be seen as a challenge (see Chapter 3, this volume, by Burdick and Dandelion).

However, judging from Nordic Friends, unprogrammed Quakers in Europe are standing solidly and faithfully in their own tradition, working on deepening their understanding and transforming into a movement that meets the spiritual and social challenges of today. This includes contact and cooperation and reciprocal learning with Quaker groups with other beliefs and practices and at the same time a strong consciousness of their own identity and mission. European Friends feel a special responsibility to nurture their own national YMs and the small new groups in continental Europe. EMES and Woodbrooke Study Centre are continuously working according to this agenda, intending to be a ploughshare in the transformation of global Quakerism in the future.

SUGGESTED FURTHER READING

Aarek, Hans Eirik. (1982). Scandinavian Contribution to Quakerism, in *Quakerism a Way of Life*. In homage to Sigrid Helliesen Lund, Ås: Kvekerforlaget.

Aarek, Wilhelm. (1974). 'Die Quäkerbewegung in Skandinavien'. In Richenda C. Scott, ed., *Die Quäker*, Stuttgart: Evangelisches Verlagswerk.

Etten, Henry van. (1938). *Chronique de la vie Quaker française 1750–1938*, Paris: Société religieuse des amis (Quakers).

Otto, Heinrich. (1974). 'Das Quakertum in Deutschland'. In Richenda C. Scott, ed., *Die Quäker*, Stuttgart, Evangelisches Verlagswerk. www.fwccemes.org/

13

❧

Quakers in Asia-Pacific

Stephanie Midori Komashin

Spanning from India in the west, up to China in the north, and down to New Zealand in the southeast, the Asia-Pacific region is home to approximately 35,000 Friends in about twenty countries. By numbers, close to 90 percent are Evangelical, 6 percent are non-pastoral Programmed, and 5 percent are Unprogrammed. This chapter looks beyond these statistics by outlining the work of Quakers and touches on Quaker-related organisations that operate in the region.

George Fox reported in 1661 that an unnamed Friend '[h]ath been three years out in the East Indies, who hath done much servis, and brings a good report of many that received his testimony'; with Fox's letter to the Kangxi emperor of the Qing dynasty in hand, three Friends attempted to reach China in the same year (Fox 1952, 420; Sykes 1997, 4). Most of the landscape of Friends in the region would find their own message in Fox's undelivered letter:

> God ... would have all to know him ... for God is Light, and this is the true Light which doth enlighten every man that cometh into the World, which is Christ the Son of God, the way to the Father ... out of the Earth, Sin, and the Fall, and Evil, and Transgression, Now this is the Light which Jesus Christ hath enlightened you ... If you receive this Light, you receive Christ ... which brings you Peace, and Unity with God, and with one another. (Fox 1706, 207–8)

Though missionary zeal is associated by some with Western-initiated colonialism and paternalism, the most common pattern of mission in this region has been spearheaded by Asians who have requested Asian, British and American Friends to come assist them – through mentoring, financing and limited staffing – in their unaided discovery of Quaker spirituality or unapologetically evangelistic vision. The first of these entreaties came from

Mariano and Cecilia D'Ortez, who surprised London Yearly Meeting (YM; later Britain YM) in 1861 as Quakers from Calcutta asking for a missionary after their comrade, William Gaumisse, had stumbled across the writings of Robert Barclay and Thomas Clarkson and they had begun meeting for worship in like fashion. London Quakers declined this request, but Frederick Mackie (1812–93) and Edward May (1820–64) of Adelaide MM travelled to affirm and assist the meeting of more than thirty committed Indians (Sykes 1997, 4, 41–43). This pattern of native request and ready response has been repeated in the Orthodox Women's Foreign Missionary Association of Philadelphia (WFMA, later Foreign Missionary Association of Friends of Philadelphia)'s 1883 Japan Mission, five of the Asian mission fields of Evangelical Friends Mission (EFM, an agency of Evangelical Friends Church – North America), and Evangelical Friends Church Southwest (EFCSW)'s 1997 Cambodia Mission. In the spirit of Fox's itinerant preaching, intra-Asia missionary fervour also runs high. Employing multicultural and multilingual assets to plant churches, Indian Friends have moved to Nepal, and Taiwanese to the Philippines, with Bhutanese and Thai nationals regularly travelling to neighbouring countries.

Asian Evangelical Friends emphasise personal salvation and the lordship of Jesus Christ, baptise, and employ pastors as do their North American counterparts; however, these similarities occur in environments of village evangelism where no one has heard of Jesus; laying on of hands for miraculous healing of illnesses takes place; and practical theology decisions are made about arranged marriages, household idols and funeral practices. Dissimilarly, Asian Friends face economic, verbal and violent communal persecution, including eviction, beatings, dismemberment and death threats that send them into hiding with the help of pastors and police. Some leaders are proud of their Quaker heritage but also of intentionally cultivating indigenous expressions. Some Unprogrammed Friends find their lack of familiarity with Western Quaker practises disconcerting. While American Evangelicals may feel slightly more at home amongst these Friends, they land outside of their comfort zones amidst the animated dancing and are astonished by weekly prayer meetings of 300 members or open-air meetings drawing 1,500 inquirers.

Non-pastoral Programmed Friends feature hymns and a sermon and conduct silent worship from time to time. Despite potential misunderstandings concerning their denial of sacraments, these Friends are legally registered as 'Christian' and 'churches' first and identify as Quaker second, lest government entities co-opt their properties for other uses. With commitment to health in mind, body and spirit, they focus on serving children by meeting basic needs and providing education, as well as raising awareness of living in harmony with nature. Programmed Friends use phrasing such as 'in love and peace of our saviour Jesus Christ' as well as 'Quaker witness,' and they maintain good rapport with both of the other demographics.

Asia-Pacific Unprogrammed Friends identify with liberal perspectives and enjoy silent meetings, spiritual nurture and penning Quaker literary works. While they look to Pendle Hill and Woodbroke study centres in the United States and Britain for guidance, their own geopolitical realities kindle rigorous living out of the peace testimony as facilitators of reconciliation. Friends undertake life-threatening and occupational risks in demonstrations to protest nuclear testing, treaty issues for indigenous peoples and military expansion and secrets.

Evangelical Friends tend to be representative of the predominantly young general population of their countries and record their numbers according to weekly average attendance in churches and 'fellowship groups' (the latter a term used in some ecclesiologies for meetings of fewer than twenty or twelve active, baptised members), whilst some Asia-Pacific Friends face shrinking and ageing membership and tend to report numbers according to membership that does not always correlate to an ability to regularly attend meetings.[1]

This chapter outlines the Quaker presence throughout the Asia-Pacific region, including an extended case study of Japan, before offering some conclusions.

AUSTRALIA AND NEW ZEALAND

James Backhouse (1794–1869) and George Washington Walker (1800–59) (London YM) formed Australasia's first meeting in Hobart in 1832 and urged the governor of New South Wales that 'it is the bounden duty to make all the restitution in their power ... for the benefit of the aborigines of Australia' (Backhouse 1838, 51). Identifying with this role as 'Conscience of the Colony', Australian Friends have assisted First Nations Peoples and Torres Strait Islanders through the First Nations Peoples Concerns Committee, Quakers for a Reconciled Australia and Quaker Service Australia (QSA), which has expanded into Asia and Africa, including its Cambodian English Language Training Program (Jordan 2016, 1–2).

Unprogrammed Australia YM, formed in 1964, contains approximately 1,000 members in seven regional meetings. Waratah Rose Gillespie (1941–2010) advocated Aboriginal sovereignty (Gillespie 2005, 3–5). Attracted to

---

[1] Some unprogrammed meetings count non-member attendees separately.

Quakerism by its peace testimony and non-condemnation, David Carline (1944-) of the Kooma-gwamu nation has protested at a Tahiti nuclear testing site, organised an alternate school for at-risk children and raised awareness that Australia remains the only Western nation lacking a treaty with Indigenous People. His Queensland Regional Meeting returned a piece of land in 1988. Carline daily waits for guidance in silence beside the river, and says, 'The essence of the Spirit is the same. The ancient Spirits, the respect of the land, and the Spirit of the country' (Carline, personal communication, 2016; Jordan 2016, 1).

New Zealand's Yearly Meeting, *Te Haahi Tuuhauwiri* ('the faith community that stands shaking in the wind of the Spirit' in the Māori language), established in 1964, has roughly 480 Unprogrammed Friends in eight Monthly Meetings. Samuel (1795–1875) and Martha Young Strong (1805–54) (London YM) started meetings in 1842 and shepherding Ann Fletcher (1833–1903) and Thomas Jackson (1832–1900) brought stability through visitation and First-Day Schools (Adams 1986, 22, 75, 82–84). Quaker Peace and Service Aotearoa/New Zealand (QPSANZ) conducts humanitarian work, such as Robert Howell (1946-)'s Indonesian police nonviolence training beginning in 1997 (Gregory, personal communication, 2016).

Australasian advocacy includes earth care and same-sex marriage. Proud features are the Friends School in Hobart, Silver Wattle Quaker Centre and the Whanganui Quaker Settlement.

BHUTAN AND BANGLADESH

Evangelical Friends Church, Bhutan (EFM), is a Yearly Meeting composed of sixty-five churches and more than fifteen fellowship groups since 2000. Approximately 1,850 Bhutanese Friends practise a rich and creative form of Quakerism contextualised for their culture, taking inspiration from the Old and New Testaments and lived out in *goh* and *kira*, their traditional dress (Cammack, personal communication, 2016).

Rupak (1970-) and Pramila Tamang (1973-) were faithful Buddhists who sought healing for Pramila's fatal illness amongst their religious leaders and were told that there was no hope (Cammack 2016). Whilst 'in desperate condition. Serving the idols and all the things', a Christian pastor offered to pray for her and shared the Gospel with them, leading to a process of healing, conversion and baptism in 1997. Pramila recounts, 'I was seeking, "Who is the only one God?" But when I received Christ, then I got peace' (Evangelical Friends Mission 2016b). Rupak's brother, Norbu Tamang (1967-), a refugee to Nepal, met John M. Vanlalhriata (Vanlal) Thiak (1951-) in EFC-Nepal YM and connected the Tamangs to him in 2000.[2] Under Vanlal's mentorship, they started a fellowship that has grown into a 300-member Friends church with ethnic dance worship, Sunday school and church-planting youth trainings (Cammack, personal communication, 2016).

Enthusiastic to live out the ways of the patriarchs and apostles, Bhutanese Friends bury their dead in the hills in place of common Bhutanese cremation. Every fellowship group displays the king's photograph on a wall. At the same time, Friends' intentional servant leadership flies countercultural to societal top-down or positional leadership. Pastors endeavour to raise self-sustaining, self-governing and self-reproducing churches through vision-casting trainings that can number fifty leaders per cohort, and they send domestic and international missionaries (Cammack, personal communication, 2016; Tamang, personal communication, 2016; Tamang and Tamang 2016).

In the ten years since Philippine Evangelical Friends International Ministries (PEFIM) recommended a Bangladeshi evangelist/discipler to EFM for church planting, Bangladesh YM (EFM) has grown to an average attendance of 580 Friends in nearly twenty churches and three fellowship groups. While Bhutanese Friends live in relative safety, Bangladeshi Friends suffer calculated, violent persecution that threatens their lives. With a number of enterprises aimed at raising the standard of living, pastors practise prayerful discernment about stewardship and pursue indigenously sourced, locally reproducible ministry without salary (Cammack, personal communication, 2016; Stansell, personal communication, 2016).[3]

CAMBODIA, MYANMAR AND THAILAND

More than 150 Cambodian Friends in eight churches are grouped within Friends Church (EFCSW) and Good News Friends Church (a collective effort of all Yearly Meetings of Guatemala, Honduras and El Salvador). Immigrants to the United States of Long Beach Friends Church (LBFC)'s Khmer adult ministry shared the Gospel with relatives during trips to their home country. Neang Soth's 'son' Yiv Poa, who became a Christian while a refugee in Thailand, started preaching and discipling in Cambodia in 1994. Soth and Friends asked LBFC for missionaries to assist and Ray and Virginia Canfield's North and Central American missionary team arrived in 1997.

---

[2] United Nations–resettled refugees Norbu and Juna Tamang (1973–) and Bhakta Tamang (1981–) have planted Bhutanese-Nepali Evangelical Friends Church – Eastern Region (EFC-ER) churches in the United States since 2015 (Tamang, personal communication, 2017).

[3] Due to security concerns involving the physical safety of Friends, names have been omitted.

Muen Chan Sokha and Ngin Sinath lead Friends learning how to share their faith amongst those who accuse them of forsaking their heritage and abandoning deceased relatives (Moore 2012, 330; Sward, personal communication, 2016).

The eighty-member Evangelical Friends International Church, Kalay in Myanmar separated from American Baptist International Ministries in 2002 and adopted Pasig Evangelical Friends Christian Church's Discipline. They conduct Programmed worship, have experimented with silent worship and are intrigued by African Friends' dance and song (Bywater 2015).

Chalee Khunakon (1973–), director of education and training, and Solomon Sanking (1976–), director of outreach, lead a Friends church of the Lahu minority group in Thailand that evangelises ethnic minorities in remote bamboo house villages where the Gospel has never been preached. Connected to Damascus Friends Church by Ben Kibbe (1978–) in 2012 through The Way Foundation (Evangelical Friends Church – Eastern Region (EFC-ER)), miraculous healings and laying on of hands in prayer are of great import to Lahu Friends, who love choirs and theological conversation (Kibbe, personal communication, 2016).

CHINA, HONG KONG AND TAIWAN

In 1886, Robert John (c. 1860–1918) and Mary Jane Catlin Davidson (1865–1942) of London YM's Friends Foreign Missionary Association (FFMA) evangelised in traditional Chinese dress and established a school and hospital in Chongqing in southwest China. Despite attacks and one beheading in the Boxer Rebellion, Friends founded Sichuan YM in 1904 with fifty-six Chinese Quakers. Stephen Yang (1911–2007) was imprisoned during the Cultural Revolution, but a government official arranged for Yang and Friends to hold Meetings in Chengdu (Mason and A.I.H. 1938, 8–9, 11–3; Co 2007, 13–4).

From 1887, Esther Hettie Butler (1851–1921) (Ohio YM (Gurneyite), later EFC-ER) founded a Nanjing girls' school and hospital, with pastor-scholar Gao (?–1929) and elder Clara Gao in church leadership. Friends took charge of Church of Christ's Luho Mission in 1900, where the chaplain and Bible women of the Peace Hospital and Chuen-Hwa Wang's clinic evangelised bed to bed (DeVol 1988, 10, 22, 165). The Semi-Annual Meeting sent domestic missionary Lydia Wu to Yunnan province in 1930 and recorded more than 1,000 members in 1934 (DeVol 1988, 191; Williams 2006, 257). Pastor Li of Nanking Friends Church and his wife were tortured to death and Lindley Chiang, pastor of Luho Church and Bible scholar, died in jail. The Chinese Communist Party confiscated their churches and combined them into the sole state-sanctioned church, the Three-Self Patriotic Movement. Some individuals still identified as Quaker in the 1980s (DeVol 1988, 190–217).

With nearly 10,000 members in more than sixty churches in six districts, Taiwan Friends Church (TFC) is the largest in the region, representing 30 per cent of Asia-Pacific Quakers. Charles (1891–1968) and Elsie V. Lambright Matti (1891–1982) and Ella Ruth Hutson (1922–2012) of the Nanjing Mission held their first sing-along in Chiayi, Formosa (later Taiwan; formally, Republic of China) in 1953. Yuijie Ma (?–1980) unofficially pastored Northside Friends Church through daily door-to-door visits to invite women to church (including miracle reports), standing guard at the church gate so women could not sneak out and leading Sunday school in the mornings; planting Lake View Chapel in the afternoons; and running Northside's evening service. Ma and husband Ching-Swan Chow planted Round Hills Friends Church in 1960 and then co-pastored Northside from 1966. Hui Ming led husband, Titus Tung, to pastor Harmony Friends Christian Church, which has an attendance of 600–700 for services, 300 for weekly prayer meetings, hour-long pre-workday morning prayer (accom-panied by 100 or so streaming video hits), a 100-member choir and an orchestra. Luho Mission's Charles E. (1903–89) and Leora Van Matre DeVol (1902–95) figured prominently in TFC's growth (DeVol 1988, 303–6, 393–95; Duh, personal communication, 2016; Lei, personal communication, 2016).

Taiwanese Friends are apt to cite Bible verses to describe Taiwan YM, first convened in 1977 and characterised as buoyant, overwhelmingly young and expressing grandeur. Friends esteem the commitment of their pastors to God, their congregations and evangelism; mutual care and unity of the Spirit within the church; believers' obedience; and fear of God (Lei 2015; Zheng and Huang, personal communication, 2016). 'In the grace of God, the Friends Church family members will continue to maintain their original aspirations and follow their ancestors' footsteps, willing to put themselves in ministry,' envisages women's fellowship and Sunday school leader Chen Yu-Jhu Zheng (1946–), summarizing TFC as '[l]ove God, love people and love to preach the gospel. Let the good news of the gospel be spread to every corner of the world' (Zheng and Huang, personal communication, 2016).

Adapting Chinese New Year *chunlian* poetry decorations, churches affix brush-painted blessings on strips of red paper around the door and gate, and they compare this to doorpost marking in the Book of Exodus. Friends develop ways to be alongside adherents of other religions, such as assisting a bereaved family's funeral preparations whilst maintaining their own faith understand-ings, for example, holding a flower rather than bowing or inhaling incense. TFC makes home visits with would-be converts to worship, pray and replace idols with a wooden cross. Its 'Beauty Life Association' manages orphanage

and senior citizen visitation, hospital volunteers, tutoring, single-parent services, a helpline and counselling (Lei, personal communication, 2016).

The Evangelical Friends Church denomination (with no affiliation to
Evangelical Friends Church International (EFCI)) is an independent
Taiwanese church that joined TFC in 1957 through Samuel Cheng's Mainland
China acquaintance with Charles DeVol but left in 1959 (Duh, personal com-
munication, 2016).

Hong Kong Friends Meeting, an Unprogrammed Monthly Meeting of
fewer than thirty members, founded Oxfam Hong Kong in 1979.

INDIA

India is home to four expressions of Quakerism, non-pastoral Programmed,
mission-affiliated Evangelical, autonomous Evangelical, and Unprogrammed.
Composed of more than 25 percent of Asia-Pacific Friends, India is a micro-
cosm of the region's diversity.

India's oldest Yearly Meeting is non-pastoral, non-sacramental Programmed
Mid-India YM in the state of Madhya Pradesh. Rachel Metcalf (1828–89)
(London YM) arrived in 1866 and Samuel Baker (1856–99) (Ireland YM
(FFMA)) introduced Programmed worship beginning in 1877. Bal Mukand
Naik (1857–1950) evangelised the Chamar shoemaker caste whilst Ojha chief
Jagraj converted forest village communities (Sykes 1997, 60–61, 78–79, 102–3).
Friends aided 11,000 victims of the 1890s famine, flood, and cholera epidemic
and rescued nearly 1,000 orphans (Sykes 1997, 119–21).

For reasons both political and religious, close to 2,000 Friends in six
churches incorporate hymns, sermons and extended time for sharing a song,
Scripture or an edifying word as Programmed worship; practise silent worship
from time to time; and read the Bible and Britain YM's *Quaker Advices and
Queries* monthly (Rhodewalt 2012a; Jonathan, personal communication, 2016).
Extended families such as the Jonathans, Roberts, Lals, Samuels and Daniels
nurture familial community through home meetings (Rhodewalt 2012b). Mid-
India YM has run Compassion International child development centres since
2008, providing daily meals, education and health support and sports training
such as football and karate to 560 children in Itarsi and Sehore. Friends serve
on the Friends School Governing Board for three Quaker-founded higher
secondary schools and a primary school to 'protect the children and . . . make
their bright future' (Jonathan, personal communication, 2016). Over the years,
Friends Rural Centre, Rasulia, Hoshangabad, has adapted from industrial
apprenticeship to adult education, cottage industries, cooperatives, well

building, village schools and no-till agriculture and water filtration (Choudhry 1977, 165–93; Sykes 1997, 269).

Mid-India YM established Sehore Leprosy Asylum in Bhopal state in 1891. A dispute over meetinghouse ownership led Bhopal MM to separate into Bhopal YM in 1966. In the aftermath of the 1984 Bhopal gas tragedy, widely considered the worst industrial accident in history, Friends initiated medical care, meals, school supplies and needlecraft training in the worst affected areas; 150 members in two churches practise weekly Programmed worship and monthly Unprogrammed worship, with goals of educating Young Friends and cultivating concern for global sufferings (Williams and Terrell 1897, 114; Preckel 2012, 198–99; Titus 2016, 1–2).

Programmed Friends organise the triennial All India Friends Gathering for problem solving, increasing understanding and strengthening unity. Their primary challenge is fluctuating government policy that jeopardises or terminates their charitable initiatives (Jonathan, personal communication, 2016; Titus 2016, 2–3).

India's largest Evangelical Friends demographic is a church network of 4,000 Friends in Bihar state (EFC-ER) who enjoy cultural music and worship style, prayer, Bible reading and preaching. Babir and Lalita Gautam and about thirty circuit rider-esque pastors discipled by Victor and Lori Tovar (on-site in 2010–11, then via Internet) started fellowships that have grown into 200 churches. They contribute wells, sanitary latrines and schools in slums to village communities (Evans, personal communication, 2016).

The Yearly Meeting of EFM Kolkata has 1,150 Friends in more than twenty churches and sixty fellowship groups in West Bengal and Uttarakhand states. D K (Diptendra Kumar) Sarkar (1951–) reports experiencing his noontime room in 1979 turn 'very dark and a small light is coming from a hole to my face. I heard a voice – "I need you."' Though shaken, he later felt Hinduism offered enough truth for India, but upon dreaming of Christ's nail-scarred hands and a voice saying, 'I died for you, nobody else,' Sarkar committed himself to Jesus as Lord. Meeting Charles (Chuck) E. Mylander (1941–) while preaching in Kolkata slums led to EFM supporting and advising the church network since 2003. Sarkar expressed, '"Friends" are known as praying people. I thank God that I have come to the right mission' (Sarkar 2013, 1–3; Cammack, personal communication, 2016).

Evangelical Friends Church, South India (EFC-ER) has 580 members in about twenty churches in Kerala state, where P. K., Mariamma, Benson and Annie Sam plant churches through institutions, public transportation hubs, open-air meetings and villages (Duh, personal communication, 2016;

Evangelical Friends Church - Eastern Region 2016a; Evangelical Friends Church - Eastern Region 2016b).

Through the Children's Refuge and Bundelkhand's earliest education and hospital for girls in Madhya Predesh state, Delia Fistler (1867–1916), Esther Baird (1861–1950), Martha (Matti) Barber and Mary Thomas (Ohio YM) raised pastors, educators, doctors and nurses beginning in 1892 – notably, the Bai, Das, Prakash and Singh families, whose descendants number among more than 300 Bundelkhand YM (EFC-ER, EFM) members in three churches that observe the liturgical year and teach Quaker testimonies (Nixon 1985, 16–18, 87, 424–25). Everett Lewis (1905–81) and Luho's Catherine Isabella DeVol Cattell (1906–86) strategised for the Yearly Meeting established in 1961, whilst William Ezra (1909–92) and Frances Hodgin DeVol (1909–96) headed medical missions (Nixon 1985, 146; 1987, 110, 121). Chhatarpur MM manages English Christian College, primary school and nursery, featuring outdoor prayer and yoga. Jack-of-all-trades Gabriel Massey (1935–) has served as chief editor of the Bundeli language Bible translation, pastor, pharmacist, school manager and director of Christian Organization for Rural Nurture, describing, 'I, being a Friend . . . [w]ait upon the Lord for His leading in Silence. Believe on the Bible as Word of God . . . With my life and service I must show forth that I belong to Jesus' (Massey, personal communication, 2016).

Karnataka YM (EFC-ER) has 250 members in five churches on the Arabian Sea V-Coast, whose Caring Hands NGO rehabilitates *devadasi* Hindu temple prostitutes by providing job skills, counselling and children's homes. India Sikkim Friends Church (Evangelical Friends Church, Bhutan) in northeast Sikkim state is a Yearly Meeting of roughly 100 members in two churches established in 2006. Fewer than ten vibrant, ethno-cultural Maithil Friends churches[4] (Evangelical Friends Church Yearly Meeting of Nepal) inhabit India's Terai plains (Cammack, personal communication, 2016; Caring Hands 2016; Duh, personal communication, 2016; Stansell, personal communication, 2016; Tamang, personal communication, 2016). Himalayan Garhwali converted through EFM's 1991–2010 Mussoorie region mission function as an autonomous Friends church network in Uttarakhand state (Hadley 1994, 20; Cammack, personal communication, 2016; Duh, personal communication, 2016).

Members of General Conference of Friends in India, founded by Shri Ranjit M. (1902–77) and Doris Chetsingh (1902–77) in 1959, collaborated with Mahatma Gandhi, Rabindranath Tagore, Horace Alexander (1889–1989) and

---

[4] Due to security concerns, this group's name is confidential.

Marjorie Sykes (1905–95), include fewer than thirty Unprogrammed Quakers separated by great distance who gather for an annual meeting (Sykes 1997, 273–74; Khurana, personal communication, 2016).

INDONESIA

Friends Church Indonesia (EFCSW) is a Yearly Meeting of approximately 4,000 members in around thirty-five churches. In 1987, William (Bill) Hekman offered to start Friends work in Indonesia for EFCSW (Friends United Meeting (FUM) until 1993). Initially, EFCSW sent Bible school students in short-term church-planting appointments, resulting in reports of supposed rapid growth – which proved to reflect Hekman recruiting churches by paying their pastors twenty dollars per month to be Friends. Though many stipendiary churches left after Hekman was removed and compensations terminated, some remained because they liked who Friends were. Superintendents Misterlian Tomana (1963–) and Arbiter Simorangkir (1968–) steadied the network whilst Suryani (Yani) S. Wattimena (1962–) and her husband Rodolf (Ruddy) Pantou (1957–2013)'s itinerant ministry success-fully rooted peacemaking, spiritual renewal and ecumenical reconciliation. Yani mobilised women in intercessory prayer through Indonesia's prayer movement and describes 'being a part of the Friends Church is such a blessing in my life. Love God and love each other is so real in Friends' (Amavisca, personal communication, 2016; Pfeiffer, personal communication, 2016).

Indonesian Friends promote peace in schools, support homeless children and medical programs for the poor and share the Gospel (Quaker Peace & Legislation Committee 2014, 6). One enthusiastic schoolteacher/pastor conceived an idea of spending time in village mosques until someone would inquire, 'You are not Muslim, are you?' Upon being asked who he was a follower of, he would then show the Koran's description of Jesus and supplement this with an account of the resurrection. By his count, two or three people would commit to following Jesus each time, with whom he continued to follow up (Amavisca, personal communication, 2016).

FROM ORTHODOX TO LIBERAL BY WAY OF WAR, A CASE STUDY OF JAPAN YEARLY MEETING

Whilst Asia-Pacific Friends typically preserve their received strain of Quakerism, Japanese Friends began as Orthodox with hymn singing and closing prayer bookending otherwise silent meetings, appropriated assorted

Quaker influences and retained some early customs within their amalgamated post-WWII identity. Japan YM numbers fewer than 110 Friends in five
Monthly Meetings composed of between five and fifty members (Yamamoto,
personal communication, 2016).

   Born a samurai, Inazo Nitobe (1862–1933) was baptised in the Sapporo
Band, an indigenous Christianity of non-pastoral, non-Programmed meetings. A Baltimore meetinghouse reminded him of *Sartor Resartus*'s description of George Fox (Nitobe 1969c). WFMA's interests in Japan and in starting
a girls' school to elevate the status of women coalesced when Nitobe and
Kanzo Uchimura strongly proposed that this was Japan's pressing need
(Nitobe 1969b, 208; Toda 2014, 61–64). WFMA sent Gurneyite Joseph
(1851–1932) and Sarah Ann Newson Cosand (1846–1915) (Kansas YM) to
form Friends' Church (*Furendo Kyoukai*) in 1885 (Angell 2002). Chuzo
Kaifu (1858–1942), preacher, evangelist, and principal of the 1887 Friends
Girls School (later, the Friends School), which begins with Daily Meeting for
Worship and ends with a hymn and moment of silence, helped found Tokyo
Meeting in 1886 (Binford 1950, 106).

   Canada YM (Orthodox, later FUM) and London YM joined the Japan
Mission in 1888 and 1891, respectively. At its largest, Japanese Quakerism
numbered around 350 members, chiefly in Ibaraki prefecture's seven
Monthly Meetings through Kwansen Yoshioka and his wife's pioneering
missionary work and Gurney (1865–1951) and Elizabeth Julia Schneider
Binford (1876–1948) (Indiana YM (Orthodox))'s Gospel Tent Meetings of
Bible, organ and brass (Sharpless 1937, 98; Binford 1950, 183–89; Brownstein
1987, 38–41).

   Baltimore MM's Nitobe and Mary P. Elkinton Nitobe (1857–1938) started
an unaffiliated meeting in Sapporo in 1893 and had a mystical experience
about founding Distant Friends Night School (Nitobe 1969a, 574; Katoh 2002,
30). Nitobe spoke at and hosted meetings, authored *Bushido, The Soul of
Japan*, served as under-secretary-general of the League of Nations and
articulated peace and anti-militarism in the Matsuyama Incident, House of
Peers, and newspaper articles (Oshiro 1995, 258–61; Satô 1995, 222–33; Ootsu
2012, 45–46, 57–64).

   After Tokyo MM's first split due to the earliest Friends having joined
under an 1885 *Confession of Faith* without a peace testimony, Cosand
restarted the pacifist Society of Friends (*Kirisuto Yuukai*) in 1895, with
Japan YM founded in 1917 (Binford 1950, 42–49; Takahashi 1995). After the
1940 Religious Bodies Law granted recognition to large Christian groups,
Japan YM merged into the United Church of Christ in Japan, which included
creed, sacraments, ordination, Shinto training and *youhai* ((imperial)

worship from afar), and in 1942 stated its support for the war (Best 1948, 51–56; Breen 2003, 266; Yamaguchi 2015, 1), but approximately twenty dissenting Friends led by Seiju Hirakawa (1874–1963), Iwao Ayusawa (1894–1972), Kikue Kurama (1910–98), Ichiro Koizumi (1912–91), Kiyoshi Ukaji (1914–98) and Toshi Ishida (1912–2002) practised resistance through underground silent meetings (Sharpless 1944, 39–41; Akashi, personal communication, 2016).

After WWII, Tamon Maeda (1884–1962) and Yasaka Takagi (1889–1984) lobbied that Emperor Hirohito not be prosecuted in the Tokyo War Crimes Trials, and Elizabeth Janet Gray Vining (1902–99) (Germantown MM) was appointed Crown Prince Akihito's tutor through American Friends Service Committee (AFSC)'s recommendation (Hoshino 2010, 31–35). Three former meetings reorganised Japan YM in 1947 under leadership of the non-cooperating Friends, who steered it towards Liberal Quakerism (Brinton and Watahiki 1958, 258, 269; Toda 2003, 16–20).

Japan YM organises the Nitobe Memorial Lecture and publishes Japanese Quaker history and thought. Japanese Friends support the Friends School, two kindergartens both named 'Small Friends Kindergarten' and featuring silent prayer in their daily programmes, Japan Friends Service Committee (JFSC, formerly Japan Friends Organisation) and Friends Old Folks Home. JFSC's Friends Setagaya Centre Building fosters preschooler/senior citizen interaction by housing Friends Nursery School (with the traditional mochi rice-cake pounding ritual and Doll Festival), Friends Home, Friends Care Centre and Shimouma Reassurance Health Centre. Offshoots are Friends LARA Nursery School and two crèches. Kamiuma and Nakamaru Day Care centres provide senior rehabilitation and dementia care along with Japanese calligraphy and ikebana (flower arranging), marking the year with a New Year's shrine visit, taiko drum and *mikoshi* (portable shrine) festival and *Bon Odori* (dance welcoming ancestral spirits) (*Otomodachi Hoikuen* [Friends Nursery School] 2015; Japan Friends Service Committee 2016; Yamamoto, personal communication, 2016).

Tokyo MM practises Unprogrammed worship with sharing from those who 'receive the working of God' or hymn requests. Tokyo Friends enjoy monthly evening worship, hymn singing, a study group and a peace round-table, and they have written statements opposing Japan's legislation on national military secrets and collective self-defence (*Kirisuto Yuukai Tokyo Gekkai* [Society of Friends Tokyo Monthly Meeting]). Mito MM introduced conscientious objection to Nagasaki atomic bombing survivor Susumu Ishitani (1931–2002), who founded COMIT (Conscientious Objection to Military Tax) and translated the historically important manga *Barefoot Gen* depicting the bombing of Hiroshima, challenging, '[P]eople say only saints such as Gandhi or Martin Luther King, Jr. can do nonviolence ... Did they act nonviolently without fears? ... We need to grow and become a George Fox, a Gandhi, a Martin Luther King, Jr., or a Stephen' (Ishitani 1986, 7; Ishitani 1992, 2–3).

While Nitobe considered Quaker spirituality best suited to Japanese sensibilities,[5] it turned out that pacifism – the testimony often seen as synonymous with Quakers today – proved the greatest challenge for Japanese Friends in the 1894 and 1941 fractures (Nitobe 1969b, 209; Brownstein 1987, 37; Furuya 1995, 69–71). Navigating evangelical Orthodox, non-evangelical Orthodox, London YM and Pendle Hill study abroad influences during the rise and fall of Japan's colonial imperialism, Japanese Friends aligned with Liberal Quakerism after WWII.

NEPAL

Nepal's 5,600 Friends are organised into two Yearly Meetings (EFM) and represent more than 15 percent of Asia-Pacific Friends. Evangelical Friends Church Yearly Meeting of Nepal, primarily in the south, has upwards of 3,000 attendees in forty churches and twenty fellowship groups, whilst EFC-Nepal YM contains nearly fifty churches and eight fellowship groups throughout the country with average attendance of 2,500 (Cammack, personal communication, 2016).

After working alongside Bundelkhand Friends in Chhatarpur hospitals and schools, John and Sangi Vanlal (1953–) of India's Mizoram state moved to Nepal in 1994 to plant EFC-Nepal YM, where Sangi's village sewing centres and tailoring shop have trained more than 600 women since 1997 (Cammack, personal communication, 2016). Despite blockages and strikes, beatings and bomb threats, their candid 2016 report characterises a church-planting ministry focused on home visits for building strong relationships:

> Evil spirits were troubling Jit Narayan Mahoto and his family, so Jit asked Pastor Maharaji for help. Maharaji shared the gospel, prayed, and the Lord delivered Jit Narayan and his family from the evil spirits. After the deliverance, Jit's family returned home and saw a cross that was suspended in midair outside their house. They viewed the cross for about an hour before

---

[5] While appreciative of the *Daodejing* and Buddhist texts, Nitobe was careful to note their differences from Quakerism, writing, 'Let it be far from me to turn Quakerism into Oriental mysticism ... George Fox and his followers conceived ... of light as a person ... We read Laotze; we read Buddhist saints ... we are brought very near to the idea of redemption, atonement, salvation ... but not the one thing essential – namely, a perfect living Personality' (Nitobe 1970, 334–35, 341).

it disappeared. All five family members accepted Jesus Christ as their Lord and Savior. This incident happened in August of 2014.

In March of this year, Jit and his wife had a dream. They saw someone calling them to preach the Good News in Bardiya ... [and] an insane 24-year-old man with long hair and nails who was bound with ropes. Jit and his wife ... headed to Bardiya, a town they had never been to ... A Christian, who was standing nearby, overheard ... [H]is son had been insane for more than three years. He led the couple to his home and opened a dark room where his son had been bound for one year ... They prayed for him, cut his long hair, trimmed his nails, and he became a normal man. Seeing this miracle, several people invited Jit and his wife to their homes ... A fellowship under the leadership of Kowasoti Friends Church has begun in the Kulieni village where the miracle took place. (Evangelical Friends Mission 2016a, 1)

Samson (1952–) and Priscilla Retnaraj (1971–)'s team has facilitated Community Health Evangelism through community clinics since 2003 and adopted a holistic community development approach to friendship evangelism, empowering villages to develop their own self-sustaining projects. Retnaraj comes alongside village leaders to identify needs – often adult literacy, but also single-day pop-up medical camps, earthquake relief and agricultural projects – and matches these with resources that the community already has to avoid creating dependency. The Gospel is shared in the context of the friendships that form, resulting in a general pattern of entire families, rather than individuals, becoming Christians (Cammack, personal communication, 2016).

PHILIPPINES

The Friends affiliated with either PEFIM's Yearly Meeting (EFC-ER, EFM) approaching 1,000 attendees in twelve churches, or Taiwan Friends Ministries and Mission in the Philippines, Inc. (TFC), of more than 500 attendees in upwards of twenty churches, focus on propagating the Gospel and church planting. Filipino Friends are perceived as Protestants who – by definition – are 'protesting' against the established Roman Catholicism (Chen, personal communication, 2016; De la Cruz, personal communication, 2016).

Jaime P. and Lydia Tabingo's house-to-house evangelism and Bible studies started PEFIM in 1977. Jaime (Jim) G. Prieto, commissioned by EFC-ER to plant churches in his home country, discovered the Tabingos already doing this and merged his mission with theirs. Filipino Friends are musical, with original Tagalog songs, worship conferences and symposiums and evangelistic concerts. Crisanto De la Cruz (1981–), executive pastor of PEFIM, served during the 2013 Bohol earthquake and Typhoon Haiyan, one of the world's strongest cyclones, and he links a personal relationship with Jesus Christ to humanitarian work. De la Cruz mobilised PEFIM to hand-carry emergency foodstuffs to Higher Ground Friends Church's village subsisting on whatever root vegetables, coconuts, and banana plant stems they could find, and returned monthly to replant. He says, '[I]t is our relationship with the Lord Jesus Christ which matters most to us ... – so *that* we would be able to appreciate more our being Friends ... [W]hat being a Friend is ... is becoming more and more vague ... [so we] identify ourselves as Christians who happen to be Friends' (De la Cruz, personal communication, 2016).

TFC sent Oliver Chen (1958–) and his wife Grace Hsieh (1959–) to launch Luzon Friends Mission in 1996.[6] Chen planted Manila Mandarin Friends Church within a year and the first Tagalog service in 1999. After Xerxes L. Casas expanded Taiwan Friends Ministries and Mission in the Philippines, the three island groups run independently. Activities include pedicab driver fellowship, literacy and agricultural technology gatherings (Chen 2003, 2006; Chen, personal communication, 2016).

SOUTH KOREA

Yoon Gu Lee (1929–2013), Shin Ai Cha, and fellow Koreans who worked with Friends Service Unit (FSU) in 1958 began an Unprogrammed Meeting for Worship, formed Seoul MM in 1964 and adopted Tandong leper village in 1966 (Lee 1969, 1984).

Sok Hon Ham (1901–89) was born in North Korea, baptised in Uchimura's *Mukyoukai* (non-church) movement in Japan; joined the South Korea March 1st Movement; joined Seoul MM in 1967 and established the National Council for the Protection of Democracy and National Congress for the Restoration of Democracy. Ham developed a *Minjung* theology of the excluded and described Korea as Queen of Suffering and Jesus as Son of Suffering, an allegory of the Korean people's mission 'to bear our load of iniquity ... [to] deliver ourselves and the world ... a sweetness that none but the bearer can hardly imagine' (Ham 1985, 182–83; see also Kim 1998, 12; Kwag, private correspondence, 2016).

---

[6] Initially incorporated by PEFIM but separated after a conflict with EFCI-AR, the two churches later drafted a memorandum of understanding and co-exist (Duh 2016b).

South Korea's two meetings containing twenty-five members meet monthly for Bible or Quakerism discussions and quarterly for Family Gatherings, aid victims of catastrophe (such as land mines) and protest military expansion and nuclear operations (Jin 2008; Kwag, personal communication, 2016).

WORSHIP GROUPS

Scattered across the Asia-Pacific region are outposts of Friends who differ from the dominant expression of Quakerism in their area, evangelise in closed countries or are geographically remote. Of the Unprogrammed worship groups ranging in size from one to forty members in Beijing, Bohol, Phnom Penh, Delhi, Singapore and Yangon, the most internationally active is the Bohol WG in the Philippines, where three Friends have conducted relief work and advocated vegetarianism, interfaith harmony, LGBT rights and environmentalism since 2009 (Henderson, private correspondence, 2016; Khurana, personal communication, 2016; Quirog, personal communication, 2016).

Christ-centred Beverley Friends Meeting (BFM), of around thirty members who received visitation and epistles from Ohio YM, was incorporated into Avon Valley General Meeting (AVGM) which itself left Australia YM in 1999. After AVGM folded in 2005 and BFM re-affiliated with Australia YM, Shane (1959–) and Valerie Moad (1969–) remain the region's only Conservative Quakers in association with the international Wider Fellowship of Conservative Friends of Ohio YM, and consider that Friends 'do the best we can to follow our Lord and Saviour Jesus Christ. Often we get it right and many times we don't but hopefully we keep trying to ... seek that Light ... [which makes] a difference in someone[']s life to feel Christ's love ... I do believe as Friends we have a good way to walk and live our faith in this world' (Moad 2011; Moad, personal communication, 2016).

A number of Evangelical Friends minister in countries of limited religious freedom as sponsored or tentmaker missionaries with the support of their Yearly Meetings (Stansell 2014, 109).

REGIONAL BODIES AND HUMANITARIAN ORGANISATIONS

The three primary regional bodies/gatherings for Friends in the Asia-Pacific region each follow a triennial fellowship cycle. The leading affiliation is with Evangelical Friends Church International – Asia Region (EFCI-AR, formerly

STEPHANIE MIDORI KOMASHIN

Evangelical Friends International), which unites more than 99 percent of Asian Evangelical Friends.[7] In addition to EFCI-AR's primary Asia Region Conference, its Friends South Asia Conference convenes roughly 200 Friends of Bhutan, India and Nepal who share ethnolinguistic ties. The second body is Friends World Committee for Consultation – Asia West Pacific Section (FWCC-AWPS), with which 15 percent of the region's Friends are affiliated. FWCC-AWPS coordinates a Triennial Gathering, Companion Meetings Meeting for Worship online, and visitation. The third, All India Friends Gathering, assembles more than sixty Programmed, Evangelical, and Unprogrammed Friends.

In addition to homegrown JFSC, QSA, QPSANZ and Caring Hands, global Quaker-initiated humanitarian relief, development, and mediation serve the region. Friends Ambulance Unit (later FSU and Quaker Peace and Social Witness) rescued Chinese and Indian civilians from 1941 by providing medical care and emergency supplies. Since entering China in 1925, post-WWII Japan relief and refugee work and civil disobedience in the Vietnam War, AFSC's shift from aid in Bangladesh, Cambodia, India, Indonesia, Laos, Myanmar, Pakistan, Thailand and Timor-Leste into peace building and intermediation organised Martin Luther King, Jr.'s 1959 India pilgrimage; has provided sustainable technologies for North Korean cooperative farms; has promoted conflict sensitivity between Chinese businesses and stake-holders; and has supported Indonesian *Jathilan* (horse dance), *Barongsai* (Chinese lion dance), and Javanese theatre peace work. A Quaker Action Group and Canadian Friends Service Committee channelled wartime medical supplies to Vietnam. Nadine Hoover (1961–), Valerie Joy (1941–), John Michaelis (1945–) and Beverley Polzin (1939–) facilitate hundreds of Alternatives to Violence workshops, visiting, trauma resiliency, discernment and ending of violence and segregation in Indonesia, Nepal, the Philippines, Australia and Aotearoa/New Zealand for the Asia West Pacific Initiative of Friends Peace Teams.

ASIA-PACIFIC FRIENDS, RISK TAKING, MISSIONAL, FOX-Y

If we ask, 'Have Asia-Pacific Friends made any difference?' I anticipate global Friends promptly agreeing on a resounding 'yes'. If we then ask, 'In what way?' we are reminded that differing convictions and motivations of Evangelical, Programmed, and Unprogrammed Friends are such that

[7] The Garhwali churches and independent Taiwanese denomination church are not affiliated.

many are 'diminished by not knowing sufficient [sic] about the world family of Friends' (Meredith 1997, 1). This chapter has attempted to reduce this knowledge gap. Conclusions include the following:

- Asia-Pacific Friends are risk takers. In a region vulnerable to religious violence, geopolitical conflict and natural disasters, many put their lives at stake to share their faith, secure a safer world and minister to victims of disaster.
- Whilst not denying the existence of West-to-East missions, Asian Friends have both initiated historical missions and led the majority of current missionary work.
- Just as the future of worldwide Quakerism is in the hands of the African and Latin American Friends (Abbott 2013, 550, 562), Asia-Pacific Friends are on a similar trajectory of rapid evangelical growth, pioneering new ways of being Quaker. Young, newly Christian and developing culturally relevant Meetings of traditional arts and hands lifted in prayer, these Friends thrive under persecution or in freedom. Church planting is a primary enterprise, often involving community development (Stansell, private correspondence, 2016).
- Management of philanthropic endeavours and safeguarding of properties amidst governmental policy shifts notwithstanding, holistic and congenial Programmed Friends steadily invest in children, environmentalism and countrywide Quaker unity.
- Unprogrammed Friends are active in peacemaking conflicts carved over centuries of injustice, mobilising to aid people in crisis and providing long-term education and training in Quaker testimonies.
- Intraregional camaraderie amongst Evangelical Asians who 'consider their work as a regional movement' (Stansell 2014, 110) and amongst Unprogrammed Quakers is unmistakable, with wariness between these two strains short on details of the other. Programmed Friends get along with both.
- Absence of scholarly attention is sorely evident. Despite Mid-India's 150+ and TFC's 60+ years of history, and no language barrier precluding consulting many national leaders, there are less than ten scholarly English works on more than 30,000 Asian Evangelical and Programmed Friends and their forebears. Scholarly and general writings have traced Western missionaries rather than illuminating Asian Friends themselves. Far more is written on the region's Unprogrammed 5 percent, suggesting ethnocentrism, but even here, stories of humanitarian workers, missionaries and immigrants can outstrip those of the native Friends.

SUGGESTED FURTHER READING

DeVol, C. E. (1988). *Fruit That Remains, The Story of the Friends Mission in China and Taiwan sponsored by The Evangelical Friends Church – Eastern Region (Formerly Ohio Yearly Meeting of Friends)*, Taipei: Dixon Press.

Saville, H. (2009). 'Friends in deed' in *50 Years of Quaker Service Australia*, Surry Hills, NSW: Quaker Service Australia.

Stansell, R. (2014). 'Friends in India and Asia', *Quaker Religious Thought* 123:11, 107–14.

Sykes, M. (1997). *An Indian Tapestry, Quaker Threads in the History of India, Pakistan & Bangladesh, From the Seventeenth Century to Independence*, ed. by G. Carnall, York: Sessions Book Trust.

PART IV

EMERGING SPIRITUALITIES

14

෴

Unprogrammed Quaker Spiritualities

Michael Birkel and Deborah L. Shaw

Religious communities constantly shift and grow in an effort to remain vital. Some changes result from interaction with wider religious and social contexts, while others begin from within. Both can be found within the contemporary unprogrammed Quaker traditions in North America. Recent decades have witnessed a resurgence of interest in spirituality in many historically Christian societies. Both within and outside historic communities of faith, spiritual practitioners have recovered resources from their own tradition and have benefited from interaction, exchange, and borrowing from others. Quakers have been a part of this wider movement, as givers and receivers.

This chapter begins with an account of a spiritual renewal among Friends that draws on a recovery of historic Quaker practices through the influence of Friends from the Conservative branch of Quakers and how this has enhanced the inward lives of other-than-Conservative Friends. Then follows a brief nod to history, noting that Friends have from their earliest days and across the centuries benefited from spiritual influences from outside the boundaries of their community. This chapter then turns to the topic of contemporary Friends who have gone a step beyond, drawing inspiration from the spirituality of other traditions, to the point of actively identifying with more than one religious community. Some Friends practice dual belonging, and this chapter considers one Muslim-Quaker, keenly influenced by the mystical element of Islam known as Sufism, and two who identify as both Buddhist and Quaker yet define that relationship in complementary ways.

Friends have a history of privileging religious experience over doctrine or systematic theological reflection, hence a preference for religious autobiography as the premier form of Quaker literature. Echoing this tendency, the primary emphasis here is on individual writers as examples of contemporary unprogrammed spiritualities.

CONSERVATIVE FRIENDS: A CASE STUDY

Recovering neglected or even forgotten portions of a community's own inheritance can offer spiritual revitalization. As an example of this reclamation that can be found in the retrieval of past spiritual practices, the Conservative tradition of Friends has in recent years experienced the rise of gifted ministers who have fostered renewal among Conservative Friends themselves and enriched the experiences of other Quakers.

The number of Friends in the United States is a small percentage of Friends worldwide, and of that, the number of Conservative Friends is even smaller. The three small Conservative Yearly Meetings may be understood as "conservers" of many of the original or long-standing practices of the Religious Society of Friends. These Yearly Meetings may be viewed as a part of the clear Conservative witness of an understanding that many across the branches are reaching back toward and that many within the Conservative traditions have never quite lost, that spiritual gifts, while sent through the conduit of a particular person, are in fact, sent to the faith community and, therefore, belong to the faith community – not to the person.

Three exemplary ministers who have shared the gifts of the Conservative tradition with the wider community of Friends and in this way have contributed to a revival of spiritual liveliness across the spectrum of Friends are William P. Taber, Deborah Fisch, and Lloyd Lee Wilson.

William Taber (1927–2005) was a much loved teacher and spiritual nurturer. He taught in Friends schools, served as a released minister in Ohio Yearly Meeting, and was a member of the faculty at Pendle Hill, a Quaker study center near Philadelphia. He had a particular talent for opening the treasures of the Conservative tradition for other Friends, including Liberal Quakers who were suspicious of ministers, cautious about Jesus, and skeptical about the value of Scripture. For generations, many Conservative Friends were hesitant to describe methods of spiritual practice, preferring that spiritual experiences be recognized intuitively by those who were reared in that tradition. William Taber was a bit of a maverick. He sensed that newcomers to Quakerism, despite their yearnings for a deeper inward life, did not have sufficient background to grasp such an indirect way of learning nor the time to make up for an early life not spent within Conservative Quaker culture. In response to this need, he departed from Conservative tradition and wrote boldly about what to do in the silence of meeting for worship and how to discern the movement of the Spirit in meetings for business (Taber 1992, 2010) He invited contemporary Quakers to read the

Bible in the company of early Friends, and he explained early Quaker spiritual terms with a clarity and warmth that fostered a desire among modern Friends to experience that spiritual reality (Taber 1984; Drayton and Taber 2015) William Taber's works continue to benefit readers, for whom they open new vistas of spiritual possibilities.

Deborah Fisch is a well-known Friend from Iowa Yearly Meeting Conservative, of which she was presiding clerk for more than a decade. Her faithful leadership of the Traveling Ministries Program of Friends General Conference from 1998 to 2015 provided spiritual leadership to its member meetings in a variety of ways. In her role Deborah would discern both the spiritual needs of the meetings requesting visitation as well as discerning the spiritual gifts of those who had been called to serve those meetings. This exercising of the role of elder, often at a distance, is an exceedingly rare and valuable gift. In early days of the Traveling Ministries Program, an accidental double booking meant that two Friends were sent to the same meeting, an "accident" that then happened every succeeding time, as all were reminded of why the disciples, and the early Friends, had been sent out in pairs. Deborah's vocal ministry is quotidian in nature, which makes sacred the ordinary and welcomes everyone to reflect on his or her own everyday experiences in the light of Divine overlay to see where God might be at work or at play.

Lloyd Lee Wilson is a minister of the gospel, writer, educator, and activist; has served as clerk of North Carolina Yearly Meeting (Conservative); and also served as clerk of that bodies' Yearly Meeting of Ministers, Elders and Overseers. Lloyd Lee has traveled extensively among Friends, waiting upon the Lord as to what his ministry and action will be when he arrives. Of lasting significance has been his publication *Essays on the Quaker Vision of Gospel Order*, first published in 1993 and now in its third printing. Friends from across the branches have eagerly responded to this exploration of Gospel Order as understood by early Quakers and contemporary Conservative Friends. ("Gospel Order" is a phrase used by earlier Friends to describe a harmonious way of being in relationship with God and community. Gospel Order implies divine intention and design in which humans participate through deep listening, discernment, and obedient response.) In this work, and in his life and witness, Lloyd Lee holds the center, resting on our beloved Friends traditions, not unquestioningly, but faithfully and lovingly, without dilution or compromise. He is asked to travel among Friends ostensibly to speak or lecture, when in reality the real purpose is often for the opportunities that take place over coffee or between sessions, when one person takes the risk to share what is deepest in his or her heart and together they offer it into the care of God.

The central quality of the spirituality of Conservative Friends being the immediate and perceptible guidance of the Holy Spirit, the tradition therefore values the intuitive dimension of the inward life and the personal narrative of direct experience. In harmony with this principle, this chapter continues with a personal account of life in the ministry as experienced by one of the authors, Deborah Shaw:

> Because spiritual gifts are to be nurtured, cared for, pruned and tended by the faith community as well as the individual – so also, this narrative is not one of an individual person, but of the faith community, writ large, not bounded by a single meeting, Yearly Meeting, or even a continent. The tending of the faith community is at times expressed through spiritual nurturers, at times through precious, unexpected "opportunities" with beloved elders or complete strangers (angels unawares), at times through the diligent pursuit of devotional reading and, of course, at times through the guidance of the Holy Spirit. I awoke early one morning with the clarity that my own life was uniquely positioned to model the conservative witness amongst Friends today in the United States. So, while loath to put myself forward in such a manner it seemed useful to the case study.
>
> Standing solidly in the second decade of the twenty-first century what influences me personally stretches at least as far back as the late 1800s to my paternal grandparents, who were born among Conservative Friends. Having just visited one of my former students who teaches Quakerism at Moorestown Friends School in New Jersey, I became very aware of standing on a point in that timeline when I came into the meeting room and Melissa introduced me to the fourth graders as the person who had taught her much of what she knew about Quakerism, just as she is one who is teaching them much of what they know about Quakerism. As the sweet fourth graders broke into applause, I became keenly aware that the way that any of us models, exercises, expresses, and teaches Quaker faith and practice stretches far into the future.
>
> The influences I have felt from Conservative Friends has translated into the work that I have done for more than twenty years with hundreds of college-aged Quakers, what I have tried to put into practice (and faith) with them, and of the work I have done in sharing during retreats and workshops here and there.
>
> While my first six years were in the liberal Philadelphia Yearly Meeting, my home life was very much a Conservative one in that we spoke plain language with one another, were conversant with Scripture, were given the sense and expectation that "there was one, even Christ Jesus, that could speak" to our condition, though my parents framed that in language that our young minds could grasp. My memory is that this was a joyful certitude of accompanying presence, a sure and comforting guide and solace. My

family was on the visitation committee for the quarter for which I credit my lifelong love of intervisitation amongst Friends.

The next significant Conservative influence on my life was from two years attendance at Olney Friends School in southeastern Ohio. Here I was exposed to the witness of many faithful lives: farmer Cliff Guindon, cook and baker Dottie Guindon, Jessie and Don Starbuck were all powerful influences. Taking Quakerism with Teacher Bill Taber, the gracious and graceful presence of Teacher Fran Taber, each day begun and ended with community worship, worshiping in Stillwater Meetinghouse. I cannot say that the influences worked on me noticeably at the time, but when I reflect on my life I can point back to that time and recognize when seeds of contemplation and letting one's life preach were planted.

Settling in North Carolina shortly after graduation from Olney, the majority of my work life has been at Guilford College (the South's only Quaker college) and my membership has been at Friendship Meeting for more than thirty years. Friendship is a member of North Carolina Yearly Meeting (Conservative) and is associated with Piedmont Friends Fellowship (Friends General Conference). Friendship is a relatively young meeting with a wide spectrum of belief fed by both Guilford College and the nearby Quaker-founded retirement facility, Friends Homes, both of which bring unprogrammed Friends from a variety of Yearly Meetings into spiritual fellowship.

SPIRITUAL NURTURE

Very early on, through both work in the Guilford College Library and through Friendship Meeting, I grew close with Carole Treadway, a luminary in the Conservative Quaker world. Building on our shared connections as Olney graduates, Carole took me under her wing and was always available as a listening heart, a spiritual mother and nurturer to me as I was far from home and family. I recently came across a note Carole wrote to me when my younger brother died, and it is exquisite in its kindness, depth, and containment of the breadth of emotion that she knew I was in. In the note Carole does not shrink back from noting how even my failures in my relationship to my brother will have brought me nearer to what God would have me be. Carole listens with Christ's ears and seeks to minister to others guided by the Inward Teacher. This informs how I try to attend to the Quaker Leadership Scholars, indeed to all with whom I come in contact. Carole's influence has spread across the branches through her years as a core teacher for The School of the Spirit's On Being a Spiritual Nurturer Program. It is a particular way of being with one another, a stillness and openness that is described as having an "opportunity" with someone, or as practicing the presence of God with another person.

TRAVELING IN THE MINISTRY

At some point in my late 30s, it was laid on my heart that I should attend an event taking place at Pendle Hill to serve as a prayerful presence for several people that I knew would be presenting. Because I was there I was able to pray with and particularly encourage one of the presenters, making it possible for her to share more authentically from her true self. This practice, which I came to call being a spiritual elder for someone, continues to be one of my leadings. In particular I have a reciprocal relationship with Ben Pink Dandelion in which I serve as his spiritual elder when he is speaking in the United States (as I am able), and he serves as my spiritual elder when I am leading retreats in Britain. Serving in this way when Ben was speaking at Southeast Yearly Meeting made members of that Yearly Meeting aware that Friends still engage in this practice, that it is not just in the history books! Very often during this kind of traveling, special "opportunities" arise to be present with Friends, to hear of burdens or joys that they are carrying and to listen deeply and attentively together to that Inward Teacher that never fails. As I leave my work at Guilford to travel in the ministry, the Quaker Leadership Scholars are invited to hold that travel in prayer and regularly inquire how things went upon my return. My husband reminds Friendship Meeting of where I am on the First Days that I am not in meeting and I know that many there are upholding what I am about in prayer. This refers back to the sense of the faith community at work in nourishing and nurturing any and all aspects of the ministry.

ELDERS

The role of elder as Friends travel in the ministry was mentioned earlier. How wonderful to have a companion to be praying for you while you speak, to help you discern the way forward if you are not feeling clear, to turn to if you falter in the midst of the ministry, to trust for absolute honesty and reflection when you have completed the task, to help you learn from the times that you may have been less than faithful. Elders in the meeting are those who discern, recognize, and name spiritual gifts in the faith community. They tend to the gifts, nourishing, pruning, nurturing, holding the bearer accountable, helping the community be a good garden. That is the ideal. I look back in wonder at myself being asked to be the clerk of the Yearly Meeting at the age of thirty-seven, which seems young, but my acquiescence was given in and through the knowledge that the elders and the community had made that discernment and that the whole body would be upholding me in the work. I recall with delight and joy the times that I have traveled as spiritual elder for Deborah Fisch and witnessed her faithful

waiting upon the Lord, sometimes standing in the midst of Friends waiting for her to speak for three to four minutes without saying a word,
waiting patiently until the Word was given, knowing that she would not
speak until she heard with her inward ear the breathings of Christ. This
modeling has taught me in my work with the students and in travels
among Friends. As Friends in times past, Quakers can ask one another
today, "How does Truth prosper with thee, Friend?" and as Friends seek to
faithfully respond, time with one another will be blessed and fruitful
according to God's purposes.

QUAKERS AND OTHER TRADITIONS: WIDER CHRISTIANITY

In parallel with this renewal from within, Friends have profited from non-
Quaker sources and traditions. Friends have profited from the spiritual
practices of other Christians. This is nothing new to Quakers, who have
from the start enjoyed the insights of the wider Christian community. Earlier
Quakers read non-Quaker mystics such as Jacob Boehme, the unknown
author of the *Imitation of Christ*, Jeanne Guyon, and others (Grubb 1863,
152; Jones 1914, 151–234; Steere 1948, 17–51; Birkel and Bach 2010). In the
eighteenth century, abolitionist Anthony Benezet read the fourth-century
Macarian Homilies (Cadbury 1934, 71). In 1813, Quakers William Backhouse
and James Janson edited a small volume on contemplative prayer, *A Guide to
True Peace: Or, the Excellency of Inward and Spiritual Prayer*, drawn on
seventeenth-century Catholic writers Jeanne Guyon, François Fénelon, and
Miguel Molinos (Birkel 2015b, 145–96). Victorian Quakers such as Caroline
Stephen appreciated the fourteenth-century Dominican mystic Johannes
Tauler (Stephen 1891, 37). Twentieth-century Quaker Douglas Steere prized
the works of the seventeenth-century French bishop François de Sales (Steere
1948, 55–86). Thomas Kelly, among others, was deeply fond of the writings of
a seventeenth-century Carmelite friar, born with the name Nicolas Herman
but more widely known as Brother Lawrence of the Resurrection (Kelly 1941,
20, 35, 75, 111).

Such influences and confluences have always been a sign of spiritual
openness and vigor among religious communities across history. In more
recent times, Quakers have appreciated the revival of *lectio divina*, a medieval
Christian practice of meditative reading of Scripture. Other Quakers have
been involved in the current renewal of spiritual direction, a practice of
spiritual guidance that has its roots in the Catholic tradition. Some of these
Quaker spiritual directors have received their training in, for example,
Ignatian methods of direction.

QUAKERS AND OTHER TRADITIONS: BEYOND CHRISTIANITY

Like other Christians, Friends have explored the gifts of other-than-Christian communities (Habito 2008; Knitter 2009). For some, this has led to a respectful borrowing of practices. For others, it has resulted in dual membership in Quakerism and another religion. Each of these poses challenges. Borrowers must consider the ethics of their actions, perhaps especially borrowers whose cultural histories include oppression and colonization of others. Dual belongers have to face the competing demands of two religious systems with their different concepts of self, reality, divinity, worship, meditation, and ethics.

QUAKERS AND MUSLIM SPIRITUALITIES

In an article in *Quaker Theology* entitled "The Journeyman – The Making of a Muslim Quaker," Brett Miller-White offers an account of his spiritual path into Quakerism and Islam (Miller-White 2004). He identifies with the mystical dimension of Sufism, though he admits that he is not always vocal about this in the mosque, acknowledging that Sufism has a complicated reputation among mainstream Muslims. Unlike some Quakers who are drawn to a Sufi ideal but without the requirement to identify as Muslim, Brett Miller-White writes of being at home with the Qur'an, the accounts of the Prophet Muhammad, and the Pillars of Islam, although he confesses that, like many Muslims, he does not regularly observe the expectation of ritual prayer five times each day. His acquaintance with Islam began with his many years of service in the Middle East as part of the Church World Service program of the National Council of Churches. He was drawn to Sufi practices of healing through sound, hence to Islam, and he undertook formal profession of Islam, the confession of faith in God and the Prophet. His background was Protestant, but traditional Christian doctrines on Christ and the Trinity had never sat well with him. He writes that he found that "Islam has perhaps a better understanding of the teachings of Jesus than Christians do." He uses the Quaker language of a divine leading when he notes, "Eventually I was led to accepting, in 2003, after having studied its wider implications, an invitation to take Shahadah – i.e. to become a Muslim."

Dual belonging was no problem from the standpoint of his Muslim identity: "Islam has never claimed to be an exclusive religion. It has been very open to the authenticity and in particular the accommodation of other religious persuasions." As for Quakerism, "I remain comfortable with my own recognition of Quakerism as a universalistic vehicle that takes one beyond the limits of Christianity. I depend fully upon the genius of Quakerism being understood as the Light of God waiting to be discovered within each soul." He describes the compatibility of his two religious communities in this way:

> Meanwhile the dichotomy of my two weekly experiences, the mosque and meeting, are not in conflict. The demands are quite similar, both being a part of like-minded people, one body willing to prostrate themselves as a whole to make contact with God and the other willing to center down together and gather in the whole to make that same contact. In my case it really works.

Other Sufis in the West, as mentioned, have forged an Islam-optional or even post-Islamic understanding of their Sufi identity. These include Murshid Samuel L. Lewis, a student of Hazrat Inayat Khan who brought a universalist understanding of Sufism to the West. The organization founded by Samuel Lewis is now known as the Dances of Universal Peace. These dances are popular among Liberal Quakers and are often offered in the course of the annual national gathering of Friends General Conference. Other Quakers are drawn to the mystical poetry of Sufism, such as the verses of Jamaluddin Rumi, recognized as the founder of the Mevlevi Sufi tradition, perhaps better known in the West as the whirling dervishes.

One of the authors (Michael Birkel) was a guest of a group of Friends who had not formally joined the Muslim community but worship with a Sufi-influenced community for Friday prayers and attend retreats with a Sufi teacher. They expressed appreciation for the mystical teachings of their shaykh and for the embodied rituals of Muslim prayer, noting that these complement what they experienced in Quakerism.

QUAKERS AND BUDDHISM IN NORTH AMERICA

Arguably the other religious tradition to which contemporary Liberal Quakers are most attracted is Buddhism. With its traditions of meditation, compassion, and nonviolence, Buddhism feels compatible to many unprogrammed Liberal Quakers. Westernized forms of Buddhism, often divested of cultural expressions, rituals, hierarchies, apotropaic or theurgic practices, and its focus on merit for non-monastics, appeals to the spiritual thirst of many North Americans who are dissatisfied with Christian and Jewish experience. Rabbi and professor Zalman Schlachter-Shalomi described this as "Buddhism for export," a tradition "stripped of the chthonic and ethnic things from Asia" (Kasimow, Keenan, and Keenan 2003, 89). His following

words on Jews who are involved in Buddhist practice could equally apply to
many Quakers who explore Buddhism:

> While it is true that we Jews have an aversion to icons that want to invite
> adoration, I don't believe that this touches Jews who are involved in
> Buddhism too much. The "Ju-Bus," people who do mostly Zen or
> Vipassana meditation, are not into the icons. I don't see too many Jews
> going to the *ao-honzon* [the main object of veneration] and chanting
> *"Namu myoho renae kyo"* ("Hail to the Lotus Sutra"). (Kasimow, Keenan,
> and Keenan 2003, 89)

Steve Smith expresses similar sentiments when he writes that, after more
than twenty years of Zen meditative practice, he anticipated an ongoing
commitment to *zazen*, "Yet I remain detached from outward forms of
Buddhist ritual. Out of deference and respect for tradition, I participate in
various religious observances ... These manifestations of traditional
Japanese Soto Zen continue to feel alien to me, however; they do not express
my own authentic religious impulses" (Smith 2003, 9–10).

North American Quaker interaction with Buddhist traditions and practitioners is nothing new. In the middle of the past century, Teresina R. Havens,
who earned a doctorate in comparative religion from Yale University in 1933,
published *Buddhist and Quaker Experiments with Truth: Quotations and
Questions for Group or Individual Study* (Havens 1950, 1992). In 1966, Quaker
philosopher Douglas Steere sought to initiate a Christian-Zen encounter
with Japanese Buddhists (Steere 1967, 16, 20–21).

Outside North America, at the dawn of the twentieth century, Japanese
Quaker Inazo Nitobe, who had studied and lived in the United States,
reflected on Buddhism and its spiritual legacies (Nitobe 1908). Mary Rose
O'Reilley's *The Barn at the End of the World: The Apprenticeship of a Quaker,
Buddhist Shepherd* is a brilliant, honest, and frequently hilarious account of
her time exploring the intricacies of sheep farming in a Minnesota barn and
learning Buddhist teachings and practices in Plum Village in France, a
community founded by Zen master Thich Nhat Hanh. Her reflections reveal
a person deeply enriched by her encounter with Buddhist thought, practice,
and practitioners (O'Reilley 2000).

Interestingly, in the title of her book she chooses to punctuate the relationship between Buddhism and Quakerism with a comma rather than a hyphen.
She is an English professor, so this was a deliberate choice. A hyphen connects,
while a comma separates. She tends to keep her discussion of Buddhism
separate from her consideration of Quakerism in this book. She does not tell
a story of formally joining the Buddhist community.

Many contemporary Friends are similarly disinclined toward multiple belonging, content to borrow from Buddhism what suits them. Thich Nhat Hanh himself has spoken on dual identity in this way, responding to the question, "Should Christians who are attracted to Buddhist teachings become Buddhists?"

Christians who know how to generate mindfulness, concentration and insight are already Buddhist ... even if they don't call themselves Buddhist, because the essence of Buddhism is mindfulness, concentration and insight ... they don't need to wear the label "Buddhist" ... When a Christian embraces the Buddhist practice correctly, he will never be uprooted from his Christian heritage ... I think there are enough Buddhists; we don't need to convert more people to Buddhism. Just taking care of the Buddhists we have now takes a lot of energy already. Many of them don't practice. So let us not worry about making more Buddhists. (Nhat Hanh 2006)

Other Quakers have chosen dual affiliation, formally joining both Buddhist and Quaker communities. Valerie Brown and Sallie King serve as two complementary approaches to dual religious identification. While both recognize affinities as well as differences between Quakerism and Buddhism, Valerie Brown has an interest in bringing the two traditions together, while Sallie King tends to keep them separate. Each offers an enriching encounter.

VALERIE BROWN

Valerie Brown identifies as both Quaker and Buddhist. Reared a Roman Catholic, she is active as a member of the Religious Society of Friends, and she was ordained by Vietnamese Zen Buddhist Master Thich Nhat Hanh as a layperson in his Tien Hiep Order. She is also a certified teacher of Kundalini yoga. Trained as an attorney and experienced as a lobbyist, she is a facilitator for the Center for Courage and Renewal, a leadership coach, and an educator in mindfulness. She has written essays that have been published as pamphlets by the press of the Quaker retreat center Pendle Hill (Brown 2006, 2010, 2013).

Valerie Brown feels led to promote traditionally Buddhist practices among Friends, particularly the practice of mindfulness as articulated by Thich Nhat Hanh. Mindfulness can enhance the Quaker quest to encounter the Light within oneself and others. Further, Buddhist meditation seeks to "hold divergent feelings and sensations in awareness," thus balancing energies in a way that can clarify the process of discernment. She identifies the Light of

God within each person with the universal Buddha nature. She finds a harmonization between Buddhist meditation and Quaker silent meeting for worship, as well as other similarities. The Buddhist practice of loving kindness is akin to Christian prayer. The Quaker peace testimony "roughly equates with the Buddha's teaching on love." The doctrine of Right Speech in the Buddhist Eightfold Path resonates with Quaker vocal ministry. She compares Quaker meeting with the Zen practice of *Chado* (tea ceremony) and notes common values of respect, purity, and tranquility. Having worked to establish a common ground between the two traditions, she then recommends that Friends can adopt some Buddhist practices. Meditation can teach Quakers a stable position through proper posture that can enhance their worship and reacquaint them with the role of the body in the spiritual life. She suggests that Buddhist practices of meditation and mindfulness and that Buddhist principle of the Four Noble Truths and the Eightfold Path "can transform and enliven Quaker spirituality." She assures Friends that in "practicing Buddhist teachings as Quakers, we recognize that we are never far from our Buddha-nature, our enlightened self" (Brown 2006, 6, 7, 9, 11, 18–19, 21–23, 26, 32).

SALLIE KING

Sallie King offers reflections on her own personal experience of dual belonging. She is not an evangelist for Buddhist practice among Friends. Instead, she shows her readers how she can be both and yet integrate them into one eloquent life. She is a scholar, especially of socially engaged Buddhism, the recent movement among some Buddhists to work for social change for greater justice (King 2005). In addition to her scholarly writing, she has been a religious activist, involved in interfaith and particularly Buddhist-Christian dialogue, in religiously based efforts to promote peace, and in spreading the message of socially engaged Buddhism in traditionally Buddhist societies where that is a novel concept.

Sallie King has written about her dual religious identity, most directly in her essay "The Mommy and the Yogi" and in her article "Religious Practice: A Zen-Quaker Internal Dialogue" (King 1994, 2003a). Growing up as a "generic Protestant" in a military family, she found it impossible to reconcile what she discerned as the pacifist teachings of Jesus with her military environment. Further, the notion of a benevolent, all-powerful deity clashed with her awareness of the vastness of human suffering. She found solace and sense in the Four Noble Truths of Buddhism, which she encountered as identifying and confronting the problem of suffering and eventually joined a

Zen Buddhist community and took up the practice of meditation, drawn to the focus on experience rather than submission to external authority. She became a scholar and professor of Buddhism. Historically, much of Buddhist literature on meditation and philosophy derives from a monastic setting. Parenting young children brought challenges that the classical tradition did not address, and she found herself attending and then joining a Quaker meeting, not as a replacement for Buddhism but rather as a complement fully compatible with it.

Sallie King finds both Zen Buddhism and Quakerism to be doctrinally flexible, locating truth primarily in experience and regarding verbal formulations and conceptual schemes as secondary and provisional. For her, the Buddhist concept of a universal Buddha nature and the Quaker belief in the Light within every person are compatible. Each tradition offers different strengths: Buddhism with its philosophy and meditative practices and Quakerism with its "manner of bringing spirituality into the worldly life of lay people." She values the egalitarian impulse in Quakerism and its practice of corporate decision making (King 2003a, 161). As a community historically grounded in the wider Christian tradition, Quakerism spoke of love, a bond or attachment to this world, and a fruit of the Spirit. This passionate love, in her experience as a mother, differed from the cool detachment of Buddhist teachings on compassion, yet it aligned with Buddhism in that it entailed a forgetting of self.

Sallie King cannot be accused of turning Quakerism into a whatever-you-want-it-to-be religion. She finds a core to Quaker faith and practice. In her essay "Friends and Other Religions," she describes Quakerism as a religion based on "an illumination that is simultaneously Christian and Universalist." It affirms "the living Spirit of God as a Reality that transcends all names and forms" and that is present universally in a people. At the same time the "language, imagery and inspiration" of Quaker faith is Christian. While Friends avoid creeds, Quaker testimonies of truth, nonviolence, equality, and simplicity, combined with the practice of submission to the guidance of the Spirit, form an identifiable center that is "clear and not to be compromised" (King 2003b, 3, 5, 6).

Sallie King is cautious about mixing the two religions inappropriately. In her experience, they offer different strengths: "If these traditions were the same, there would not be any point to me in practicing both of them. They are compatible, but not the same at all" (King 1994, 161). She readily acknowledges that Buddhism is prominent in her conceptualization of religious categories of thought, such as emptiness, but Buddhism has emphasized this philosophical dimension more than Quakerism has – and Buddhism rather than Quakerism has been the focus of her professional scholarly undertakings. At the same time, she freely confesses that she has found it impossible to accept much of Buddhist doctrine on karma and reincarnation. She tells of admitting this to a Zen teacher, whose response was that if such teachings do not work for her, she should ignore them (King 1994, 160). Again, doctrinal formulations are not the core of either Buddhism or Quakerism. Instead the focus is on action. Buddha nature is not so much a concept as a set of actions that invites everyone to act like a Buddha and to lessen the suffering of the world. This is akin to her description of the core of Quakerism as the living out of ethical principles or testimonies. This concern with principled, compassionate living that seeks to better the world is witnessed in Sallie King's scholarship. She is deeply trained in classical Chinese and Japanese texts, but much of her work as a scholar and as a religious activist focuses on socially engaged Buddhism, as noted earlier.

Reflecting on these two Buddhist Quakers, it might be fair to say that Valerie Brown's concern is to bring Buddhist practices to Quakerism in order to enrich Quaker spirituality, while Sallie King has a concern as an activist to encourage Buddhists to engage in reforms for social justice – an area of concern that has historically been much more central to Quakers than to Buddhists. Taken together, they demonstrate two possibilities for Quaker and Buddhist elements to enhance the inward life of contemplation and the outward life of social change.

CONCLUSION

At first glance, the two kinds of spiritual renewal described in this chapter may seem to have little in common. Where might these two meet? At the extremes of either, they do not. Some Quakers become attracted to the Conservative tradition because it offers support for an unabashedly Christian way of being a Friend. One of the authors (Michael Birkel) has been an occasional visitor to Conservative Friends in Ohio Yearly Meeting in Barnesville, Ohio, for many years; very often in worship, he has heard vocal ministry on John 14:6, always cited in the King James Version: "Jesus saith unto him, I am the way, the truth, and the life: no man cometh unto the Father, but by me," offering a clear witness to Christ as the only way. Ohio Yearly Meeting, it could be argued, may be the group of Conservative Friends most deeply influenced by wider evangelical Christianity. It is difficult to imagine at least some of these Friends approving of non-Christian influences on Quakerism – but that is only one end of the Conservative spectrum.

One place where these two strands of centeredness in Christian identity and openness to learning from other religious communities have met is at Pendle Hill, the Quaker study center mentioned earlier. Two important figures in the history of that community were Howard Brinton and Douglas Steere (Steere 1973; Angell 2013). Both were of strong Christian identity, and both engaged in efforts to promote interfaith understanding, particularly with the religions of South and East Asia. Howard Brinton had a strong Wilburite background, which is one strand within Conservative Quakerism; in his writings he sought to reclaim a positive reputation for what is called Quietism within Quakerism, with which the Conservative tradition is keenly identified and which was poorly esteemed by his mentor Rufus Jones (Brinton 1952, 66–72, 181–87). It was during his years at Pendle Hill that William Taber, mentioned earlier, had the most impact on non-Conservative Friends, holding up for them the gifts of that branch of Quakers. Pendle Hill has also been a place that has regularly hosted events led by Deborah Shaw and by Valerie Brown. What unites all these Friends is their profound interest in the mystical expression of the religious life, whether the source of that mystical dimension is articulated in terms drawn from Quaker or from other traditions.

From its start, the Quaker heritage has been one of both universalism and Christian particularity: the Light that enlightens everyone was understood as the Light of Christ that entered human history. The complexity of this dual focus has always come to expression in a variety of spiritual vitalities. The Quaker tradition is not static but rather unfolding, and its interactions with other traditions, as well as renewals from within, serve as witness to this quality.

SUGGESTED FURTHER READING

Brown, Valerie. (2006). *The Mindful Quaker: A Brief Introduction to Buddhist Wisdom for Friends*, Wallingford, PA: Pendle Hill Publications.

Drayton, Brian, and Taber Jr., William P. (2015). *A Language for the Inward Landscape: Spiritual Wisdom from the Quaker Movement*, Philadelphia: Tract Association of Friends.

King, Sallie B. (1994). "Religious Practice: A Zen-Quaker Internal Dialogue," *Buddhist-Christian Studies* 14: 157–62.

Taber, William P. (1992). *Four Doors to Meeting for Worship*, Wallingford, PA: Pendle Hill Publications.

Wilson, Lloyd Lee. (2007). *Essays on the Quaker Vision of Gospel Order*, Philadelphia: Quaker Press of FGC.

15

 catch-word ornament

Quakers and Non-theism

Dan Christy Randazzo

INTRODUCTION

Non-theism is a minority tradition within the worldwide Religious Society of Friends (RSOF), with the vast majority of self-defined non-theist Friends hailing from either Britain or the United States. The term 'non-theism' can best be understood as a compromise term, for it encompasses a very wide theological and conceptual tent, the members of which hold a dizzying array of positions on the existence of God, how 'God' can be defined or understood, the main components of Quaker identity, and what level of priority to give each of those components for the construction of 'Quakerness'. Nothing unites all non-theists except a sense that they do not view the construct of 'God' as a personal, monotheist deity. Non-theism is knowingly constructed as an undefined definition in an effort to be as inclusive as possible for all people who seek to claim a Quaker identity, yet who cannot ascribe to any form of personal monotheism. Many non-theist Friends use the label as shorthand for explaining their view of Quakerism, yet do so reluctantly, recognising that while there are non-theists in the RSOF, those non-theists often hold very different views from one another.

Non-theism is, at its core, a product of Liberal Quakerism, present throughout the world, wherever Liberal Quakerism exists. Non-theistic thought in Liberal Quakerism most often reflects the context of Britain Yearly Meeting, and the Friends General Conference in the United States, however, as the majority of non-theist writers are either British or North American.

The existence of non-theism within Liberal Quakerism is connected to the increased diversity of belief within Liberal Quakerism in the latter half of the twentieth century. At the beginning of the century, Liberal Quakers were generally Christocentric. Over time, and particularly by the middle of the century, Universalist theology took hold within Liberal Quakerism. This was met with significant critique at first; yet soon Universalism claimed space within Liberal Quakerism alongside Christocentrism. Eventually, Christocentrism was marginalised, as Liberal Quakerism became largely Universalist. This trend towards questioning the core assumptions of Liberal Quakerism has not been completed, and the current tension lies over the question of God.

This development is reflected in the development of Universalist groups in both Britain and the United States. As these groups developed and gained acceptance within Liberal Quakerism, non-theism embedded itself within the groups, as the only available outlet for non-theists to develop community within the RSOF. The groups provided a home for non-theists and aided in the development of both community and of non-theist thought. The relationships between non-theists and other Universalists were not always easy, however, due to the diversity inherent in Universalist Quaker theology. Yet, Universalist Friends were generally welcoming to non-theist members as well as giving space in their journals to the expression of non-theist voices. Thus, as Universalism developed as a distinct tradition within Liberal Quakerism, non-theism was also given space to develop.

Non-theism is therefore a tradition whose perspectives on the Religious Society of Friends, theological concerns and understanding of the fundamental priorities of Quakerism are coloured by Liberal Quaker theology and practice and have been shaped by the attempt to find a place in a religious tradition which places the presence of God within each person as its most fundamental theological claim. Non-theist writing reflects these concerns, with a determined focus on demonstrating that the roots of non-theism go deep within Quaker history and theology. This effort seeks to not only demonstrate that the theological openness of Liberal Quakerism allows space for non-theist theological interpretations, but that Liberal Quakerism should be mainly focused on practice and ethical concerns. Success in this endeavour would render differences on the existence or non-existence of God less meaningful for Quaker identity, leading to a new form of Quakerism which places the question of God as an interesting side aspect for a religious faith focused entirely on the present, lived reality.

This chapter sketches out these themes by focusing on non-theist perspectives, including non-theist publications as well as non-theist writings within Universalist publications. This chapter includes a discussion on ways which non-theists have chosen to define themselves; interpretations of Quaker history and identity; assessments of the priority of reason and Quaker practice as core aspects of both theist and non-theist Quakerism;

and a potential outline for a unique a/theology for non-theism, including avenues where non-theist Friends have demonstrated efforts to bridge the theist/non-theist divide, and potential areas of future development in non-theist thought.

DEFINITIONS OF NON-THEISM

Most Quaker non-theists tend to view 'God' as a human construct. They see Quakerism as a way of life shaped by the Testimonies, Quaker worship and business practice. Non-theists define religion as the means of placing these aspects of Quaker life within a certain community of meaning. The perspective of Quaker non-theism toward theistic belief can be placed on a spectrum of perspective from: a dangerous superstition, through a relatively harmless (if outmoded) silliness and finally towards a legitimate and potentially powerful way of understanding human existence.

David Boulton, a noted non-theist Quaker, has made multiple attempts at establishing a common definition. He defines non-theism as 'the absence of belief in deity/ies, in the existence of God (where "existence" is understood in the realist, objective sense), especially belief in one supreme divine Creator' (Boulton 2006, 6). Boulton describes the development of the term as a process of accepting the 'least disliked option', where other terms, such as 'atheist', 'humanist' and 'naturalist' were all deemed either too controversial or as carrying unnecessary negative stigma, thus being ineffective umbrella terms for an option which Boulton sees as rejecting the theistic concept of 'God' (2006, 7). Boulton emphasises rejection in part because he does not view theistic constructions of God as real, instead proclaiming that God is a human construct, serving human needs. He proclaims that he has deep respect for the concept of 'God', in that within all expressions of 'God' are the symbolic and poetic metaphors which signify 'the sum of our human values, the imagined embodiment of our human ideals, the focus of our ultimate concern'. God is 'no more, but, gloriously, no less, than all that makes up the human spirit' (Boulton 2006, 8). However, he also stresses the need to reject theistic conceptions of God because he sees belief in such conceptions to be dangerous, leading to such harmful human behaviours as religiously based violence, exclusion, and intolerance (Boulton 2006, 9–10).

In this, he is in line with John Linton, the non-theist Universalist who established the Quaker Universalist Group (QUG) in Britain. In an early edition of *The Universalist*, the main journal for the QUG, Linton suggested that he was much better off for having given up his 'delusions' about the existence of God, along with his faith (1984, 17). He then claimed that religious faith often causes more violence than what he termed 'reason', thus demonstrating the necessity for the RSOF, in particular, to give up all divisions based on religious faith. For Linton, this stemmed both from an aversion to Christian truth claims as well as a strong agnostic stance towards the question of 'Truth'. Thus, the openness and willingness to listen to all religious perspectives of Quaker Universalism appealed to him and inspired him to aid in the growth of Quaker Universalism. Yet, he viewed this pursuit as more than just an effort at greater inclusion within Liberal Quakerism as it existed. Instead, he sought to have Quakerism not only welcome agnostics especially, due to what Linton viewed as similar underlying attitudes and ethical viewpoints, but also as part of an overall turn in Quakerism towards ethical Universalism and specifically away from Christianity (Linton 1994, 74). Linton would therefore define Quaker non-theism as not only intellectually open and focused on ethics but also explicitly agnostic, Universalist and highly critical of Christianity. Notably, Linton desired that this change would occur as a natural evolution of the Society; Linton claimed, in terms of Universalists specifically, that 'QUG members don't seek a schism within Quakerism, nor to "twist the Society" to its view' (1979, 1).

Not all non-theists ascribe to this evangelistic impulse. Bowen Alpern, a self-described atheist Friend, views the theist/non-theist divide in Quakerism as by far the least important divide amongst Friends. In fact, he claims that the division caused by this divide is actually a distraction from the Quaker effort to help create the peaceable kingdom, which is so vitally important that the RSOF must quickly adapt so that it can become whole, growing as a community in such a way that it can transcend its divisions, all at a much more rapid pace than Quakers might be comfortable with (B. Alpern 2006, 83–84). This reflects his core view that Quakerism is a way of life based on the ethics of peace-making, which needs to adopt an 'all hands on deck' approach. He thus views theological diversity as a positive thing, as long as that diversity is rooted in the common purpose of the Quaker life. This reflects a common trend amongst non-theist Friends to define religion as those structures and practices which serve to connect people together in community. Robin Alpern suggests this definition of religion as the most appropriate, as the religious life both derives meaning and structure from, and provides the same to, a community of like-minded people seeking to live by a certain set of principles (R. Alpern 2006, 19).

A corollary to Bowen Alpern's vision of a theologically diverse and ethically unified Quakerism would be an emphasis on the Quaker rejection of creeds, and a resulting openness towards theological diversity and insistence on privacy about individual belief, which have emerged in Liberal Quaker theological thought. A significant portion of non-theists emphasise the latter as key to their understanding of Quakerism. Representative of this trend, Tim Miles stated that this privacy renders the content of his individual religious belief irrelevant, meaning that his Quaker identity did not necessitate any agreement on issues of theology or belief with other Quakers (2006, 116).

This does not mean that theological belief is immaterial to non-theist Friends, however. A significant thread in non-theist discourse is the need to allow the contours of religious belief to be 'left up to mystery', as Hubert J. Morel-Seytoux argues (2006, 129). This emphasis on mystery runs counter to Boulton's stated certainty about the non-existence of God beyond a human construct, for mystery implies that there are, at least, areas of deliberate uncertainty in the minds of some non-theists regarding the concept of 'God'. The emphasis on building unity around Quaker Testimonies and business practice, particularly in Alpern's vision, also runs counter to Boulton's and Linton's desires to actively engage theistic belief with the intent of removing it from the RSOF. There exists at the heart of non-theism a potential paradox, therefore, for which some non-theists (including Linton) have suggested different ways of reconciling. The end of the chapter revisits this question as it plots out a future for non-theists.

NON-THEIST HISTORIOGRAPHY

Non-theism emerged as a definable aspect of Quakerism with the rise of Universalism within Liberal Quakerism in the early twentieth century, yet non-theists claim a long heritage of religious scepticism, dating back to the mid-seventeenth century. Os Cresson, a Quaker naturalist, devoted a significant portion of his recent work *Quaker and Naturalist Too* to exploring what he terms the 'roots' (historical development of scepticism as a key aspect of Quaker thought) and 'flowers' (the resulting development of Quaker non-theism as a community and a school of thought) of Quaker non-theism. While Cresson acknowledges that the vast majority of people listed as 'roots' of non-theism likely held strongly theistic beliefs, the thinkers who he claims laid the foundation for Quaker scepticism held beliefs that aided in the expansion of the boundaries for Quaker identity and thus 'helped make Friends more inclusive' (2014, 65).

By expanding the bounds of Quaker non-theist history beyond explicitly non-theist thinkers, Cresson allows non-theists to lay claim to a significant portion of the Quaker heritage that might otherwise be reserved exclusively for theist Quakers. This kind of creative re-appropriation reflects many aspects of the creation of non-theist identity, in that non-theist Quakers are often forced to develop their own understanding of what it means to be Quaker in a tradition which places significant value on its earliest thinkers, all of whom were undeniably theist. Reflecting this, Boulton has made an attempt to suggest that George Fox's vision of God was 'more inner light than outer superman', a perspective which Boulton claims was denounced as 'atheism' by 'religious traditionalists' (2012, 2). When, and in what manner, these traditionalists made these statements is not expanded upon, however. Similarly, both Boulton and Cresson lay claim to other notable Friends and friends of Friends, with Gerrard Winstanley, the Diggers, the Manchester Free Friends, Lucretia Mott and Henry Cadbury mentioned most often in their writings.

These efforts have endured some critique from other Quakers who view some of these theories to be, at best, historically inaccurate. Representative of this trend, and referring to efforts to locate the modern Liberal Quaker willingness to 'seek' without a specific intent to find a particular vision of God, Patrick Nugent claims that just would not make sense in the past: the early Seekers wanted to find something specific, related to the conversion moment which occurred when the Seeker found and had a definitive transformation due to a 'definitive intervention by Jesus Christ' (2012, 53). Similarly, Nugent claims that non-theist efforts to locate even a proto-non-theism in George Fox's thought are incorrect. Nugent claims that Fox simply cannot be accused of atheism in the way that Boulton suggests. The same applies to Lucretia Mott: Nugent notes that non-theist attempts to locate within Mott's defence of Universalist belief a proto-non-theism does not take into account Mott's continued insistence, throughout her life, on the existence of God. Finally, Nugent argues that 'a thorough read of the first 150 years of Quaker history cannot sustain non-theism as authentically Quaker', meaning that non-theism cannot be rooted in early Quaker thought, and instead must be seen as a much more recent development (2012, 51). This does not imply that Nugent fails to see value in non-theism; in fact, he claims that there is much theological potential with non-theism.

This also reflected the views of Kingdon Swayne (1920–2009), who was an influential non-theist Quaker Universalist and a member of the Quaker Universalist Fellowship (QUF), the main Quaker Universalist group in the United States. Swayne claimed that while he did not 'mean to cut us off from our roots', that the intense focus on locating Universalist beliefs (which he includes himself in), and thus gaining legitimacy from, the views of early Friends is unhelpful (1986, 10). This is due to what Swayne terms the 'enormous intellectual gulf' standing between late twentieth-century Friends and the mid-seventeenth century. Not only has the modern world been shaped by intervening centuries of religious thought, Swayne argues, it would also be far too difficult to effectively, and accurately, translate complex religious concepts and language across that same divide. Modern Friends should therefore avoid adopting an 'idolatrous' attitude towards the early Friends and instead focus their efforts on building a modern Quakerism from modern thought.

Following Swayne's guidance, focusing on the development of non-theist thought in the twentieth century reveals a fascinating heritage. Non-theists have identified certain Quakers as either influential on later non-theism or whose own non-theist writing contributed to the development of non-theist thought. Most prominent amongst these was Henry Cadbury (Boulton and Cresson 2006, 98). While Cadbury was quiet about his scepticism of theistic belief during his career, he would give his classes a copy of a paper he had written defending non-supernatural experience within Quakerism. Cadbury took pains to fully acknowledge that many, even a majority of Quakers can have experiences of a supernatural God. Yet, he admitted that he had rarely, if ever, had such an experience. Instead, he developed what he understood to be his own way of being Quaker, based on Quaker values, leading to a 'way of life' (Cadbury 2000, 30).

The first non-theist organisation which sought to align itself with Quakerism was the Humanist Society of Friends (HSOF), begun by Lowell Coate, in 1939. The HSOF was not explicitly Quaker, yet it included numerous Friends amongst its members and intentionally strove to align itself with Liberal Quaker values. Strong emphasis was placed on humanism as the core philosophy for the group, with a concomitant emphasis on peace, reflecting the strong influence of the Quaker members. The HSOF offered a vision of religious humanism which was 'scientific' and 'intensely focused' on the current situation of people's lives. As leader, and editor of the HSOF newsletter *The Humanist Friend,* Coate offered a definition for religion as devotion to a principle, an ideal, without belief in dogmas. Coate emphasised the necessity of having a list of 'superior and ideal human characteristics' which manifested themselves in work for social change (1939, 1). Demonstrating the seriousness with which HSOF held its Quaker connection, *The Humanist Friend* would reprint letters from notable Friends on issues of concern. Representative of this trend is a letter from Rufus Jones on the humanitarian crisis presented by the Second World War, and the challenge for Friends to focus not on abstract ideologies but on the practical changes that Friends could make to the lives of people affected by war (Jones 1939, 7). Notably, the HSOF sought to maintain its connection with Friends over the next seventy years. It was not until 2003 that the HSOF board decided to remove 'Of Friends' from its title, due to a desire to demonstrate how its mission had gradually evolved into serving the wider humanist community (http://thehumanistsociety.org/about/history/).

The most prominent discussions of non-theism, until at least 1976, were mainly critical of non-theism. They include two Pendle Hill Pamphlets (Carol R. Murphy's 1946 pamphlet, *The Faith of An Ex-Agnostic*, number 46, and Alexander C. Purdy's 1967 pamphlet, *The Reality of God: Thoughts on the 'Death of God' Controversy*, number 154), and one Swarthmore Lecture (William Homan Thorpe's 1968 lecture, *Quakers and Humanists*). All three volumes are especially insistent upon the incompatibility of Quakerism to non-theism in any form. Several Swarthmore Lectures were given which introduced non-theist concerns and issues, however, and have been noted as having been greatly influential on the development of non-theist thought. Particularly influential were Arthur Stanley Eddington's 1929 lecture, *Science and the Unseen World*, as it demonstrated the inherent amenability of Quaker thought to scientific method and thought; John MacMurray's 1965 lecture, *Search for Reality in Religion*, as it sought to apply a rationalist philosophy perspective on Quakerism, which MacMurray noted was a generally experiential religion; and Richard S. Peters's 1972 lecture, *Reason, Morality and Religion*, as it demonstrated that reason could be utilised to develop a religion focused on structuring the present life around reasonable moral values.

By the late 1970s, Universalism was beginning to receive a greater level of acceptance amongst Liberal Friends, with non-theists at the forefront of the development of both the QUG and the QUF. Corresponding with this trend was Janet Scott's 1980 lecture *What Canst Thou Say? Towards a Quaker Theology*, noted as the first time that Christianity was decentred as the sole focus of Liberal Quaker theology (Davie 1997, 218). These movements, in tandem, emboldened Universalists, and by extension, non-theists, to reimagine Quaker theological possibilities.

The first official recognition and effort to serve the needs of non-theist Friends occurred with the first non-theist workshop, entitled 'Nontheistic Friends', held at Friends General Conference (FGC) Annual Gathering in 1976 (Boulton 2012, 35). No any other official RSOF acknowledgement of non-theism occurred until the 1996 FGC Annual Gathering, when one workshop, entitled 'Nontheism Amongst Friends', was held. At least one workshop on a non-theist topic was held annually until 2012, which was also the year that Nontheist Friends Fellowship was established in Britain. Other seminars and conferences were held from 1996 to 2012, at both Pendle Hill in the United States and Woodbrooke Quaker Studies Centre in Britain, which solidified the sense of non-theism as not only a valid expression of but also a valid theological alternative to theism for Liberal Friends (Buglass 2011, 31–33).

NON-THEIST INTERPRETATION OF QUAKER IDENTITY

There is no one unifying interpretation of Quaker identity, and expression of the importance of that identity amongst non-theists, beyond the fact that they all feel as if they are Quaker. Some non-theist Friends state it as a plain correlation: their values align with what those of the RSOF; they feel at home amongst Quakers; and Quaker worship gives them a sense of connection, community and meaning. As these are the most important markers of Quaker identity for these Friends, they believe these markers are sufficient. They are Quaker by dint of the fact that they 'feel' like a Quaker (Filiacci 2006, 117). An unspoken aspect of this approach is that they are not troubled by the existence and testimony of theist Friends in meeting. Other non-theist Friends feel more compelled to insist on proclaiming either the value of non-theist perspectives or the challenges they encounter with theistic belief.

Marian Kaplan Shapiro is representative of this perspective. Shapiro claims that she views Jesus as an effective moral teacher yet is deeply uncomfortable with any language which expresses the value of following Jesus as 'Christ', 'Lord' or any other honorific related to his status as 'messiah' or as supernatural deity. This extends to testimony in meeting to that effect, to which she feels compelled to respond by 'speaking her truth' about its inherent dangers (Shapiro 2006, 132). Despite this, Shapiro has experienced two seemingly paradoxical realities: not only has she consistently been treated well and welcomed by theists in meeting, she also has been forced to acknowledge that she is envious of the security that theism seems to provide believers. Shapiro has chosen to simply allow this paradox to exist, proclaiming simply that 'I *am* a Friend' (2006, 132).

Many non-theist Friends have not experienced such an untroubled welcome as non-theists, however. For Robin and Bowen Alpern, this is related to a negative experience of being asked to leave their meeting after proclaiming their non-theism publicly (R. Alpern 2006, 24). Yet, for others their trouble resides with the seeming paradox at the heart of Quaker non-theism: how can a person who does not ascribe to a belief in God or deity/ies be a full member of a religious society which holds as its central theological tenet that all people can experience a direct and transforming experience of God? As with all aspects of Quaker non-theism, there is a vast diversity of ways non-theists have approached this problem.

Kingdon Swayne approaches it by laying out what he views as the five concepts which can be utilised in an effort to unite all Liberal Quakers: responsiveness to a religious impulse and a desire to engage in religious community; personal freedom following a religious impulse; acceptance of meeting for worship as a core element of Quaker spirituality; tolerance for diversity of religious metaphorical language; and, finally, having 'one's life speak' in an active way (Swayne 1987, 10). In this way, he is able to effectively dodge the question of belief by focusing on the performance of Quakerism, which in Swayne's construction, depends on both a desire to be in community (one can assume that this includes theists) as well as an insistence on tolerance for theological diversity. In this way, Swayne can reverse the direction of critical inquiry back towards theists and claim that theist Friends must follow the same rules as non-theist Friends.

Robin Alpern provided an effective demonstration of taking this tactic – reversing the critical mirror – to react to the most common response to her claiming a non-theist identity, 'Why Not Join the Unitarians?' This question is presented as both a straightforward query as well as a dismissive suggestion about the supposed blasé attitude which Unitarians are assumed to take towards theological content, a stance which the imaginary interlocutor appears to claim Alpern holds as well. This challenge is often presented as a theist critique of non-theism: if you desire to remain Quaker, you must present an argument which effectively deals with the centredness of theist belief in Liberal Quaker theology. Alpern elects to respond to this question by changing the terms of the question. She claims that far from being a diversion from Quaker belief, her non-theism is actually a response to her training and formation as a Quaker, most especially in both Quaker practice and the values which undergird it (Alpern 1997, 24). She then lists core Quaker values and practices, and the way that each one has led her towards non-theism. She refers to the impact of plain speech on her theology, in that it led her to query the concept of 'God' as potentially too complex to be truly 'Quaker'. She extends this willingness to critically engage authority to her critique, and eventual rejection, of the teachings of George Fox as well. This develops into a thoroughgoing house clearing, as she follows the Quaker teaching to shun empty forms and to live a true life and proclaims that everything be swept away, including long-standing traditions – even belief in God – if shown to be empty. She views talk about God as inherently empty, as such talk does not specifically lead to the direct act of making a better world.

Thus she demonstrates her command of Swayne's technique of using some Quaker essentials to critique other essentials. She argues that as she was taught that communal discernment is essential, that her development of these beliefs while engaged in communal discernment leads to the inescapable conclusion that they must, in fact, be 'true', at least in some sense. She claims that as all humans desire companionship and community, her unwillingness to speak the language of God in worship does not necessarily mean that she and by extension all atheists and agnostics are not able to understand truly being 'gathered' in worship. She then attacks the core aspect of that assumption by stating that rejecting her religious potential is to deny her humanity.

She completes the reversal of the critical mirror by claims that the true 'parasites' (an epithet that she claims has been directed her way previously) are not non-theists who gain a sense of the religious by being members of Quakers but are instead those theists whose belief in God only exists because they are amongst company who believe. By not contributing their doubts about God to the community, she suggests that theists want to feed off the good feelings of general agreement, thus avoiding the discomfort of controversy. Finally, she claims that when one states a final belief that he or she has arrived at through seeking, one stops seeking and thus the belief causes that person to become ossified.

In this, Alpern argues that taking continuing revelation to its logical conclusion demands that Quakers should never settle on a final belief, especially belief in 'God'. The obvious response is whether this includes the lack of belief in a deity, however. While Alpern does demonstrate how reversing the critical mirror and engaging with core Liberal Quaker concepts can create new theological possibilities, and also develop non-theist expressions of Quaker identity, her methodological approach rests on a potentially challenging core assumption: that everyone has doubts about the existence of God. Quaker theists firmly claiming a faith in God's existence, unmarked by doubt, might prove challenging to her methodology.

THE A/THEOLOGY OF NON-THEISM

This chapter has provided examples of non-theist theological engagement, including constructions of who, or what, the concept of 'God' might mean to individual non-theist Friends. Effectively, if any theological language can be imagined that is not belief in a personal, interventionist monotheist supernatural God, non-theism has the potential of engaging with it.

This does not leave non-theist theology at an impasse, forever forced to listen to new and different visions of an individual's experience, or lack of experience, with 'God', and failing to develop any cohesive critical language to bring to bear. Quaker philosopher Jeffrey Dudiak offers a potential way forward by continuing the method established in this chapter of reversing the question at hand: whether, in fact, theism and a/theism are binary. He begins his engagement by unsettling the modern assumption of a binary by reframing the question in terms of pre-modern religious language. He claims that atheism and theism, in their modern forms, are only possible in a secular, modern world where faith ('surrendered immersion in a world of ineluctable meanings', as he defines it) has lost meaning (Dudiak 2012, 26). The possibility that one can either 'possess' belief or unbelief, and that this is first a vitally important question, or even an option to humans, arose in a modern, secular age (Dudiak 2012, 26). Faith is now dependent on both belief and unbelief. Dudiak admits that the age of reason did offer liberation from often crushing religious structures, yet he insists that some things have been lost in this transition.

First amongst these is a change in the focus of subjectivity. In the pre-modern religious imaginary, to be a subject was to be 'subject to', a passive being upon whom forces acted which were transcendent. Now, subject is the external 'subject of', an object to be perceived or acted upon. What 'exists' is no longer lived as gift but is dependent upon the judgement of thought and reason, which in turn gauges its existence/non-existence as well as its value. Dudiak claims that this is a shift from a medieval focus on ontology to a modernist focus on epistemology; recast, this is the shift from faith to belief, as belief is inherently a question of assent to a statement of fact. The emphasis is also no longer on the place which the knower has within the world, but what the meaning of world is over against the knower. A result of this shift is that belief in God is prerequisite for finding selves in God's world. A corollary to this is a shift from faith as trusting immersion in a world which gives meaning, as context for belief, to belief (and thus knowledge and assent) as prerequisite for faith. Thus, it is now foolish to have faith in God without belief. The result of this shift is the creation of a/theism, which places the highest priority on reason and the ability to answer to reason, for a focus on belief implies a focus on knowledge, which in turn necessitates reason.

Dudiak suggests that modernity therefore places the 'knowing subject-known object' as foundational, and limits ways of understanding God (2012, 30). This occurs because modernism has led both theism and non-theism to accept the natural/supernatural distinction, meaning that any construction of 'God' must fall along this binary. A denial of supernatural reduces God to a human projection in the form of a metaphor or story (immanent naturalism), whereas limiting God to a supernatural object means transcendent theism is the only way to imagine a theistic God. This supernatural transcendent creates theistic claims that are literally in-credible, in that they are non-credible and irrational, and thus impossible to believe. The end result is that both sides wind up failing to have a vision of God worth spending any time or attention dealing with. Dudiak argues that the most productive way forward would be to dismiss the modern binary as foundational to any God-talk or relationship. Instead, Quakers should decentre human emphasis on 'seeing', or understanding (judging the credibility of objective facts), and commit to being called by 'hearing' the voice of God.

Shannon Craigo-Snell suggests that Quakerism already possesses a number of elements which bridge the division between modern and pre-modern concerns, which could provide the kind of bridging theology/atheology which non-theists argue is essential for the future of a Liberal Quakerism with non-theism as an integral component (2012, 49). Most pertinent of her suggestions are these: experience and reasoning (pre-modern and modern ways of engaging with one's place in the world) are both already present in Quaker worship, a reluctance to separate private from public (thus, 'having one's life speak') and the corollary insistence that religion extends to every sphere of personal and communal life. I would argue that a final component that brings these aspects together is a rejection of the personal/communal binary, relating to the Light: as the Light Within is available to each individual person, it is thus also available to the entire community, binding together the community in an interdependent web.

Resonances of this exist within the narratives of non-theist a/theology, even in those narratives which seem most antithetical to a theistic perspective. The two themes which present the most potential for interlocking with this effort include 'God' as cosmos and 'God' as human values.

Non-theist visions of the cosmos are varied, yet generally encompass the entirety of what is known to exist in the physical universe. Non-theist Friends who focus on God as 'cosmos' emphasise the experience of interconnection and mystery that they feel when they attempt to reside within the entire creation. Carolyn Nicholson Terrell relates a story from childhood which has continued to shape her perspective in this overpowering sense of overwhelm, which she claims inspires the sense of awe theists relate when they worship God. She claims that she heard a voice saying that God 'didn't create the world, he came along with it' (Terrell 2006, 114). She has always interpreted the message as teaching that God is all of the creation, the energy that existed from the beginning of time. There are interesting overlaps here with pantheism, with God as the forces which move the universe and give it life. Similar to that is David B. Lawrence's perspective, which he terms 'hylozoism'. He defines it as the idea that life/consciousness pervades everything in the cosmos. God is thus whatever essence or force animates all life in the universe. This force is still entirely physical, and a manifestation of the physical world, yet is still awe-inspiring (Lawrence 2006, 119).

Gudron Moller (a Quaker from Aotearoa/New Zealand Yearly Meeting) references the interconnection amongst all beings yet adds an emphasis on human evolution. Moller claims an identity as an agnostic humanist rather than non-theist as the emphasis on the 'unknown/uncertain' in agnosticism leaves space open to new ideas (2006, 127). Moller pushes against giving Fox's terminology for God (including, one may assume, Fox's vision of the 'Light') the greatest weight as doing so limits the horizons for new formulations and conceptions of 'God'. Moller stresses a seeming paradox between God as wholly human and God as a mystical, transforming power which resides in humans and gives humans strength to see a new world. This power is linked to the interconnection between all beings and is something which likely evolved with humanity. Moller references British Quaker Alex Wildwood's ideas of human evolution and maturation away from external, supernatural God towards something which celebrates the human connection with earth in life-giving creative expression.

Finally, George Amoss Jr. has taken as his theological project the development of ways of repurposing traditional Quaker language, including Christian language, in ways that bridge the seeming gap between non-theism and theism, in an effort to honour the experience of theists while also honouring his own. Reflecting this, Amoss references the construct of the Light in a way that is suggestive of interdependent presence. Amoss stresses that the Light is not a possession, or something to believe *in* (reflecting Dudiak's concerns) but is instead an experience to reside within. Residing in this Light will result in transformation for both our personal lives as well as our communal lives. We are then capable of leading to a way of life demonstrative of this same Light within (Amoss 1989, 21–24).

Amoss has developed this theme in significant detail since 1989, cataloguing his work on his website, Postmodern Quaker. Amoss has applied his method to his most recent project, *Quaker Faith and Practice for the 21st Century*. This document retains traditional Quaker Christological language, while interpreting that language through the lens of both Liberal Quaker theology and Amoss's vision of non-theism within Liberal Quakerism. Amoss expressly seeks to develop a methodology which respects and reflects the experience of both theism and non-theism (2016). He develops a construct of the Light as an experience to reside within, which will result in both individual and communal transformation. He utilises Christian language to describe the experience of Light, and the manner of the resulting transformation, without actually claiming any 'Christological' meaning.

Roland Warren suggests a way to bridge both the vision of 'God' as cosmos as well as 'God' as human value. Warren suggests that God is something 'created' by humans to explain the relation between humans and their experience of objective circumstances (2002, 6). God is what we create to explain the relationships that we experience between ourselves, our world, and the transcendent ideals that we hew to. God is therefore a product of the human mind, but not only so, in that God does not exist for humans outside of human perception. In other words, God is a framework applied to a set of experiences, circumstances and objective realities to make sense of our world, as well as the inexplicable. At its core, this is the 'religious experience'. Warren claims that while everyone has the potential for a religious experience, not everyone develops the hermeneutic for framing and understanding the experience in relation to a 'God'. In this sense, he reflects the concerns of Boulton, Linton and other non-theists who stress that 'God' is purely a human construct.

Warren offers something new, however, when he suggests that the root of sentience and consciousness cannot be found within the physical world. Instead, it seems to lie in another plane of existence, while of course being very present in the physical world, and rooted to it: when the physical body is dead, consciousness goes away. The natural world includes both the physical world and the realm of consciousness, mental processes and ideas. Reflecting Moller and Wildwood, Warren suggests that the experience of encountering the 'transcendent' or feeling a deep connection to God could simply be another step along the path of human evolution. Humans are therefore already evolved enough to engage in encountering these extra-physical planes of existence. This need not be the supernatural, per se; it could just be another plane of existence in the natural world, the realm of 'spirit', which humans are trying to grope their way towards understanding (Warren 2002, 16). 'Religion' has laid claim to this realm, but it can be understood in other ways.

This section suggested multiple avenues for future development in non-theist thought, in terms of both the creation of a uniquely Quaker non-theist a/theology and dialogue with Quaker theists (including Christian theists). Dudiak's suggestion that theism and non-theism have a common path forward within Liberal Quakerism framed this discussion, demonstrating that both theists and non-theists have the potential to gain from engagement with each other. Warren presents a vision for engagement which places the concerns of non-theists as a priority in the encounter, while Amoss presents the vision most concerned with seeking an equal space within Quakerism for the concerns and perspectives of both theists and non-theists.

CONCLUSION

This chapter has proposed future avenues for non-theism to grow: its self-definition, historiography and approach to history; interpretations of Quaker identity which engage in critical readings of a non-theistic Quaker imaginary; and the engagement of both non-theism and theism as equal partners in the development of Liberal Quaker theology. Non-theism is a complex umbrella term encapsulating multiple spectra: the value of theistic constructions within Liberal Quakerism, the role of belief in the definition of non-theist identity and meaning, and the capacity of non-theism to craft its own theological thought. Non-theism has not only already made contributions to the development of Liberal Quaker theology, especially in the role it played in the development of Universalist Quakerism, but it also has the potential for building bridges with Christocentric Liberal Quakerism in terms of a common theological language and imaginary. Moving forward, however, non-theism can only continue to make effective contributions to the development of Liberal Quakerism if it remains in dialogue with both Universalist and Christian Liberal Quakerism; following voices rejecting the value of theism will divorce non-theism from the rich theological history of Liberal Quakerism and imperil future development of non-theism within Liberal Quakerism.

SUGGESTED FURTHER READING

Amoss, George. *The Postmodern Quaker*, https://postmodernquaker.wordpress.com/
Boulton, David (ed.). (2006). *Godless for God's Sake: Nontheism in Contemporary Quakerism*, Dent: Dales Historical Monographs.
Cresson, O. (2014). *Quaker and Naturalist Too*, Iowa City: Morning Walk Press.
Website of Nontheist Friends, www.nontheistfriends.org/

❧

16

Evangelical Quakerism and Global Christianity

Jon R. Kershner

The majority of Quakers do not reside in Europe or North America, but in Africa, Latin America, and Asia, the regions and cultures also known as the "Majority World." Contemporary Quakers worldwide are predominately evangelical and are often referred to as the Friends Church. This evangelicalism can be defined in terms of its theology and in the structure of its worship services, which often resemble evangelical Protestant services with a sermon by a pastor and singing. Theologically, evangelical Friends emphasize evangelism; charismatic or heart-felt worship; a belief in human depravity and the need for redemption; and, especially among Majority World evangelical Friends, the coupling of spiritual and social ministries. The majority of Quakers in Europe and North America are evangelical and programmed. Nearly all Majority World Quakers are evangelical and programmed. Among Quakers who identify as being evangelical Christians are those who belong to Yearly Meetings or organizations that include the title "evangelical," as in Evangelical Friends Church International. Other Quakers identify as evangelical Christians but are a part of Quaker organizations that are not officially evangelical, as in Friends United Meeting (see the section on "Evangelical Friends Organizations" later). Throughout this chapter, the term "Evangelical Friends" will refer specifically to those issues and activities that belong specifically to Evangelical Friends Church International. The lowercase "evangelical Friends/Quakers" is a broader terms and refers to all Quakers who self-identify as evangelical Christians, whatever their organizational associations. Yearly Meeting names or parent organization names are also used to distinguishing among the various groupings of evangelical Quakers.

The growth of Quakerism in the Majority World, and of evangelicalism within Quakerism, parallels the larger trend in global Christianity, in which the numerical center of Christianity has moved outside of Western contexts and is dominated by evangelical spirituality. Globally, as of 2015, there were nearly one billion evangelicals and Pentecostals, and the growth trends of these movements are approximately twice the rate of the global population as a whole. However, the number of evangelicals is probably underreported, since many members of mainline congregations in the Majority World fit definitions of evangelicalism, even though their official denominational affiliation does not self-define that way (Johnson et al. 2015, 29; Tienou 2007, 213). Likewise, the vast majority of Christians reside in the Majority World, where growth trends are also outpacing global population growth (Johnson et al. 2015, 29). As a result, evangelical Christianity is situated to continue its rapid growth for some time, as are evangelical Friends in the Majority World.

This chapter examines evangelical Friends in their present-day situation in three primary sections. The first section defines evangelicalism generally and then applies that definition to evangelical Friends, tracing their development over time. The second section identifies the main ecclesial bodies populated by evangelical Quakers, their primary responsibilities and missions, and their prominence around the world. The final main section discusses the differences and similarities between evangelical Friends and the wider Quaker communion. These similarities and differences are analyzed in terms of two main headings: (1) spirituality, worship, and authority; and (2) social justice and morality. The chapter then concludes by describing cultural challenges faced by evangelical Friends and the theological trajectories that are finding resonance in many communities around the globe.

EVANGELICAL THEOLOGY AND DEVELOPMENT

While evangelicals share a common ethos and core theological presuppositions, these are enculturated in varying ways according to a particular church's historical period, tradition, and geographic location.

Timothy Larsen argues that an evangelical can be defined as follows:

1. "an orthodox Protestant
2. who stands in the tradition of the global Christian network arising from the eighteenth century revival movements associated with John Wesley and George Whitefield;
3. who has a preeminent place for the Bible in her or his Christian life as the divinely inspired, final authority in matters of faith and practice;
4. who stresses reconciliation with God through the atoning work of Jesus Christ on the cross;
5. and who stresses the work of the Holy Spirit in the life of an individual to bring about conversion and an ongoing life of fellowship with God and

service to God and others, including the duty of all believers to participate in the task of proclaiming the gospel to all people." (Larsen 2007, 1)

This definition identifies both the key features of evangelical theology (preeminence of the Bible, the atoning work of Jesus on the cross, and the need for conversion and evangelism) and a particular historical tradition with many variations (orthodox Protestantism and the revivalism of Whitefield and Wesley). Evangelicalism is best understood as a protest movement within Christianity. Historically, the evangelical message has been addressed to a purportedly Christian society that was not Christian enough and needed to be convinced and convicted of its unbelieving (Walls 1996, 81).

Evangelical Friends would agree with each of the tenets of evangelicalism cited by Larsen. Among the wider Quaker communion, evangelical Friends can usually be distinguished by both the theological points Larsen delineates and by form of worship. The present-day branches of Quakerism (e.g., Liberal, Conservative, Evangelical) are often differentiated by the interrelated categories of theology and method of conducting worship, with Orthodox and Liberal Quakers practicing a non-pastoral, unprogrammed form of worship. Like other evangelical denominations, evangelical Friends churches, which are all programmed and pastoral, believe that one's relationship with God is the defining factor of true worship instead of a particular form of worship, such as unprogrammed silence, and can be variable from church to church, and even, Sunday to Sunday. For evangelical Friends, Quakerism is a Christian religion and worship should have an evangelistic element to proclaim salvation through Christ. Moreover, evangelical Friends believe that God is active in the pastor's planning of the worship service (Hamm 2003, 78).

One aspect that distinguishes evangelical Friends from other evangelical groups is the heightened sense of universal ministry, or the belief that all members are ministers whether or not they are paid pastors. Thus, evangelical Friends churches can feature significant participation in worship services from non-clergy members of the congregation. Some evangelical worship services also have times of unprogrammed silence, or "open worship," ranging from a couple of minutes up to fifteen minutes. During open worship, anyone may speak. Some churches include additional times set aside for testimony or prayer requests from the congregation. Many churches occasionally invite members of the congregation to give the sermon. Moreover, Evangelical Friends mostly view all members as ministers within their communities, while the pastor has a particular (but not superior) ministry of teaching and administration for the day-to-day operations of the church. Friends churches that emphasize the universal ministry claim the practice to be derived from the historic Quaker tradition in which there were no official clergy and all members were tasked with ministering according to the "measure" of divine guidance they had received (Barclay 2002, 46–47).

Pink Dandelion has argued that evangelical Quakerism is diverse, with various groups being influenced by external influences, including modernism, Holiness spirituality, and fundamentalism (2007, 190). Evangelical Friends, today, often point back to George Fox (1624–91) – key founder of Quakerism in the mid-seventeenth century – as an inspiration for their evangelicalism, especially his concern for the need for total conversion and redemption in Christ. The *Faith and Practice* of Evangelical Friends Church – Mid-America frames Quaker roots in this evangelical framework, beginning a section on the history of Friends noting that Fox "studied the Bible so thoroughly that he learned much of it by memory." He finally "found inner peace through trusting Jesus Christ as his Savior," which led him to then "tell others about the Gospel of Christ as God's way to free people from sin. As Fox shared the reality he had found, others responded and joined him in spreading the good news of salvation" (*Faith and Practice: The Book of Discipline. Evangelical Friends Church – Mid-America*, 1). This description of Quaker history corresponds with definitions of evangelicalism: (1) primacy of Scripture, (2) salvation in Christ, (3) human need for redemption/conversion, and (4) importance of evangelism. Even though evangelicalism as a clearly defined reform movement was still almost a hundred years in the future, Evangelical Friends can see the roots of contemporary evangelical Quakerism in Quaker origins of the 1650s.

One moment in nineteenth-century Quaker history remains definitive for evangelical Friends. In 1887, a group of moderate evangelical Friends gathered in Richmond, Indiana, to reflect on the pressures of both Holiness revivalism and modernism. Holiness revivalism was a mid-nineteenth-century movement that saw the introduction of the pastoral system among evangelical Friends and taught that the culmination of faith was a fully sanctified life. Modernism among Quakers refers to the trend of incorporating higher biblical criticism and viewing culture as something that could be engaged constructively. The fruit of the 1887 conference was the Richmond "Declaration of Faith." This document retained Quaker testimonies in regard to emphasizing spiritual sacraments and peace, but it also reflected the theological tenor of the Holiness revivals and was firmly entrenched in orthodox Christianity. At the time, some of the radical evangelical Friends swept up in revivalism wanted to eliminate much of the historic Quaker understanding of sanctification and faith. The Declaration of Faith took a moderate position; none of the groups at the conference got everything it wanted. After the conference, other Quaker groups expressed concern that the Declaration of Faith seemed to resemble a creed. Despite the controversy, the Declaration of Faith remains an essential theological framework for evangelical Friends (Hamm 2003, 53–4; Roberts 2013, 109). Evangelical Friends' Yearly Meetings continue to include the Declaration of Faith in their Books of Discipline, "Faith and Practice," alongside other evangelical Protestant statements, including that of the National Association of Evangelicals (Dandelion 2007, 191). The National Association of Evangelicals was founded in 1942 as a way for evangelical groups to work together across denominational lines toward common goals of evangelism and toward supporting conservative Christian social values. These two documents are seen as important expressions of evangelical Quakerism.

Global Christianity tends to be evangelical; however, as a result of distinct cultural and philosophical contexts, it has differing emphases from Western evangelicalism. While there is no single manifestation of Majority World Christianity, there are broadly accurate characteristics. In general, Majority World Christians tend to give greater authority to the Bible than do Western Christians, especially in regard to morality, supernatural forces, and the ongoing relevance of prophecy (Jenkins 2006, 4–5). These more literalist readings of the Bible are true of Majority World Christians even when they are part of denominations that are typically seen as liberal in a Western context, such as Anglicans or Methodists. Philip Jenkins argues that this more conservative approach to the Bible is due in part to the fact that many Majority World Christians identify with the social, political, and economic realities of the biblical world. Poverty, famine, state oppression, and persecution are part of the daily realities for many Majority World Christians, which leads them to distrust the secular order and put their dependence on God for hope and survival (Jenkins 2006, 5). In addition to more literalist approaches to the Bible, Majority World Christians

1) share a strong supernatural orientation (including experiences with visions, demonic/angelic interventions and healings);
2) are sensitive to Christian responsibilities to address issues of poverty and social justice;
3) are experienced in articulating the uniqueness of their faith in a religiously pluralist environment;
4) are likely to emphasize the communal dimensions of the Bible and Christianity; and
5) emphasize evangelism and personal salvation. (Jenkins 2007, 8; Tennent 2007, 15)

These theological characteristics explain, in part, why it is that the Christian groups that have been most successful at establishing churches in the Majority World are traditional Roman Catholicism and evangelical or Pentecostal Protestantism, which focus on applied Christianity and supernaturalism and call for high degrees of commitment (Jenkins 2007, 8; Sanneh 2008, 167).

EVANGELICAL FRIENDS ORGANIZATION

Most evangelical Friends are members of either Evangelical Friends Church International (EFCI) or Friends United Meeting (FUM), with some other evangelical Yearly Meetings remaining independent from either organization.

EFCI was formed in 1989 out of earlier iterations of Evangelical Friends associations. EFCI seeks to coordinate resources across its 140,000 members in twenty-four countries, divided into five international regions: Africa, Asia, Europe, Latin America, and North America. The regional directors from each of these international regions form the International Council. The two largest regions in terms of membership are Africa (50,000–60,000 members, most of these in Rwanda, Congo, and Burundi) and Latin America (~55,000 members, most of these in Bolivia and Guatemala) (Evangelical Friends Church International n.d.). The purpose statement of Evangelical Friends Church – North America (EFC–NA) describes both the evangelical theology and ministry networks that characterize all EFCI regions: "to work together in Christian ministry based on biblical principles to develop personnel and resources that will enable the member regions to fulfill the Great Commission [Mt. 28:19–20]" (Evans 2014, 75).

In addition to organizing ministries internationally, EFCI also defines the theological boundaries of the group. EFCI's belief statement is within the mainstream of evangelical Christianity, with very little to identify it as an explicitly Quaker organization. One reason for this is that Quaker "testimonies" and practices are interpreted and practiced in different ways depending on the needs of the local culture. With the cultural diversity and international focus of EFCI, the common denominator is a belief structure that resembles other evangelical Protestants, featuring the following:

1) Trinitarian formula for God as described in the Bible;
2) Jesus is divine, lived perfectly, died sacrificially and was resurrected, and is the "only acceptable payment for the penalty of mankind's rebellion and wrongdoing";
3) the Holy Spirit empowers believers to follow Jesus' pattern on earth;

4) the Bible is "the written word of God" and "fully authoritative in all it says";

5) Humanity was created for full relationship with God, but that relationship was destroyed through disobedience and can only be repaired through Jesus' sacrifice;

6) the Church is the "living presence of Jesus in the world" as seen in evangelism and service. (Friends Beliefs n.d.)

Evangelical Friends recognize themselves as one expression of the larger global evangelical movement and, so, can work ecumenically with other groups that share these common statements.

Many evangelical Friends view their Quaker heritage and testimonies as an important contribution to global Christianity. Thus, local EFCI churches are often intentional about translating their Quaker expression into a particular local context, but the form that translation takes varies from location to location. As a result, EFCI focuses on maintaining the evangelical theological doctrines that they feel must precede any particularity of expression. This outlook is a main difference between evangelical Yearly Meetings, on one hand, and Liberal and Conservative Quaker Yearly Meetings, on the other hand, which might argue that giving primacy to a set of doctrines is credalism and that the particular form of unprogrammed Quaker worship is the true means through which Quakerism is experienced.

The largest and most involved ministry of EFC-NA is Evangelical Friends Mission, the internationally focused mission training and sending organization. Evangelical Friends Mission raises more money, has an annual budget of $2 million, and employs more workers than any other commission within EFC-NA (Evans 2014, 77). Its stated mission "is to fuel a worldwide movement of people who seek first the kingdom of God, planting churches that live and die to carry out the Great Commission in the spirit of the Great Commandment" (Evangelical Friends Mission n.d.). The purpose of Evangelical Friends Mission is not to produce Quakers but to evangelize with the Gospel, and Quaker testimonies are presented as an important, but supplemental, part of a new believer's discipleship. In some Majority World countries, the evangelism efforts of evangelical Friends missionaries (who are often Indigenous evangelists) would not look very different from the missions of other denominations. It is as new converts learn more about their faith that Friends theologies of inward spiritual experience, peace making, and gender equality become a part of the message (Cammack 2015).

FUM is the umbrella organization for many evangelical Friends worldwide; but whereas all member churches of EFCI are theologically evangelical, this is not the case with FUM. FUM describes itself as a "collection of Christ-centered Quakers," but FUM Yearly Meetings and local meetings show great theological variation. Of the 184,000 reported FUM members, 15,000 are dual-affiliated with Friends General Conference (FGC), an association of Liberal Quakers. While FUM is generally pastoral and programmed, some individual meetings have less programming than others and those dual-affiliated with FGC are most likely not evangelical and often are unprogrammed or semi-programmed. However, the majority of FUM in America is evangelical; even more so, the vast majority of FUM Yearly Meetings in the Majority World are also evangelical. Membership in FUM is not determined by adherence to a set of beliefs, as is the case with EFCI. Instead, FUM provides resources and facilitates partnerships among member Yearly Meetings wherever they might be located on the theological spectrum. Thus, FUM unites some evangelical and non-evangelical Yearly Meetings. Collaboration between EFCI Yearly Meetings and evangelical FUM Yearly Meetings is inconsistent, at least in part because EFCI Yearly Meetings are wary of the non-evangelical influences within FUM and, so, tend to focus on their own networks.

In addition to EFCI and FUM, there are independent evangelical Yearly Meetings. For example, Central Yearly Meeting formed in 1926 from churches in Indiana and Kansas that deemed FUM too liberal (Roberts 2013, 112). Central Yearly Meeting is not formally connected with any other Quaker body. Likewise, there are at least five independent Yearly Meetings in Bolivia that freely participate in EFCI conferences but are not counted in EFCI statistics. These five Bolivian independent Yearly Meetings total more than 30,000 members (Latin America/America Latina n.d.; Roberts 2013, 120).

EVANGELICAL FRIENDS AND THE LARGER QUAKER COMMUNION

While there is local variation, evangelical Friends globally tend to view themselves as a part of God's universal work of salvation and, so, think favorably of other evangelical groups that share core evangelical values. Moreover, Majority World Quakers share the same points of emphases as other Majority World Christians. This is particularly true in regard to expressive worship, the role of the Bible in shaping morality, a heightened sense that prayer and spiritual forces are shaping everyday life, and the social impacts of the Gospel (Jenkins 2007, 8; Tennent 2007, 15). East African Friends hold their Quaker heritage as very important but view themselves as "part of the larger Christian church, which is the body of Christ in the world ... to express the good news of Jesus Christ in each of our

communities and to the rest of the world, so that others may be saved"
(*Christian Faith and Practice in the Friends Church, Friends United Meeting
in East Africa*, 5). However, many evangelical Friends are articulate about the
need for a faith that "is both Quaker and evangelical," though the way that is
manifested would be a matter of interpretation (Punshon 1996, 209).

Spirituality, Worship, and Authority

Spirituality and worship are key similarities and differences among Quaker
traditions. This section highlights the structure of worship services and
underlying spirituality, and the authority of personal experience and the
Bible among Quaker traditions.

For evangelical Friends, worship is grounded in gratitude for salvation in
Christ and is heavily laden with biblical teachings. Revelatory dreams, healings, and prophetic pronouncements are a common feature of evangelical
Friends in the Majority World. In India, a man named Mukul converted to
Christianity after the congregation of Gopalpur Friends Church successfully
prayed for the healing of his dying son (Sarkar 2015a, 1). Upon conversion,
Kenyan Friend Oliver Kisaka Simiyu was cured of asthma and allergies and
given spiritual gifts of the "Holy Spirit" to confirm the authenticity of his new
faith, including "speaking in tongues, and healing the sick. These experiences
were unmistakable demonstrations of the power of God in my life" (Simiyu
2004, 47). Reminiscent of early Quaker experiences of "quaking" in the Spirit,
observers at Yearly Meeting sessions in Kenya have seen "God's power
[come] upon many Friends so much so that some shook and others spoke
in tongues" (Simiyu 2004, 54).

While most evangelical Friends in the West would deem these types of
charismatic spiritual experiences as theoretically possible, few Western evangelicals have experienced them. In the Majority World, where Pentecostalism
is the dominant expression of evangelical Christianity, a heightened degree of
spiritualism is part of the enculturation process. Indeed, in Asia and Africa,
most converts come from those inculcated in indigenous spirituality, which
has sometimes developed deep resonances with Pentecostal and evangelical
faith (Angell 2006, 120; Chan 2007, 226–27; Welling 2013, 314). In other cases,
such as in some Friends communities in South America, Indigenous religions
continue to distract converts from adherence to Christianity and pose a
challenge for local church leaders (Thomas 2014, 117).

Because of the cultural resonance of expressive spirituality, in many places
evangelical Friends worship features dancing; energetic singing; and exuberant, vocalized prayer. Worship services among evangelical Friends in the

Majority World can last several hours or more. Among the programmed churches of North America, worship resembles other Protestant services, usually lasting one hour, but seem mild compared to the charismatic expression of Friends in the Majority World (Stansell 2009, 108). Many evangelical Friends view fervent, expressive worship in singing as that most authentic way to unite one's outward practice of faith with one's inward spiritual reality (Mamani 2010, 4).

Expressive worship is also an area of tensions among evangelical Friends. In East Africa, for most of the twentieth century, worship services resembled the style and temper of American evangelicalism, featuring hymns and clearly defined roles in worship centered on the pastor. However, at the beginning of the twenty-first century, young Kenyan and Burundian Friends have challenged this tradition and called for greater freedom in worship and the adoption of new spiritual practices (Amoyi Lanogwa 2010, 32; Phylis 2010, 6). Simiyu argues that Friends should allow "greater flexibility" in their spiritual practices so that young Friends can adopt Pentecostal modes of worship, including fervent all night prayer services (Simiyu 2004, 55). He encapsulates the task of enculturation and the process of alignment in which Majority World evangelical Friends have innovated on the Western Quaker tradition:

> [Living spiritually] is not about maintaining traditions, though traditions are important; it is about understanding God's way today. To be led by the Spirit of God is not to work exactly as [George] Fox worked, but to accomplish God's work in our hour as the Spirit will lead us today. This does not mean that Fox was wrong, or that we can't learn from his generation, or that we can't do things as they did. It only means that we understand what we mean when we say the Spirit is leading us. (Simiyu 2004, 58)

Majority World evangelical Friends own their Quaker message and are the key agents in translating it into their cultural context, often in ways that might seem contrary to the Quaker tradition among Western Quakers.

Yet, for many evangelical Friends churches, the historic Quaker testimonies are deemed "nonessentials," which can be helpful but can be set aside to reach out to more people. However, for many evangelical Friends, Quaker testimonies of simplicity and peace are integrated into their public witness. In some Majority World countries, especially in Asia, evangelical Friends commonly perform water baptism as a public sign of an inward spiritual reality. For Friends in India, the use of water in baptism is sometimes justified according to the spirit of early Quakerism (Sarkar 2015b, 1). For example, early Quakers rejected the physical sacraments in their Christendom context because the outward ritual was disconnected from the inward spiritual reality. However, in places such as

India and Nepal, where Christians are a persecuted minority, the performance of baptism with water is symbolic of a new life and has real consequences for a convert's relationship to her or his community, such as exclusion from cultural practices deemed inconsistent with Christianity, losing one's job, and financial jeopardy. In other places, evangelical Quakers may perform water baptisms for a wide range of reasons, including cultural expectations, or a new convert's personal request.

In EFC-NA, many church worship services increasingly resemble non-denominational worship services with a worship band, songs not different from other evangelical worship services, and a casual teaching sermon from a pastor. Unprogrammed open worship is often optional, if offered at all. As American evangelicalism has trended toward emphases on technologically sophisticated, culturally engaging, and energetic worship services featuring electric guitars and chorus singing, larger Evangelical Friends churches have followed suit. However, there is considerable diversity among the types of worship among Evangelical Friends churches in the United States. Yorba Linda Friends Church (Evangelical Friends Church – Southwest), which could be considered a megachurch with its weekly attendance of more than 4,000, multiple weekly worship services, and amphitheater-style sanctuary, demonstrates one attempt at integrating evangelical nondenominationalism with the Friends heritage. Yorba Linda Friends Church does not claim Quakerism as the primary source of its identity; instead, it encourages people to develop a personal relationship with Jesus Christ. Yet, they do imply Quaker teachings, without labeling them as such. For example, they cite the spiritual reality of ongoing "communion" with God and the baptism of the Holy Spirit as the true reality of the ordinances and sufficient in themselves. However, the church does regularly provide opportunity for participating in the physical elements of water and wafer "for those whose conscience would lead them to partake" (Foundational Beliefs, n.d.).

By contrast, another EFC-NA church, North Seattle Friends Church (Northwest Yearly Meeting) has an average attendance of about thirty people and features open worship of at least fifteen minutes, and often much longer, according to the "leadings" of the Spirit each Sunday. Sometimes there is no sermon, or else the pastor feels "led" to not give the prepared sermon. At other times, sermons specifically focus on applying Quaker testimonies to present-day events. For North Seattle Friends Church members, striving to articulate a specifically Quaker spirituality is crucial to their identity as Christians. A visitor to Yorba Linda Friends Church and North Seattle Friends Church would probably conclude the two churches were of completely different denominations. Both churches, and many other EFC-NA

churches, are negotiating the changing cultural climates of post-denomina-
tionalism, secularism, evangelicalism, and modernism in their own way with
the spiritual and personnel resources at hand. They adapt their Quaker
heritage in ways that speak to the changing needs of their congregations.
All of these dimensions mean that there is a high degree of variability among
the worship expressions, ministries, and resources of EFC-NA churches.

In some cases, EFC-NA churches are responding to the changing demographic needs of their communities by becoming increasingly multicultural and
even multilingual. EFC-NA contains at least thirty Spanish-speaking congregations (Byrne n.d.), and others whose primary languages are Korean, Khmer, and
Farsi. Many of the Spanish-speaking churches in the United States are derived
from Friends churches in Latin America, originally started by EFC-NA missions
(Pickard 2014, 128). The worship service schedule for Long Beach Friends
Church (Evangelical Friends Church – Southwest) demonstrates the changes
in demographics occurring in some locations with a multicultural community:

9am
English Worship
Khmer Sunday School
Children's Sunday School (9:25am)

11am
Khmer Worship
Children's Jr. Church
Youth Sunday School

4pm
Latino Worship (Who We Are, n.d.)

Three language groups in a single congregation is not typical of EFC-NA
churches, but the growth of Friends in the Majority World and immigration
patterns have led to cross-cultural contact within American Evangelical
Friends churches. The full impact of this growing multiculturalism within
EFC-NA is still emerging, but some American Evangelical Friends are hope-
ful that Majority World Quaker missionaries and immigrants will bring a
new evangelistic vitality to American Evangelical Friends.

Even though there are considerable differences in the worship practices
and underlying spirituality of Majority World evangelical Friends and North
American evangelicals Friends, the largest difference is between evangelical
Friends globally and unprogrammed Friends. For unprogrammed Friends,
worship characterized by silence and speaking out of silence is not only seen
as the highest form of Quaker worship but corresponds with a non-credal,

apophatic approach to the Divine and faith. One description of worship in unprogrammed Britain Yearly Meeting's *Faith & Practice* reflects how personal experience is the primary means for encountering religious enlightenment: "To me, worship is recognizing and communing with the divine whether it is within myself, in others, or in the world. The pre-condition of worship is my belief in worth-ship, my own and that of other people" (*Quaker Faith and Practice* 1999, sec. 2.08). The approach to worship implied in this quote is not necessarily Christian and is not rooted in the Bible. For evangelical Friends, individual experience is interpreted through the Bible and a belief in a transcendent God that provided the means of salvation, without which all are lost to eternal condemnation. Evangelical worship is focused on gratitude to this active and transcendent God and to submitting one's life to God, which has identifiable lifestyle hallmarks including sexual purity, honesty, avoiding alcohol, and evangelism. This contrasts with the common sentiment among unprogrammed Friends that worship is primarily about listening for the innate worth that resides in all people already. Yet, other unprogrammed Friends, such as Thomas Kelly (1893–1941), have maintained a spiritual theology that evangelical Friends interpret as Christocentric and even as an expression of a robust integration of evangelical and Quaker theology. Kelly did not identify himself as an evangelical, but his writings are read widely among evangelical Quakers.

In the case of Liberal Yearly Meetings, worship and theology are always a "'towards' kind of activity" that emphasizes the role of the individual in seeking, if not finding, God or theological truth. By contrast, evangelical Friends view theology and religious truth as given from God, and God is a knowable and certain referent in their theology (Dandelion 2007, 244).

One primary area of contention between evangelical Friends and Liberal Friends is on the nature and authority of the Bible. Most unprogrammed Friends tend to have lower views of the Bible's authority and its relevance for contemporary Quakerism. The focus among unprogrammed Friends on individual spiritual experience is primary and does not need to agree with biblical concepts. Evangelical Friends might differ on particular interpretations of the Bible but would grant it great authority for their spiritual and social lives. While sojourning at Pendle Hill in Pennsylvania, Kenyan Friend Simiyu was "greatly disturbed" to hear that some Quakers prioritize individual "leadings" above the teachings of Scripture (Simiyu 2004, 53). While a uniting spiritual feature across Quaker traditions is the view that authentic faith must be appropriated inwardly and not only a matter of reciting a creed or of performing rituals, evangelical Friends believe the Bible is authoritative in revealing God's will and its message should be appropriated inwardly. For evangelical

Friends, a true understanding of God's leading would never conflict with the teachings of the Bible.

Social Justice and Morality

At the end of the twentieth century, evangelical Friends reinvigorated a commitment to working for social justice as an essential part of the Gospel message (Welling 2013, 320). This section looks at the specific cases of the role of women among Friends, peace making, and sexuality.

Evangelical, Liberal, and Conservative Friends officially support women as ministers, but there practices vary greatly. In FUM and EFC-NA, women sometimes serve as pastors. However, churches make their own hiring decisions, which means the preferences of church leaders and local search committees become the functional position on women in ministry. Many evangelical Friends churches have never had a woman as a pastor, though this fact would not always derive from an overt and intentional church policy. In some cases, though, the teachings of individual Friends churches have prohibited women serving as pastors (Fager and Souza 2014).

In 2015, Bware Yearly Meeting in Kenya (FUM) became the first East African Yearly Meeting to appoint a woman as Presiding Clerk of the yearly meeting ("First woman to serve as Presiding Clerk of a Yearly Meeting in East Africa," 2015). In 2011, Northwest Yearly Meeting (EFC-NA) appointed a woman as Superintendent of the Yearly Meeting for the first time, the highest administrative and pastoral position in the Yearly Meeting (Spencer 2011). Friends' women in Burundi and Kenya have new economic opportunities and have risen to political prominence. In Nepal and Kenya, Evangelical Friends' converts and missionaries have challenged discriminatory dowries and male favoritism (Angell 2006, 115–17; Roberts 2013, 122). In India, husband and wife evangelists work as partners in ministry (Roberts 2013, 122). Evangelical Friends Mission sees its work as enhancing the equality of women around the world (Cammack 2015). Nonetheless, evangelical Quaker women are not as likely to be pastors or hold important positions as are men, and in some places women ministers face considerable resistance from the wider culture (Roberts 2013, 122).

Friends of every tradition are united in a testimony to peace and non-violence, though not all Quakers are strict pacifists. Kenyan Friends teach Christian nonviolence and love of enemy (Christian Faith and Practice in the Friends Church, Friends United Meeting in East Africa, n.d. 6). After the Burundian and Rwandan genocides of the 1990s, Friends united to care for widows and orphans and have been leaders in trauma healing

(Niyonzima and Fendall 2001, 105–6; Roberts 2013, 122). When ethnic conflict broke out in East Africa in 2007–8, African Friends gave refuge to persecuted people, even though they knew it could cause them material suffering (Abbott 2013, 562). Majority World Friends face religious violence, economic oppression, and political unrest firsthand, and they find their faith to be a spiritual and physical support to them. Evangelical Friends seek to integrate social action with personal holiness, supporting the human rights of Dalit castes in India and providing medicine, education, and shelter according to local needs (Roberts 2013, 121–22; Sarkar 2015c, 1, 2015d, 1). They describe nonviolence and working for justice in the face of various forms of persecution and suffering as an important part of their obedience to God (Cammack 2015).

At present, the greatest area of conflict between Quaker traditions regards human sexuality. Liberal Friends tend to be politically and socially liberal and accepting of homosexual practice, whereas Conservative and evangelical Friends tend to be politically and socially conservative or traditional (Dandelion 2007, 244). Conservative Friends have differing views on homosexuality, but evangelical Friends are almost unified in their rejection of homosexual practice. All Evangelical Friends Yearly Meeting's *Faith and Practices* prohibit homosexual practice. Mid-America Yearly Meeting's (EFC-NA) *Faith and Practice* defines homosexuality as an "evil" that will bring about "God's judgment" against those who "practice and encourage such activity" (*Faith and Practice: The Book of Discipline. Evangelical Friends Church - Mid-America*, n.d., 19–20). While the official position of evangelical Friends prohibits homosexual practice, the number of young adult evangelical Friends who either support the full inclusion of homosexuals into the life of the church or do not view homosexual behavior as an automatic disqualifier for faithful living is larger than among evangelical Friends as a whole.

In 2013, the majority evangelical Indiana Yearly Meeting (FUM) split due to differing perspectives on how much authority the Yearly Meeting could legitimately exercise over local churches. The specific instance in which the question of authority arose was the decisions by one church, five years prior, to become affirming of homosexual relationships, a position that opposed Indiana Yearly Meeting's official stance. The evangelical meetings in Indiana Yearly Meeting, insisting that this local church's affirmation of homosexual relationships had to be condemned, initiated a process resulting in the eventual separation (as a body) of fifteen meetings. Evangelical churches remained in Indiana Yearly Meeting, while moderate and progressive-leaning Friends formed a new organization, the New Association of Friends (History of the New Association of Friends, n.d.). However, the churches that switched from Indiana Yearly Meeting to the New Association did so because they believed churches should have greater ability for self-determination whatever their social and theological convictions (Angell 2014). In 2015, similar controversies in North Carolina Yearly Meeting (FUM) and Northwest Yearly Meeting (EFC-NA) exposed other splits over issues of Yearly Meeting authority and church autonomy, homosexuality, and biblical authority (Fager 2015).

Evangelical Friends in the Majority World do not face the same divisions over human sexuality as are present in American Christianity; they are united in their views of traditional marriage. In 2012, the Presiding Clerk of Friends Church Kenya, an organization that covers all of the Kenyan Yearly Meetings, issued a press release on "Quakers and Homosexuality." He condemned the acceptance of homosexual practice among Liberal Friends as "re-branding sexual immorality to mean human rights" and abandoning God to please one's "own selfish desires" (Malenge 2013). This statement prompted a response from the socially and theologically progressive journal *Quaker Theology* in the United States, which called for Malenge to reconsider and defend his statement and invited responses from other North American Quakers across the theological spectrum, though only one response from a member of an evangelical Yearly Meeting was made (Fager 2013). That response from an Evangelical Friend rejects the way homosexual actions are sometimes viewed by evangelicals as a sin of a higher order and contends, instead, that homosexual relationships should be understood within the context of all sexual sins described in the Bible (Heathman 2013). The deep division between evangelical Friends and Liberal Friends, and sometimes Conservative Friends, on the nature of biblical authority and interpretation is so decisive that many evangelical Friends do not bother engaging across traditions on these issues (for attempts at uniting Quaker traditions and the Christ-cenetred but inclusive Freedom Friends group, see Daniels and Woods, Chapter 17, this volume).

CONCLUSION

As the twenty-first century progresses, evangelical Friends will continue to wrestle with the legacies of the Quaker tradition, and whether or not the wider Quaker communion is a meaningful point of connection. For some socially and theologically progressive North American evangelical Friends, connections with the wider Quaker communion will be important and movements such as Convergent Friends will facilitate these interactions. Evangelical Friends in the United States will continue to express their faith in ways that respond to perceived cultural threats and needs. The results will vary considerably from church to church and from Yearly Meeting to Yearly Meeting. In EFC-NA and FUM Meetings in the United States, disagreement about biblical interpretation and the "culture wars" will lead to further divisions. The influence of Protestant evangelicalism, and theological differences among Friends, will lead some churches to increasingly affiliate with the larger evangelical culture. Many smaller evangelical Friends churches, like most small churches in the United States, will struggle to survive. More and more non-English-speaking evangelical Friends churches will emerge in partnership to, or in place of, existing evangelical Friends churches.

Evangelical Friends in the Majority World are mixed concerning their connection to the wider Quaker communion. In some places, the history of Friends and the diversity of Quaker traditions are honored. Cuban Friend Heredio Santos speaks for many when he says that despite differences in belief and practice, "we feel part of one single world-wide Quaker family, together with silent Friends and all the other Friends in the world" (Santos 1991, 10). Other Majority World Friends are unaware that there are other Quaker traditions outside of their evangelical contacts, or else they wish to distinguish themselves from the perceived unbiblical practices they find among some parts of the wider Quaker communion. In the poor communities of India, for example, where religious persecution is a reality and poverty is rampant, evangelists' primary concern is on the spiritual and physical needs around them.

Majority World Friends will continue to grow in numbers and continue to enculturate the Quaker tradition into their own contexts. In some cases, such as among young Friends in Kenya, this will likely mean more expressiveness in worship and a greater willingness to incorporate Pentecostal practices. Majority World Friends will become missionary-sending churches. Their message will be similar to that of other Majority World Christians, and ecumenical dialogues and ministries among various evangelical groups will continue to provide infrastructure for ministry. Majority World Friends are generally uninterested whether these evangelistic emphases are accepted as legitimate Quaker expressions by Quakers in the West; it is their lived experience and deep conviction that a conservative Christian message is true and the best expression of Quakerism. In fact, the ongoing de-Westernization of Christianity as a whole parallels the de-Westernization of Quakerism and will continue to introduce new expressions of Quakerism in culturally enculturated ways, even though sometimes these new expressions of Quakerism may seem to be counter to Western Quaker practices.

Evangelical Friends missionary networks and resources will continue to unite evangelical Friends around the world. As the West becomes increasingly secularized and social anomie becomes more widespread, Europe and North America will become seen as mission fields. Majority World Quakers could very well help Westerners enculturate Friends heritage for a post-Christian, post-denominational, postmodern context.

SUGGESTED FURTHER READING

Conti, A., Curtis, C., Daniels, C. W., Hart, H., Katreen Hoggatt, S., Jadin, E. et al. (eds.). (2010). *Spirit Rising: Young Quaker Voices*, Philadelphia: Quaker Press of Friends General Conference.

Abbott, M. P. and Senger Parsons, P. (eds.). (2004). *Walk Worthy of Your Calling: Quakers and the Travelling Ministry*, Richmond, IN: Friends United Press.

Roberts, A. (2013). "Evangelical Friends, 1887–2010," in *The Oxford Handbook of Quaker Studies*, ed. by S. Angell and P. Dandelion, Oxford: Oxford University Press, pp. 108–25.

Stansell, R. (2009). *Missions by the Spirit: Learning from Quaker Examples*, Newberg, OR: Barclay Press.

Welling, J. S. (2013). "Mission," in *The Oxford Handbook of Quaker Studies*, ed. by S. Angell and P. Dandelion, Oxford: Oxford University Press, pp. 306–20.

Convergent Friends

Renewal, Hybridity, and Dialogue in Twenty-first-Century Quakerism

C. Wess Daniels and Greg Woods

INTRODUCTION

In this chapter, the sector of Quakerism labeled as 'convergent Friends' is explored linguistically, historically, and in terms of how it manifests today within contemporary Western Quakerism. Convergent Friends, fueled by the use of social media, combine insights from the emerging church movement and traditional understandings of the Quaker faith to hold both conservative and emergent impulses in tension with dialogue around differences present within modern Quakerism.

I DEFINING CONVERGENCE WITHIN A QUAKER CONTEXT

Convergent Friends, as a term specifically applied to an emerging pattern some identify within Quakerism, was coined by San Francisco Quaker Robin Mohr in 2005. Shortly thereafter, she argued "convergent"

> Describes Friends who are seeking a deeper understanding of our Quaker heritage and a more authentic life in the kingdom of God on Earth, radically inclusive of all who seek to live this life. It includes, among others, Friends from the politically liberal end of the evangelical branch, the Christian end of the unprogrammed branch, and the more outgoing end of the Conservative branch. It includes folks who aren't sure what they believe about Jesus and Christ, but who aren't afraid to wrestle with this question. It includes people who think that a lot of Quaker anachronisms are silly but who are willing to experiment to see which are spiritual disciplines that still hold life and power to transform and improve us ... Linguistically, it

alludes to an affinity for both Conservative Friends and the Emergent Church. (Mohr 2006b)

"Convergent" is a *portmanteau*, a word that combines two words to create a new meaning. It is a composite of "conservative" and "emergent," as in "conver/gent," describing those Quakers whose commitments seek to hold in tension two impulses: conserving that which is most alive within their particular branch of Quakerism, while also being emergent or innovative in ways that distinguish it from other expressions within the Quaker tradition. Therefore, *tradition* and *context* are essential in the framework for convergent Friends. Add to these two impulses a third: *dialogue.* Convergent Friends are committed to learning through dialogue with Quakers and non-Quakers alike. In dialogue, convergent Friends bring together people, ideas, and/or practices as a potential source for renewing their own expression of Quakerism.

Because of this, convergence is a hybrid Quakerism, transgressing the boundaries of established Quakerism (cf. Dandelion 2008: 108–9). In this way, convergent Friends create an "intersection of Quaker theology, practice and dialogue between evangelical, [conservative] and liberal, programmed and unprogrammed, Christian and non-Christian Friends all being blown in the same director by the 'winds of the Spirit'" (Daniels 2012: 87). Quakers drawn to convergent Friends tend to be, in the words of Robin Mohr, Friends on the "Politically liberal end of the evangelical branch, the Christian end of the unprogrammed branch, and the more outgoing end of the Conservative branch" (Mohr 2006b). There are convergent Friends who experiment with forms of art or liturgy in worship, teach Bible study, offer Christ-centered messages within meetings where this is an unusual or unwelcome practice, or rediscover early Quaker practices and writings in meetings that have lost a sense of history and tradition. They may find ways to incorporate ideas or practices from other Quaker streams or other religious traditions into their own while still remaining rooted within their particular branch. Convergent Friends represent a self-aware movement that attempts to bring about renewal through the application of these three impulses: tradition, context, and dialogue.

Finally, convergent Friends cannot be understood outside of their Western postmodern context and the global information culture that enables the sharing and participating in communities across time and space (Bolger 2007). The "emergent" thread within conv/ergent refers to the initial influence of the emerging church, a nondenominational grouping of churches that sought to be contextual within postmodernity, hold to a "generous orthodoxy," and focus on living the way of Jesus rather than holding to a dogmatic doctrine-oriented faith (Gibbs and Bolger 2005). Convergent Friends take context seriously as the catalyst through which renewal takes place within the tradition (Daniels 2015: 105). For instance, Freedom Friends Church, a convergent Friends church in Salem, Oregon, wrote the first and only *Quaker Faith and Practice* explicitly for a postmodern context (Freedom Friends Church 2009: 1).

Global information culture also sets the backdrop for the emergence of convergent Friends. The growing accessibility of the World Wide Web created the opportunity for new relationships to form: "The grassroots nature of the Internet enabled the cultivation of a contemporary Quaker community that traveled institutional, geographical, and theological distances" (Daniels 2011a: 87). While relationships were not confined to weblogs and social networks, such tools became a primary way of building and communicating for convergent Friends. In 2009, Elizabeth A. Oppenheimer published a collection of fifty-eight articles she collected from Quaker bloggers in *Writing Cheerfully on the Web: A Quaker Blog Reader*. This collection offered a snapshot into the burgeoning online Quaker community, incorporated a broad range of Quaker perspectives and provided an easy access into the convergent conversation for those who were not online or did not know where to start.

II   THE LONG ARC OF CONVERGENT QUAKERISM

Peggy Senger Morrison (then Parsons) outlines convergence as *hybrid* Quakerism: when a break is made along the fault line of a community, not everyone fits nicely into one side or the other (2009). There are many who have come before who did not fit neatly into the boxes of institutional Quakerism, or Christianity more generally. Therefore, it is not surprising to find a long line of "convergent" Friends stemming back to the middle of the nineteenth century. Even if they were not always called by the same name, and even if some of these Friends were thought to be "divergent" at the time, these convergent Friends sought to hold in tension the poles of their tradition within changing cultural contexts. As Morrison writes:

> [Convergent] is not about making a new place, or stream, or institution.
>   I think it is a sensibility, a perspective, a desire,
>   a proclivity, if you will.
>   It is fearless, nonviolent, non-competitive,
>   cross border engagement
>   for the purpose of deepening the spiritual life. (Parsons 2009)

While a need remains for a more in-depth historical analysis, following are a few of the many examples that chart "convergence" within Western Quakerism.[1] The 1820s to the 1860s was a time of great disruption within the Quaker tradition. As a result the three major streams of Quakerism developed: Hicksite, Gurneyite, and Wilburite.[2] Each of these streams hold significance within convergent Friends; each impulse has aspects that can be built upon. The conservative part of convergent stems not so much from a direct line to the Wilburite tradition, but rather from a shared impulse to conserve and value the tradition. Lloyd Lee Wilson, author of *Quaker Vision of Gospel Order* (1993), a Conservative Friend from North Carolina, has influenced convergent Friends in reclaiming the idea of "Gospel Order" and other Christian themes from within a more Conservative framework. Lewis Benson's *Catholic Quakerism* (1966) and the subsequent creation of the New Foundation Fellowship are other examples of this move toward renewal through reclaiming the tradition of radical, prophetic Quakerism.

Another example of Friends trying to bring about renewal through a revisioning of the tradition as they witnessed it in their time is found in Charles Fager's *Remaking Friends: How Progressive Friends Changed Quakerism and Helped Save America (1822–1940)* (2014). Fager charts the course of progressive Friends, an offshoot of Hicksite Friends, whose ingenuity not only challenged the gradualist Friends on the issue of slavery as they embodied themes that later came to be called the "Social Gospel." They also helped to create the basis upon which the 1926 Friends General Conference Uniformed Discipline was formed (Fager 2014). Progressive Friends and the Indiana Yearly Meeting of Anti-Slavery Friends are examples of how convergence is not simply about bringing Quakers together, but rather about reimagining the Quaker tradition in response to changing

[1] The earliest reference to "convergent" within a Quaker context appears in St. Louis in 1970. At an FWCC-sponsored event, 135 Friends from twenty-four American Yearly Meetings gathered to discuss the question of renewal under the topic of "The Future of Friends." It was at this conference that the words "emergent" and "convergent" were first used in relation to the renewal within the Quaker tradition: "What is the purpose of the Faith and Life movement among American Friends? (a) To come into unity through agreeing in a collective statement of our common faith? (b) To reconstruct the theology or find again the spirit of early Quakers? (c) To know the present state of our Society through what might be called 'comparative Quakerism': a study of the various theological types and points of view to be found in our Yearly Meetings and associations? (d) To seek through meeting together and dialogue between the various strands of current Quakerdom new life and light under the leading of the Holy Spirit – something that might be called 'convergent' or 'emergent' Quakerism" (Jones 1971)? This reference points to "convergent" Quakerism as Spirit-led, emergent within culture, and strengthened through the differences found among Friends through the practice of dialogue.
[2] For a more in-depth look at the shaping of nineteenth-century Quakerism see Hamm 1988.

cultural contexts.[3] On the other side of the Quaker family tree (Gurneyite), Carole Spencer describes Holiness Friend Hannah Whitall Smith (1832–1911) as a "woman who defies classification even today, whose life embodied multiple identities and contradictions" (Spencer 2013). Smith, in her 1903 autobiography, wrote: "I have always rather enjoyed being considered a heretic, and have never wanted to be endorsed by any one. I have felt that to be endorsed was to be bound, and that it was better, for me at least, to be a free lance, with no hindrances to my absolute mental and spiritual freedom" (Spencer 2013).

Despite being someone loved by conservative Christians, Smith was not only an Orthodox Quaker and Holiness preacher; she was also a Universalist in her views about heaven and hell as well as a "progressive, even radical in politics, a fierce feminist who marched with her daughters for woman's suffrage. Later in life she gave labor union speeches and explored Christian socialism" (Spencer 2013).

One significant event in the lineage of convergent Friends is known as the "Manchester conference," in England in 1895. Here Quaker leaders and scholars came together to discuss the future of Quakerism and to respond to the challenges they faced brought on by rapidly changing culture, the growing influence of the natural sciences and the historical critical method of interpreting the Bible. Martin Davie writes of the conference:

> Response to these challenges among British Quakers, as among Christians in general, was mixed. Some rejected them in their entirety and held on to their traditional beliefs. Some shifted towards fundamentalism. Some abandoned Christian belief altogether. Modernists saw these challenges as presenting an opportunity to develop a new form of Christian and Quaker theology that was more intellectually and spiritually credible. (Davie 2011: 213)

In 1897, Modernist/Renewal Friends Rufus Jones, William Braithwaite, and John Wilhelm Rowntree took up the challenge and set out to develop a more thoroughly modernist, and therefore relevant, Quakerism in an attempt to renew the tradition within their changing cultural context.[4] These men set upon the monumental task of rewriting Quaker history in a comprehensive seven-volume set. Dandelion writes, "[Jones] aimed for a

---

[3] Cf. McDaniel and Julye 2009, 92–95.

[4] Pink Dandelion writes, "Renewal Quakerism was in some ways a natural development of Gurney 'world-accepting' Quakerism. It wanted to move on from the peculiarities and have a modern Quakerism of its time, 'renewed,' and work with other Christians in bringing about the Kingdom. Theologically, they were post-millennial, that is, they believed humanity would prepare the way for the rule of the saints and the subsequent Second Coming of Christ" (Dandelion 2008, 30).

new reliance on tradition and history, the understanding of Quakerism as essentially about group mysticism, and a commitment to the social gospel; he hoped he could unite different persuasions around this renewed vision" (Dandelion 2007: 122–23).[5]

Large scale efforts to organize a rapidly diversifying Quaker community can be found in the creation of early-twentieth-century Quaker organizations such as the American Friends Service Committee (1917), Five Years Meeting (1902), and Friends World Committee for Consultation world gathering in Philadelphia (1937).[6] In-depth descriptions of each of these is outside the purview of this chapter, but each excelled in different areas of the convergent sensibility: the desire to remain connected to the Quaker tradition, the response to cultural needs, and the desire to create dialogue across the branches of Friends.[7]

Smaller-scale efforts, often led by individuals, have played a critical role in the move toward convergence as well. Some Monthly and Yearly Meetings, rent apart by Orthodox-Hicksite splits, reunified beginning in 1945. Other

---

[5] The impact of Jones's work upon Gurneyite and Hicksite Quakerism was deeply influential (Dandelion 2005, 65). Dandelion outlines the four key threads of influence upon the shifting landscape of Quakerism: "The first was that experience, not Scripture, was primary, and gave authority for belief and action. The second was that faith needed to be relevant to the age. Quakerism was not again to be stuck with anachronistic peculiarities or indeed an intellectually suspect dependence on Scripture. Third, given the second, Friends were to be open to new Light from whatever quarter it may come. Fourth, these Quakers adopted the idea of progressivism, the belief that new revelation had greater authority than old (an idea Isicheir first identifies with Quakerism in 1874)" (Dandelion 2005, 66). While "convergent" as a term applied to renewal work among Quakers was not in circulation in the time of Jones, it is clear that he was working with the three impulses the characterize convergent Friends and that his "sensibility, perspective, and desire" mirror the convergent impulse even if his methods and outcomes were different.

[6] Convergent Friends have been aware of the important work of FWCC from the beginning and while deeply valuing that work have attempted to differentiate their work from that of FWCC in the past: "This may all sound very similar to what FWCC has been doing for years, and it is. Over the last 70 years, FWCC has done important work facilitating communication among Friends of all persuasions. However, FWCC has approached the work from an institutional level, while the convergent Friends conversation has been at the personal level. It is as though FWCC is ordinarily about walking through the officially approved doors and talking in the formal parlors of our Religious Society, while convergence has been more like hanging out in the kitchen or on the back porch" (Mohr and Daniels 2007).

[7] To be clear, the current convergent model of renewal is not about reunification whether through doctrinal statements or realignments around practice as Everett Cattell suggested in his "The Future of Friends" talk in 1966 (Cattell 1966), nor is every attempt at renewal a "convergent renewal." Convergence is renewal by keeping tradition, context, and dialogue at the forefront and refusing to employ one at the expense of the others. While not every attempt does this equally well, from a convergent perspective, each attempt is valuable in its own right as an experiment in moving in the right direction. Contemporary convergent Friends have not encouraged the creation of new institutions.

groups emerged during this time that have in one way or another attempted renewal through emphasizing one or more of the three convergent impulses: Quaker Theological Discussion Group (1958) continued to wrestle with the challenges brought on by the modernist-fundamentalist splits within Orthodox Quakerism in order to, as Paul Anderson writes, provide "a vehicle of sustained theological reflection among Friends of all persuasions, seeking to address issues of long-term and timely interest from a Quaker point of view ... [with] the hope of spiritual renewal" (Anderson 2014, 3). Other attempts were Elton Trueblood's Yokefellows (1950s), which sought spiritual renewal through seven disciplines and eventually became a prison ministry; Lewis Benson's New Fellowship Foundation, which believed that seventeenth-century Quakerism was a prophetic movement and sought to retrieve that vitality through close study of Early Quaker writings, the practice of traveling ministry, and other older Quaker practices; the creation of Earlham School of Religion by Wilmer Copper in 1960 was another attempt at rebuilding vitality among Friends. More current attempts at renewal within unprogrammed Quakerism are the creation of the *Quaker Theology Journal* which is edited by Chuck Fager, Stephen Angell, and Ann Riggs and set out to perform the "ongoing work of self-examination and definition which any living faith community faces [and] to prepare ourselves to take a fuller and more constructive part in the many opportunities for ecumenical and interfaith dialogue which are now available" (Fager 1999); *Quaker Quest* from Britain Yearly Meeting and Rex Ambler's *Experiment with Light* in the United Kingdom are some of the key attempts.

Direct correlations to modern day convergent Friends link back to Young Friends gatherings at Guilford College in 1954 and in 1975 at regular Youthquake meetings, which primarily drew unprogrammed and Evangelical Friends together (Abbott 2012, 382). In 1977, the Wichita gathering aimed to bring Latin American Friends to an "All Friends" gathering but faltered over conflicts around sexual diversity (Fager 2016a). Then FWCC World Gathering in 1985 led to the creation of a Portland, Oregon, area Quaker women's group called, "Multwood" (see Abbott, Chapter 18, this volume). Two Quaker women, one Evangelical and one Liberal, participating in both the 1985 World Gathering of Young Friends at Guilford College and Friends World Conference for Consultation Triennial in Oaxtepec, Mexico, became friends as they traveled in the ministry in the Pacific Northwest sharing about their experiences at these gatherings (Abbott 1995, 4). Out of this grew a desire to create deeper relationships and explore the strength of their differences among women as part of the two yearly meetings in the Northwest, Northwest Yearly Meeting (programmed) and Pacific Northwest Yearly Meeting (unprogrammed).

Consequently, women from Multnomah Monthly Meeting and Reedwood Friends Church, along with women from West Hills Friends, and South Salem Church began meeting regularly (Abbott 1995, 5).

Out of the fertile ground Multwood nurtured into being, two significant projects were born, both setting the stage and example for future convergent endeavors: the Pacific Northwest Quaker Women's Theology Conference (PNQWTC) and Freedom Friends Church (FFC). The PNQWTC, which started in 1992, is written about far more extensively elsewhere in Chapter 18 and in Pamela Calvert's important, "'How Blessed It Is for the Sisters to Meet': Historical Roots of the Pacific Northwest Quaker Women's Theology Conference" (Calvert 2003). Women in Multiword and the PNQWTC continue to work toward forging new relationships and building bridges where Quaker difference is understood as a strength and building on narrative theology that has fertilized convergent Quakerism on the West Coast.

III   THE EMERGENCE OF CONTEMPORARY CONVERGENT FRIENDS

Next we outline four examples of convergent Friends within contemporary Quakerism, where it originated from and how it is being manifested today. All of these examples here are of groups that self-describe as convergent and offer a glimpse into the different levels of how individuals and organizations can be convergent. These groups are working with the tradition, context, and dialogue threads of convergence in different ways, but each works to reclaim the Quaker tradition and life as a contextually relevant faith in the world and to build dialogue across differences.

A   Convergent Friends and the Quaker Blogosphere

Convergent Friends as a more focused conversation on renewal of the tradition and dialogue across Quaker differences became even more organized in 2005. In the comments on the blog post "Quaker History as a Uniting Force" (Mohr 2005), Peggy Senger Morrison (then Parsons) invited Robin Mohr to come to the 2006 Quaker Heritage Day, where she, Marge Abbott, and Alivia Biko were being led "towards talking about The Future of the Friends Movement, Quaker Renewal and Outreach and Quaker cross-pollination." These three women also played a key role in the creation of Freedom Friends Church, a convergent Quaker meeting (see Section B). Later the overall topic of Quaker Heritage Day shifted slightly, but these Friends, and many others including Chris Mohr, Chad Stephenson, Max Hansen, Wess and Emily

Daniels, all met in March at the conference for the first time and ate dinner together at the Mohr household in San Francisco for what would became the first of many convergent Friends gatherings (Mohr 2006a). In October 2006, Mohr, who is now the general secretary of the Friends World Committee for Consultation Section of the Americas, a global Quaker body that overlays much of the convergent mission, wrote of the gathering in Friends Journal saying,

> This spring I hosted an unusual dinner party: nine Quakers from Ohio, Oregon, and California, gathered for fellowship, dialogue, and take-out pizza at my apartment in San Francisco. Our ages ranged from four to 60-something. We were polite, charming, and friendly, yet we asked and answered some hard questions. We talked about Jesus and gay rights, about fear and righteousness, about finding our own paths within the Quaker tradition, sometimes on well-worn tracks and sometimes by blazing new trails. (2006a, 1)

The relationships established that weekend were significant in the early life of convergent Friends. These small home gatherings made up of Quakers from various branches became a more regular format for convergent Friends in the coming years, with meetings like this happening in places such as Los Angeles, Portland, Boston, and other places in the Northeast; Greensboro, NC; Indiana; Ohio; Seattle; Atlanta; London; and Birmingham, England.

What drew many of these Friends together in the first place were their weblogs or blogs. Following what Henry Jenkins calls "Convergence Culture," where older notions of passive use of media are traded in for more participatory engagement and consumers become producers (Jenkins 2006), convergent Friends are Quakers who leverage social media and the Internet as a vehicle to create relationships across Quaker branches, as well as a platform for writing about their faith in new cultural contexts. Blogs could be seen as digital forms of earlier zines and early Quaker pamphlets and these connections between the early Quaker "Publishers of Truth" and convergent bloggers was not lost on these Friends (Daniels 2015, 83–86). Quaker author and blogger Brent Bill writes,

> While much of our past work has been via traditional print media, today's Publishers of Truth are making our mark in the realm of social networking – Facebook, Myspace, Twitter, LinkedIn and, of course, the blogosphere. This phenomenon of blogging is one of the most democratic forms of expression for Friends today and the number of Quaker blogs must surely almost match the number of pamphlets produced by the earliest Friendly writers. (Oppenheimer 2009)

Beyond using blogs for publishing ideas about Quakerism in the twenty-first century, these Friends used this "communal media" to establish new pathways to relationships: "In the same way, convergent Friends utilize communal media to construct a community that bypasses traditional Quaker structures, such as Yearly Meetings and top down organizations" (Daniels 2010a, 240). Blogging was never a requirement to participate in convergent Friends, but it was where a large part of the conversation took place because many of these Friends were separated geographically and institutionally. Blogging became a form of experimenting with ideas, testing connections between one's Quakerism and its implications for embodiment, and building connections through dialogue. Comments on one's blog were a way to get instant feedback, to learn and hear stories about other Friends' perspectives in a safe way that bypassed the traditional stereotypes and labels that are often obstacles to creating relationships.

In 2006, QuakerQuaker.org was launched by Quaker blogger and editor Martin Kelley (Kelley 2016). Kelley has long played an important role in helping to connect Quaker bloggers since at least 2004 with his "Subjective Guide to Quaker Websites"; but it was the creation of QuakerQuaker.org in 2006 that helped centralize that effort that continues today. The initial guide was a list of Quaker bloggers with links back to their blogs that Kelley knew about and collected on his website, "The Quaker Ranter." From there it developed further into the aggregated website as QuakerQuaker.org where "explicitly Quaker, timely and interesting" articles were posted to the front page by editors of the site. This had the effect of highlighting interesting blog posts and encouraging Friends to blog, to get onto the front page of QuakerQuaker.org meant that there were hundreds of Quakers visiting that blog. Further, QuakerQuaker became something of an online meeting-house. It is no longer just a blog aggregator but a full-blown social media website where people have their own profile pages, write their blogs right on the site, use discussion forums, and more. By 2016, QuakerQuaker brought together more than 3,200 members from around the world on the site.

While the work on convergence has been done by individuals in Quakerism for more than one hundred years, these online and offline relationships enabled the ideas and the work of convergent Friends to congeal and spread in new ways. Convergent Friends gatherings have been held at Conservative, Liberal, and Evangelical Yearly Meetings and Monthly Meetings and retreat centers such as Ben Lomond Quaker Center, Pendle Hill, and Woodbrooke Quaker Study Centre. Numerous articles and books have been written about convergent Friends, and organizations and meetings have begun using the language of convergence as a descriptor of their work.[8] Following are just a few examples.

B   Freedom Friends Church

Freedom Friends Church is an independent Monthly Meeting that has been around for more than ten years and has written the first convergent and open-sourced *Faith and Practice*. It was a work of love long before it ever was a tangible reality. In 1999, when Peggy Morrison and Alivia Biko were traveling together in the ministry, they realized their shared dream of some-day starting a Christ-centered church that also welcomed sexual diversity and was deeply rooted in the Quaker tradition. Eventually Morrison and Biko would meet Jane Wheeler, an unprogrammed Quaker from the Northwest, and learned that she too shared a similar vision so they asked her to join the effort. These three women met to discern how and when a meeting like this might take shape, in worship and discussion, a leading was seasoned, and the call became clear (Daniels 2015, 165).

The vision for what Freedom Friends was to look like is written in the opening of their *Faith and Practice*:

> Freedom Friends Church was formed in 2004 by three Friends in response to the perceived call of the Present Christ. Early in the formation process we realized that we needed to be able to articulate that call in a way that highlighted our deep resonances with traditional Quakerism and our unique interpretation of how those traditions could be lived out in a post-modern age. This Faith and Practice is one of our attempts to articulate our call.
>
> We are a uniting meeting, having received members by transfer from Friends General Conference, Friends United Meeting and Evangelical Friends International. But equally important to our call is the fact that a majority of our members are new to Quakerism. Teaching the ways of Friends is an important part of our mission. We set out to be Christ-centered, Quaker, and inclusive. We are semi-programmed, lightly pastoral and socially progressive. We believe in continuing revelation. Our Faith and Practice reflects all these things. (Freedom Friends Church 2009: 1)

---

[8] A few honorable mentions are Friendly Water for the World, Way of the Spirit, the Reconciliation Project that is a part of the Good News Associates, and the Ramallah Friends Meeting, which all describe their work as convergent or have been described in that way by other convergent Friends (Hallward 2013, 78–79). The first three are all also located within the Pacific Northwest.

From the outset, Freedom Friends Church was a model of what a convergent Friends meeting looks like as it aimed to be a "uniting meeting" that drew Friends together from Friends General Conference, Friends United Meeting, and Evangelical Friends Eastern Region while building on the Quaker tradition within a new postmodern cultural context. They aimed to do this through what they and others have called a "generous orthodoxy."

Starting a meeting such as Freedom Friends did not come without its challenges. A meeting that welcomed sexual diversity was out of compliance with the Northwest Yearly Meeting Faith and Practice, the yearly meeting that Biko and Morrison were both a part of and where Morrison's recording was held. They knew that a meeting like this would face serious obstacles and create tensions with their Yearly Meeting, as questions around faith and practice, the Bible, and sexual diversity were debated in the Northwest Yearly Meeting and other programmed Yearly Meetings in the United States (Fager and Souza 2014). On the other side, a Quaker meeting that had a pastor and was explicitly Christ-centered would face obstacles in the nearby liberal unprogrammed North Pacific Yearly Meeting. Thus, these women had to approach the creation of Freedom Friends with great care, not wanting to be critical of anyone else, as Morrison reported, "We add to the fabric; we're not a breach in the fabric" (Daniels 2015, 169).

Knowing that to proceed was a great step of faith, they called together a meeting for clearness on February 6, 2004. They met with both programmed and unprogrammed Quaker women from Northwest Yearly Meeting, North Pacific Yearly Meeting, and Pacific Yearly Meeting, many of whom were active in Multwood and the Pacific Northwest Quaker Women's Theology Conference During the weekend they met at a monastery in Mt. Angel, Oregon, where they waited for the leading of the "Present Christ" as they prayed, worshiped, and listened together. Finally, clearness emerged. There was no way that this meeting fitted within either of the Yearly Meetings in the Northwest. The best way forward was to be independent so that they could remain in relationship with both as a testimony to what was possible (Daniels 2015, 169).

As a convergent meeting, Freedom Friends is unique among Friends meetings. Not only is it theologically different, bringing together threads from programmed and unprogrammed traditions in new ways, it is also different in its structure and practice. Its semi-programmed liturgy is highly participatory and relies on all members to be engaged and contribute to the overall meeting for worship (Daniels 2015, 174–78). During a meeting for worship they sing songs, have a time of congregational prayer or "gratitudes and petitions," and participate in "expectant" or silent worship for about forty-five minutes. Their meetinghouse contains an art table that is available during the meeting for people to use if they are interested in using art as part of their expression of worship. There is also a black box that has inspirational quotes in it that one can read during the meeting to help focus listening. For Freedom Friends, the point is not to stress the beauty of silence but the practice of listening: "This is why they consider themselves 'fidgeter friendly.' 'You can get up and walk around meeting. You can knit. You can read. You can paint at the art table. We don't try and get better and better at silence we try and get better at centering in the midst of the noise'" (Daniels 2015, 178). Through all of this, Freedom Friends has a pastor, but she is not paid and she does not preach on Sunday. The pastor guides the meeting for worship as a host of the worship space and can speak out of the silence if led, but no prepared message is brought. A key role for the pastor is to help the meeting learn how to listen to the Present Christ in their midst.

As with other convergent Friends, Freedom Friends has moved away from consumer-oriented religion to a participatory framework both in terms of its worship and in the creation of its *Faith and Practice*. Its *Faith and Practice* is one of Freedom Friends most important contributions to the Quaker tradition because it transgresses so many boundaries and is truly unique in the Quaker landscape (Daniels 2015, 188). Its creation took five years of hard work with involvement by the whole meeting. Morrison laid out the ideas for the initial three sections during a retreat before Freedom Friends stated, but once the community was formed everyone was involved.

Morrison wrote:

> Our Faith and Practice is the expression of the way we already live in community. We wrote it to give the church continuance through time, as a guideline for those yet to come. They can use it as long as it speaks to them though we also know it will be changed and altered as new truths come to light. We also hope it will encourage other people who love God. We want others who hold our values to know they are not alone, to help give them language for what they have not been able to speak. We want people to know that all different types of people with various economic statuses, sexualities, educations, theologies, and temperaments, really can form one community and love God together. (Morrison, quoted in Daniels 2015, 189)

Inviting the community into the process was a way for them to express their gifts and be drawn deeper into the life of the meeting. Through participating in the creation of content, investment in a community deepens (Daniels 2015, 64–75). Besides recognizing that their *Faith and Practice* is an open work that will continue to evolve, it names a "progressive Christian faith" while fostering theological hospitality: "We have great theological diversity in our meeting and this expression of faith is a center for us – a campfire to sit around, each at their own comfortable place and distance" (Freedom Friends Church 2009, 1). The *Faith and Practice* covers their basic beliefs around Christ, Spirit, the Bible, the church, and more ways that are consistent with basic Quaker teachings. There are other parts of the *Faith and Practice* that cover more unique topics among Christ-centered Quakers such as its section on sexuality (Freedom Friends Church 2009, 2–8),[9] and its section on the renunciations of slavery, fundamentalism, and evil.[10] Overall, Freedom Friends as a Quaker meeting and as seen in its *Faith and Practice* is a good example of how convergent Friends "remix" the Quaker tradition, drawing on various threads of the tradition and leveraging them in new ways within their context.

C   Quaker Voluntary Service

Quaker Voluntary Service is a national Quaker organization whose work is not only inspired by the work of convergent Friends but also has a number of people who identify as convergent on its board of directors. While Christina Repoley was attending Guilford College, she was a part of the Quaker Leadership Scholars Program (QLSP), a program for Guilford students rooted in Quaker worship and values. Through her experience in the QLSP, she felt moved to deepen her Quaker experience. When she graduated from Guilford College in 2002, Repoley was "on fire to make a difference in the world and to live [her] Quaker faith" (Repoley 2013). After college, Christina moved to Philadelphia, Pennsylvania, for an internship with a

---

[9] "We hold dear the gift of our sexuality, which is given to all persons regardless of gender identity, orientation, or marital status. Because sexuality and spirituality are closely related, all believers are called to be thoughtful stewards of their sexuality. We believe that fully intimate sexual relations are intended to be expressed within long-term, committed, monogamous relationships, and then always with dignity and love. Sexuality that is de-humanizing, promiscuous, violent, non-consensual, manipulative, or predatory in nature is always harmful" (Freedom Friends Church 2009: 9).

[10] About slavery (3–1) it says: "to slavery of addictions" and any other form of bondage that keeps people free; Fundamentalism (3–2): "We believe that God calls human souls in more ways than we can imagine, and that God abides with anyone who seeks God in spirit and in truth, regardless of how they name God"; and about Evil (3–3): "[We] do renounce our only true enemy, sometimes called satan, the accuser of the children of God, the father of lies. We renounce all his acts, temptations and deceits. We pledge ourselves to the fight against him and against the consequences of his lies: slavery, hatred, despair, envy, and greed. This is called 'The War of the Lamb', in scripture and Quaker tradition" (Freedom Friends Church 2009: 11–12).

now-defunct progressive Christian magazine, *Other Side*, and to live in a Catholic Worker House.

During her time in Philadelphia, she became friends with several young adult Mennonites and heard about their memorable and transformative experiences they had through Mennonite Volunteer Service, a yearlong service program offered by Mennonite Mission Network for young adults. Repoley wondered why these experiences did not exist for young adult Quakers, as well.

Repoley knew that Quaker organizations, including American Friends Service Committee, used to offer programs for young adults to perform service, but by the mid-2000s most of these programs had been discontinued. The remaining programs that Repoley could find "seemed so small. I noticed that many were not directly recruiting Quakers and most did not contain any faith component. Plus, they were not connected to each other, making it difficult to find them all at once" (2013). Out of frustration for the lack of options for Quaker young adults to live out their faith and be supported, Repoley started dreaming of what a Quaker yearlong volunteer service program might look like.

Repoley believed that God was leading her to start a program for young adult Friends; she embarked on a long journey. Along the way, she found others who were interested in her vision and they formed a committee that became the board that ultimately founded Quaker Voluntary Service (QVS) in 2011 and opened the first house the following year in Atlanta, Georgia, where Repoley is now located. Shortly before the opening of the Atlanta QVS House, Repoley was named the first full-time executive director of the organization.

During the 2015–2016 program year (August-July), twenty-four Fellows (the term that QVS uses for its volunteers) lived in four houses in Atlanta, Georgia; Boston, Massachusetts; Philadelphia, Pennsylvania; and Portland, Oregon (Quaker Voluntary Service 2016). The model that QVS uses is similar to other yearlong faith-based programs in the United States, like Mennonite Voluntary Service. In this model, young adults live in intentional community for a year with other volunteers, receive a monthly stipend, and work full time for a nearby nonprofit of some type.

Quaker Voluntary Service is convergent in how it seeks to make apprentices of the Quaker tradition within contemporary context while fostering dialogue among the various branches of Quakerism. Each service program varies in how exactly the yearlong program operates. Within the QVS model, the program is deeply rooted within the Friends tradition. Each house is intentionally under the care of a Quaker body. host Quaker bodies currently support the four QVS houses, by an individual Monthly Meeting (Atlanta and Boston), a group of Monthly Meetings/Friends churches (Portland), or a Quarterly Meeting (Philadelphia). Each fellow is matched with a spiritual nurturer for the year, a Quaker who is part of the wider body that oversees their house. The houses are expected to abide by Quaker discernment practices as they hold house business meetings, and they are expected to have a regular time for worship as a house. Lastly, specific times are set aside throughout the year to more fully explore Quaker values through speakers and shared learning.

Furthermore, like other convergent projects, earlier models of Quaker service influence the QVS programming. Part of the original vision for QVS was to be a program where young adult Friends from different branches would come and serve together. Repoley found inspiration for this type of model from how the American Friends Service Committee (AFSC) started in 1917. In that instance, Friends from the Hicksite and Orthodox branches came together to find a way for young Quaker men to serve their alternative service in World War I. For years afterward, through both alternative service and the work camp programs that AFSC and then other Quaker organizations began offering, Friends from different branches were able to come together to serve together and build relationships.

By starting QVS, Repoley wanted to provide young adults similar experiences to these models because she had learned from past participants of the AFSC programs that these experiences allow for greater dialogue between the different Friends traditions. Also as Repoley was learning about the breath of Quaker tradition and diversity at Guilford College, she discovered that she was only taught about some aspects of Quakerism during her childhood. Having grown up in an unprogrammed meeting, Charlotte Friends Meeting in North Carolina, the main messages of Quakerism she was taught were about liberal politics and social justice. She felt deprived from not being taught about the Bible and about theology. She believed that the Bible and theology were just as important to Quakerism as social justice and politics. In designing QVS with others, Repoley especially wanted to have both elements as crucial parts of the program to help ground young adults in the full breadth of Friends tradition. As a result, many QVS Fellows who come from the unprogrammed tradition as Repoley did study the Bible and talk about theology for the first time ever during their year in the program.

The convergence of young adult Friends from different traditions that Repoley had dreamed about has yet to be fully realized within QVS. Only about half of the Fellows each program year even identify as Quaker. Most of the Fellows, who do identify as Quaker, have come from the unprogrammed Friends tradition, usually associated with Friends General Conference. In the first four program years (2012–2015) of the QVS, only four Evangelical Friends and two Friends United Meeting (FUM) Friends have served as QVS Fellows (Repoley 2016). QVS has struggled to appeal to young adults from the Evangelical, FUM, and Conservative Friends traditions. There has yet to be a Fellow from the Conservative tradition. For Repoley, it is still an important aspiration for QVS to be more convergent.[11] The original vision of QVS was, and is still, to have a national network of houses, so there are plans to expand to more cities in the coming years (Repoley 2016). Still, with all it has done so far as a convergent project, QVS is already increasing conversations and relationships between Friends of different traditions through service, much like AFSC was doing in the twentieth century.

D   Convergent Friends Worship Gathering Pacific Northwest

As mentioned earlier, Portland, Oregon, metro area has a great diversity of Friends, more so than most other areas of the United States. The Portland area has both unprogrammed Monthly Meetings from North Pacific Yearly Meeting and evangelical churches from Northwest Yearly Meeting. Because of the interbranch work already being done in the Portland area, through groups mentioned earlier, such as Multwood and Pacific North West Quaker Women's Theology Conference, and their own personal experiences with the wider convergent Friends movement, Carol Joy Brendlinger of West Hills Friends Church and C. Wess Daniels of Camas Friends Church created a monthly convergent worship in 2012 open to anyone in the Portland area.

Up to that point, convergent Friends gatherings had happened more sporadically, such as the one in San Francisco in 2006, and were less planned. Often convergent gatherings were one-time events and took place whenever traveling Friends would be in an area where another branch of Friends was residing. Therefore, Brendlinger and Daniels had a desire for having a Convergent Friends group that was more local and would meet regularly.

---

[11]   One reason for the lack of Friends' diversity within QVS is the lack of programmed and Evangelical Friends directly involved in QVS houses. Only Portland has the involvement of Evangelical Friends with the local QVS house. There, two unprogrammed Friends meetings from North Pacific Yearly Meeting and two Evangelical Friends churches from Northwest Yearly Meeting joined to provide care and local oversight for the Portland QVS house. These two factors directly affect the availability to reach out to young adults within programmed and Evangelical traditions in recruiting efforts. The QVS staff and board still do make an effort to reach out to programmed and Evangelical yearly meetings and regularly visit and connect with colleges and universities sponsored by those yearly meetings.

They also desired a group that was open to any Quaker who wanted to come, no matter his or her affiliation, age, gender, or sexual orientation.

Before starting a local convergent Friends group, Brendlinger and Daniels met with the elders at Camas Friends Church in Camas, Washington, a suburb of Vancouver, where Daniels was serving at the time as the released minister (Daniels 2011b), to discuss their calling from God to start a convergent group in the Northwest. Then, with the blessing of the elders, Brendlinger and Daniels held the first local gathering of Convergent Friends February 26, 2012, at Camas Friends (Daniels 2012). Around twenty-five Friends from meetings and churches across the Portland Metro area attended this first gathering. More than four years later, the group, now known as Convergent Friends Pacific Northwest, was continuing to meet on the fourth Sunday of each month.[12] Over the four years, people from at least thirteen churches/meetings have attended the gatherings, so the group has connected with many Friends in their area. This is the first successful attempt at getting an established local convergent Friends group to meet regularly.[13]

For any convergent Friends group to be ongoing, attenders need to have a mutual desire for relationships with people of differing theological beliefs. In this vein, during their gatherings, the Convergent Friends Pacific Northwest does not try to wrestle with theological issues to find some sort of agreement or common ground. It knows that attenders of the gatherings have a wide

---

[12] Here is a short explanation of what happens at these gatherings: the gatherings are held at a different meetinghouse every month; someone from the host meeting decides the format for that night. The format is completely open but a default "liturgy" has emerged. First, the host of the meeting welcomes people. Then for the first fifteen to twenty minutes, participants are invited to read passages of the Bible they feel "led" to share out of the silence. The next forty-five minutes is "waiting worship," though sometimes the Bible reading flows into this portion as well. Next, the host of the program shares a query for "worship sharing," which is similar to a question for discussion in a worshipful or reflective way. That goes on for the next twenty-five minutes or so. Last are general announcements and light business, such as where they will meet the next month. Overall, the time of worship lasts for about ninety minutes. Tea and coffee and snacks are usually provided before and after the meeting as well to encourage conversation and connection.

[13] The program for the convergent Friends gatherings is fairly consistent each time. Each month, a different Friends church or Friends meeting will host the group. The whole program runs about an hour and a half from 6:30 p.m. to 8 p.m. with time for fellowship afterward. First, the host meeting/church will greet everyone. Then, someone will introduce a query for the evening followed by either a Scripture reading or a song. (If a Friends church hosts, it usually opens with a Scripture reading, and if a Friends meeting hosts, it usually opens with a song.) Following the reading or song comes a time for centering and silent worship. This leads into a time of worship sharing on the query that was shared at the beginning of the meeting. Usually, the attendance at these gatherings ranges from fifteen to thirty people each month and some attenders drive from an hour away to attend (Silliman 2016).

range of beliefs and will not all agree theologically. Part of its purpose statement, written by attender Alivia Biko from Freedom Friends Church, on the Convergent Friends Pacific Northwest Facebook group says: "[W]e are a diverse people. We welcome respectful dialogue. We welcome all viewpoints and opinions, so long as they are presented in a respectful and kind manner" (Biko 2016). With this understanding, during their gatherings, they focus on simply worshipping together, gently exposing their traditions with one another, and seeking God/the Inner Light (depending on their theological preference). One frequenter attender, Norma Silliman of Camas Friends, finds the worship at the gatherings to be "deep and meaningful" and the gatherings have helped her to develop a broader understanding of the diversity within Friends (Silliman 2016).

While within the Northwest some Friends Churches are not interested in any connection with unprogrammed Friends and some unprogrammed Friends are not interested in having any connection with Evangelical Friends, this convergent Friends group has succeeded because of already established longtime relationships among attenders of the monthly gatherings.

CONCLUSION

This "hybrid" Quakerism that cuts across the nineteenth-century divisions points to an arguably emergent period taking place within Western Quakers where "convergence" may not just describe one particular group within Quakerism, but a growing trend across all Quaker divisions. Aided greatly by the availability of the social web and convergence culture, this appears to still be largely a Western phenomenon. On the other hand, the involvement of Quakers from the Global South, the strong presence of youth leadership in those parts of Quakerdom, and the reality that these Quakers are already hybrid due to their radically different cultural contexts from Western, white Quakerism, points to the possibility of underlying synergy. Two areas for further study present themselves, one is mapping a "convergent model of renewal" over Western Quaker history and developing that lineage further; a second, much needed area is to investigate these issues and connections, as well as differences, among Global Quakers. Is renewal an issue elsewhere in the world among Friends? If so, how does renewal work among Friends outside the West? In either case, convergence as described in this chapter is one grassroots movement for change and renewal that is having an impact certainly among Friends in the West and quite possibly globally.

SUGGESTED FURTHER READING

Abbott, Margery Post. (2010). *To Be Broken and Tender: A Quaker Theology for Today*, Portland, OR: Friends Bulletin Corp.

Daniels, C. Wess. (2015). *Convergent Model of Renewal: Remixing the Quaker Tradition in a Participatory Culture*, Eugene, OR: Pickwick Publications.

Gibbs, Eddie and Bolger Ryan K. (2005). *Emerging Churches: Creating Christian Community in Postmodern Cultures*, Grand Rapids, MI: Baker Academic.

Oppenheimer, Elizabeth A. (2009). *Writing Cheerfully on the Web: A Quaker Blog Reader*, Philadelphia: Quaker Books of Friends General Conference.

Parsons, Peggy Senger. (2014). *Miracle Motors: A Pert Near True Story.* 2nd ed. Unction Press.

Intra-Quaker Ecumenism

Women's Reconciling Work in the Pacific Northwest and Kenya

Margery Post Abbott

The early twenty-first century is again a time of pressure for separations among Friends in the United States and in Kenya. These, the largest national groupings of Quakers worldwide, have strikingly different contexts for separations but share at least one commonality. Since the late 1980s groups of women found ways to worship and pray together, build strong friendships, and find healing amid painful stresses.

This chapter explores some ongoing efforts among Quaker women to sustain and nurture relationships across the varied and at times conflicting traditions of Friends. The primary example offered here is that of women in the Pacific Northwest (PNW) of the United States where the two Yearly Meetings are at the opposite ends of Friends' theological spectrum. Women have met together in the PNW since 1985, building on decades of efforts by Friends World Committee for Consultation to bring together both men and women with varied success. The Pacific Northwest Quaker Women's Theological Conferences have been held biennially since 1995 and have been a model for similar gatherings in the South Central United States. These efforts will be compared to the work of the United Society for Friends Women (USFW), which has been a leader in connecting across Yearly Meetings, especially in Kenya where the tensions and pressures separating Friends are substantially different from those in the United States.

Given the breadth of the cultural and theological contexts for Friends, it would be surprising if any one explanation fit worldwide. Thus, I offer three approaches for considering these efforts among Quaker women. First is the concept of exploring the borderlands between evangelical and liberal Friends, a theme that seems particularly apt for the PNW and the South Central region.

A second dimension relates to reaffirming the testimony of equality, particularly in the evangelical meetings. The third is the peace testimony: "How can we witness to peace in the world if we cannot love, or even at times be civil to other Friends?" in the words of one PNW Friend. Friends face this issue in the context of a world where too often politically related violence erupts and lives are at stake when people allow relationships to break down and refuse to accept the humanity of the other. Potentially the ongoing willingness to listen to one another and unite despite differences can be a significant witness to the world.

SETTING THE STAGE

In the Pacific Northwest of the United States, a small group of women began meeting monthly in 1985 and they continue to do so to this day. There are two Yearly Meetings in the region: Northwest Yearly Meeting of Friends Church (NWYM), the much larger body that was constituted in 1893 and is part of Evangelical Friends Church International. North Pacific Yearly Meeting (NPYM) is largely a product of post–World War II migration to the region and was established in 1973. It consists largely of politically and theologically liberal Friends who first joined Quakers as adults and remains an independent body. For much of their history there has been relatively little interaction between the two Yearly Meetings except for some gatherings sponsored by Friends World Committee for Consultation (FWCC), usually held in the Portland, Oregon, region.

The interactions described in this chapter focus on the period from1985 to 2016. I write as a participant-observer who was part of the small group that formed in 1985 and co-clerked the planning committee for the first Pacific Northwest Women's Theological Conference held in 1995. I also enjoyed the banquet at the 1991 World Conference that was jointly planned by Kenyan women from Yearly Meetings across that nation, despite the resistance to cooperation from the men. These women also committed themselves to ongoing prayer meetings that crossed Yearly Meeting lines.

In 1985, Cilde Grover, an evangelical Friend, and Annis Bleeke, from a liberal meeting, formed a friendship as they traveled in Oregon and Washington, reporting on Grover's experiences at the World Gathering of Young Friends and Bleeke's experience at the FWCC Triennial, a gathering of representatives from Yearly Meetings worldwide. Together they dreamed of sharing on an ongoing basis the challenge and richness of their encounters with Friends of different traditions. They started "Multwood," a gathering of women from their respective meetings; Reedwood Friends Church; and Multnomah Monthly Meeting, some of whose Friends had worked together organizing o the FWCC Regional Gatherings. The original stated purpose of these Monthly Meetings was to encourage one another in our individual ministries and leadership roles within the Religious Society of Friends.

Since that original vision in 1985, an ongoing group of women has met monthly and has expanded to include women from many of the other meetings and churches within an hour's drive of Portland. Over the years a fluid group of women has entered into this work of reaching across Yearly Meeting lines, offering mutual support and building strong friendships.

REACHING OUT ACROSS THE PACIFIC NORTHWEST

In the early 1990s, the roots of the Women's Conferences grew out of both the energy and hope that came from Multwood and the mix of hope and frustrations arising out of years of FWCC regional gatherings for men and women. Several people involved in initiating the women's conferences helped organize the Western Gathering of Friends in 1992 – an event designed to bring together Friends from all seven Yearly Meetings west of the Rocky Mountains. This gathering was a good experience for those who attended, yet it attracted almost no evangelical Friends except for those invited to speak. This was the discouraging culmination of years of work organizing FWCC gatherings with limited success in including NWYM participants. The FWCC staff person for the PNW, a member of Reedwood Friends Church, expressed the resistance she encountered in her own Yearly Meeting in a 1994 letter to the organizers of the first Women's Conference. People spoke of cost as an obstacle, yet she could find only one taker when she offered to pay most of the cost herself. Her own pastor would not advertise the event or encourage people to attend, and she found increasingly that no evangelicals would attend any cross–Yearly Meeting event unless they were on the program.

Several PNW women were still determined to build trust and relationships across Yearly Meetings. They became excited about the potential for a conference where their common experiences as women could provide the basis for developing new bonds of friendship and space to explore their theological differences and similarities. Barbara Bazett (Canadian Yearly Meeting, CYM), Jane Foraker-Thompson (NPYM), and Celia Mueller (NWYM) had recently attended the 1990 International Quaker Women's Theology Conference at Woodbrooke in England. The possibility of a similar event quickly gained momentum. The local skills gained in organizing the Western Gathering and the Multwood experience of Portland women gave hopes of gaining more than token participation by evangelicals.

Starting in fall 1992, annual retreats brought together approximately twenty women, with equal numbers from Northwest, North Pacific Yearly Meetings, plus two from Canada to test the concept of a larger gathering. An important dimension was to determine if the evangelical women were committed enough to these events to personally recruit others from NWYM, as experience had shown that working through institutional channels would not work. The conferences would only go forward if attendance from the different traditions were balanced.

Despite strong resistance from some participants, especially from NPYM, to the concept of theology, the decision was made to claim this word and to assert the value of narrative theology as integral to the Friends' tradition of handing down our faith through published journals. The format of the retreats was thus centered on each individual's sense of calling encounter with God (however named) and on what each individual could affirm about her faith. This limited arguments over abstractions and meanings of words, as individuals came to see God at work in each other's lives without having to defend particular belief systems. Other simple actions to break down prejudices included such things as not noting home churches or meetings on name tags.

Both at these early retreats and at the initial conference, all speakers were asked to reflect on either historic Quaker or biblical women and address how these women influenced their lives. This approach was meant to help break down the century and more of continuing rejection of the Bible by some Friends and a distrust of Spirit and focus on right doctrine for others. This opened up space for a wider exploration of our joint faith and dimensions of it that had been lost. At the first conference many of us had to question our own hostility to evangelism. One evangelical speaker even found herself setting aside an academic paper and finding she needed to speak what she heard from the Spirit in light of the theme "What Canst Thou Say?: Blessed are Those Who hear and understand the Word of God and Follow It" (Luke 11:27, 28).

In June 1995, sixty-three women gathered at the theological conference that had been envisioned three years earlier. This PNW conference program was built around concepts used at the 1990 Woodbrooke conference and expanded with the experience of the annual retreats. The organizers committed to finding a leadership role for each person present. They encouraged each woman to speak from her own experience of all that is Holy. To quote from the flyer for the 1995 conference:

As women from divergent Friends traditions, we strive to articulate that which has been meaningful in the expression and development of our faith.

We are open to God's leadings and willing to make a commitment to prepare, to risk, and to be open to learning from one another. Our purposes in coming together are:

- To grow in the knowledge and love of God, trusting that the Inward Teacher, the Christ within, the Inner Light, the Holy Spirit, will be present to guide us;
- To create a place where it is possible to talk openly from different perspectives with love and honesty, and without rancor or tempering to accommodate perceptions of what might be acceptable;
- To use narrative theology, that is the stories of faith, as a means of integrating experience and understanding; and
- To encourage articulation of experiences and beliefs, both verbally and in writing, expecting that we will bring what we learn back into our home communities of faith.

The PNW women borrowed from the Woodbrooke gathering the requirement that each participant submit a piece in writing responding to the theme. These writings are shared with all participants in advance. Although this practice scared some away, it continues to build trust and set an atmosphere where each person is free to speak deeply out of her faith and her experience of God. One great surprise was the difficulty in determining from the papers alone who was evangelical and who was from the liberal tradition.

No formal organization supports these events, generally held near Portland, which have occurred biennially between 1995 and 2016. Each year an epistle is written to Friends Everywhere. Continuation depends on women volunteering at the end of a conference to organize the next one. At the first gathering, each plenary had one woman from each tradition offering a formal paper on a biblical or Quaker woman and speaking to why this woman was important in her faith journey. Only the proceedings of the 1995 conference were published.

EXPLORING THE BORDERLANDS

Pam Calvert, a member of Pacific Yearly Meeting, has written about the activities of PNW women, emphasizing the inclusive and non-hierarchal dimensions of the gatherings. Calvert theorizes about these gatherings as borderlands. Drawing on the work of the Hispanic feminist scholar Gloria Anzaldúa, Calvert places the women's gatherings "in the midst of this western range war between evangelicals and liberals that has been going on for more than a century" (Calvert 2003, 42).

Anzaldúa argues that borderlands exist in the space where two cultures brush up against each other. Those who occupy a borderland must create a new language to be able to fully communicate, given the different experiences and cultures that come together. Such language grows as individuals build relationships and come to trust one another. Friends in the United States do occupy different cultures. At times, substantial effort is needed to become open to the validity of the varied interpretations of their joint heritage. The PNW conferences, and those in the South Central region (discussed next) readily fit in this model of borderlands and do much to build such bridges.

SOUTH CENTRAL WOMEN'S CONFERENCES

In 1999, a second women's conference was formed drawing from South Central, Great Plains, and Mid-America Yearly Meetings. Its first session held in the South Central United States relied initially on the experience of the women from the PNW. Half of the participants of this Quaker Women's Conference on Faith and Spirituality came from unprogrammed meetings and half from Evangelical Friends International or Friends United Meeting churches. Tina Coffin, co-clerk of this event, wrote me in 2016 stating that they decided not to bring up the most divisive subjects: homosexuality, abortion, and the infallibility of Scripture: "We were there to build bridges; those topics could be addressed later, once we had built trust."

These Midwestern women met biennially until 2011 with close to fifty participants each year. But Mid-America Yearly Meeting was less supportive than other bodies. The absence of evangelical women willing to serve on a planning committee led to the end of the gatherings. Coffin asked herself:

Did we succeed in building bridges; is there a greater understanding of each other's faith on both sides of the divide? At one of the last conferences, the two clerks ... spoke openly about their deep friendship and how they had been enriched by the experience of the conferences. At that time, it brought tears to my eyes. But it is hard to gauge the long-term effect of this work.

Friends in Oklahoma held Quaker Day events in 2015 and 2016 with a mix of participants from churches and unprogrammed meetings. Coffin notes: "Perhaps the work we women did has played some role in the willingness to be with each other."

The South Central experience brings to mind the experience in the PNW in the 1980s and 1990s when resistance to evangelical participation in cross–Yearly Meeting gatherings was high. Some resistance still exists: the 2012 and

2014 PNW conferences were noted to have had significantly more women from unprogrammed meetings attending. More balanced participation is a goal for future events.

TWENTY YEARS ON: PERSPECTIVES FROM PNW
PARTICIPANTS

The PNW Women's Conferences now have a twenty-year-plus history, the most recent being held in 2016. To get a better sense of how the participants viewed these events in terms of their effect on their own lives, their Yearly Meetings, and perhaps more widely, I queried participants in the first event and the 2014 event. I emailed a half-dozen open-ended queries to everyone whose address I could obtain and received responses from just under half the participants for whom I had a valid address, or nineteen from the 1995 conference and thirty-nine from the larger 2014 conference. More responses came come from NPYM participants (59 percent of the total for both years), partly reflecting the greater percentage of liberal women at the 2014 conference.

Not surprisingly, given the way the Women's Conferences were established, most participants described the purpose of the events in terms of building relationships, building bridges, and learning from one another. Several people emphasized the need to repair the breaks within Quakerism and to discover a wholeness to their faith that had been lost amid the divisions. A few mentioned the common ground for Quakers that could be found in looking to their origins.

Honesty, "heartfelt mutual appreciation," and the sharing of faith stories were central along with breaking down prejudices and taking time to listen for God together. The most striking shift over time was that a significant number of the women at the 2014 event raised up living Friends' peace testimony as an essential dimension of the conferences, whereas only one of the original participants mentioned this. My sense is that the 1995 conference felt so experimental and risky for many that there was little focus on larger potential implications.

Almost every participant mentioned some way in which her life was changed. At times these were outward changes – for instance, one lapsed Friend began attending worship, another became a pastor. Others went on to take on significant staff or volunteer roles in FWCC. Another Friend noted that these conferences made possible the formation of the Way of the Spirit, a spiritual nurture program that draws from both traditions. For a few, a new ability to speak out was important. Identifying potential leaders and mentoring them in their calling have become an important consequence of these events. Scanning lists of attendees over the years, it is easy to note two who became clerks of Friends Committee on National Legislation, top executives in FWCC's world office and American office, as well as a clerk of the FWCC Section of the Americas.

Many referred to the deep relationships that grew out of these ongoing events. To some degree, this was made possible by the sense of empathy for the other and a broadened view of what being a Quaker meant. Often, the changes noted were internal as individuals came to terms with their own prejudices or found a sense of healing from past harsh experiences within the broader Christian church. The borderlands became real here and fostered growth for many. Such healing and growth take time and the extended history of these conferences provides this base.

Several people noted that these gatherings laid the groundwork for Convergent Friends worship and other cross–Yearly Meeting activities in the PNW involving both men and women. Wess Daniels and Greg Woods address this in more detail in Chapter 17 of this volume. Some believe that without these gatherings and the trust they established across the varied traditions, it would not have been possible for Northwest Yearly Meeting to join FWCC in 2002 and then resist efforts by some theological conservatives to withdraw in 2005. Anna Baker, a member of NWYM who was on the planning committee for several of the conferences, served as West Coast staff for FWCC and was active in developing support for this organization.

A few participants mentioned a shift within NWYM toward openness to gays and lesbians in the 2010s. Other changes mentioned by evangelical respondents were the greater awareness and appreciation of Quaker "distinctives" such as silent worship, the manner of doing business, and the testimonies, particularly among younger Friends, despite some resistance within the larger body. Several respondents from the more liberal branch of Friends mentioned the decrease in anti-Christian feeling. More Christian women have been willing to speak out about the ground of their faith in their home meetings, and NPYM even invited a Quaker pastor to be its Friend-in-Residence at one annual session. Overall, there has been an increased understanding and respect for one another.

EQUALITY

Testimony to equality of women in the ministry characterized the very first Friends. But even among Friends of the first generation, this was not always an easy witness as one of the first controversies was in part over the formation of women's business meetings. The view of Fox and Fell prevailed with the main body, and the women's meetings continued as a significant feature through much of the nineteenth century in North America and Europe, and through much of the twentieth century in Africa. During the twentieth century in the United States, theologically conservative evangelical Quakers, including NWYM, became more like their non-Quaker brethren and recognition of women's gifts in the ministry nearly disappeared for a time. The role of these conferences in rediscovering women's ministerial gifts was a factor in the success of the women's gatherings in this region. As more evangelical women stepped into pastoral positions, liberal women also took on major roles in national or international Quaker organizations, and several women have since been supported by their meetings in a variety of ministries.

Despite great gains, the tendency even among Quakers to devalue the voices of women and restrict their access to full equality is still alive in the twenty-first century. The Epistle from the 2010 conference specifically noted the sexism that younger women were encountering as they sought support for their ministries.

WHY NO MEN?

The women who helped establish the conference in the PNW were clear from the start that it should not include men. Their common struggles had the power to draw Friends together, despite the general resistance of evangelicals to engage with liberal Friends. As it turned out, having a network of women that bypassed the largely male pastors proved central in reaching this goal.

Women from both Yearly Meetings experienced openness, trust, freedom, authenticity, and joy from the women-only setting. Some respondents commented that men approach religion leading with the head, not the heart and often "talk over" women without listening to them. Participants sensed that a group of women could build relationships and mutual trust more easily than was possible in a mixed group. Many were very conscious of how women "get" certain issues, such as sexual assault, making it much easier to speak of things that are intensely painful or private.

Dorsey Green, a respondent who is a professional psychologist and author, wrote the following:

> I think women in general are, in our culture, more relational than most men. In my experience women are willing to talk with, not at, each other more easily. As a result, we develop relationships first and then wade into talking and differing about the big issues. This lays down a foundation for

listening to each other and trusting that what someone says is their tender experience, not a contest.

[a NWYM Friend] said that NWYM is so hierarchical that the women would stop talking as much and the men would take over. Research, such as J. Dan Rothwell's *In Mixed Company,* shows that in most mixed groups men talk more than women, so we would risk losing the space we have to be ourselves with each other.

Thus, one benefit of the conferences is that they give women practice in these skills and confidence to speak out.

NURTURING LEADERSHIP

In the 2014 group, a half-dozen respondents mentioned nurturing women in leadership as an important part of a women-only gathering. Surprisingly, this was not mentioned among the 1995 women. Yet one of the factors in the formation of the Multwood group was the limited opportunity for women in the ministry in Northwest Yearly Meeting. Globally, leadership for women is very much a living concern, and there is evidence that separate meetings for women are critical in raising up the role of women in the ministry, be it in England and the United States beginning in the 1600s or Kenya after the arrival of Quaker missionaries in the twentieth century.

The website for the Herbert Hoover National Historic Site in Iowa features Ruthie Tippin, former pastor of the West Branch Friends Church, who states that the separate women's Meetings were intended

to give women opportunities to learn how to lead, to learn how to clerk or chair a meeting, to take roles in leadership within their community [which they best exercise on their own]. And from that came this divided business meeting concept, and it flourished, and it strengthened women's voices; it strengthened women's place in leadership, not only in the Friends church, but in all of life.

When East Africa Yearly Meeting was formed in 1946, tribal loyalties were balanced in selecting men for various leadership positions, but women were largely excluded. Women lobbied hard for their own Yearly Meeting, which formed in 1952 for the purpose of "spiritual renewal and empowerment through preaching and interpreting the Bible." This group affiliated with USFW in 1967 (Abbott 2012, 370).

Esther Mombo, deputy vice-chancellor at St. Paul's College near Nairobi and speaker on behalf of the Africa Section at the 2012 World Conference of Friends held in Kenya, wrote the following in response to one of my queries about the role of women in creating and sustaining relationships among Kenyan Friends:

> The exclusion of women from the leadership of the first yearly meeting created in 1946 helped the women to be free from the later wrangles of the Quaker meeting. The Quaker meetings were influenced by the local cultures in excluding women from the leadership of the meetings from onset. But the women with the support of missionaries created separate meetings which were held on Thursdays hence the name *Haramisi* and *jumaa* meetings. These meetings were for prayers and education of women on issues that affected them as women but also a space of learning how to be a Quaker. The meetings grew to become meetings in each village and monthly meetings. These meetings became a basis for the formation of the women's yearly meeting formed in 1952. The women's yearly meeting ran as a separate meeting but within the main yearly meeting. Its structure was not different from the structures of the main meeting but it gave the women space to articulate their issues and to find ways of dealing with them. (Mombo 1999,

Here again, the positive role of setting up opportunities for women to meet, worship, and organize without men was helpful in allowing women to claim their own sense of ministry and a place in the church.

A PLACE FOR WOMEN/SPACE FOR CHRIST

The women who have come together over the decades have sought each other out for multiple reasons particular to their individual journeys. In addition, two pivotal preconditions arising out of the history of Friends are relevant. Northwest Yearly Meeting Friends became swept up in the Holiness Movement of the late nineteenth century and then became part of the subsequent shift toward a more generic evangelicalism. As this happened, the Quaker distinctives, including the equal ministry of women, became viewed as irrelevant, or even as obstacles to accepting Jesus as savior. Thus, by the later part of the twentieth century, few opportunities were open for women to undertake ministry.

In contrast, in North Pacific Yearly Meeting women take on many leadership roles, although at times this seems like a subtle sexism when women are willing to take on time-consuming tasks that men reject. These liberal meetings attracted many individuals who felt severely damaged by their experience of Christianity or who saw Christianity as irrelevant in today's world. Thus, Friends who were open about faith in Jesus were often denied equal freedom to speak about their faith or even openly consider the possibility of a call to ministry.

Thus participants in the Women's Conferences find aspects of Quaker faith and practice that are not present in their own communities: for the evangelical women, this would be support of those with a call to ministry; for liberal women, it would be a place to heal while exploring or enriching their own Christianity. Awareness of the depth of prejudice regarding Christianity among liberal Friends remains important for personal growth and for reconciliation. I am one whose calling has been nurtured by the evangelical women I once denigrated.

The pattern of evangelical support for women in the ministry can be gleaned from their Yearly Meeting records. Peggy Senger Morrison, a past conference participant, has researched NWYM records identifying all the women recorded as ministers or serving as pastors from 1893 to 1999. Prior to the World War II, more than a quarter of the recorded ministers were women, with the peak coming in 1917 with 44 percent. By the 1990s, the percentage hovered around 12 percent. Similarly with pastors: during the World War I, more than a quarter of the pastors were women. As the century went on, the numbers dropped below 15 percent. By the late 1970s, one or no women pastors were listed some years. The pattern is shifting in the twenty-first century.

Anna Baker of NWYM, another participant, found that 32 percent of those recorded as ministers between 2000 and 2015 were women. Of the 146 total recorded ministers in the yearly meeting in 2014, 23 (16 percent) were women. Information on churches in the Yearly Meeting accessed through the NWYM website in 2016 indicates that of the approximately 80 listed as senior or sole pastor, one-quarter are women. These numbers show distinct movement from the 1970s and 1980s. Baker, who served on the NWYM Board of Ministry for approximately twenty years, reports that in the 1970s and 1980s the focus was on recording those with a proclamation ministry, that is, those who were pastors and preaching regularly. With few women pastors, there was little perceived reason for recording women at that time. In the twenty-first century there have been more opportunities for women and a willingness to record other forms of ministry such as teaching.

PEACE MAKING BEGINS AT HOME

Elise Boulding, the twentieth-century North American sociologist and peace activist, argued extensively for grounding the peace testimony in the home as a training ground (Boulding 1989, 110). The practice of conflict resolution and "conflict maturing" as Boulding named it, starts with these most intimate relationships and then can be applied more and more widely in the more public areas of life. Women worldwide have modeled behavior consistent with the belief of those in the PNW that Friends cannot credibly witness peace to the world when they cannot live it in their own faith community.

As noted earlier, several 2014 participants in the PNW conference cited Friends' peace testimony as an important reason behind the efforts of women to build relationships between evangelicals and liberals. In the Pacific Northwest, Quakers of both traditions long disparaged the others as not being "real" Quakers and at best ignored each other for much of the twentieth century. As serious disagreements over issues of authority and acceptance of gays and lesbians increased across the United States, women in the PNW sought ways to build new connections. In the Midwest, Indiana women hope to hold together existing relationships in the aftermath of the separation of Indiana Yearly Meeting. In Kenya, in contrast, the women actively reach across tribal differences that threaten violence in their nation.

USFW: INDIANA WOMEN SUSTAINING RELATIONSHIP AMID SEPARATIONS

The vision of Eliza Armstrong Cox, who formed the Women's Missionary Society in 1881, evolved into the United Society of Friends Women (USFW), a lasting product of the nineteenth-century efforts to foster mission work abroad. At that time women were achieving equal status within their Friends meetings and seeking political and civic equity within North American and British societies (Abbott 2012, 348).

Women in Indiana have sustained USFW as one body, despite the 2013 separation of Indiana Yearly Meeting (IYM) over issues of authority. (One successor retained the name "Indiana Yearly Meeting," while the smaller successor adopted the name of "New Association of Friends.") Pam Ferguson, an Indiana pastor long active in USFW, responded in 2016 to my inquiries, first sharing the optimism of ongoing relationship: "There were no hesitations when the split became official for the USFW to change their name to Indiana USFW (as opposed to Indiana Yearly Meeting USFW) and include any women's groups from across Indiana, both New Association and IYM. There was no opposition in this and many of us assumed things would continue as they had been."

Penny Sitler, presiding clerk, Indiana USFW noted in February 2016 correspondence with me that their counterpart, Quaker Men, had not divided. She did not separate men from women in actions taken in Indiana but saw the unity of USFW holding because "Supporting missions is and has always been our organization's focus. We do not address issues of govern-ance and theology, so division truly seemed unnecessary."

However, resistance arose to efforts of women and men from the New Association to sustain their joint efforts for mission work and fellowship with the ongoing part of Indiana Yearly Meeting. Ferguson encountered Friends in Indiana who reject fellowship with Friends who do not believe the way "we" believe. She noted that "the United Society of Friends Women has been marginalized because of their hopes to remain united." This has been aggravated by an aging constituency that has not been able to attract younger women, stresses that affect many churches in the region as well.

Sitler worries about the future and offers the following sense of the condition of USFW:

> Indiana USFW faces many challenges, as sharing our affiliation means that we have the same number of people to communicate with, but more channels are required to reach them. Our relationships with the two organizations are more tenuous than our former close relationship within IYM. Further, and unrelated to the division, our local circles are dwindling in size and number.

These stresses exist elsewhere. For instance, North Carolina Yearly Meeting has the largest USFW chapter with more than 800 members, yet it is in decline as Friends there separate. Ferguson notes that she has had "phone calls from churches in North Carolina who have left the Yearly Meeting and wondered if their Women's group could remain part of the International USFW. While we encourage that, the fragmentation of Yearly Meeting churches always seems to end up in a decline of involvement and financial support."

Finding ways to remain in fellowship when yearly meetings cannot has not been simple. Both USFW and Quaker Men have met for years with a commit-ment to share their faith in the mission field and to help those in need. As lines get redrawn organizationally and theologically, a toll is taken on those who wish to actively live out the command to love neighbor as self, both when others draw lines in the sand and as congregations age and cultures change.

KENYAN SEPARATIONS AND UNITED SOCIETY OF FRIENDS WOMEN KENYA (USFWK)

In North America, peaceful relations among Friends are disturbed mainly by disagreements, separations, and at times verbal abuse, in a nation where there has been physical violence based on gender differences. In

Kenya, internal disagreements take on a different flavor at times, particularly around the 2007 elections, when there was physical violence between tribal groups. Tribal loyalties have been factors in many of the separations among Friends, making the ability to sustain relationships all the more important. Friends, men as well as women, have sought to temper and, when possible, prevent the violence that erupts over elections and other causes. Thus, when placed in a worldwide context, the ability to communicate and to trust other Friends is of even greater importance and provides a wider lens for considering the ongoing efforts to build a beloved community. This work is not unique to women by any means, but the work of women has been distinctive enough to draw attention and merit further reflection.

Over the years, tribal relationships were important in the creation of multiple Yearly Meetings in Kenya. These pressures were aggravated by ongoing control in the hands of a few powerful men. Many have noted the realities of gender oppression as well (Angell 2006, 128). Malesi Kinaro, former executive secretary for FWCC, Africa Section, a respondent to my queries, set the reconciling work of Kenyan women in the context of the sometimes harsh disagreements among the men. She wrote of how in 1974 Friends gathered at Lugulu for a regional gathering. The buses full of singing people found themselves surrounded by armed police, roughly bundled back into the buses, and sent home. In her words, "Acrimony had thus been born among Friends in Kenya."

Esther Mombo notes how the pressure for separate Yearly Meetings, combined with resistance from the East Africa Yearly Meeting (EAYM) leadership, led to forced separations beginning in the 1970s. The reasons were aggravated by "the assumption that the Luyia group in which the Quaker church was established was a homogenous group. It was not, as it had distinctive groups who spoke a language that was similar, but there were differences even in the languages."

The depths of the distrust have run deep. Kinaro notes that in this time period, many efforts by Friends United Meeting at times seemed to bring reconciliation; but when representatives returned home, they found their work rejected. She tells how these efforts led the women to try something new, noting that "many within the churches were against these splits but they remained the 'silent majority'": "Hope came in the form of a few leaders of the USFW from various Yearly Meetings. They decided that since dialogue and mediation had failed they were going to make a direct appeal to their God through joint prayers." Instead of arguing, demanding that they be heard or forming a faction, the women simply prayed. Without regard to tribe, language, or other external differences, they met on the ground that united them in God's love.

THE WOMEN'S PRAYER MEETINGS

In June 1989 communications among Kenyan Yearly Meetings were strained. Nine women from Kenya en route to North Carolina for an International USFW/Quaker Men's Triennial met at the airport to confer on what the women might do to sustain the Friends church nationwide. Slowly this idea grew. Gladys Kang'ahi, the first USFWK presiding clerk, notes that the Africa Night banquet at the 1991 Friends World Conference at Chavakali was another pivotal event for the women. This energy was consolidated at an event organized by the National Council of Churches for Friends Women, Central Province, where common struggles were shared and relationships formed. Later in 1992 a first overnight fasting prayer was held at Kaimosi. Early organizers included Leah Ganira from Central Yearly Meeting, Norah Musundi from EAYM North, Sabwa, from EAYM (South), Gladys Kang'ahi from Nairobi Yearly Meeting, and Florence Waswa from Kakamega Yearly Meeting.

Kang'ahi states, "These people agreed to humble themselves and let God lead them and to seek for Christ's strength to be patient, tolerant, loving, forgiving and prayerful." Triennial gatherings have occurred every three years since 1997. She reports that they seek equitable sharing of everything – leadership, tasks, visitations –because they have remained conscious that this was one of the earlier obstacles. She adds, "Special prayer meetings were held around the country in rotational manner, each hosting no less than 1,800 women for a single day" (Abbott 2012, 349). Kinaro writes:

This was a most innovative reconciliation method. No round table discussions were held therefore no resolutions were passed. The women simply met, had a cup of tea and spent the night praying. They would part the following morning. They moved from one yearly meeting to the next. The YM leaders wouldn't stop them because all they were doing was praying and who would stop people from praying if you claimed to be a Christian? They heard preaching, they sang songs and they prayed ... Resentment and suspicions were removed. Fellowship was restored. This movement took the men by surprise but eventually they recognized how genuine these women were. As wives talked about these prayer times the men who had been so difficult to change began to change.

Kang'ahi writes in summary:

The role of USFW in uniting Friends and addressing the disagreement that exists has been the greatest challenge for everyone. The environment is conducive now and women are supportive of each other. Frequent seminars have been encouraged at all levels as much as possible. They try to have equitable sharing of everything – positions in leadership, tasks, visitations – because they have remained conscious to the fact that this was one of the earlier obstacles. To sustain and build connections is done by being constantly in touch. Acknowledging and strengthening a hand of love, confirming our unity through prayer.

Kang'ahi states that Quaker Men now have an active prayer movement with rotating leadership. There are now 25 women pastors and about 120 women evangelists in Kenya; thus despite challenges, leadership roles have opened for women. The work of the women also contributed to rebuilding relationships among Kenyan Yearly Meetings and the creation of a reconstituted Friends Church Kenya. The women also shared many ongoing efforts such as care of orphans and widows, prison relief, and Right Sharing of World Resources projects that strengthened their connections (Angell 2006, 129).

WHY THE WOMEN UNITED

Esther Mombo, whose PhD thesis looked at Kenyan Quaker women, wrote me with her perspective on why the women were able to unite. She found that they were "spared from having wrangles because they had nothing to fight over as they were on the margins." Her analysis echoes Pam Calvert's work on women in the PNW that introduced the concept of borderlands: women who were in between, who were not defending the status quo but able to explore other dimensions of their own tradition, pray together and build relationships that bridged the differences. Kenyan women also had experience making new connections as they might be brought into different clans or tribes when they married and could bring this experience into church relationships.

Kenyan women were able to be innovative because they had no conventional power. Mombo states, "The women's Meeting did not have territory to fight over, they did not own property, they were on the margins of everything so they would relate with each other differently." Mombo argues that being "excluded from the guardianship of wealth and property in EAYM had positive implications for women in the long run." Eventually women were able to find ways to build relationships and demonstrate the power of prayer and love when the men were locked in conflict. She goes on to speak of the freedom women experienced: "Because no property was handed over to them the women were saved from the time-consuming discussions on property, which affected the men in EAYM. The exclusion gave women room to be involved with activities that they were passionate about in the growth of their meeting."

WOMEN AND PEACE MAKING IN KENYA

In the interviews she did for her PhD thesis, Mombo spoke to women leaders about the separations. She wrote me that these women

> chose to start prayers in private with each other. They chose to meet for prayers with each other even when they knew that their husbands, some of whom were leaders of the different splinter yearly meetings, were not talking to each other. The women chose to pray for a church they said was going up in flames. The meetings had no other business but to pray, for the families, the leaders of the meetings who could not talk to each other and the nation. These meetings for prayer developed into deeper fellowships among women and their numbers increased. So women from enemy yearly meetings, different clans, came together and prayed.

Turning first to prayer is central to Friends' peace testimony. While political dimensions may be important, Friends have always known peace making to be grounded in the Light of Christ, which shows the way to let go of greed, hostility, and artificial differences. The women in Kenya understood this as central to a unified church. Similarly the women in the PNW have learned to find healing in worshipping together and hearing about how God is at work among them.

CONCLUSION

Regular conferences in the PNW and the South Central region have explored the borderlands between the varied traditions of Quaker faith. They shared a common purpose of building bridges across Yearly Meetings near the extremes of the Quaker theological spectrum. Healing has happened, from the wounds of an underlying sexism in NWYM, the resistance to Christianity in NPYM, and the periodic hostility between these two bodies.

These women are not looking to reunite – the differences run deep – but many have found a richness of faith not fully present in either tradition alone. Together they have found support for their ministries that was not present in their home communities and developed the skills that help them claim full equality as pastors and ministers.

At least some have found ways to live out the peace testimony within the church, to be able to witness to the world, and to demonstrate how they love one another even in the face of pressures for separation. Some of the fruits of this work are seen in the many activities of Convergent Friends in the PNW and actions such as intervisitation by Friends from meetings that had been affirming of LGBT Friends with those churches that had been most convinced that homosexuality is a sin. This kind of gentle listening has its parallels elsewhere such as Baltimore Yearly Meeting's Intervisitation Committee whose men and women have met with conservative churches within Friends United Meeting over similar issues.

Indiana women do not fit easily into my categories, but they share a passion for mission work. Both the women and Quaker Men seek to continue unified in that work despite the split that has recently occurred in their Yearly Meeting, building on their common culture and long years of friendship.

Women in Kenya shared a common lack of power and were often marginalized despite the Quaker testimony of equality. They recognized that by praying together, they could join together in building a strong network nationwide, independent of tribal struggles and power plays. In Kenya, the women offer a model of another way of relating to one another than what the culture provides. Kenyans, both men and women, have been developing and expanding their peace work in recent decades, seeking to diffuse tensions in their communities that have often led to violence. Healing and Reconciliation Workshops are among the many actions taken. Quakers have also been active in election monitoring and other actions to diffuse tensions before violence erupts (Lumb 2012, 82). The bonds built among women can only reinforce these efforts and act as concrete examples others can point to as a witness to Jesus's teaching being lived out among them.

SUGGESTED FURTHER READING

Crawford, Patricia. (1993). *Women and Religion in England 1500–1720*, London and New York: Routledge.

Hewitt, Nancy A. (1984). *Women's Activism and Social Change: Rochester, New York 1822–1872*, Ithaca and London: Cornell University Press.

Caiazza, Amy, Hess, Cynthia, Clevenger, Casey, and Carlberg, Angela. (2008). *The Challenge to Act: How Progressive Women Activists Reframe American Democracy*, Washington, DC: Institute for Women's Policy Research.

Mombo, Esther. (1999). "Haramisi and Jumaa: The Story of the Women's Meetings in East Africa Yearly Meeting 1902–1979," *The Woodbrooke Journal* Autumn (5).

Mombo, Esther and Joziasse, Heleen (eds.) (2011). *If You Have No Voice, Just Sing: Narratives of Women's Lives and Theological Education at St. Paul's University,* Kenya: Zapf Chancery Publishers Africa Ltd.

Quaker Women's Group. (1986). *Bringing the Invisible into the Light: Some Quaker Feminists Speak of Their Experience,* London: Quaker Home Service.

Steven, Helen. (2005). *No Extraordinary Power: Prayer, Stillness and Activism,* London: Quaker Books.

Trevett, Christine. (1991). *Women and Quakerism in the 17th Century,* York: The Ebor Press.

Willard, Linda. (2008). *Quakers in Conflict,* Mustand, OK: Tate Publishing & Enterprises, LLC.

References

A Brief History of Their Work from the Beginning to the Year Nineteen Hundred and Twelve. Richmond, IN: American Friends Board of Foreign Missions; digitized 2007: https://archive.org/stream/foreignmissionwoooameriala/foreignmissionwoooamer iala_djvu.txt Accessed 1 December 2016.

"A Note of Conscription." (1915). *The Friend*, vol. LXXV, no. 24 p. 455.

Abbott, M. P. (1995). *An Experiment in Faith: Quaker Women Transcending Differences*, Wallingford, PA: Pendle Hill Publications.

Abbott, M. P. (2012). "Friends World Committee for Consultation (FWCC)." In M. P. Abbott et al., *Historical Dictionary of the Friends (Quakers)*. Lanham, MD: Scarecrow Press, pp. 382–83.

Abbott, M. P. (2013). "Global Quakerism and the Future of Friends." In S. W. Angell and B. P. Dandelion, eds., *The Oxford Handbook of Quaker Studies*. Oxford: Oxford University Press, pp. 549–64.

Abbott, M. P., Chijioke, M. E., Dandelion, P., and Oliver, J. W., Jr. eds. (2003). *The Historical Dictionary of the Friends (Quakers)*. Lanham, MD: Scarecrow Press.

Abbott, M. P., Chijioke, M. E., Dandelion, P., and Oliver, J. W., Jr. eds. (2012). *The Historical Dictionary of the Friends (Quakers)*, 2nd ed. Lanham, MD: The Scarecrow Press.

AFSC and the Nobel Peace Prize. (n.d) www.afsc.org/nobel-peace-prize, accessed September 5, 2016.

AFSC Board Minutes, June 11, 1917. AFSC Archives, Box, "AFSC Minutes 1917–1921," Folder, "AFSC Minutes General Meeting 1917."

Aldrich, R., Dean, D., and Gordon, P. (2013). *Education and Policy in England in the Twentieth Century*. London: Routledge.

Allen, R. C. (2004). "In Search of a New Jerusalem: A Preliminary Investigation into the Causes and Impact of Welsh Quaker Emigration to Pennsylvania, c.1660 – 1750," *Quaker Studies* 9:1, 31–53.

Allen, R. C. (2007a). *Quaker Communities in Early Modern Wales: From Resistance to Respectability*. Cardiff: University of Wales Press.

Allen, R. C. (2007b). "'Turning Hearts to Break Off the Yoke of Oppression': The Travels and Sufferings of Christopher Meidel c. 1659 – c. 1715," *Quaker Studies* 12:1, 54–72.

Allen, R. C. (2013). "Restoration Quakerism." In S. Angell and P. Dandelion, eds., *The Oxford Handbook of Quaker Studies*. Oxford: Oxford University Press, pp. 29–46.

Allen, R. C. and Moore, R. A. (forthcoming). *The Quakers 1656–1723: The Evolution of an Alternative Community*. State Park: Penn State University Press.

Allen, W., Grellet, W., and Grellet, S. (1818). Udvikling af de Grundsætninger og Forskrifter som iagttages og følges af det religiøse Samfund af Venner almindeligt kjendt under Navn af Qvækere som bor i Christiania og i og ved Stavanger. Christiania. Opfostringshusets Bogtrykkerie.

Alpern, B. (2006). "Listening to the Kingdom." In D. Boulton, ed., *Godless for God's Sake: Nontheism in Contemporary Quakerism*. Dent: Dales Historical Monographs, pp. 73–86.

Alpern, R. (1997). "Why Not Join the Unitarians?" *Universalist Friends* 28 (Spring), 23–28.

Alpern, R. (2006). "What's a Nice Nontheist Like You Doing Here?" In D. Boulton ed., *Godless for God's Sake: Nontheism in Contemporary Quakerism*. Dent: Dales Historical Monographs, pp. 19–29.

Amoss Jr., G. (1989). "Experience and Belief," *Universalist Friends* 12 (Spring), 21–24.

Amoss Jr., G. (2016). "Faith and Practice, PDF Available." *Postmodern Quaker*, https://postmodernquaker.wordpress.com/2016/02/21/faith-practice-pdf-available/, accessed August 4, 2016.

An Address on Some Growing Evils of the Day, Especially Demoralizing Literature and Art, from the Representatives of the Religious Society of Friends for Pennsylvania, New Jersey, and Delaware, Second Month, 10 1882 (1882) Philadelphia: Friends Book Store.

Anderson, A. and Anderson, L. (2014). "The Future of Friends in Central America." *Quaker Religious Thought*, # 123–124, pp. 130–35.

Anderson, P. (2014). "Quaker Religious Thought," *Quaker Religious Thought* 111 (August): 1–7.

Angell, S. W. (2002). "Joseph and Sarah Cosand and the Formation of the Friends' Mission in Japan, 1885–1901." Earlham School of Religion Dean's Lecture, Earlham School of Religion. Unpublished paper, available from the author.

Angell, S. W. (2003). "The Catechisms of George Fox," *Quaker Theology* 9: 90–107.

Angell, S. W. (2006). "Quaker Women in Kenya and Human Rights Issues." In R.D. Smith, ed., *Freedom's Distant Shores: American Protestants and Post-Colonial Alliances with Africa*. Waco, TX: Baylor University Press, pp. 111–30.

Angell, S. W. (2011). "Current Conflicts in Two Midwestern Friends Meetings," *Quaker Theology* 18 (Fall-Winter): 1–28.

Angell, S. W. (2013). "Howard Brinton in Theological Context." Appendix in Anthony Manousos, *Howard and Anna Brinton: Re-Inventors of Quakers in the Twentieth Century*. Philadelphia: Quaker-Bridge Media of Friends General Conference, pp. 247–266.

Angell, S. W. (2014). "Separation Accomplished: New Beginnings for a New Association of Friends and a 'Reconfigured' Indiana Yearly Meeting," *Quaker Theology* 24 (Winter-Spring): 60–83.

Angell, S. W. (2015). "George Fox University and West Hills Friends: Controversy and Conflict in Northwest Yearly Meeting," *Quaker Theology* 27 (Summer-Fall): 9–53.

Appelbaum, P. (2009). *From Kingdom to Commune: Protestant Pacifist Culture between World War I and the Vietnam War.* Chapel Hill: University of North Carolina Press.

Appleby, A. B. (1978). *Famine in Tudor and Stuart England.* Stanford: Stanford University Press.

Armitage, E. N. (1896). *The Quaker Poets of Great Britain and Ireland.* London: William Andrews and Co.

Ayllón, J. (1924). Letter published in *The Harvester,* January 1925, pp. 3–4.

Ayoub, R. (2005). "The Persecution of 'an Innocent People' in Seventeenth-Century England," *Quaker Studies* 10:1, 46–66.

Backhouse, J. (1833). *A Concise Apology for the Peculiarities of the Society of Friends, Commonly Called Quakers, in Their Language, Costume and Manners.* Hobart Town: James Ross.

Backhouse, J. (1838). "To Major General Richard Bourke, K. C. B., Governor in Chief of New South Wales." In vol. I of *Extracts from the Letters of James Backhouse, Now Engaged in a Religious Visit to Van Dieman's Land, and New South Wales. Accompanied by George Washington Walker,* 3rd ed. London: Harvey and Darton, pp. 50–53.

Balby (Doncaster) Friends Meeting website: www.doncasterquakers.org.uk/node/7 (accessed July 3, 2016).

Balfour, I. (2002). *The Rhetoric of Romantic Prophecy.* Stanford: Stanford University Press

Barbour, H. and Frost, J. W. (1988). *The Quakers.* New York: Greenwood Press.

Barbour, H. and Frost, J. W. (1994). *The Quakers.* 2nd ed. Richmond, IN: Friends United Press.

Barbour, H. and Roberts, A. O., eds. (1973). *Early Quaker Writings, 1650–1700.* Grand Rapids, MI: Eerdmans.

Barbour, H. and Roberts, A. O., eds. (2004). *Early Quaker Writings, 1650–1700,* 2nd ed. Wallingford, PA: Pendle Hill Publications.

Barbour, H., Densmore, C., Moger, E. H., Sorel, N. C., Van Wagner, A. D., and Worrall, A. J., eds. (1995). *Quaker Crosscurrents: Three Hundred Years of Friends in the New York Yearly Meetings.* Syracuse, NY: Syracuse University Press.

Barclay, A. R. (1841). *Letters, &c., of Early Friends, Illustrative of the History of the Society from Nearly Its Origin to about the Period of George Fox's Decease, with Documents Respecting Its Early Discipline, Also Epistles of Counsel and Exhortation, &c.,* London: Harvey and Darton.

Barclay, R. (1827). *An Apology for the True Christian Divinity, Being an Explanation and Vindication of the Principles and Doctrines of the People called Quakers.* New York: Samuel Wood and Sons.

Barclay, R. (2002/1678). *An Apology for the True Christian Divinity.* Glenside, PA: Quaker Heritage Press.

Barton, B. (1818). *The Convict's Appeal.* London: Darton, Harvey, Darton.

Barton, L., ed. (1822). *Poems by Bernard Barton* in *Blackwood's Edinburgh Magazine,* 66:12, 767–74.

Barton, L., ed. (1850). *Memoirs, Letters, and Poems of Bernard Barton.* Philadelphia: Lindsey and Blakiston.

Bassuk, D. (1987). *Abraham Lincoln and the Quakers.* Wallingford, PA: Pendle Hill Publications.

Beadenkopf, B. W. (2010). "Why Do the Obamas, Bidens, and Clintons Choose Friends Schools?" *Friends Journal*, October, pp. 16, 38.

Bello, W. (1986). *Visions of a Warless World: Perspectives on Peace from Divergent Traditions: The Hopes They Share, the Obstacles They Face*. Washington: FCNL Education Fund, Inc.

Benson, Lewis. (1966). *Catholic Quakerism*, Gloucester, UK: printed for the author.

Bernet, C. (2010). "Quaker Missionary Work in Germany from 1790 until 1899. List of all Anglo-American Visitors," *The Journal of the Friends Historical Society*, 62:1, 25–41.

Bernet, C. (2011). *Deutsche Quäkerbibliographie*. Nordhausen, Verlag Traugott Bautz GmbH.

Best, E. V. (1948). *"The United Church of Christ in Japan: An Analysis of the Background of and Trends toward Unity in Religion and State Resulting in the Creation of the United Protestant Church in Japan,"* unpublished master's thesis, Paper 329, Graduate Thesis Collection, Butler University.

Biko, A. (2016). "Purpose – Convergent Friends Pacific Northwest." Facebook.com. www.facebook.com/notes/convergent-friends-pacific-northwest/purpose-cfpnw/10151381190794701. Accessed March 10, 2016.

Bill, J. B. (2008). *Western Yearly Meeting, 1858–2008, 150th Anniversary: The History of Western Yearly Meeting from Its Founding to Its Sesquicentennial*. Plainfield, IN: Western Yearly Meeting of Friends.

Binford, G. (1950). *As I Remember It: Forty-three Years in Japan*. Richmond, IN: Friends Book Store.

Birkel, M. L. (2015a). "Immediate Revelation, Kabbalah, and Magic: The Primacy of Experience in the Theology of George Keith." In S. Angell and P. Dandelion, eds., *Early Quakers and Their Theological Thought, 1647–1723*. New York: Cambridge University Press, pp. 256–272.

Birkel, M. L. (2015b). "Quaker Silent Prayer." In Louis Komjathy, ed., *Contemplative Literature: A Comparative Sourcebook on Meditation and Contemplative Prayer*. New York: State University of New York Press, pp. 145–96.

Birkel, M. L., and Bach, J. (2010). *Genius for the Transcendent: Mystical Writings of Jakob Boehme*, Boston: Shambhala.

Bishop, E. (2004). "Peace and Land: A Challenge to Quakerism," doctoral work based at Sunderland University, available from the author.

Bittle, W. (1986). *James Nayler, 1618–1660: The Quaker Indicted by Parliament*. York: Sessions Book Trust.

Blair, K. (2012). *Form and Faith in Victorian Poetry and Religion*. Oxford: Oxford University Press.

Bolger, R. K. (2007). "Practice Movements in Global Information Culture: Looking Back to McGavran and Finding a Way Forward," *Missiology* 35:2, 181–194.

Boulding, E. (1989). *One Small Plot of Heaven: Reflections on Family Life by a Quaker Sociologist*. Wallingford, PA: Pendle Hill Publications.

Boulton, D. (2006). "For God's Sake? An Introduction." In D. Boulton, ed., *Godless for God's Sake: Nontheism in Contemporary Quakerism*. Dent: Dales Historical Monographs, pp. 5–18.

Boulton, D. (2012). "Nontheism among Friends: Its Emergence and Meaning," *Quaker Religious Thought* 118: 35–44.

Boulton, D. and Cresson, O. (2006). "The Making of a Nontheist Tradition." In D. Boulton, ed., *Godless for God's Sake: Nontheism in Contemporary Quakerism.* Dent: Dales Historical Monographs, pp. 87–100.

Braithwaite, A. W. (1939). "Precedent and Present Testimony." *The Friend.* pp. 195–96.

Braithwaite, C. (1995). *Conscientious Objection: To Compulsions Under the Law.* York: William Sessions.

Braithwaite, W. C. (1912). *The Beginnings of Quakerism.* London: Macmillan and Co.

Breen, J. (2003). "Shinto and Christianity: A History of Conflict and Compromise." In Vol. X of M. R. Mullins, ed., *Handbook of Christianity in Japan.* Leiden, The Netherlands: Brill, pp. 249–76.

Brightwell, C. L. (1854). *Memorials of the Life of Amelia Opie.* Norwich: Fletcher and Alexander.

Brinton, H. H. (1952). *Friends for 300 Years.* New York: Harper & Brothers.

Brinton, H. H., and Bacon, M. H. (2002). *Friends for 350 Years.* Wallingford, PA: Pendle Hill Publications.

Brinton, H. H. and Watahiki J. (1958). "Reconstruction of a Yearly Meeting," *Friends Journal* 4:17, 258, 269–70.

Britain Yearly Meeting (1995). *Quaker Faith and Practice: The Book of Christian Discipline of the Yearly Meeting of the Religious Society of Friends (Quakers) in Britain,* London: Britain Yearly Meeting.

British Quaker Survey.(2013). Data Held at the Centre for Research in Quaker Studies, Woodbrooke Quaker Study Centre.

Brock, P. (1968). *Pioneers of the Peaceable Kingdom: The Quaker Peace Testimony from the Colonial Era to the First World War.* Princeton: Princeton University Press.

Brock, P. (1990). *The Quaker Peace Testimony, 1660 to 1914.* York: Sessions.

Brock, P. and Young, N. (1999). *Pacifism in the Twentieth Century.* Syracuse: Syracuse University Press.

Bronner, E. B. (1986). "Quaker Discipline and Order, 1680–1720: Philadelphia Yearly Meeting and London Yearly Meeting." In R. S. Dunn and M. M. Dunn, eds., *The World of William Penn.* Philadelphia: University of Pennsylvania Press, pp. 322–36.

Brown, T. S. (1963). *When Friends Attend to Business.* Philadelphia: Philadelphia Yearly Meeting.

Brown, V. (2006). *The Mindful Quaker: A Brief Introduction to Buddhist Wisdom for Friends.* Wallingford, PA: Pendle Hill Publications.

Brown, V. (2010). *Living from the Center: Mindfulness Meditation and Centering for Friends.* Wallingford, PA: Pendle Hill Publications.

Brown, V. (2013). *Heartfulness: Renewing Heart, Mind, and Spirit on Retreat and Beyond.* Wallingford, PA: Pendle Hill Publications.

Brownstein, M. C. (1987). "Our Man in Mito – Yoshioka Kwansen and the First Quaker Missionaries in Japan," *The Japan Christian Quarterly* 53:1, 33–41.

Buglass, D. (2011). "What Next for Quaker Nontheism?: A Note on the Gathering at Woodbrooke College, February, 2010," *The Universalist* 92 (June): 31–33.

Burdick, T. J. (2013). *"Neo-Evangelical Identity within American Religious Society of Friends(Quakers): Oregon Yearly Meeting, 1919–1947."* Unpublished doctoral thesis, University of Birmingham, accessible via http://etheses.bham.ac.uk/4152/.

Burgis, T. (2015). *The Looting Machine: Warlords, Oligarchs, Corporations, Smugglers, and the Theft of Africa's Wealth.* New York: Public Affairs.

Burrough, E. (1672). *A Warning from the Lord to the Inhabitant of Underbarrow* (1654). In *The Memorable Works of a Son of Thunder and Consolation: Namely, That True Prophet, and Faithful Servant of God.* London: [no publisher].

Butler, J. (1974). "'Gospel Order Improved:' The Keithian Schism and the Exercise of Quaker Ministerial Authority in Pennsylvania," *William and Mary Quarterly* 31:3, 431–52.

Butler, J. (1978). "Power, Authority, and the Origins of American Denominational Order: The English Churches in the Delaware Valley, 1680–1730," *Transactions of the American Philosophical Society* 68:2, 1–85.

Butterworth, D. N. (2015). *Celluloid Friends: Cinematic Friends, Real and Imagined (1922–2012)*, Amazon Press, n.p.

Byrne, D. (n.d.). "Directory." Coalition for Hispanic Ministries. www.institutoalma .org/directorio/index.html#English (accessed February 3, 2016).

Bywater, M. (2015, September). "Quakers in Kalay, Myanmar," *The Australian Friend* 129(3). Retrieved from http://australianfriend.org/quakers-in-kalay-myanmar/

Cadbury, H. J. (1934). "Anthony Benezet's Library," *Bulletin of the Friends Historical Association* 23: 63–75.

Cadbury, H. J. (2000). "My Personal Religion," *Universalist Friends* 35 (Winter): 22–31.

California Yearly Meeting Minutes - 1921 & 1931. Whittier, CA: California Yearly Meeting of Friends Church.

Calvert, P. (2003). "'How Blessed It Is for the Sisters to Meet': Historical Roots of the Pacific Northwest Quaker Women's Theology Conference," *Quaker History* 92:2, 19–51.

Campbell Stewart, W. A. (1971). *Quakers and Education as Seen in Their Schools in England.* London: Kennikat Press.

Canadian Yearly Meeting. (1982). *Minutes of Canadian Yearly Meeting of the Religious Society of Friends,* Toronto: Canadian Yearly Meeting.

Canadian Yearly Meeting. (2016). *Personnel Policy Manual,* Ottawa: Canadian Yearly Meeting.

Canadian Yearly Meeting of the Religious Society of Friends. (2011). *Faith and Practice,* Ottawa: Canadian Yearly Meeting.

Caring Hands. (2016). Ministries. Retrieved from http://caringhandsindia.com/ ministries/

Carroll, K. L. (2010). "Persecution and Persecutors of Maryland Quakers, 1658–1661," *Quaker History* 99:1, 15–31.

Cattell, E. L. (1959). "Passion for Unity: A Critical Survey of Contemporary Quakerdom." Speech given at the 1959 gathering of the Association of Evangelical Friends in Newberg, Oregon. Reprinted in *Concern,* 1:3 (Fall): 3–18.

Cattell, E. L. (1966). "The Future of Friends," *Quaker Religious Thought* 16 (January): 10–14.

Cattell, E. L. (1970). "A New Approach for Friends." In *What Future for Friends? Report of the St. Louis Conference: A Gathering of Concerned Friends.* St. Louis, MO: Friends World Committee for Consultation.

Cattell, E. L. (2015) *The Spirit of Holiness,* 2nd ed., ed. Wayne Evans. Newberg, OR: Barclay Press.

Cave, E. and Morley, R., eds. (2000). *Faith in Action: Quaker Social Testimony.* London: Quaker Home Service.

Cazden, E. (1997). *The Modernist Reinvention of Quakerism: The Independent Meetings in New England, 1920–1950*. Unpublished M.A. Thesis, Andover Newton Theological School.

Cazden, E. (2013). "Quakers, Slavery, Anti-slavery, and Race." In S. Angell and P. Dandelion, eds., *The Oxford Handbook of Quaker Studies*. Oxford: Oxford University Press, pp. 347–62.

Chan, S. (2007). "Evangelical Theology in Asian Contexts." In T. Larsen and D. Treier, eds., *The Cambridge Companion to Evangelical Theology*. Cambridge: Cambridge University Press, pp. 225–40.

Chandler, E. M. (1836). *The Poetical Works of Elizabeth Margaret Chandler: With a Memoir of Her Life and Character, by Benjamin Lundy*. Philadelphia: Lemuel Howell.

Chandler, S. (1998). "Indigenous People' Rights," *The Canadian Friend* 94:2, 10.

Chen, O. (2003, October 4). *Ba Nian Xuanjiao Feilubin* [Eight Years as a Missionary to the Philippines]. Retrieved from www.geocities.ws/olich_58/missionipilippines8yrs.htm

Chen, O. (2006, January 21). *Feilubin Xuanjiao Shuzhi Shouce Di21qi* [Philippines Mission Debriefing Handbook No. 21]. Retrieved from www.geocities.ws/olich_58/missionipilippinesnbook21.htm

Chernus, I. (n.d.). *Reinhold Niebuhr's Critique of Nonviolence*. http://colorado.edu/ReligioiusStudies/chernus/Niebuhr.htm [accessed August 17, 2016].

Cho, N. J. and Niblett, M. (2016). "Daughters of Eve: The Labouring-class Autobiographical Hermeneutics of Two Romantic-Era English Prophetesses, Dorothy Gott (*c.*1748–1812) and Joanna Southcott (1750–1814)," *Romanticism* 22(1), 107–121.

Choudhry, B. (1977). "Report on Friend's Rural Centre, Rasulia." In B. Choudry and I. P. Desai, *History of Rural Development in Modern India*, vol. 2. New Delhi: Impex India, pp. 159–220.

Christian Faith and Practice in the Friends Church. (n.d.). Friends United Meeting in East Africa. www.quakerinfo.com/eastafricafandp2012.pdf (accessed September 20, 2017)

Chrystal, P. (2013). *The Rowntree Family of York: A Social History*. Pickering: Blackthorn Press.

Clarke, E. (2011). "Hymns, Psalms, and Controversy in the Seventeenth-Century." In I. Rivers and D. Wykes, eds., *Dissenting Praise: Religious Dissent and the Hymns in England and Wales*. Oxford: Oxford University Press, pp. 13–32.

Clarkson, T. (1806). *A Portraiture of Quakerism, as Taken from a View of the Moral Education, Discipline, Peculiar Customs, Religious Principles, Political and Civil Economy, and Character of the Society of Friends*, 3 vols. London: Longman, Hurst, Rees, and Orme.

Co, K. (2007, June). "Stephen Yang Obituary," *AWPS Newsletter* 74: 13–14.

Coate, L. (1939). "A Review of the First Yearly Meeting," *Humanist Friend* 1 (November-December): 1–4.

Collins, P. J. (1996). "'Plaining': The Social and Cognitive Process of Symbolization in the Religious Society of Friends (Quakers)," *Journal of Contemporary Religion* 11:3, 277–88.

Collins, P. J. (2000). "Quaker Plaining as Critical Aesthetic," *Quaker Studies* 5: 121–39.

Comfort, W. W. (1949). *Quakers in the Modern World*. New York: Macmillan.

Conference of All Friends Held in London August 12 to 20, Official Report (1920). London: Conference Continuation Committee for the Friends' Bookshop.

Connell, J. (2013). "'Brethren of the Same Household of Faith': The Story of Division among Conservative and Revivalist Quakers at White Lick Quarterly Meeting." Unpublished paper, Friends Collection, Earlham College.

Cook, S. (2000). "Pilgrims' Progresses: Derivative Texts and the Seventeenth-Century Reader." In D. Gay, J. G. Randall, and A. Zinck, eds., *Awakening Words: John Bunyan and the Language of Community*. Newark: University of Delaware Press, pp. 186–201.

Cooper, W. A. (1985). *The E.S.R. Story: A Quaker Dream Come True*. Richmond, IN: Earlham School of Religion.

Cooper, W. A. (1990). *A Living Faith*. Richmond, IN: Friends United Press.

Cooper, W. A. (2001/1990). *A Living Faith: An Historical and Comparative Study of Quaker Beliefs*, 2nd ed. Richmond, IN: Friends United Press.

Corder, S. (1853). *Life of Elizabeth Fry*. Philadelphia: Henry Longstreath.

Corns, T. N. and Loewenstein, D., eds. (1995). *The Emergence of Quaker Writing: Dissenting Literature in Seventeenth-Century England*. London: Frank Cass and Co. Ltd.

Cosgrave, I. (2013). "Untrustworthy Reproductions and Doctored Archives: Undoing the Sins of a Victorian Biographer." In C. Smith and L. Stead, eds., *The Boundaries of the Literary Archive: Reclamation and Representation*. Aldershot: Ashgate, pp. 61–74.

Craigo-Snell, S. (2012). "Response to David Boulton and Jeffrey Dudiak," *Quaker Religious Thought* 118: 45–50.

Crawford, P. (1985). "Women's Published Writings, 1600–1700." In Mary Prior, ed., *Women in English Society 1500–1800*, London: Methuen, pp. 211–12.

Cresson, O. (2014). *Quaker and Naturalist Too*, Iowa City, IA: Morning Walk Press.

Crisp, S. (1777). *A Short History of a Long Travel from Babylon to Bethal*. London: [no publisher].

Curle, A. (1981). *True Justice: Quaker Peace Makers and Peace Making*. London: Quaker Home Service.

Damrosch, L. (1996). *The Sorrows of the Quaker Jesus: James Nayler and the Puritan Crackdown on the Free Spirit*. Cambridge, MA: Harvard University Press.

Dandelion, P. (1996). *A Sociological Analysis of the Theology of Quakers: The Silent Revolution*. Lewiston, NY: Edwin Mellen Press.

Dandelion, P. (2005). *The Liturgies of Quakerism*. Aldershot: Ashgate.

Dandelion, P. (2007). *An Introduction to Quakerism*. Cambridge: Cambridge University Press.

Dandelion, P. (2008). *The Quakers: A Very Short Introduction*. Oxford: Oxford University Press.

Dandelion, P. (2010). "Guarded Domesticity and Engagement with 'the World': The Separate Spheres of Quaker Quietism," *Common Knowledge* 16:1, 95–109.

Dandelion, B.P. (2014). *Open for Transformation: Being Quaker*. London: Quaker Books.

Daniels, C. W. (2010a). "Convergent Friends: The Emergence of Postmodern Quakerism." *Quaker Studies* 14/2: 236–250.

Daniels, C. W. (2011a). "Convergent Friends." In M. P. Abbott et al., *Historical Dictionary of the Friends (Quakers)*. Lanham, MD: Scarecrow Press.

Daniels, C. W. (2015). *A Convergent Model of Renewal: Remixing the Quaker Tradition in a Participatory Culture.* Eugene, OR. Wipf and Stock Publishers.

Davie, M. (1997). *British Quaker Theology since 1895.* Lampeter: Edwin Mellen Press.

Davie, M. (2011). "Manchester Conference." In M. P. Abbott et al., eds., *Historical Dictionary of the Friends (Quakers).* Lanham, MD. Scarecrow Press, pp. 212–13.

Davies, A. (2000). *The Quakers in English Society, 1655–1725.* Oxford: Oxford University Press.

Davis, R., ed. (1953). *Woodbrooke 1903–1953.* London: Bannisdale Press.

Densmore, C. (2007). "Swarthmore College." In J. W. Oliver Jr., et al., eds., *Founded by Friends: The Quaker Heritage of Fifteen American Colleges and Universities.* Lanham, MD: Scarecrow Press, pp. 57–68.

DeVol, C. E. (1988). *Fruit That Remains: The Story of the Friends Mission in China and Taiwan sponsored by The Evangelical Friends Church – Eastern Region (Formerly Ohio Yearly Meeting of Friends).* Taipei: Dixon Press.

Dillon, G. (1963). "Alliance – Association," *Concern* 4:4 (October): 1–4.

Dorland, A. G. (1968). *The Quakers in Canada: A History.* Toronto, ONT: Ryerson Press.

Dorrien, G. (2003). *The Making of American Liberal Theology: Idealism, Realism and Modernity 1900–1950.* Louisville, KY: Westminster John Knox Press.

Drayton, B., and Taber, W. P., Jr. (2015). *A Language for the Inward Landscape: Spiritual Wisdom from the Quaker Movement.* Philadelphia: Tract Association of Friends.

Dudiak, J. (2012). "Quakers and Non/Theism: Questions and Prospects." *Quaker Religious Thought* 118: 25–34.

Ellis, S. S. (1858). *Friends at Their Own Fireside: Or, Pictures of the Private Lives of the People Called Quakers,* 2 vols. London: Richard Bentley.

Ellwood, T. (1712). *Davideis: The Life of David King of Israel: A Sacred Poem in Five Books.* London: [no publisher].

Erickson, G. G. (2007). "Guilford College." In J. W. Oliver Jr. et al., eds., *Founded by Friends: The Quaker Heritage of Fifteen American Colleges and Universities.* Lanham, MD: Scarecrow Press, pp. 21–42.

Etten, H. van (1938). *Chronique de la vie Quaker française 1750–1938,* Paris: Société religieuse des amis (Quakers).

Evangelical Friends Church – Eastern Region. (2016). Benson & Annie Sam. Retrieved from http://efcer.org/missions/sams-ba

Evangelical Friends Church – Eastern Region. (2016). PK & Mariamma Sam. Retrieved from http://efcer.org/missions/sams-pkm

Evangelical Friends Church International. (n.d.). http://evangelicalfriends.org (accessed December 30, 2015).

Evangelical Friends Midwest Yearly Meeting. (2010). *Faith and Practice: The Book of Discipline.* Available from www.efcmaym.org/wp-content/uploads/2012/01/FP-PART-III.pdf (accessed December 12, 2015).

Evangelical Friends Mission. (n.d.). Evangelical Friends Mission. http://www.friends mission.com/ (accessed December 18, 2015).

Evangelical Friends Mission. (2016). *EFM Bhutan, Tamang Igniting the Hope,* YouTube video, Arvada, CO: Evangelical Friends Mission.

Evans, K. and Cheevers, S. (2003). *A True Account of the Great Tryals and Cruel Sufferings Undergone by Those True Servants of God Katherine Evans and Sarah Cheevers,* S. Villani, ed., Pisa: Scuola Normale Superiore.

Evans, W. (2014). "Evangelical Friends," *Quaker Religious Thought* 123:4, 75–84.

Fager, C. (1992). *Fire in the Valley: Quaker Ghost Stories*. Falls Church: Kimo Press.

Fager, C. (1999). "Editor's Introduction." *Quaker Theology*: October.

Fager, C. (2002). *Without Apology: The Heroes, the Heritage and the Hope of Liberal Quakerism*. Fayetteville, NC: Kimo Press.

Fager, C. (2013). "A Letter to Zablon Malenge," *Quaker Theology* 12:2.

Fager, C. (2014). *Remaking Friends: How Progressive Friends Changed Quakerism & Helped Save America, 1822–1940*. Durham, NC: Kimo Press.

Fager, C. (2015). "Thunder in Carolina, Part Two: North Carolina Yearly Meeting – FUM and 'Unity' vs. Uniformity," *Quaker Theology* 14:2.

Fager, C. (2016a). "Re-Re-Re-Inventing the Wheel: 170 Years of 'Convergent' Quakerism." *A Friendly Letter*. March 19. http://afriendlyletter.com/re-re-re-invent ing-the-wheel-170-years-of-convergent-quakerism. Accessed September 19, 2017.

Fager, C. (2016b). "Back from the Brink: North Carolina Yearly Meeting Says No to a Split," *Quaker Theology* 29 (Summer-Fall): 50–78.

Fager, C. (2017). "Two Blockbusters: Northwest YM to Split over LGBT Issues; & a Lawsuit Coming?" *A Friendly Letter*, 28 January 2017, http://afriendlyletter.com/two-blockbus ters-northwest-ym-split-lgbt-welcome-lawsuit-coming/ (accessed January 28, 2017).

Fager, C. and Souza, J. (2014). "Northwest Yearly Meeting and 'Shattering' Conflict: Chapter One," *Quaker Theology* 13(24): 1–15.

Faith and Practice: The Book of Discipline. Evangelical Friends Church – Mid-America, (n.d.). www.efcmaym.org/faith-and-practice. Accessed September 19, 2017.

Farnworth, R. (1653). *A Message from the Lord to All That Despise the Ordinance of Christ*. London: [no publisher]

Filiaci, A. (2006). "Don't Ask, Don't Tell." In D. Boulton, ed., *Godless for God's Sake: Nontheism in Contemporary Quakerism*. Dent: Dales Historical Monographs, pp.116–17.

Fisher, S., Addi, D.I., Ludin, J., Smith, R., Williams, S. and Williams, S. (2000). *Working with Conflict: Skills & Strategies for Action*. London and Birmingham: Zed Books and Responding to Conflict.

Flanagan, E. (2015). *Renewable: One Woman's Search for Simplicity, Faithfulness, and Hope*. Berkeley: She Writes Press.

Forbes, S. S. (1982). "Quaker Tribalism." In M. Zuckerman, ed., *Friends and Neighbors: Group Life in America's First Plural Society*. Philadelphia: Temple University Press, pp. 145–73.

Forbush, B. (1956). *Elias Hicks: Quaker Liberal*. New York: Columbia University Press.

"Foundational Beliefs," (n.d.) [Yorba Linda] Friends Church. www.friendschurchyl .com/about/who-we-are/foundational-beliefs (accessed December 30, 2015).

Fox, G. (1658). *A Catechisme for Children*. London: Thomas Simmons.

Fox, G. (1659). *Primer for the Schollers and Doctors of Europe*. London: Thomas Simmons.

Fox, G. (1660). *A Declaration from the Harmless & Innocent People of God, Called, Quakers against All Sedition Plotters & Fighters in the World: For the Removing of the Ground of Jealousie and Suspition from Both Magistrates and People in the Kingdome, Concerning Wars and Frighting: Presented unto the King, upon the 21th Day of the 11th Moneth, 1660*, London.

Fox, G. (1706). FOR THE EMPEROR OF CHINA, And his Subordinate KINGS AND PRINCES. From the People of God in England, in English called Quakers. By G. F. In

Gospel-Truth Demonstrated, in a COLLECTION of Doctrinal BOOKS, Given forth by that Faithful Minister of Jesus Christ, GEORGE FOX: Containing PRINCIPLES, Essential to Christianity and Salvation, held among the People called QUAKERS, London: T. Sowle, in White-Hart-Court, in Gracious-Street, pp.207–9.

Fox, G. (1952). *The Journal of George Fox,* J. L. Nickalls, ed., Cambridge: Cambridge University Press.

Fox, M. (1710). "Epistle to Friends from Swarthmoor Hall, 4th month, 1698," from *A Brief Collection of Remarkable Passages,* London.

Francis, E. (2004). "Healing Relief . . . without Detriment to Modest Reserve . . . ': Keble, Women's Poetry and Victorian Cultural Theory." In K. Blair, ed., *John Keble in Context.* London: Anthem, pp. 115–24.

Freedom Friends Church. (2009). *Faith and Practice of Freedom Friends Church.* 1st ed. Salem, OR. http://freedomfriends.org/FF-What.htm.

Freeman, M. (2013). "Quakers, Business, and Philanthropy." In S. Angell and P. Dandelion, eds., *The Oxford Handbook of Quaker Studies.* Oxford University Press, pp. 420–33.

Fremon, J. (2001). "'Meeting for learning' at Princeton Friends School." *Friends Journal,* January, pp. 12–13.

"Friends Ambulance Unit (FAU) in WWI." (2016). Available from www.quakersinthe world.org/quaker-in-action/252 (accessed February 17, 2016].

"Friends and Enlistment." (1914). *The Friend,* pp. 932–33.

"Friends Beliefs." (n.d.). Evangelical Friends Church International. www.evangelical friends.org/beliefs (accessed December 15, 2015).

"Friends in the New Century." (1901). *Friends' Intelligencer,* 1st Mo. 5, p. 6.

Friends Meeting of San Antonio (Texas) website: www.sanantonioquakers.org/meet inghouse/meetinghouse.htm (accessed July 3, 2016).

Froese, Paul and Bader, Christopher. (2007). "God in America: Why Theology Is Not Simply the Concern of Philosophers," *Journal for the Scientific Study of Religion* 46 (Dec.): 465–81.

Frost, J. W. (1973). *The Quaker Family in Colonial America; a Portrait of the Society of Friends.* New York: St. Martin's Press.

Frost, J. W. (1992). "'Our Deeds Carry Our Message': The Early History of the American Friends Service Committee," *Quaker History* 81:1, 9–11.

Frost, J. W. (2003). "From Plainness to Simplicity: Changing Quaker Ideals for Material Culture." In Emma Lapsansky-Werner and Anne Verplanck, eds., *Quaker Aesthetics: Reflections on a Quaker Ethic in American Design and Consumption.* Philadelphia: University of Pennsylvania Press, pp. 16–42.

Furuya, J. (1995). "Graduate Student and Quaker." In J. F. Howes, ed., *Nitobe Inazō: Japan's Bridge Across the Pacific.* Boulder: Westview Press, Inc., pp. 55–76.

FWCC. (2007). Map, "Find Quakers Around the World." Available in PDF format from Friends World Committee for Consultation.

FWCC. (2012). Map, "Find Quakers Around the World." Available in PDF format from Friends World Committee for Consultation.

FWCC. (2012). "Kabarak Call for Peace and EcoJustice," *Friends World News,* p. 5, July.

FWCC. (2016). *Living Sustainably and Sustaining Life on Earth – The Minute from the Plenary.* http://fwcc.world/fwcc-news/living-sustainably-and-sustaining-life-on-earth-the-minute-from-the-plenary (accessed October 29, 2016).

Gallagher, C. (2006). "The Rise of Fictionality." In F. Morretti, ed., *The Novel*, Volume 1: *History, Geography, and Culture*. Princeton: Princeton University Press, pp. 336–63.

Garman, M., J. Applegate, M. Benefiel, and D. Meredith, eds. (1996). *Hidden in Plain Sight: Quaker Women's Writings, 1650–1700*. Wallingford, PA: Pendle Hill Press.

Garratt, A. (1927). *A History of the Society of Friends (Quakers) in Canada*. Toronto: Macmillan Company of Canada.

General Conference of Friends. (1887). *Proceedings, Including Declaration of Christian Doctrine, of the General Conference of Friends, Held in Richmond, Ind., U.S.A.* Richmond, IN: Nicholson & Bro.

Genovese, H. (2015). "Not a Myth: Quakers and Racial Justice," *Quaker Studies* 19(2), 243–59.

Gibbs, E. and Bolger, R. K. (2005). *Emerging Churches: Creating Christian Community in Postmodern Cultures*. Grand Rapids, MI: Baker Academic.

Gill, C. (2005). *Women in the Seventeenth-Century Quaker Community: A Literary Study of Political Identities, 1650–1700*. Aldershot: Ashgate.

Gillespie, W. R. (2005). *About Aboriginal Sovereignty: Seeking New Understandings, New Pathways*. Canberra: Yearly Meeting Quaker Indigenous Concerns Committee of the Religious Society of Friends (Quakers) in Australia.

Gilpin, T. (1848). *Exiles in Virginia with Observations on the Conduct of the Society of Friends during the Revolutionary War, Comprising the Official Papers of the Government Relating to That period, 1777–1778*. Philadelphia: [no publisher]. [C. Sherman].

Glimt fra dansk kvækerhistorie. I anledning af 100-året for Vennernes Samfund – Kvækerne i Danmark 1875–1975. (1975). (Glimpses of Danish Quaker History at the centennial of the Religious Society of Friends in Denmark 1875-1975) Copenhagen, Vennernes Samfund, Kvækerne.

Gragg, L. (2009). *Quaker Community on Barbados: Challenging the Culture of the Planter Class*. Columbia: University of Missouri Press.

Graves, M. P. (1996). "The Anti-Theatrical Prejudice and the Quakers: A Late Twentieth Century Perspective." In P. N. Anderson and H. R. Macy (eds.), *Truth's Bright Embrace: Essays and Poems in Honor of Arthur O. Roberts*. Newberg, OR: George Fox University Press, pp. 239–55.

Graves, B. C. (1999). *Americanizing Cuba by Cubanizing Protestantism: The Cuba Mission of American Friends, 1900–1948*. Unpublished MA thesis, University of Texas in Austin.

Greaves, R. L. (1969). "The early Quakers as Advocates of Educational Reform," *Quaker History* 58: 22–30.

Greaves, R. L. (1986). *Deliver Us from Evil: The Radical Underground in Britain, 1660–1663*, New York: Oxford University Press.

Greaves, R. L. (1992). "Shattered Expectations? George Fox, the Quakers, and the Restoration State, 1660-1685," *Albion: A Quarterly Journal Concerned with British Studies* 24:2, 237–59.

Greaves, R. L. (2001). "Seditious Sectaries or 'Sober and Useful Inhabitants'? Changing Conceptions of the Quakers in Early Modern Britain," *Albion: A Quarterly Journal Concerned with British Studies* 33:1, 24–50.

Greenwood, J. O. (1978). *Signs of Life: Art and Religious Experience*. London: Friends Home Service Committee.

Gregg, H. (1990). "John Bright: Called to the Lord's Service," *Quaker Religious Thought* 24:3, 8–30.

Gross, P. and Lerner, L. (2012). "Talking in All: A Conversation on Poetry and Quakerism Between Philip Gross and Laurence Lerner," *Quaker Studies* 17:1, 110–30.

Grubb, S. L. (1863). *A Brief Account of the Life and Religious Labors of Sarah Grubb, (formerly Sarah Lynes): A Minister of the Gospel in the Society of Friends.* Philadelphia: Friends' Book Store.

Gurney, J. J. and Fry, E. G. (1819). *Notes on a Visit Made to Some of the Prisons in Scotland, and the North of England . . . in Company with E. Fry.* London: n.p.

Gurney, J. J. (1845). *Thoughts on Habit and Discipline*, 3rd ed. London: Hamilton, Adams and Co.

Gurney, J. J. (1860). *On Plainness of Speech, Behaviour & Apparel.* London: Richard Barrett.

Gwyn, D. (2014a). *Personality and Place: The Life and Times of Pendle Hill.* Philadelphia: Plain Press.

Gwyn, D. (2014b). *A Sustainable Life: Quaker Faith and Practice in the Renewal of Creation.* Philadelphia: FGC Quakerpress.

Gwyn, D. (2015). "Seventeenth-Century Context and Quaker Beginnings." In S. Angell and P. Dandelion, eds., *Early Quakers and Their Theological Thought, 1647–1723.* Cambridge: Cambridge University Press, pp. 13–31.

Habito, R. (2008). *Living Zen, Loving God.* Boston: Wisdom.

Hadley, N. (1994). "Evangelical Friends Mission (EFM)." In *Northwest Yearly Meeting of Friends Minutes, 1994* (pp. 19–21). Newberg, OR: Northwest Yearly Meeting of Friends, Paper 99, George Fox University Archives, http://digitalcommons.george fox.edu/nwym_minutes/99

Hagglund, B. (2013). "Quakers and Print Culture." In S. Angell and P. Dandelion, eds., *The Oxford Handbook of Quaker Studies.* Oxford: Oxford University Press, pp. 477–91.

Hagglund, B. (2015). "Quakers and the Printing Press." In S. Angell and P. Dandelion, eds., *Early Quakers and Their Theological Thought, 1643–1723.* Cambridge: Cambridge University Press, pp. 32–47.

Haidt, J. (2012). *The Righteous Mind: Why Good People Are Divided by Politics and Religion.* New York: Pantheon Books.

Haines, D. L. (2000). "Friends General Conference: A Brief Historical Overview," *Quaker History* 89 (Fall), 1–16.

Hall, D. (1992). "'The Fiery Tryal of Their Infalliable Examination': Self Control in the Regulation of Quaker Publishing in England from the 1670s to the mid-19th century." In R. Myers and M. Harris, eds., *Censorship and the Control of Print in England and France1600–1910.* Winchester: St. Paul's Bibliographies, pp. 59–86.

Hallward, M. C. (2013). "The Ramallah Friends Meeting: Examining One Hundred Years of Peace and Justice Work," *Quaker Studies* 18:1, 76–95.

Ham, S. (1983). "War Is the Most Extreme Luxury: The Voice of Ham Sokhon," Seoul: Seoul Monthly Meeting of Society of Friends.

Ham, S. (1985). *Queen of Suffering: A Spiritual History of Korea*, E. S. Yu, trans., London: Friends World Committee for Consultation.

Hamm, T. D. (1988). *The Transformation of American Quakerism: Orthodox Friends, 1800–1907.* Bloomington: Indiana University Press.

Hamm, T. D. (1994). "Hicksite Quakers and the Antebellum Nonresistance Movement," *Church History* 63: 557–69.

Hamm, T. D. (1997). *Earlham College: A History, 1847–1997*. Bloomington: Indiana University Press.

Hamm, T. D. (2000). "The Hicksite Quaker World, 1875–1900." *Quaker History*, 89 (Fall), 17–41.

Hamm, T. D. (2002). "'A Protest against Protestantism': Hicksite Friends and the Bible in the Nineteenth Century," *Quaker Studie*, 6 (March): 175–94.

Hamm, T. D. (2003). *The Quakers in America*. New York: Columbia University Press, 2003.

Hamm, T. D. (2007). "Earlham College." In J. W. Oliver Jr., et al., *Founded by Friends: The Quaker Heritage of Fifteen American Colleges and Universities*. Lanham, MD: Scarecrow Press, pp. 43–56.

Hamm, T. D. (2009). "Friends United Meeting and its Identity: An Interpretative History," *Quaker Life*, January/February: 10–15.

Hamm, T. D. (2010). *The Road to ESR: or, the Long, Tangled, and Often Confusing Story of How Friends Came to Embrace Theological Education*. Richmond, IN: Earlham School of Religion.

Hamm, T. D. (2013). "Hicksite, Orthodox, and Evangelical Quakerism, 1805–1887." In S. Angell and P. Dandelion, eds., *The Oxford Handbook of Quaker Studies*. Oxford: Oxford University Press, pp. 63–77.

Hamm, T. D., Marconi, M., Salinas, G. K., and Whitman, B. (2000). "The Decline of Quaker Pacifism in the Twentieth Century: Indiana Yearly Meeting of Friends as a Case Study," *Indiana Magazine of History* XCVI (March): 45–71.

Havens, T. R. (1950). *Buddhist and Quaker Experiments with Truth; Quotations and Questions for Group or Individual Study*. Philadelphia: Religious Education Committee, Friends General Conference.

Havens, T. R. (1992). *Mind What Stirs in Your Heart*. Wallingford, PA: Pendle Hill Publications.

Haverford (2016). The York Retreat & Other Asylums. ch. 5 http://qmh.haverford.edu/york/ (accessed September 5, 2016).

Healey, R. R. (2006). *From Quaker to Upper Canadian Faith and Community among Yonge Street Friends, 1801–1850*. Montreal and Kingston: McGill-Queen's University Press.

Healey, R. R. (2011). "'I Am Getting a Considerable of a Canadian They Tell Me': Connected Understandings in the Nineteenth-Century Quaker Atlantic," *Quaker Studies* 15:2, 227–45.

Healey, R. R. (2013). "Quietist Quakerism, c. 1692–1805." In S. Angell and P. Dandelion eds., *The Oxford Handbook of Quaker Studies*. Oxford: Oxford University Press, pp. 47–62.

Healey, R. R. (2015). "From Apocalyptic Prophecy to Tolerable Faithfulness: George Whitehead and a Theology for the Eschaton Deferred." In S. Angell and P. Dandelion, eds., *Early Quakers and Their Theological Thought, 1647–1723*. Cambridge: Cambridge University Press, pp. 273–92.

Healey, R. R. (forthcoming). "Into the Eighteenth Century." In R. C. Allen and R. Moore, eds., *The Quakers 1656–1723: The Evolution of an Alternative Community*. State Park: Pennsylvania State University Press.

Heathman, M. (2013). "Response." *Quaker Theology* 12(2). http://quakertheology.org/QT-23-Friends-Church-Kenya-vs-Homosexuals-Text-and-Responses-Quaker-Theology-Number-23.html (accessed September 20, 2017).

Hedstrom, M. S. (2004). "Rufus Jones and Mysticism for the Masses," *Cross Currents* 54:2, 31–44.

Herman, B. L. (2003). "Eighteenth-Century Quaker Houses in the Delaware Valley and the Aesthetics of Practice." In E. Lapsansky-Werner and A. Verplanck, eds., *Quaker Aesthetics: Reflections on a Quaker Ethic in American Design and Consumption*. Philadelphia: University of Pennsylvania Press, pp. 188–211.

Hicks, E. (1834). *Letters of Elias Hicks. Including also a Few Short Essays, Written on Several Occasions, Mostly Illustrative of His Doctrinal Views*. New York: Isaac T. Hopper.

Higgins, E. F. (2016). "Going Naked as a Sign: Quaker Utopianism and the Alien Other." In J. W. Hood ed., *Quakers and Literature*. Longmeadow, MA; Philadelphia, PA; Windsor, CT: Friends Association For Higher Education, pp. 90–100.

Hilty, H. (1977). *Friends in Cuba*. Richmond, IN: Friends United Press.

Himmelfarb, G. (1997). "The Age of Philanthropy," *Wilson Quarterly* 21 (Spring): 48–55.

Hinds, H. (2015). "Unity and Universality in the Theology of George Fox." In S. Angell and P. Dandelion, eds., *Early Quakers and Their Theological Thought, 1647–1723*. Cambridge: Cambridge University Press, pp. 48–63.

Hinshaw, G. P. (2013). "Five Years Meeting and Friends United Meeting, 1887–2010." In S. Angell and P. Dandelion, eds., *The Oxford Handbook of Quaker Studies*, Oxford: Oxford University Press, pp. 93–107.

Hirst, M. (1972/1923). *The Quakers in Peace and War*. New York: Garland.

"History of Monteverde and the Quakers." (n.d.). www.monteverdetours.com/history-of-monteverde.html (accessed September 20, 2017).

"History of the New Association of Friends." (n.d.). New Association of Friends. www.newassociationoffriends.org/the-origins-of-our-yearly-meeting (accessed December 20, 2015).

Hobby, E. A. (1995). "Handmaids of the Lord and Mothers in Israel: Early Vindications of Quaker Women's Prophecy," in N. T. Corns and D. Loewenstein, eds., *The Emergence of Quaker Writing: Dissenting Literature in Seventeenth-Century England*. London and Portland, Frank Cass and Company, pp. 88–98.

Hodges, J. A., O'Donnell, J. H., and Oliver, J. W. (2003). *Cradles of Conscience: Ohio's Independent Colleges and Universities*. Kent: The Kent State University Press.

Holmes, E. (2007). "Friends University." In J. W. Oliver Jr., et al., *Founded by Friends: The Quaker Heritage of Fifteen American Colleges and Universities*. Lanham, MD: Scarecrow Press, pp. 223–40.

Homan, R. (2013). "Quakers and Visual Culture." In S. Angell and P. Dandelion eds., *The Oxford Handbook of Quaker Studies*. Oxford: Oxford University Press, pp. 492–506.

Hood, A. (1996). "The Material World of Cloth: Production and Use in Eighteenth-Century Rural Pennsylvania," *William and Mary Quarterly* 53:1 (January), 43–56.

Hood, J. W. (2016). "Introduction: Quakers and Literature." In J. W. Hood, ed., *Quakers and Literature*. Longmeadow, MA; Philadelphia, PA; Windsor, CT: Friends Association For Higher Education, pp. 1–10.

Horle, C. W. (1988). *The Quakers and the English Legal System, 1660–1688*. Philadelphia: University of Pennsylvania Press.

Hoshino, K. (2010). "*Why an American Quaker Tutor for the Crown Prince? An Imperial Household's Strategy to Save Emperor Hirohito in MacArthur's Japan.*" Unpublished master's thesis, University of Pittsburgh, Pittsburgh.

Hoskins, L. (1950). Letter to Roy Clampitt, dated April 7. AFSC Archives, General. Philadelphia.

Hume, T. C. (1933). "Prophet of Disillusion," *The Christian Century* 4, January, 18–19.

Hunt, N. (1961). *Two Early Political Associations: The Quakers and the Dissenting Deputies in the Age of Sir Robert Walpole*. Oxford: Clarendon Press.

Imani, A. (2001). "Brand New." *Friends Journal*, January, 20–23.

Indiana Yearly Meeting Minutes–1921. Richmond IN: Indiana Yearly Meeting of Friends, 1921.

Ingle, H. L., ed. (1984). "'A Ball That Has Rolled Beyond Our Reach': The Consequences of Hicksite Reform, 1830, as Seen in an Exchange of Letters," *Delaware History*, 21 (Fall-Winter), 127–37.

Ingle, H. L. (1986). *Quakers in Conflict: The Hicksite Reformation*, Knoxville: University of Tennessee Press.

Ingle, H. L. (1994). *First among Friends: George Fox and the Creation of Quakerism*, Oxford: Oxford University Press.

Ingle, H. L. (2010). "Class Privilege and Schools among Modern Friends," *Friends Journal*, October, 14–15.

Ingle, H. L. (2015). *Nixon's First Cover-Up: The Religious Life of a Quaker President*. Columbia: University of Missouri Press.

Iowa Yearly Meeting Minutes – 1996. Oskaloosa, IA: Iowa Yearly Meeting of the Society of Friends, 1996.

Ishitani, S. (1986). *Looking for Meanings of My A-Bomb Experience in Nagasaki*, Toorak, VIC: The Religious Society of Friends (Quakers) in Australia, Incorporated.

Ishitani, S. (1992). *Self-Giving Love: From an Address on Justice, Peace and the Integrity of Creation*. Philadelphia: The Wider Quaker Fellowship of Friends World Committee, Section of the Americas.

Isichei, E. (1970). *Victorian Quakers*. Oxford: Oxford University Press.

Jahn, G. (1947). "Award Ceremony Speech." /www.nobelprize.org/nobel_prizes/peace/laureates/1947/ (accessed January 11, 2017).

Japan Friends Service Committee. (2016, November 1). *Shisetsu Ichiran* [Facilities List]. Retrieved from www.n-friends.or.jp/sisetu/sisetu

Jasper, D. (2016). *Engaging North Korea: Building toward Dialogue with U.S. Government-Sponsored People-to-People Exchange Programs*. Philadelphia, PA: American Friends Service Committee.

Jenkins, H. (2006). *Convergence Culture*. New York: New York University Press.

Jenkins, H. M. (1901). "Friends in the New Century," *Friends' Intelligencer*, 6.

Jenkins, P. (2007). *The Next Christendom: The Coming of Global Christianity, Revised and Expanded Edition*. New York: Oxford University Press.

Jin, B.-K. (2008). *History of Korean Quakers*. Retrieved from http://blog.daum.net/wadans/7787944

Johns, D. L. (1992). "Everett L. Cattell and a Theology of Christian Missions," *Quaker Religious Thought* 78: 5–17.

Johns, D. L. (2013). "Worship and Sacraments." In S. Angell and P. Dandelion, eds., *Oxford Handbook of Quaker Studies*. Oxford: Oxford University Press, pp. 260–73.

Johnson, O. and Burling, W. (2001). *The Colonial American Stage, 1665–1774: A Documentary Calendar*. Madison, NJ: Fairleigh Dickinson University.

Johnson, T. E. and Savidge, D. (2009). *Performing the Sacred (Engaging Culture): Theology and Theatre in Dialogue*. Grand Rapids, MI: Baker Academic.

Johnson, T.M., Zurlo, G.A., Hickman, A.W., and Crossing, P.F. (2015). "Christianity 2015: Religious Diversity and Personal Contact," *International Bulletin for Missionary Research* 39:28–29.

Jolliff, W. (2007). "Driven by Darkness, Drawn by Light: The Progression of Faith in the Poetry of John Greenleaf Whittier." In J. Leach-Scully and P. Dandelion, eds., *Good and Evil: Quaker Perspectives*. Aldershot: Ashgate, pp. 153–62.

Jones, A. (2010). *Forty Favourite Hymns*. London: Arrow Books.

Jones, C. H. (1946). *American Friends in World Missions*. Elgin, IL: Brethren Publishing House.

Jones, R. M. (1914). *Spiritual Reformers in the 16th & 17th Centuries*. London: Macmillan.

Jones, R. M. (1920). *A Service of Love in War Time: American Friends Relief Work in Europe, 1917–1919*. New York: Macmillan.

Jones, R. M. (1921). *The Later Periods of Quakerism*. London: Macmillan.

Jones, R. M. (1927). *The Faith and Practice of the Quakers*. London, Methuen & Co.

Jones, R. M. (1939). "To Friends in America: A Brief Message from Rufus Jones," *Humanist Friend* 1 (November–December), 7.

Jones, T. C. (1971). *Quaker Understanding of Christ and Authority*. Philadelphia: Faith and Life Movement.

Jones, R. M. (2009/1903). *George Fox, An Autobiography*. Ithaca: Cornell University Press.

Jordan, J. (2016). *FWCC AWPS Questionairre*. Surry Hills, NSW: Religious Society of Friends (Quakers) in Australia.

Jung, J. (2006). *Ham Sokhon's Pacifism and The Reunification of Korea: A Quaker Theology of Peace*. Lewiston, NY: Edwin Mellen Press.

Justice, H. (1905). *Life and Ancestry of Warner Mifflin, Friend – Philanthropist – Patriot*. Philadelphia: Ferris and Leach.

Juterczenka, S. (2007). "Crossing Borders and Negotiating Boundaries: The Seventeenth-Century European Missions and Persecution," *Quaker Studies* 12:1, 39–53.

Kandie, P. (2015). "The Road to Economic Progress Has Been Slow, But Can Be Hastened," *The Star* (Nairobi), June 4. www.the-star.co.ke/news/2015/06/04/the-road-to-economic-progress-has-been-slow-but-can-be-hastened_c1146821 (accessed September 22, 2017)

Kansas Yearly Meeting Minutes–1919 & 1937. Wichita: Kansas Yearly Meeting of Friends.

Kashatus, W. C. (1997). *A Virtuous Education: Penn's Vision for Philadelphia Schools*. Wallingford, PA: Pendle Hill Publications.

Kasimow, H., Keenan, J. P., and Keenan, L. K. (2003). *Beside Still Waters: Jews, Christians, and the Way of the Buddha*. Boston: Wisdom.

Katoh, T. (2002). *Sofu Nitobe Inazo no Koto: 2001-nen Shin Nitobe Inazo Kinen Kouza Kouen [About My Grandfather, Inazo Nitobe: 2001 New Inazo Nitobe Memorial*

Lecture], Tokyo: Kirisuto Yuukai Nihon Nenkai [Japan Yearly Meeting of the Society of Friends].

Keble, J. (1912). *Keble's Lectures on Poetry, 1832–1841*. 2 vols., E. K. Francis (trans.) Oxford: Clarendon Press.

Keiser, R. M. (2014). "Quaker Institutional Identity," *Friends Journal*, April, 22–23.

Keiser, R. M. (2015). "Felt Reality in Practical Living and Innovative Thinking: Mary and Isaac Penington's Journey from Puritan Anguish to Quaker Truth." In Stephen W. Angell and Pink Dandelion, eds., *Early Quakers and Their Theological Thought, 1647–1723*. Cambridge: Cambridge University Press.

Keith, G. (1692). *Some Reasons and Causes of the Late Seperation [sic]*. Philadelphia: William Bradford.

Keith, G. (1696). *An Exact Narrative of the Proceedings at Turners-Hall, the 11th of June 1696*, London.

Keith, G. (1697). *A Second Narrative of the Proceedings at Turners-Hall, the 29th of the Month Called April, 1697*. London: Printed for B. Aylmer.

Keith, G. (1698). *A Third Narrative of the Proceedings at Turner's Hall the Twenty First Day of April 1698*. London: Printed for C. Brome.

Keith, G. (1700). *George Keith's Fourth Narrative of His Proceedings at Turners-Hall Divided into Three Parts*. London: Printed for B. Aylmer.

Keith, G. (1701). *George Keith's Fifth Narrative*. London: Printed for B. Aylmer.

Keith, G. and Budd, T. (1692) *A True Copy of Three Judgments Given Forth by a Party of Men, Called Quakers at Philadelphia, against George Keith and His Friends. With Two Answers to the Said Judgments*. Philadelphia: William Bradford.

Kelley, M. (2016). "QuakerQuaker.org." www.quakerquaker.org, accessed April 5, 2016.

Kelly, T. (1992). *A History of Adult Education in Great Britain from the Middle Ages to the Twentieth Century*. Liverpool: Liverpool University Press.

Kelly, T. R. (1941). *A Testament of Devotion*. New York: Harper and Bros.

Kennedy, T. C. (1996). "Quaker Women and the Pacifist Impulse in Britain, 1900–1920." In Harvey L. Dyck, ed., *The Pacifist Impulse in Historical Perspective*. Toronto: University of Toronto Press, pp. 182–206.

Kennedy, T. C. (2001). *British Quakerism, 1860–1920: The Transformation of a Religious Community*. New York: Oxford University Press.

Kennedy, T. C. (2009). *A History of Southland College: The Society of Friends and Black Education in Arkansas*. Fayetteville: University of Arkansas Press.

Kenworthy, L. S. (1987). *Quaker Education: A Source Book*. Kennett Square, PA: Quaker Publications.

Kershner, J. R. (2013). "The Valiant Sixty-First? John Woolman's Apocalyptic Eschatology and the Restoration of the Lamb's War," *Quaker Studies* 18:1, 23–49.

Kett, A. V. (2014). "'Without the Consumers of Slave Products, There Would Be No Slaves': Quaker Women, Antislavery Activism, and Free-Labor Cotton Dress in the 1850s." In B. Carey and G. Plank, eds., *Quakers and Abolition*. Urbana: University of Illinois Press, pp. 56–72.

Kiley, A. and Fairbanks, J. (2007). "Whittier College." In J. W. Oliver et al., eds., *Founded by Friends: The Quaker Heritage of Fifteen American Colleges and Universities*. Lanham, MD: Scarecrow Press, pp. 187–202.

Kim, S.-S. (1998). "*An Examination of the Life and Legacy of a Korean Quaker, Ham Sokhon (1901–1989): Voice of the People and Pioneer of Religious Pluralism in Twentieth Century Korea*," unpublished doctoral thesis, University of Sheffield.

Kimball, H. and Kimball, B. (2002). *Go into All the World: A Centennial Celebration of Friends in East Africa*. Richmond, IN: Friends United Press.

King, M. (2014). *Quakernomics: An Ethical Capitalism*. London: Anthem Press.

King, S. B. (1994). "Religious Practice: A Zen-Quaker Internal Dialogue," *Buddhist-Christian Studies* 14, 157–62.

King, S. B. (2003a), "The Mommy and the Yogi." In H. Kasimov, J. Keenan, and L. Keenan, *Beside Still Waters: Jews, Christians, and the Way of the Buddha*. Boston: Wisdom, pp. 157–70.

King, S. B. (2003b), *Friends and Other Religions*. Philadelphia: Quaker Books of FGC.

King, S. B. (2005), *Being Benevolence: The Social Ethics of Engaged Buddhism*. Honolulu: University of Hawaii Press.

Kirby, M. W. (1984). *Men of Business and Politics: The Rise and Fall of the Quaker Pease Dynasty of North-East England, 1700–1943*. London: Allen & Unwin.

Kirisuto Yuukai Tokyo Gekkai [Society of Friends Tokyo Monthly Meeting]. (n.d.). *Yuukai to ha* [What Is the Society of Friends?]. Retrieved from http://quaker-tokyo .sakura.ne.jp/yuukaitoha.html

Knitter, P. (2009). *Without Buddha I Could Not Be a Christian*. Oxford: Oneworld.

Knohe, D. "Records of AFSC's Civilian Public Service (April 1941–August 1946)." *SCPC, AFSC/CPS, Document Group 02*.

Kraak, D. E. (2000). "Variations on 'Plainness': Quaker Dress in Eighteenth-Century Philadelphia," *Journal of the Costume Society* 34: 51–63.

Labouchere, R. (1988). *Abiah Darby 1716–1794 of Coalbrookdale: Wife of Abraham Darby II*. York: William Sessions.

Labouchere, R. (1993). *Deborah Darby of Coalbrookdale, 1754–1810: Her Visits to America, Ireland, Scotland, Wales, England and the Channel Isles*. York: William Sessions.

Lacey, P. A. (1998). *Growing into Goodness: Essays on Quaker Education*. Wallingford, PA: Pendle Hill Publications and Friends Council on Education.

Landes, J. (2015). *London Quakers in the Trans-Atlantic World: The Creation of an Early Modern Community*. London: Palgrave.

Lapsansky, E. (2003). "Past Plainness to Present Simplicity: Search for a Quaker Identity." In E. J. Lapsansky and A. A. Verplanck eds., *Quaker Aesthetics: Reflections on a Quaker Ethic in American Design and Consumption*. Philadelphia: University of Pennsylvania Press, pp. 1–15.

Lapsansky, E. (2013). "Plainness and Simplicity." In S. Angell and P. Dandelion, eds., *The Oxford Handbook of Quaker Studies*. Oxford: Oxford University Press, pp. 335–46.

Lapsansky-Werner, E. J. and Verplanck, A. A. (2003). *Quaker Aesthetics: Reflections on a Quaker Ethic in American Design and Consumption*. Philadelphia: University of Pennsylvania Press.

Larsen, T. (2007). "Defining and Locating Evangelicalism." In T. Larsen and D. Treier, eds., *The Cambridge Companion to Evangelical Theology*. Cambridge: Cambridge University Press, pp. 1–14.

Larson, R. (1999). *Daughters of Light: Quaker Women Preaching and Prophesying in the Colonies and Abroad, 1700–1775*, New York: Knopf.

LaVoie, C. (2003). "Quaker Beliefs and Practices and the Eighteenth-Century Development of the Friends Meeting House in the Delaware Valley." In E. Lapsansky-Werner and A. Verplanck, eds., *Quaker Aesthetics: Reflections on a Quaker Ethic in American Design and Consumption*. Philadelphia: University of Pennsylvania Press, pp. 156–87.

"Latin America/America Latina." (n.d.). Evangelical Friends Church International. www.evangelicalfriends.org/latin-america (accessed December 27, 2015).

Lawrence, D. B. (2006). "Life Permeating The Cosmos." In D. Boulton, ed., *Godless for God's Sake: Nontheism in Contemporary Quakerism*. Dent: Dales Historical Monographs, pp. 118–19.

Lawson, T. (1680). *A Mite into the Treasury*. London: Andrew Sowle.

Lee, H. W. (1969). *Friends in Korea*. Wallingford, PA: Pendle Hill. Retrieved from http://blog.daum.net/wadans/7787976

Lee, Y.-G. (1984). "Quakers in Korea," *Friends Journal* 30:2, 9.

Lei, D. (2015). 3 Visions for the Leading Clerk of Taiwan Friends Church Yearly Meeting, Taiwan Friends Church Yearly Meeting. In private communication to S. M. Komashin. March 16.

Lettsom, J. (1784). *The Works of John Fothergill*. London: Charles Dilly.

Levy, B. (1988). *Quakers and the American Family British Settlement in the Delaware Valley*. New York: Oxford University Press.

Lewy, G. (1988). *Peace and Revolution: The Moral Crisis of American Pacifism*, Grand Rapids, MI: William B. Eerdmans Publishing Company.

Lichti, J. I. (2008). *Houses on the Sand? Pacifist Denominations in Nazi Germany*. New York: Peter Lang.

Linton, J. (1984). "Nothing Divides Us," *The Universalist* 12 (July), 16–20.

Linton, J. (1994). *Athwart the Storm: Prose and Poems*, York: William Sessions Limited.

Linton. J. (1979). "Editorial," *The Universalist* 2 (July), 1–4.

"Listen to Them Breathing." (2011) Radio 4. August 30, 2011, 23: 30.

Lippard, George. (1845). *The Quaker City*. Philadelphia: T. B. Peterson.

Lloyd, B. (2007). "The Paradox of Quaker Theatre." *New Theatre Quarterly* 27(3), 219–28.

London Yearly Meeting. (1806). *A Collection of the Epistles from the Yearly Meeting of Friends in London to the Quarterly and Monthly Meetings in Great-Britain, Ireland, and Elsewhere from 1675 to 1805: Being from the First Establishment of That Meeting to the Present Time*. Baltimore: Cole and Hewes.

London Yearly Meeting. (1802). *Extracts from the Minutes and Advices of the Yearly Meeting of Friends, Held in London from Its First Institution, Second Edition*. London: London Yearly Meeting.

London Yearly Meeting. (1818). *Epistles from the Yearly Meeting of Friends Held in London*. London: W. & S. Graves.

London Yearly Meeting. (1822). *Extracts from the Minutes and Advices of the Yearly Meeting of Friends Held in London from Its First Institution*. London: London Yearly Meeting.

London Yearly Meeting. (1834). *Rules of Discipline of the Religious Society of Friends, with Advices: Being Extracts from the Minutes and Epistles of Their Yearly Meeting,*

Held in London, from Its First Institution, Third Edition. London: Darton and Harvey.

London Yearly Meeting. (1858). *Epistles from the Yearly Meeting of Friends Held in London,* vol. 1. London: Edward Marsh.

London Yearly Meeting (1861). *Extracts from the Minutes and Epistles of the Yearly Meeting of the Religious Society of Friends, Held in London, from Its First Institution to the Present Time, Relating to Christian Doctrine, Practice and Discipline.* London: The Yearly Meeting of the Religious Society of Friends.

London Yearly Meeting. (1883). *Book of Christian Discipline of the Religious Society of Friends in Great Britain; Consisting of Extracts on Doctrine, Practice and Church Government, from the Epistles and Other Documents Issued under the Sanction of the Yearly Meeting Held in London from Its First Institution in 1672 to the Year 1883.* London: Samuel Harris.

London Yearly Meeting. (1922). *Christian Life Faith and Thought in the Society of Friends: Being the First Part of the Christian Discipline of the Religious Society of Friends in Great Britain.* London: Central Offices of the Religious Society of Friends.

London Yearly Meeting. (1923). *Extracts from the Minutes and Proceedings of the London Yearly Meeting of Friends.* London.

London Yearly Meeting. (1925). *Christian Practice: Being the Second Part of Christian Discipline in the Religious Society of Friends in Great Britain.* London: Religious Society of Friends.

London Yearly Meeting. (1945). *Proceedings.* London: London Yearly Meeting.

London Yearly Meeting. (1960). *Christian Faith and Practice in the Experience of the Society of Friends.* London: London Yearly Meeting of the Religious Society of Friends.

London Yearly Meeting. (1949–52). *Minutes.* London: London Yearly Meeting.

Loukes, H. (1958). *Friends and Their Children.* London: George G. Harrap.

Loveman, K. (2008). *Reading Fictions, 1660–1740: Deception in English Literary and Political Culture.* Aldershot: Ashgate.

Lowman, E. B. and Barker, A. J. (2015). *Settler: Identity and Colonialism in 21st Century Canada.* Halifax and Winnipeg: Fernwood.

Lucas, E. V. (1893). *Bernard Barton and His Friends: A Record of Quiet Lives.* London: E. Hicks.

Lumb, J. (2012). *Ending Cycles of Violence: Kenyan Quaker Peacemaking Response after the 2007 Election.* Washington, DC: Madera Press.

Lurie, A. (2000). *The Language of Clothes.* New York: Henry Holt.

MacGregor, M. E. (1844). "Amelia Alderson Opie: Worldling and Friend," *Smith College Studies in Modern Languages* 14:1–2 (October 1932–January 1933).

Mack, P. (1992). *Visionary Women: Ecstatic Prophecy in Seventeenth-Century England.* Berkeley: University of California Press.

Mack, P. (2003). "Religion, Feminism, and the Problem of Agency: Reflections on Eighteenth-Century Quakerism," *Signs* 29:1, 149–77.

Magesa, L. (2013). *What Is Not Sacred? African Spirituality.* Maryknoll, NY: Orbis.

Malenge, Z. (2013). "Quakers and Homosexuality Press Statement," *Quaker Theology* 12:2.

Manning, D. (2009). "Accusations of Blasphemy in English Anti-Quaker Polemic, c. 1660–1701," *Quaker Studies* 14:1, 27–56.

Marder, B. L. (1979). *Stewards of the Land: The American Farm School and Modern Greece.* New York: Columbia University Press.

Marder, B. L. (1979). *Stewards of the Land: The American Farm School and Greece in the Twentieth Century.* Macon, GA: Mercer University Press.

Marietta, J. D. (2007). *The Reformation of American Quakerism, 1748–1783.* Philadelphia: University of Pennsylvania Press.

Marsden, G. M. (2006/1980). *Fundamentalism and American Culture,* new ed. Oxford: Oxford University Press.

Martin, C. J. L. (2003). "Tradition Versus Innovation: The Hat, Wilkinson-Story and Keithian Controversies," *Quaker Studies* 8:1, 5–22.

Mason, E. (2004). "'Her Silence Speaks': Keble's Female Heirs." In K. Blair ed., *John Keble in Context.* London: Anthem, pp. 125–42.

Mason, I., and A.I.H. (1938). "Friends in Szechwan," *The West China Missionary News* 40:2, 8–14.

Massey, V. (1999). *The Clouded Quaker Star: James Nayler, 1618–1660.* York: Sessions Book Trust.

Masterman, J. H. B. (1920). *The Story of the English Towns: Birmingham.* London: Society for Promoting Christian Knowledge.

Mbiti, J. S. (1990). *African Religions and Philosophy,* 2nd ed. London: Heinemann.

McDaniel, D. and Julye, V. (2009). *Fit for Freedom, Not for Friendship: Quakers, African Americans, and the Myth of Racial Justice.* Philadelphia: Quaker Press of Friends General Conference.

McGrath, A. E. (2015). "Anglicanism and Pan-Evangelicalism." In M. D. Chapman, S. Clark, and M. Percy, eds., *The Oxford Handbook of Anglican Studies.* Oxford: Oxford University Press, pp. 314–25.

McHenry, I. (2010). "Sparks and Spaces: Lived Experiences in Friends' Schools." *Friends Journal,* October, 11–13.

Mekeel, A. J. (1996). *The Quakers and the American Revolution.* York: Sessions Book Trust.

Meredith, R. G. (1997). *Learning of One Another: The Quaker Encounter with Other Cultures and Religions.* North Hobart, TAS: Backhouse Lecture Committee, The Religious Society of Friends (Quakers) in Australia.

Miles, T. (2006). "Silence Qualified by Parables." In D. Boulton, ed., *Godless for God's Sake: Nontheism in Contemporary Quakerism.* Dent: Dales Historical Monographs, pp. 115–16.

Miller, J. (2005). "'A Suffering People': English Quakers and Their Neighbours c. 1650–c. 1700," *Past & Present* 188:1, 71–103.

Miller, L. McK. (1999). *Witness for Humanity: A Biography of Clarence E. Pickett.* Wallingford, PA: Pendle Hill.

Miller-White, B. (2004). "The Journeyman – The Making of a Muslim Quaker," *Quaker Theology* 10, Spring-Summer, www.quaker.org/quest/issue-10-muslim-white-01.htm

Minear, M. (1987). *Richmond, 1887: A Quaker Drama Unfolds.* Richmond, IN: Friends United Press.

Minutes of the Five Years Meeting of Friends–1902, 1922, 1940 & 1950. Richmond, IN: Five Years Meeting.

Moad, S. (2011). "Is Plain Plain? Or Is Plain a Pain?: Reply by Shane Moad," *QuakerQuaker.* April 19. Retrieved from www.quakerquaker.org/group/ohioym/

forum/topics/is-plain-plain-or-is-plain-a?commentId=2360685%3AComment%
3A46001&xg_source=activity&groupId=2360685%3AGroup%3A14273

Mock, R. (2004). *Loving without Giving In: Christian Responses to Terrorism and Tyranny*. Telford, PA: Cascadia Publishing House.

Mohr, R. (2005). "Quaker History as a Uniting Force? What Canst Thou Say." http://robinmsf.blogspot.com/2005/10/quaker-history-as-uniting-force.html

Mohr, R. (2006a). "A Convergence of Friends," *Friends Journal* 52:10, 1–4.

Mohr, R. (2006b). "Robinopedia: Convergent Friends." http://robinmsf.blogspot.com/2006/01/robinopedia-convergent-friends.html. Accessed January 26, 2016.

Mohr, R. and Daniels, C. W. (2007). "Convergence Among Friends: From the 'Kitchen' to the 'Parlor' – Friends Journal." www.Friendsjournal.org/2007140/. Accessed March 19, 2016.

Moller, G. (2006). "Cold-shouldered by Quaker Silence." In D. Boulton, ed., *Godless for God's Sake: Nontheism in Contemporary Quakerism*. Dent: Dales Historical Monographs, pp. 126–28.

Moore, H. (2012). "Southeast Asia." In M. P. Abbott, M. E. Chijioke, P. Dandelion, and J. W. Oliver Jr., eds., *Historical Dictionary of the Friends (Quakers)*, 2nd ed. London: The Scarecrow Press, Inc., p. 330.

Moore, R. A. (2000). *The Light in Their Consciences: Early Quakers in Britain, 1646–1666*, University Park: Pennsylvania State University Press.

Moore, R. (2005). "Seventeenth Century Published Quaker Verse." *Quaker Studies* 9:1, 5–16.

Moore, R. (2013). "Seventeenth-century Context and Quaker Beginnings." In S. Angell and P. Dandelion, eds., *The Oxford Handbook of Quaker Studies*. Oxford University Press, pp. 13–28.

Morel-Seytoux, H. J. (2006). "God Was on Trial – and the Verdict Was Guilty." In D. Boulton, ed., *Godless for God's Sake: Nontheism in Contemporary Quakerism*. Dent: Dales Historical Monographs, pp. 128–30.

Moretti, F., ed. (2006). *The Novel*, Vol. 1: *History, Geography, and Culture*. Princeton: Princeton University Press.

Nash, G. B. (1986). "The Early Merchants of Philadelphia: The Formation and Disintegration of a Founding Elite." In R. S. Dunn and M. M. Dunn, eds., *The World of William Penn*. Philadelphia: University of Pennsylvania Press, pp. 337–62.

Nash, L. (1979). "Review of A. O. Roberts, Tomorrow Is Growing Old: Stories of the Quakers in Alaska," *Quaker History* 68: 115–116.

Nebraska Yearly Meeting Minutes – 1956, 1957 (1957). Central City, Nebraska: Nebraska: Nebraska Yearly Meeting of Friends.

Neelon, D. (2009). *James Nayler: Revolutionary to Prophet*. Becket, MA: Leadings Press.

Nellis, M. and Waugh, M. (2013). "Quakers and Penal Reform." In S. Angell and P. Dandelion, eds., *The Oxford Handbook of Quaker Studies*. Oxford: Oxford University Press, pp. 377–91.

Nhat Hanh, T. (2006). "The Art of Prayer," April, http://plumvillage.org/thich-nhat-hanh-interviews/thich-nhat-hanh-answers-weekly-magazine/

Niebuhr, R. (1932). *Moral Man and Immoral Society: A Study in Ethics and Politics*. http://media.sabda.org/alkitab-2/ReligionOnline.org%20Books/Niebuhr,%20Reinhold%20-%20Moral%20Man%20and%20Immoral%20Society%20-%20Study%20in.pdf (accessed August 17, 2016).

Nitobe, I. (1908). *Bushido, the Soul of Japan*. Tokyo: Teibi Publications.

Nitobe, I. (1969). "Japan and Its Needs." In *Articles to the "Friends" Review* in Vol. XXIII of *Nitobe Inazo Zenshuu* [The Complete Works of Inazo Nitobe], Tokyo: Kyo Bun Kwan [Christian Literature Society of Japan], pp. 207–9.

Nitobe, I. (1969). "Letter." In *Articles to the "Interchange"* in Vol. XXIII of *Nitobe Inazo Zenshuu* [The Complete Works of Inazo Nitobe], Tokyo: Kyo Bun Kwan [Christian Literature Society of Japan], pp. 246–48.

Nitobe, I. (1969). "Why I Became a Friend." In *Articles to the "Interchange"* in Vol. XXIII of *Nitobe Inazo Zenshuu* [The Complete Works of Inazo Nitobe], Tokyo: Kyo Bun Kwan [Christian Literature Society of Japan], pp. 242–45.

Nitobe, I. (1969). "To Brother Joseph: Sapporo, Feb. 19, 1893." In *Letters to the Elkintons* in Vol. XXIII of *Nitobe Inazo Zenshuu* [The Complete Works of Inazo Nitobe], Tokyo: Kyo Bun Kwan [Christian Literature Society of Japan], pp. 574–76.

Nitobe, I. (1970). "A Japanese View of Quakerism." In *Lectures on Japan: An Outline of the Development of the Japanese People and Their Culture* in Vol. XV of *Nitobe Inazo Zenshuu* [The Complete Works of Inazo Nitobe], Tokyo: Kyo Bun Kwan [Christian Literature Society of Japan], pp. 332–51.

Nixon, E. A. (1985). *A Century of Planting: A History of the American Friends Mission in India*. Canton, OH: Friends Foreign Missionary Society, Evangelical Friends Church – Eastern Region.

Nixon, E. A. (1987). *On the Cutting Edge: The Story of a Surgeon and His Family Who Served Country Folk to Kings in Four Nations*. Canton, OH: The Barclay Press.

Niyonzima, D. and Fendall, L. (2001). *Unlocking Horns: Reconciliation in Burundi*. Newberg, OR: Barclay Press.

Nordau, M. (1993). *Degeneration*. Lincoln: University of Nebraska Press.

Northwest Yearly Meeting of Friends Church 2012, *Faith and Practice: A Book of Christian Discipline*, http://nwfriends.org/faith-practice/ (accessed 28 July 2016).

Norway (1865). Census. Digitalarkivet.no/census/search/1865 (accessed September 27, 2017).

Nugent, P. J. (2012). "Response to Papers on Theism (Just a Little) and Non-Theism (Much More)," *Quaker Religious Thought* 118: 51–56.

O'Donnell, E. A. (2013). "Quakers and Education." In S. Angell and P. Dandelion, eds., *The Oxford Handbook of Quaker Studies*. Oxford: Oxford University Press, pp. 405–19.

Oliver, J. W., Jr. (2007). "Malone College." In J. W. Oliver Jr. et al., eds., *Founded by Friends: The Quaker heritage of Fifteen American Colleges and Universities*. Lanham, MD: Scarecrow Press, pp. 203–22.

Oliver, J. W., Jr., Cherry, C. L., and Cherry, C., eds. (2007). *Founded by Friends: The Quaker heritage of Fifteen American Colleges and Universities*. Lanham, MD: Scarecrow Press.

"On Fiction Reading" (1882). In *A Series of Tracts on Moral and Religious Subjects*. 3 vols. Philadelphia: The Tract Association of Friends, vol. 3, No. 134.

Ootsu, M. (2012). *Kirisuto Yuukai Nihon Nenkai to Nitobe Inazo: 2012-nen Shin Nitobe Inazo Kinen Kouza Kouen [Japan Yearly Meeting of the Society of Friends and Inazo Nitobe: 2012 New Inazo Nitobe Memorial Lecture]*. Tokyo: Kirisuto Yuukai Nihon Nenkai [Japan Yearly Meeting of the Society of Friends].

Opie, A. (1825). *Illustrations of Lying, in All Its Branches*. London: Longman, Hurst, Rees, Orme, Brown and Green.

Opie, A., King, S., and Pierce, J. B. (2003). *Father and Daughter with Dangers of Coquetry*. Peterborough, ONT: Broadview Press.

Oppenheimer, E. A. (2009). *Writing Cheerfully on the Web: A Quaker Blog*. Philadelphia: Quaker Books of Friends General Conference.

Oregon Yearly Meeting Minutes–1919, 1920 & 1926. Newberg, OR: Friends Church of Oregon Yearly Meeting.

O'Reilley, M. R. (2000). *The Barn at the End of the World: The Apprenticeship of a Quaker, Buddhist Shepherd*. Minneapolis: Milkweed Editions.

Orobator, A. E. (2008). *Theology Brewed in an African Pot*. Maryknoll, NY: Orbis Press.

Oshiro, G. (1995). "The End: 1929–1933." In J. F. Howes, ed., *Nitobe Inazô: Japan's Bridge Across the Pacific*. Boulder: Westview Press, Inc., pp. 253–78.

Otomodachi Hoikuen [Friends Nursery School] (2015). *Ichinen no Gyouji* [Annual Events]. Retrieved from www.otomodachi-hoikuen.jp/event.html

Otto, H. (1974). "Das Quakertum in Deutschland." In Richenda C. Scott, ed., *Die Quäker*. Stuttgart: Evangelisches Verlagswerk

Our Mission. www.eqat.org/our_mission, accessed September 5, 2016.

Painter, L. K. (1966). *The Hill of Vision: The Story of the Quaker Movement in East Africa 1902–1965*. Kaimosi, Kenya: East Africa Yearly Meeting.

Parsons, P. S. (2009). "Why I Like the Idea of Convergence." In E. A. Oppenheimer, ed., *Writing Cheerfully on the Web: A Quaker Blog*. Philadelphia: Quaker Books of Friends General Conference, pp. 136–39.

Pasquali, V. (2015). "The Poorest Countries in the World." *Global Finance Magazine*. www.gfmag.com/global-data/economic-data/the-poorest-countries-in-the-world?page=12 (accessed December 1, 2016).

Peace Testimony Subgroup of QPS Peace Committee 1993, *The Quaker Peace Testimony: A Workbook for Individuals and Groups*, London: Communications and Fundraising Department of the Religious Society of Friends.

Penn, W. (1726). *A Collection of the Works of William Penn*. 2 vols. London: J. Sowle.

Penn, W. (1682). *No Cross, No Crown: A Discourse Showing the Nature and Discipline of the Holy Cross of Christ*. London: Andrew Sowle.

Pestana, C. G. (1993). "The Quaker Executions as Myth and History," *Journal of American History* 80: 2, 441–69.

Pestana, C. G. (2015). "The Conventionality of the Notorious John Perrot." In S. Angell and P. Dandelion, eds., *Early Quakers and Their Theological Thought, 1647–1723*. Cambridge: Cambridge University Press, pp. 173–89.

Peters, K. (1995). "Patterns of Quaker Authorship, 1652-1656." In T. N. Corns and D. Loewenstein, eds., *The Emergence of Quaker Writing: Dissenting Literature in Seventeenth Century England*. London: Frank Cass, pp. 6–24.

Peters, K. (2005). *Print Culture and the Early Quakers*. Cambridge: Cambridge University Press.

Peterson, D. F. (2007). "Haverford College." In J. W. Oliver Jr. et al., *Founded by Friends: The Quaker Heritage of Fifteen American Colleges and Universities*. Lanham, MD: Scarecrow Press, pp. 1–20.

Philadelphia Yearly Meeting (Hicksite). *Minutes, 1830*.

Phylis, L. (2010). "Cultural Activities." In A. Conti, C. Curtis, C. W. Daniels et al., eds., *Spirit Rising: Young Quaker Voices*. Philadelphia: Quaker Press of Friends General Conference, p. 6.

Pickard, D.G. (2014). "Friends in Central America," *Quaker Religious Thought* 123:4, 125–29.

Pickett, C. E. (1953). *For More than Bread: An Autobiographical Account of Twenty-Two Years' Work with the American Friends Service Committee.* Boston: Little, Brown and Company.

"Plain Quakers" websites: https://plainquakers.org/ (accessed August 20, 2016); www .quakerjane.com/spirit.friends/plain_dress-.html (accessed August 20, 2016).

Plank, G. G. (2012). *John Woolman's Path to the Peaceable Kingdom a Quaker in the British Empire.* Philadelphia: University of Pennsylvania Press.

Pratt, D. H. (1985). *English Quakers and the First Industrial Revolution: A Study of the Quaker Community in Four Industrial Counties, Lancashire, York, Warwick, and Gloucester, 1750–1830.* New York: Garland.

Preckel, C. (2012). "Healing the People and the Princes: Hospitals, Hakīms and Doctors in Bhopal." In Vol. VII of F. Speziale, ed., *Hospitals in Iran and India, 1500-1950s.* Leiden, The Netherlands: Brill, pp. 191–214.

Preston, J. and Joffe, P. (2016). "Truth and Reconciliation: The Importance of Examining Genocide," *Quaker Concern* 42: 1, 1, 6.

Price, J. M. (1986). "The Great Quaker Business Families of Eighteenth-Century London: The Rise and Fall of a Sectarian Patriciate." In R. S. Dunn and M. M. Dunn, eds., *The World of William Penn.* Philadelphia: University of Pennsylvania Press, pp. 363–99.

Punshon, J. (1984). *Portrait in Grey: A Short History of the Quakers,* London: Quaker Home Service.

Punshon, J. (1996). "Some Reflections on Quaker and the Evangelical Spirit." In P. Anderson and H. Macy, eds., *Truth's Bright Embrace: Essays and Poems in Honor of Arthur O. Roberts,* Newberg, OR: George Fox University Press, pp. 205–20.

Punshon, J. (2001). *Reasons for Hope: The Faith and Future of the Friends Church.* Richmond, IN: Friends United Press.

Putnam, R. D. and Campbell, D. E. (2010). *American Grace: How Religion Divides and Unites Us.* New York: Simon and Schuster.

Pyper, H. S. (2015). "Robert Barclay: The Art of Apologetics." In S. Angell and P. Dandelion, eds., *Early Quakers and Their Theological Thought, 1647–1723.* Cambridge: Cambridge University Press, pp. 207–23.

Quaker Earthcare Vision & Witness, www.quakerearthcare.org/article/quaker-earth care-vision-witness (accessed September 5, 2016).

Quaker Faith and Practice, 2nd ed. (1999). The Yearly Meeting of the Religious Society of Friends (Quakers) in Britain, London.

Quaker Faith and Practice: The Book of Christian Discipline of the Yearly Meeting of the Religious Society of Friends (Quakers) in Britain (2013) London: Yearly Meeting of the Religious Society of Friends Quakers in Britain.

Quaker Peace & Legislation Committee. (2014). *QPLC Discussion Paper: Indonesia and Australia,* Canberra, ACT: Religious Society of Friends (Quakers) in Australia, Inc.

Quaker Voluntary Service. (2016). "QVS Fellows." www.quakervoluntaryservice.org/ current-fellows/ (Accessed March 10, 2016).

Quakers in the World. website: www.quakersintheworld.org/quakers-in-action/134 (accessed August 12, 2016).

Quakers in the World. (n.d.). "Quakers in Jamaica and Barbados." http://www.quaker sintheworld.org/quakers-in-action/268/Quakers-in-Jamaica-and-Barbados (accessed September 20, 2017).

Quaker Peace & Legislation Committee. (2014). *QPLC Discussion Paper: Indonesia and Australia*, Canberra, ACT: Religious Society of Friends (Quakers) in Australia, Inc.

QUNO (Quaker United Nations Office). (n.d.). "About Us" www.quno.org/about (accessed September 5, 2016).

Rae, J. (1970). *Conscience & Politics: The British Government and the Conscientious Objector to Military Service 1916~1919*, London: Oxford University Press.

Rae, J. T. (1903). *The Temperance Record*, vol. 1, new series. London: Richard J. James.

Raistrick, A. (1953). *Dynasty of Iron Founders: The Darbys and Coalbrookdale*. New York: Longmans, Green.

Rasmussen, A. M. B. (1995). *A History of the Quaker Movement in Africa*. New York: I. B. Tauris.

Rathborne, S. G. (1902–3). *Old Broadbrim Weekly*. New York: Street & Smith.

Reay, B. (1985). *The Quakers and the English Revolution*. New York: St. Martin's Press.

Repoley, C. (2013). "Coming Alive: Discerning the Next Chapter of Quaker Service – Friends Journal," December. www.friendsjournal.org/coming-alive-discerning-next-chapter-quaker-service/ (accessed September 16, 2016).

Repoley, C. (2016). Phone Interview with Greg Woods.

Report of Fourth Triennial Conference of Evangelical Friends. (1956). Pp. 44–48. Archive located at George Fox University in Arthur Roberts' Papers, Box #2, folder 2.1.1. Newberg, Oregon.

Reynolds, D. (2016). "Quaker Literature: Is There Such a Thing?" In J. W. Hood, ed., *Quakers and Literature*. Longmeadow, MA; Philadelphia, PA; Windsor, CT: Friends Association For Higher Education, pp. 80–89.

Rhodewalt, S. (2012). Request More about These Topics from India. Nov. 5. Retrieved from http://indiafriendsworkinggroup.blogspot.com/2012/11/request-more-about-these-topics-from.html

Rhodewalt, S. (2012). "All Is Well." Oct. 28. Retrieved from http://indiafriendswor kinggroup.blogspot.com/2012/10/all-is-well.html

Riggs, A. K. (2011). "Is Warsaw Close Enough? Reading Yoder's *Nonviolence–A Brief History* in Kenya," *Conrad Grebel Review* 29:3, 10–21.

Riggs, A. K. (2014). "Friends in Eastern Africa," *Quaker Religious Thought* 123–24 (November): 85–92.

Robbins, K. (1979). *John Bright*. London: Routledge & Kegan Paul.

Roberts, A. O. (1975). *The Association of Evangelical Friends: A Story of Quaker Renewal in the Twentieth Century*. Newberg, OR: Barclay Press.

Roberts, A. O. (1978). *Tomorrow Is Growing Old: Stories of the Quakers in Alaska*. Newberg, OR: Barclay Press.

Roberts, A. O. (2013) "Evangelical Quakers, 1887–2010." In S. Angell and P. Dandelion, eds., *Oxford Handbook of Quaker Studies*. Oxford: Oxford University Press, pp. 108–25.

Roberts, H. (2004). "Friends in Business: Researching the History of Quaker Involvement in Industry and Commerce," *Quaker Studies* 8:2, 172–93.

Roberts, T. (n.d.). "Western Yearly Meeting Statistics–Comprehensive."

Robinson, G. (1715). *A Brief History of the Voyage of Katherine Evans and Sarah Cheevers*. London: J. Sowle.

Robinson, W. (1891). *Friends of a Half Century: Fifty Memorials with Portraits of Members of the Society of Friends, 1840–1890*, London: Edward Hicks.

Rogers, P. (2011). "Bradford Peace Studies, on Global Conflict and Sustainable Security Part 1" www.youtube.com/watch?v=FzwN7pwn1bY (accessed February 16, 2016).

Ross, R. (2006). *Returning to the Teachings: Exploring Aboriginal Justice*, Toronto, ONT: Penguin Group (Canada).

Ross, I. (1996). *Margaret Fell, Mother of Quakerism*, 3rd edn. York: Sessions Book Trust.

Rowntree Society, "Friends Ambulance Unit." Available from The Rowntree Society www.rowntreesociety.org.uk/friends-ambulance-unit/ (accessed July 27, 2016).

Rowntree, J. S. (1859). *Quakerism Past and Present: Being an Inquiry into the Causes of its Decline in Great Britain and Ireland*. London: Smith, Elder and Co.

Ruth, S. (2011). "Making the Quaker Connection," *The Friend* [Online] Available at *https://thefriend.org/article/making-the-quaker-connection* (accessed November 30, 2016).

Sanneh, L. (2008). *Disciples of All Nations: Pillars of World Christianity*. New York: Oxford University Press.

Santos, H. (1991). "A Bridge of Love/Un Puente De Amor." Keynote Address, New England Yearly Meeting.

Sarkar, D. K. (2013). *Testimony – D K*, Kolkata: Evangelical Friends Mission.

Sarkar, D.K. (2015a). "Malda." [Newletter].

Sarkar, D.K. (2015b). Questions to D. K. Sarkar.[Email].

Sarkar, D.K. (2015c). "Emmanuel Hostel." [Newsletter].

Sarkar, D.K. (2015d). "The Story of Gazole Child Development Center." [Newsletter].

Satô, M. (1995). "Journalism: The Last Bridge." In J. F. Howes, ed., *Nitobe Inazô: Japan's Bridge Across the Pacific*, Boulder: Westview Press, Inc., pp. 217–236.

Scattergood Friends School. (2016). *The History of Scattergood Friends School*. www .scattergood.org/our-school/quaker-values (accessed August 30, 2016)

Schellenberg J. and Switzer, D. M. (1998), "Interview with Joan Slonczewski," in *Challenging Destiny: New Fantasy and Science Fiction*. www.challengingdestiny .com/interviews/slonczewski.htm

Schmidt, J. M. (1991). *Souls or the Social Order*. Brooklyn, NY: Carlson Publishing Inc.

Schmitt, H. A. (1997). *Quakers and Nazis: Inner Light in Outer Darkness*. Columbia: University of Missouri Press.

SCPC Conscientious Objection/Objectors (1970–1999), Box 7, Folder Subject File: Conscientious Objection: Foreign Sources, 1970–1979).

Selleck, G. A. (1976). *Quakers in Boston, 1656–1964: Three Centuries of Friends in Boston and Cambridge*. Cambridge, MA: Friends Meeting at Cambridge.

Selleck, L. (1995). *Gentle Invaders: Quaker Women Educators and Racial Issues during the Civil War and Reconstruction*. Richmond. IN: Friends United Press.

Shapiro, M. K. (2006). "God – 'The Guru I Do Not Want to Worship.'" In D. Boulton, ed., *Godless for God's Sake: Nontheism in Contemporary Quakerism*. Dent: Dales Historical Monographs, pp. 132–33.

Sharpless, E. F. (1944). *Quakerism in Japan: A Brief Account of the Origins and Development of the Religious Society of Friends in Japan*. Philadelphia: Friends World Committee for Consultation.

Shelley, P. S. (1840). *Essays, Letters from Abroad, Translations and Fragments*. ed. by M. Shelley, London: Edward Moxon.

Shilston, T. G. (2012). "Thomas Venner: Fifth Monarchist or Maverick?" *Social History* 37: 1, 55–64.

Silliman, Norma. (2016). Phone Interview with Greg Woods.

Simiyu, O. K. (2004). "Convicted and Set Afire." In M. P. Abbott and P. Senger Parsons, eds., *Walk Worthy of Your Calling: Quakers and the Travelling Ministry*. Richmond, IN: Friends United Press, pp. 45–58.

Slonczweski, J. (1986). *A Door into Ocean*. London: Women's Press.

Smith, B. (2007). "The Testimony of Martha Simmonds, Quaker," *Quaker Studies* 12:1, 26–38.

Smith, S. (2003). *A Quaker in the Zendo*. Wallingford, PA: Pendle Hill.

Socknat, T. P. (1987). *Witness Against War: Pacifism in Canada 1900–1945*. Toronto: University of Toronto Press.

Soderlund, J. R. (1985). *Quakers & Slavery: A Divided Spirit*. Princeton, NJ: Princeton University Press.

Southern, A. (2011). "The Rowntree History Series and the Growth of Liberal Quakerism," *Quaker Studies* 16:1 (September), 7–73.

Spear, T. (2003). "Neo-traditionalism and the Limits of Invention in British Colonial Africa," *Journal of African History* 44:3–27.

Specht, N. J. (2010). "'Being a Peaceable Man, I Have Suffered Much Persecution': The American Revolution and Its Effects on Quaker Religious Identity," *Quaker History* 99: 2, 37–48.

Spencer, C. D. (2007). *Holiness, the Soul of Quakerism: An Historical Analysis of the Theology of Holiness in the Quaker Tradition*. Eugene, OR: Wipf & Stock.

Spencer, C. D. (2011). "Report from Northwest Yearly Meeting, July 2011," Earlham School of Religion. http://esrquaker.blogspot.com/2011/08/report-from-northwest-yearly-meeting.html (accessed January 18, 2016).

Spencer, C. D. (2013) "Learning and Leading: Meet Hannah Whitall Smith, a 'Convergent Friend' at the Turn of the Nineteenth Century." Earlham School of Religion. http://esrquaker.blogspot.com/2013/10/meet-hannah-whitall-smith-convergent.html (accessed March 15, 2016).

Spencer, C. D. (2015). "The Man Who 'Set Himself as a Sign': James Nayler's Incarnational Theology." In S. Angell and P. Dandelion, eds., *Early Quakers and Their Theological Thought, 1647–1723*. Cambridge: Cambridge University Press, 64–82.

Stansell, R. (2009). *Missions by the Spirit: Learning from Quaker Examples*. Newberg, OR: Barclay Press.

Stansell, R. (2014). "Friends in India and Asia," *Quaker Religious Thought* 123:11, 107–14.

Steere, D. V. (1943). *On Beginning from Within / On Listening to Another*. New York: Harper & Row.

Steere, D. V. (1948). *Doors into Life: Through Five Devotional Classics*. New York: Harper.

Steere, D. V. (1967). *On Being Present Where You Are*. Wallingford, PA: Pendle Hill Publications.

Steere, D. V. (1973). *Mutual Irradiation*. Wallingford, PA: Pendle Hill.

Stenographer's report of the Five Years Meeting of the Society of Friends in America. (1912). Archive located at Earlham College, Richmond, Indiana.

Stephen, C. (1891). *Quaker Strongholds.* 3rd ed. London: E. Hicks Jr.

Stern, T. N. (1992). "Jesse Holmes, liberal Quaker," *Friends Journal*, June, 21–23.

Stieren, C. (1998). *Crossing Borders: Canadian Friends and International Affairs, 1931–1997*, Canadian Quaker Pamphlet Series no 47. Argenta, BC: Argenta Friends Press.

Stowe, H. B. (1852). *Uncle Tom's Cabin.* London: J. Cassell.

Stubbs, T. (1659). "A Declaration of Life and Power in Me." In *Certain Papers Given Forth in the Spirit of Truth which Witness against the Wisdom of the World and Unrighteousness of Men*, London: [no publisher].

Swayne, K. (1986). "Universalism or Latitudinarianism," *Universalist Friends* 7 (Fall), 8–11.

Swayne, K. (1987). "A Comment on Daniel Seeger's Unity and Diversity in Our Spiritual Family," *Universalist Friends* 8 (Spring), 8–11.

Swennerfelt, R. (2016). *Rising to the Challenge: The Transition Movement and People of Faith*, Albany, CA: QIF Focus Books.

Swennerfelt, R. (n.d.). *Why Transition.* Retrieved September 5, 2016, from Quakers in Transition. https://quakersintransition.wordpress.com/why-transition/

Swift, D. E. (1962). *Joseph John Gurney: Banker, Reformer, & Quaker.* Middleton: Wesleyan University Press.

Sykes, M. (1997). *An Indian Tapestry: Quaker Threads in the History of India, Pakistan & Bangladesh: From the Seventeenth Century to Independence*, G. Carnall, ed., York, UK: Sessions Book Trust.

Szi, C. (2015). "Throughout the Years: Race at Haverford College." http://wrprchristi naszi.weebly.com/early-years.html (accessed April 21, 2016).

Taber, F. I. (2010). *The Witness of Conservative Friends: William and Frances Taber.* Philadelphia: Wider Quaker Fellowship.

Taber, W. P. (1984). *The Prophetic Stream.* Wallingford, PA: Pendle Hill Publications.

Taber, W. P. (1992), *Four Doors to Meeting for Worship.* Wallingford, PA: Pendle Hill Publications.

Taber, W. P., and Birkel, M. L. (2010). *The Mind of Christ: Bill Taber on Meeting for Business.* Wallingford, PA: Pendle Hill Publications.

Takahashi, M. (1995). *Nisshin Sensou to Furendo Kyoukai* [The First Sino-Japanese War and the Friends Church]. *Touhou Gakuen Daigaku Tanki Daigaku-Bu Kiyou [Bulletin of Toho Gakuen College of Drama and Music]*, 13, 11–22.

Tamang, R., and Tamang, P. (2016). News from Bhutan: The Land of the Thunder Dragon. August.

Taylor, J. (1647). *The World Turn'd Upside Down, or, A Briefe Description of the Ridiculous Fashions of These Distracted Times.* London: Printed for John Smith.

Tennent, T. (2007). *Theology in the Context of World Christianity: How the Global Church Is Influencing the Way We Think About and Discuss Theology.* Grand Rapids, MI: Zondervan.

Terrell, C. N. (2006). "The Energy That Was Present in the Beginning." In D. Boulton, ed., *Godless for God's Sake: Nontheism in Contemporary Quakerism.* Dent: Dales Historical Monographs, p. 114.

The Bay Psalm Book: Being a Fascimile Reprint of the First Edition, Printed by Stephen Daye at Cambridge in New England (2011/1640). Carlisle, MA: Applewood Books.

The Book of Discipline of Ohio Yearly Meeting of the Religious Society of Friends [Online] Available at www.ohioyearlymeeting.org/wp-content/uploads/2011/09/OYMDiscipline-2014.pdf (accessed November 2, 2016).

The Humanist Society, http://thehumanistsociety.org/about/history/

The Old Discipline: Nineteenth-Century Friends' Disciplines in America. (1999). Glenside, PA: Quaker Heritage Press.

The Revised Discipline Approved by the Yearly Meeting of Friends, held in Baltimore, for the Western-Shore of Maryland and the Adjacent Parts of Pennsylvania and Virginia, in the Year One Thousand Seven Hundred and Ninety-Three. (1794). https://quod.lib.umich.edu/e/evans/N20594.0001.001?view=toc

Thirsk, J. (1990). *Chapters from the Agrarian History of England and Wales, 1500–1750.* Cambridge: Cambridge University Press.

Thomas, D. (1907). *In The Witness and Training School News* 1:2, 7.

Thomas, H. (2014). "Friends in South America," In *Quaker Religious Thought*, 123–124, 115–24.

Thomas, N., ed. (2012). *De encuentro a ministerio: la vida y fe de los Amigos latinoamericanos.* La Paz, Bolivia: CALA.

Thomson, M. (2006). *Toward a Culture of Peace: Can We Afford to Pay the Price.* Argenta, BC: Argenta Friends Press.

Tienou, T. (2007). "Evangelical Theology in African Contexts." In T. Larsen and D. Treier, eds., *The Cambridge Companion to Evangelical Theology.* Cambridge: Cambridge University Press, pp. 213–24.

Titus, R. (2016). *Goals*, Bhopal, MP: Bhopal Yearly Meeting.

"To Men and Women of Goodwill in the British Empire." 1914, *The Friend*, Vol. LXXIV, no. 33, p. 599.

Toda, T. (2003). *Firaderufia· Furendo to Nihon Nenkai 1900 ~ 1947* [Philadelphia Friends and Japan Yearly Meeting 1900–1947]. *Yamanashi Kenritsu Joshi Tanki Daigaku Kiyou* [Bulletin of Yamanashi Prefectural Junior College for Women]. Pp. 11–22, 36.

Toda, T. (2014). *Firaderufia ni Okeru Shiba Shiro – Nichibei Kouryuu no Kiten toshite –* [Shiba Shiro as a Hub of the Earliest Interactions between Japan and Philadelphia]. *Yamanashi Kokusai Kenkyuu (Kokusai Seisaku Gakubu Kiyou) [Yamanashi Glocal Policy Research (Glocal Policy Faculty Bulletin)].* Pp. 9, 60–69.

Tolles, F. B. (1948/1963). *Meeting House and Counting House: The Quaker Merchants of Colonial Philadelphia, 1682–1763.* Chapel Hill: University of North Carolina Press.

Trevett, C. (2000). *Quaker Women Prophets in England and Wales, 1650–1700.* Lewiston, NY: Edwin Mellen Press.

Trueblood, D. E. (1966) *The People Called Quakers.* New York: Harper & Row.

Trueblood, D. E. (1974). *While It Is Day: An Autobiography.* New York: Harper and Row.

Truth and Reconciliation Commission (TRC) of Canada. (2015). *Final Report of the Truth and Reconciliation Commission of Canada, Vol. I: Summary: Honouring the Truth, Reconciling for the Future.* Toronto: James Lorimer & Company Ltd.

Tyrrell, A. (1987). *Joseph Sturge and the Moral Radical Party in Early Victorian Britain.* London: Christopher Helm.

Underiner, T. (2012). "Plain Speech Acts: Reading Quakerism with Theatre and Performance Studies." in L. Gharavi, ed., *Religion, Theatre, and Performance: Acts of Faith*. New York and London: Routledge, pp. 100–14.

Union Bible College Catalog 2016–2018 [Online]. Available at https://ubca.org/aca demics/catalog/ (accessed November 2, 2016).

UNDRIP (United Nations Declaration on the Rights of Indigenous Peoples) (2007). United Nations. www.un.org/development/desa/indigenouspeoples/declaration-on-the-rights-of-indigenous-peoples.html (accessed September 18, 2017).

Valenze, D. (2006). *The Social Life of Money in the English Past*. Cambridge: Cambridge University Press.

Vann, R. T. (1969). "Nurture and Conversion in the Early Quaker Family," *Journal of Marriage and Family* 31:4, 639–43.

Vernon, S. (2000). *In-transit: The Story of a Journey*. Belize City: Angelus Press.

Vining, E. G. (1955). *The Virginia Exiles*. Philadelphia and New York: J. B. Lippincott Co.

Vining, E. G. (1960). "Penn and the Poets." In A. Brinton, ed., *Then and Now: Quaker Essays: Historical and Contemporary by Friends of Henry Joel Cadbury*. Freeport, NJ: Books for Libraries Press, pp. 95–118.

Wafula, R. J. (2016). "From Mud Huts to Yearly Meetings: Africa Has the World's Largest Concentration of Quakers Today," *Christian History* 117: 36.

Wahl, A. J. (1979). *Jesse Herman Holmes, 1864–1962: A Quaker's Affirmation for Man*. Richmond, IN: Friends United Press.

Walker, C. C., ed. (1968). *Quakers and the Draft: What Friends Are Saying and Doing about Selective Service*. Philadelphia: Friends Coordinating Committee on Peace.

Walls, A. (1996). *The Missionary Movement in Christian History: Studies in the Transmission of Faith*. Maryknoll, NY: Orbis Books.

Walton, G. A. (1917). "Wartime Thought For Quakers," *Friends' Intelligencer* 74:21, 324.

Walvin, J. (1997). *The Quakers: Money and Morals*. London: John Murray.

Walvin, J. (2014). "The Slave Trade, Quakers, and British Abolition." In Brycchan Carey and Geoffrey Plank, eds., *Quakers and Abolition*. Urbana: University of Illinois Press, pp. 165–79.

Warren, R. L. (2002). *Journey Through Skepticism*. Wallingford, PA: Pendle Hill Publications.

Watson, J. R. (1997). *The English Hymn: A Critical and Historical Study*. Oxford: Clarendon Press.

Watts, M. R. (2015). *The Dissenters*, Vol. III: *The Crisis and Conscience of Nonconformity*. Oxford: Oxford University Press.

Weaver, H. D., Jr., Kriese, P., and Angell, S. W. (2011). *Black Fire: African American Quakers on Spirituality and Human Rights*. Philadelphia: Quaker Press of Friends General Conference.

Webb, S. (2013). "Poetry through Quaker Eyes," *The Friends Quarterly* 40:3, 10–22.

Weddle, M. B. (2001). *Walking in the Way of Peace: Quaker Pacifism in the Seventeenth Century*. Oxford: Oxford University Press.

Welling, J. S. (2013) "Mission." In S. Angell and P. Dandelion, eds., *The Oxford Handbook of Quaker Studies*. Oxford: Oxford University Press, pp. 306–20.

West, J. (2003/1945). *The Friendly Persuasion*. San Diego, CA: Harvest Books.

Western Yearly Meeting Minute–1922. (1922). Plainfield, IN: Western Yearly Meeting of Friends Church.

Western Yearly Meeting. (1881). *The Discipline of the Society of Friends of Western Yearly Meeting*. Richmond, IN: Nicholson and Bros., 1881.

Western Yearly Meeting. (2016). "2015 State of Society Report." In *Western Yearly Meeting of Friends Church: Resource & Minute Book, 2016*. Plainfield, IN: Western Yearly Meeting of Friends Church.

Whitehead, G. (1830/1693). *The Christian Doctrine and Society of People Called Quakers Cleared &c.* In S. Tuke, ed., *Memoirs of George Whitehead*. York: W. Alexander and Son, Vol. 2, pp. 331–56.

Whitehead, G. (1697). *An Antidote against the Venome of The Snake in the Grass*. London: Printed for Thomas Northcott.

Whittier, J. G. (1873). *The Complete Poetical Works of John Greenleaf Whittier*. Boston: James R. Osgood and Company.

"Who We Are," (n.d.). Long Beach Friends Church. www.lbfc.org/about/ (accessed December 30, 2015).

Wider Quaker Fellowship. (2013) *From Encounter to Ministry: The Life and Faith of Latin American Friends*. Philadelphia: Friends World Committee for Consultation.

Willcuts, J. L. (1963). "Evangelical Friends Alliance," *Concern*, 4: 4 October, 5–8.

Williams, J. H., and Terrell, C. D. (1897). Friends' Mission Work in India. In London Yearly Meeting (Society of Friends), ed., *Report of the Proceedings of the Conference at Darlington on Foreign Missions Held, by Direction of London Yearly Meeting, 1896*, London: West, Newman and Co., pp. 111–17.

Williams, W. R. (2006). *The Rich Heritage of Quakerism*, 2nd ed. Newberg, OR: Barclay Press.

Winchester, A. J. L. (1991). "Ministers, Merchants and Migrants: Cumberland Friends and North America in the Eighteenth Century," *Quaker History* 80:2, 85–99.

Wolfson Centre for Archival Research. (n.d.). MS466/1/1/10/1/5, Elizabeth Cadbury, speech at the Manchester Conference (Society of Friends).

Woolman, J. (1883/1774). *A Journal of John Woolman*. Philadelphia: Friends Books.

Worrall, A. J. (1980). *Quakers in the Colonial Northeast*. Hanover, NH: University Press of New England.

Wright, L. (1932). *The Literary Life of the Early Friends, 1650–1725*. New York: Columbia University Press.

Wrigley, E. A. and Schofield, R. (1989). *The Population History of England, 1541–1871: A Reconstruction*. Cambridge: Cambridge University Press.

Yamaguchi, Y. (2015). "A Review of the Origin of Evangelicals in Japan upon the 70th Anniversary of the End of World War II," *Japan Update* 70:1–2. Autumn.

Yarrow C. H. M. (1978). *Quaker Experiences in International Conciliation*. New Haven, CT: Yale University Press.

Zarembka, D. (2015). "Dialoguing with Terrorists," *Friends Journal* 61:7, 21–22, 49.

Zaru, J. (2008). *Occupied with Nonviolence: A Palestinian Woman Speaks*. Minneapolis, MN: Fortress Press.

Zug, James. (2009). "The Color of Our Skin: Quakerism and Integration at Sidwell Friends School," *Quaker History* 98: 35–47.

Index

Printed in the USA
CPSIA information can be obtained
at www.ICGtesting.com
LVHW050521300723
753818LV00003B/12